Waikīkī Dreams

SPORT AND SOCIETY

Series Editors
Aram Goudsouzian
Jaime Schultz

Founding Editors
Benjamin G. Rader
Randy Roberts

*For a list of books in the series, please see
our website at www.press.uillinois.edu.*

Waikīkī Dreams

How California Appropriated Hawaiian Beach Culture

PATRICK MOSER

UNIVERSITY OF ILLINOIS PRESS
Urbana, Chicago, and Springfield

Library of Congress Cataloging-in-Publication Data
Names: Moser, Patrick (Patrick J.), 1963– author.
Title: Waikīkī dreams : how California appropriated Hawaiian
   beach culture / Patrick Moser.
Description: Urbana : University of Illinois Press, [2024] |
   Series: Sport and society | Includes bibliographical references
   and index.
Identifiers: LCCN 2023049703 (print) | LCCN 2023049704
   (ebook) | ISBN 9780252045912 (cloth : acid-free paper) |
   ISBN 9780252088018 (paperback : acid-free paper) | ISBN
   9780252056789 (ebook)
Subjects: LCSH: Surfing—Social aspects—California,
   Southern—History. | Popular culture—California,
   Southern—History—20th century. | Racism against
   Indigenous peoples—Social aspects—California,
   Southern. | Settler colonialism—California—History. |
   Depressions—1929—California. | White nationalism—
   California—History. | World War, 1939–1945—Influence.
   | Surfers—California, Southern—Biography.
Classification: LCC GV839.65.C2 M67 2024 (print) | LCC
   GV839.65.C2 (ebook) | DDC 797.3/207949—dc23/
   eng/20231201
LC record available at https://lccn.loc.gov/2023049703
LC ebook record available at https://lccn.loc.gov/2023049704

For Craig Lockwood, who saw all the changes, knew all the players, and made his own distinct contributions to California beach culture.

Contents

Acknowledgments

I am very grateful to the California Surf Museum for access to its collections and the welcoming staff and volunteers: Jane Schmauss, Jim Kempton, Camille Cacas, Tara Lee Torburn, and Rick Wilson. The Surfing Heritage and Culture Center also opened its collections, with special help from Barry Haun, Linda Michael, and KeAnne Langford. Craig Lockwood introduced me to Spencer Croul and Mike Funk, who were extremely generous in sharing Croul's deep archives and providing many photographs. Chris Mauro was especially helpful, introducing me to his many contacts for photographs and permissions. Many thanks to Rick Blake and Huntington Beach's International Surfing Museum, which provided access to the scrapbook of the San Onofre Surfing Wahines and several photographs. A host of friends, colleagues, acquaintances, and collectors have shared their material and special knowledge of surf history along the way: Dina Gilio-Whitaker, Arthur Verge, Peter Westwick, Scott Laderman, Scott Hulet, Grant Ellis, Tim Cooley, Matt Warshaw, Sandy Hall, Craig Stecyk, Tim DeLaVega, John Clark, Tom Adler, Mark Fragale, Cary Weiss, Jens Jensen, Scott Hulet, Joe Tabler, Malcolm Gault-Williams, Gary Lynch, Lisa Peterson, Wilson Butte, Michael Scott Moore, Lee Ohanian, Ian Lind, JP Van Swae, Bob Pearson, Barney Largner, Georgia Chronopoulous, Tom Covello, and Steve Foster. My thanks to John Grannis, Carl Ackerman, and Norman and John Ball for photographic reproductions.

I benefitted from a year sabbatical leave to complete research and writing and appreciate the support of my colleagues at Drury University: Beth Harville, Jennifer Silva Brown, Kevin Henderson, Cathy Blunk, Charlyn Ingwerson, Jennifer Joslin, Katie Gilbert, Jo Van Arkel, Peter Meidlinger, Elizabeth Nichols, Tim Robbins, and Tony Smith. I am grateful to Rich

Schur for asking me to teach a class on California Beach Culture for Drury's Honors Program and to the following students who read draft versions of book chapters: Emma Allison, Mat Colling, Kelsi Gelle, Alex Ince, Lauren McQuerter, Zoey Mueller, Anna Pfaff, and Drew Tasset. I am especially indebted to Beth Harville and Kevin Henderson for providing extra funds for photo permissions and usage. The librarians at Drury University have been extremely supportive and helpful in processing numerous research materials: William Garvin, Phyllis Holzenberg, Katherine Bohnenkamper, Barbi Dickensheet, Holli Henslee, and Jacqueline Tygart. My thanks to colleagues Rebecca Miller and Sarah Jones for help scanning photographs.

I have relied on the expertise of many librarians, archivists, and other professionals beyond Drury to track down historical information, including Michael Holland (Los Angeles City Clerk's office); Susan Lamb (Santa Monica Public Library); Bill Riddle and Michael Dolgushkin (California State Library); Kelly Riddle and Frank Harris (Los Angeles County Library); Terri Garst (Los Angeles Public Library); Alyssa Bellew and Ansley Davies (Los Angeles Department of Parks and Recreation); Peter T. Young (Hoʻokuleana LLC); Nicole Mooradian (Los Angeles Department of Beaches and Harbors); Stacy Beard (California Department of Parks and Recreation); Tanesha L. Hudson (Hermosa Beach City Clerk's Office); Lola Aguilar (California State Park Archives); Martha Juede and Robby Mazza (Malibu Adamson House Foundation); Melissa Nykanen and Brendan Morris (Pepperdine University Libraries); Angelica Illueca (Witkin State Law Library); Tristan Willenburg (Historical Society of Long Beach); Eric Kilgore (National Archives at Saint Louis); John Kearns and Sara Crown (Santa Monica History Museum); Jim Harris (Santa Monica Pier); David Willis (Santa Monica City Clerk's Office); Monique Sugimoto (Palos Verdes Library District), Jill Thrasher (Sherman Library and Gardens), and Luisa Haddad (Special Collections, University of California, Santa Cruz). Many thanks to Paul Wormser for the tour of Corona del Mar and Newport Harbor.

I greatly appreciate the help and expertise of the team at the University of Illinois Press: Daniel Nasset, Michael Roux, Heather Gernenz, Mariah Mendes Schaefer, Jennie Fisher, Tad Ringo, Kevin Cunningham, Roberta Sparenberg, and Angela Burton. My thanks to Walt Evans for his keen copyediting skills. Thanks to Tracy Dalton for her work on the index.

A final thank you to friends and family who provided lodging and good company during my research trips to the west coast: Chris and Pati Moser, Steve and Jackie Moser, Miles and Julia Butler, Jack Moser, Pam and Pat Pesetti, Terry and Jerry Christenson, Kathy Moser and Cynthia Bologna,

Cynthia Conway and Eduardo Cuevas, Michael Scott Moore, Tanya and Steve Dennis, and Tim Cooley and Ruth Hellier. Greg Schneider and Theresa Moser generously sheltered me for weeks on end and provide lasting friendship. I am so grateful to my family here in Springfield, Missouri, for their love and support—Ryan Moser and Linda Trinh Moser.

A Note on Hawaiian Language

I have followed contemporary usage in writing Hawaiian words and names by including diacritical marks (the ʻokina and kahakō) that guide standard pronunciation. However, when referring to or quoting primary historical sources that do not use these marks (e.g., "Waikiki Beach Patrol"), I have preserved the original.

Introduction

We had ukes and guitars, and one fella had a
trumpet, and we used to have big luaus. After
we'd surf, we'd go back to the beach and just eat,
then we'd play Hawaiian songs till midnight or so.
Just Hawaiian music because that's all we liked.
We used to listen to this radio program called
Hawaii Calls, it was broadcast out of Waikiki, and
we'd all dream about going to Hawaii.[1]
—Calvin "Tulie" Clark, Palos Verdes Surfing Club

A storm brews in the South Pacific, sending waves thousands of miles across the ocean to break on the shores of California in the summertime. Waves come from other directions, of course, during other seasons, and they are often bigger and better shaped. But summer waves are special. They speak to our collective fantasies in ways unmatched by winter surf. It's why Rincon, some fifty miles north of Malibu and often a superior wave, sits in relative obscurity outside the surf community while its flashy sibling, Surfrider Beach, commands the world's attention when it comes to California dreamin'. Yes, Malibu's fame partly owes to the Hollywood stars who live right around the corner from the break. And yes, it's also the influence of Los Angeles, longtime mecca of hope and health despite the gritty details of living beside millions of people. But here's the real reason why Malibu shines so brightly: it breaks best in the summer, not in the winter like Rincon. Cold water and wetsuits just aren't sexy. Sunshine, tan skin, athletic young bodies performing dazzling maneuvers in warm waves—that's sexy. More than a century of marketing has told us so. That image is based on Western fantasies of the people and places of the South Pacific, where the waves come from.

Hawai'i, in the path of those waves, forms part of the tropical fantasy largely because of Waikīkī, which also faces toward the South Pacific and breaks best in the summertime. But honestly, the islands are so temperate that mainlanders imagine them existing in a state of perpetual summer, their palm trees, trade winds, and year-round warm water beckoning to the imagination.[2] Few eras summoned the dream of Waikīkī more strongly than the Great Depression, when mass unemployment, poverty, and displacement fueled strong desires for a faraway life of romance and easy recreation. With the promise of developing these ideas in later chapters, we can make a couple of statements here about the general impact of the Great Depression on California beach culture. First, high unemployment rates gave young people the gift of time, which allowed them to spend more days at the beach developing their sports and leisure activities. Second, beach culture also thrived during the 1930s because beaches were both a cheap form of leisure and readily accessible to the majority-white population in Southern California.

The story of California beach culture's growth during the Great Depression really begins in the 1920s with the influence of Native Hawaiian Duke Kahanamoku. Beach culture has existed, of course, as long as people have lived on the California coast.[3] Native American communities occupied and worked the Southland's coastal areas for thousands of years—some of their ancestors still do today—from the Kumeyaay in present-day San Diego to the Chumash in the northern counties of Los Angeles, Ventura, and Santa Barbara. The long history of settler colonialism in California—Spanish, Mexican, and American—cleaved indigenous peoples from their ancestral lands, specific examples of which are treated in Part Two. Generally speaking, settler colonialism represents the precondition for the beach culture that is the focus of this study.[4] That culture first developed in Southern California upon the arrival of mixed-race Hawaiian George Freeth (1883–1919), whose combination of surfing and lifeguarding changed people's perspective about the beach. Over nearly a dozen years working as a lifeguard and swim coach in the Golden State (1907–1919), Freeth showed Southern Californians that the surf zone, while certainly dangerous and the cause of many drownings, also offered them a tremendous amount of pleasure. His development of lifeguard programs from Los Angeles to San Diego, which included teaching lifeguards to surf to become more effective rescuers, created the foundation of California beach culture as we recognize it today, from *Gidget* and the Beach Boys to *Baywatch* and the billion-dollar surf industry. Freeth's sudden death in the 1918–1919 flu pandemic created a void soon filled by his friend and protégé, Duke Kahanamoku.[5]

An all-around waterman and Olympic champion, Duke spent the latter half of the 1920s playing small roles in Hollywood. When he wasn't on location in Wyoming filming a western, or traveling to Southern California's Channel Islands to play a South Seas chief, he spread enthusiasm for beach culture by giving surfing exhibitions and making headlines with dramatic rescues, how-to articles on bodysurfing, and teaching water sports to top Hollywood personalities. His fame, good looks, humble personality, and athletic abilities captured the attention of an entire generation of Californians and encouraged them to swim and surf the way he did.[6] Duke's Hollywood experience encapsulates in many ways the contradictory impulses that run through California beach culture of the 1930s: a reverence for all things Hawaiian that typically stopped short at the color line. Hollywood promoted South Seas films while denying Kahanamoku and other islanders leading roles because of their skin color. In a similar fashion, surfing clubs and municipal lifeguard organizations, whose heroes and role models were Native Hawaiians and mixed-race Hawaiians, excluded people of color (and women) from their ranks as a matter of practice. This disconnect between embracing an ideal of Native Hawaiian culture and yet ignoring substantive relationships with Native Hawaiians themselves surfaces time and again among the leading beach influencers of the era.

Beach culture developed so strongly in Southern California in the 1920s and 1930s because the region became one of the nation's biggest manufacturing centers. California beach culture was literally built in Los Angeles—surfboards, paddleboards, lifesaving gear, water camera housings, to name a few. The most iconic products to come off the assembly lines—Pacific System Homes surfboards and Tom Blake paddleboards—played a part in the complex dynamic that was essentially colonial in nature: appropriating the tradition of indigenous people in a way that cast them as extras in their own cultural production. The result was a California surfboard manufacturer that became the purveyor of traditional Native Hawaiian craft. Once Native Hawaiians are separated from their own cultural products, space is left open for others to fill that gap. Historian Kevin Starr describes how Californians of the 1920s materialized their dreams of health and prosperity through great building projects across the state.[7] The same was true for individuals looking to fulfill personal dreams that centered on Waikīkī. In the most extreme case—that of mainland surfer Tom Blake—the dream was not simply to idealize the life of a Native Hawaiian, but to actually become one himself.

As California beach culture depended upon mechanisms of settler colonialism, so too Blake's appropriation of Native Hawaiian identity. In both cases—and we'll have more to say about these issues throughout the study—the ultimate motivation can be traced back to deep-seated cultural imperatives to both remove and replace indigenous peoples. Because settler colonialism, as a structure and ongoing process rather than a finite historical event, has enduring consequences, we can retrace our steps a bit and reason that one of those consequences manifested itself in the lack of substantive relationships between Southern Californians of the era and their Native Hawaiian counterparts.[8] That is to say, the disconnect between white Southern Californians and indigenous Hawaiians would be an expected outcome of a broader system that placed the two populations at odds. One would have to work actively against prevailing social biases and structures to develop meaningful bonds across cultures.

Tom Blake became one of five influencers, along with John "Doc" Ball, Preston "Pete" Peterson, Mary Ann Hawkins, and Lorrin "Whitey" Harrison, who took the lead in developing beach culture in California by building things both material (surfboards, outrigger canoes, lifesaving gear) and immaterial (clubs and social networks). The do-it-yourself mentality that permeated the Great Depression spurred these five and others to fabricate what they needed to spend time at the beach and to celebrate what we would call today a beach "lifestyle"—from surf racks and surf shacks to club newsletters, photographs, and books. Each of the five was strongly influenced by Duke and other Native Hawaiians, and each had occasion to visit Hawai'i at various times in the 1930s. These excursions gave them nominal firsthand knowledge of Waikīkī and Native Hawaiian culture, which increased their influence and reputations as trendsetters. The knowledge and enthusiasm they brought back mixed with a veritable storm of South Seas popularity in music, film, and dance that inundated Southern California and established Los Angeles as the hottest outpost of Hawaiian culture.

Midway through the Great Depression—1935—is a good year to suspend for a moment to consider the fruitful cross-pollination happening between Honolulu and Los Angeles. Despite general economic devastation, California had become a juggernaut for the nation by this time, rising to the top ranks in aviation, oil production, general manufacturing, population growth, real estate development, and, of course, the golden goose of Hollywood. Tom Blake, a Hollywood man himself, shone brightly in 1935. In May, *National Geographic* devoted eight full pages to his Hawaiian photographs of surfing and canoeing.[9] In June, Honolulu's Paradise of the Pacific Press released Blake's influential book, *Hawaiian Surfboard,* which included a historical overview of surfing, along with nearly fifty illustrations. By September, Santa Monica lifeguard captain George Watkins estimated that 350 surfboards and paddleboards were being used on his beaches, and he planned to send lifeguard Chauncey Granstrom to Honolulu with five of them "in order to demonstrate what has been done in this city in developing the finer points" of riding waves.[10] Blake's new hollow paddleboard design—standard lifesaving gear in Southern California by 1935—and the innovative use of balsa in surfboard construction, gave Watkins the idea of sharing techniques with lifeguards and surfers in the islands. Blake took that responsibility on himself when he left for Hawai'i in December 1935 and secured a job with the Waikiki Beach Patrol.[11]

The *Honolulu Star-Bulletin* was interested enough in Hollywood's Hawaiian community in the summer of 1935 to start a gossip column entitled "Hawaiians at Hollywood." Penned by Georgia Stiffler (wife of Hawaiian steel guitar player Sol Ho'opi'i), the column ran weekly for two and a half years and provided updates on the South Seas craze "sweeping Hollywood like a kona storm."[12] The "Hawaiian colony," as they called themselves, consisted primarily of musicians, dancers, and actors (and their families) who made a living in the movie industry and local club scene. Stiffler listed a sampling of the most recent night spots to open in the Los Angeles area in 1935: the Tropical Hut, the Hawaiian Hut, the Little Grass Shack, the Seven Seas, the Beachcombers, the Tropics, and the Aloha Buffet.[13] She was essentially recording the beginning of Tiki culture in Los Angeles, a fad pushed by MGM studios that year in two of their films, *Last of the Pagans* and *Mutiny on the Bounty* (this latter won the Academy Award for Best Picture). The genre became so popular that each of the major studios would soon have at least one South Seas film in production every year. Stiffler's husband, Sol Ho'opi'i, recorded "Sweet Leilani" in 1935, a song that would win an Academy Award after Bing Crosby sang it in *Waikiki Wedding* (1937). Hollywood's biggest star, Shirley Temple, was named honorary captain of the Waikiki Beach Patrol when she visited Honolulu in the summer of 1935, complete with her own pint-sized surfboard.

The most famous of the surf clubs, the Palos Verdes Surfing Club, formed in 1935, as did the West Coast Paddleboard Association, an umbrella organization that supported surfing and paddleboarding competition until 1941. The near-completion of the Newport Harbor jetty in 1935 meant that Corona del Mar was definitely *out* as Southern California's most famous surfing spot—put on the map by Duke himself—and San Onofre was definitely *in* as its replacement. San Onofre became (and remains) the keeper of the Waikīkī flame, the beach where the aloha spirit burns brightest in the entire state of California. And finally, of course, *Hawaii Calls* debuted in Los Angeles in November 1935.[14] The weekly radio program played live Hawaiian music directly from the shores of Waikīkī, with the sound of the surf opening the broadcast at the Moana Hotel. Waikīkī was no longer twenty-five hundred miles away from Los Angeles. It was as close as your radio dial every Monday night at 9:30 P.M. on station KHJ.

Los Angeles turned into a hotbed of Hawaiian culture in the 1930s, the fertile soil in which California beach culture thrived until Pearl Harbor seized the world's attention on December 7, 1941, after which much of California beach culture shut down. During the preceding decade, however, California exerted increasing control over images of Native Hawaiians through its movie, tourist, and surfboard industries. Matson Navigation Company, based in San Francisco, owned the steamships and major Waikīkī hotels that catered to Hawai'i's tourists, the majority of whom came from California.[15] The movie studios, of course, and the majority of "Hawaiian" night clubs, were run by Californians. The official surfboard company of Waikīkī's iconic Outrigger Canoe Club, which provided "Genuine Hawaiian surfboards" to the equally iconic Waikīkī beachboys, was California's Pacific System Homes. The first builder of Tom Blake's "Hawaiian Hollow and Paddle Surf Boards" was the Thomas Rogers Company, based in Venice, California. The general upshot of California's "kona storm," to echo Georgia Stiffler, meant that Californians were selling California-made "Hawaiian" products mostly to other Californians (and other mainlanders). The effect was to generate the kind of colonial attitude toward Native Hawaiians that arises in the title of the *Santa Monica Outlook*'s article on Captain Watkins sending Chauncey Granstrom to the islands: "SANTA MONICANS TO TEACH HAWAIIANS SURFBOARDING ART." The newspaper headline expresses a basic symptom of settler colonialism by appropriating cultural knowledge—in this case of Native Hawaiian surfing—and then bestowing it back upon the indigenous population. In this dynamic, Santa Monicans take possession of the art of surfing, part of an invidious colonial process that ultimately seeks the replacement of natives themselves.[16]

A number of Hawaiians did well in California during the height of the South Seas fad. Mamo Clark, for example, starred opposite Clark Gable in *Mutiny on the Bounty* and landed plum roles in Hollywood over the next few years. Two Honoluluans, Tony Guerrero and "Whistlin' Willie" Ornellas, owned the Hawaiian Hut.[17] The top musicians and hula dancers of the period—Sol Ho'opi'i, Lani and Dick McIntire, Mabel Akoa, among others—earned lucrative salaries because their talents were in such high demand for movies, nightclubs, and radio programs. Despite this success, the general co-opting of Native Hawaiian culture extended to Waikīkī itself in the form of a 1938 Pasadena Rose Parade float crewed by members of the Palos Verdes Surfing Club. The float, entitled "Little Waikiki" ("Doc" Ball's moniker for Bluff Cove), carried Eleanor Roach doing the hula, and Mary Ann Hawkins standing on a surfboard, while eight "bronzed Palos Verdians" escorted them the length of the parade route.[18] The float and its passengers acted out the theme that year ("Fantasy Playland") in a way that exemplified the steady conquest of Hawai'i, which in another two decades would become the fiftieth state. In the ultimate colonial fantasy playland,

Native Hawaiians were erased completely, replaced by white mainlanders who assumed their identities and managed to transport a version of Waikīkī to their local community. At first glance, such a reading of teenagers on a parade float might seem absurd. The young people involved would not have interpreted their actions this way, nor would they likely have condoned any such proceeding. But their dress, their actions, their disconnect from the people, places, and traditions they were trying so hard to emulate aligned them with a broader social and political march that pushed that fantasy toward reality.

Three beach centers—Palos Verdes, San Onofre, and Malibu—helped shape the ideal of Waikīkī surf into a recreational activity that became particularly Californian. Depression-era surfers at each break were looking for waves that rolled like those beneath Diamond Head, but the specific geography of California—the river mouths at San Onofre and Malibu, for example—transformed those southern swells into waves that were unique to their respective surf spots. The long rides at Bluff Cove, San Onofre, and Malibu may have recalled Waikīkī in a general way, but the cobblestones and other geologic factors created surf that had its own particular demands. Californians derived their surfing heritage entirely from Hawai'i, but the necessity to adapt to the demands of local surf spots forced them to begin building their own beach culture. The most obvious example is the role that automobiles played in the development of surfing. Cars didn't really factor into the surf life at Waikīkī—locals and tourists had relatively easy access to the waves. But California surf spots were spread out, and surfboards were heavy, so wheels became a necessity. Car culture begat accessories like surf racks, tires to burn on the beach after a cold winter session, and terms like "klunker" for a used surfboard.[19] The era's premier surf photographer in California, "Doc" Ball, framed his photographs with Waikīkī in mind, but the coves, cliffs, piers, and beaches that filled his lens captured a nascent culture establishing its own traditions.

No one had stronger Waikīkī dreams than Tom Blake, and his *Hawaiian Surfboard*—part history, part memoir, part how-to manual—tracks that dream in vivid detail. A first of its kind in surf culture, the book became a kind of gospel for later historians who cited him chapter and verse as they outlined a vision of surf history that largely fell into step with a colonial narrative that cast Anglo-Americans as the rescuers of Native Hawaiian culture, and of surfing in particular.[20] Blake's invention of his own native legend in *Hawaiian Surfboard* not only betrays the Hollywood influence of South Seas films on his writing—Blake himself worked in the studios over several decades—but also situates him in a centuries-long national pastime of "playing Indian," to cite Phillip J. Deloria's study, where white

Americans construct identities based on the appropriation and eradication of indigenous peoples.[21] Blake's Waikīkī dream serves as a cautionary tale, then, one that has resonated strongly with white mainlanders over the years perhaps because he is telling a story that, at heart, many of us want to believe.

World War II drained California beaches of many young people who enlisted in the military, and still others joined the war effort as civilians in the Southland's booming aviation and shipbuilding industries. Gas rationing restricted excursions to the coast, and though most beaches remained open to the public, a heavy military presence owing to fears of a Japanese invasion probably further discouraged ocean recreation at a time when the nation's energy remained focused on defeating Adolph Hitler and the Axis powers. Down but not out, California beach culture bided its time and even maintained some momentum despite the sudden evaporation of surfing clubs and contests, Hawaiian-themed social events, and the brutal reality of a South Pacific bathed in war. California beach culture had gained solid traction in the early 1930s when lifeguard organizations incorporated Blake's hollow paddleboards as lifesaving gear, thus ensuring a nexus of young men who regularly trained and competed on the craft. By maintaining their skills in ocean rescue and the use of watercraft, lifeguard programs ensured the continuity of beach culture during and after the most destructive event of the twentieth century. The new materials that came out of war technology—plastic foam and fiberglass—soon emerged in the home workshops of a younger generation of shapers in Southern California. These protégés of prewar surfers, inspired in their turn by the lure of Hawai'i, became the builders of a new beach culture that turned Malibu into the center of the surfing world as California looked toward the 1950s.

California Beach Culture in the 1920s—The Decade of Duke

"The Duke's performance was the most superhuman rescue act and the finest display of surfboard riding that has ever been seen in the world, I believe."[1]
—J. A. Porter, Newport Beach chief of police

Early Saturday morning on June 14, 1925, Antar Deraga, a government weather forecaster and lifeguard in the budding resort community of Corona del Mar, hung a checkered "distress" flag near the entrance of Newport Harbor as a warning to ships' captains of the dangerous conditions. Swells were breaking across the nineteen-hundred-foot jetty that marked the entrance to the harbor "with greater force than he had ever seen them," reported the *Santa Ana Register* the following day.[2] The flag was still flying on Sunday morning when Myron Bland, a merchant from the inland town of Riverside in neighboring Los Angeles County, arrived with sixteen passengers to lead a daylong fishing trip. Bland later stated at the coroner's inquest that he didn't see the warning signal and that no one had alerted him to the conditions.

At 6:45 that morning, Bland was motoring the forty-foot *Thelma* around the end of the jetty when three enormous swells rolled in from the southwest. He managed to guide the boat over the first one; the second broke the cabin glass, and saltwater swamped the engine down below. Bland rushed to the engine room, desperate to keep the motor running, when the third wave—reportedly over twenty-feet high—crashed into the ship and rolled it over. Passengers were thrown into the ocean. The ones who managed to cling to the rails were pummeled by the white water, which dragged the *Thelma* toward shore and wrecked it on a sandbar fronting the Corona del Mar bathhouse.

Duke Kahanamoku with unknown woman—likely at Corona del Mar, circa 1925. (Friends of the Malibu Library Historical Collection/Los Angeles County Library.)

Twelve of the passengers were fortunate that famed Hawaiian swimmer Duke Kahanamoku (1890–1968) happened to be on the beach that day. He and three friends from the Los Angeles Athletic Club—Owen Hale, Gerard Vultee, and William Hurwig—had driven down on Saturday and camped overnight so they could surf the big waves rolling off the sandbar. When Duke spotted the boat in trouble, he quickly grabbed his surfboard and paddled out. In multiple trips, he and the other surfers pulled the floundering passengers from the water and ferried them to shore, where Deraga and Captain Thomas Sheffield, manager of the local bathhouse, hauled the men onto the beach. The *Santa Ana Register* reported that Duke, "with his mighty swimming strokes, seemed to be all around the boat at all times, and whenever a head bobbed up, he was there, to grab the drowning man and to place him on a surf board."[3] Survivor F. W. Hock told the newspaper that they all would have perished if not for Duke: "The Hawaiian was a wizard, and he seemed to have everything in his hands, as we were fighting, out there in the water."[4]

Unfortunately, five of the men drowned, including eighteen-year-old Edgar Morris (a student) and his older brother Jonathan (a clerk). Jonathan Morris's father-in-law, E. E. McClain (a machinist), also drowned. Several of the passengers had arrived on the beach unconscious, and Deraga's wife Helen, and Mary Grigsby, a nurse, were credited with saving their lives.

Beyond the heroism of Duke and the other men and women, the event offers an opportunity to gauge not only how beach culture had been developing in Southern California since George Freeth arrived in 1907 and built its core around lifeguarding and surfing, but also where beach culture was headed as the Roaring Twenties gave way to the Great Depression. It would be another decade before beach culture, and surfing in particular, became part and parcel of California's regional identity. The path in that evolution, however, skirted crucial landmarks along the way, including the development of coastal engineering projects, the marketing of beach resorts and athletic clubs, and the glamour of Hollywood. As Southern California opened its seashores and embraced Pacific Island cultures—Hawaiian in particular—there was also a closing down and fencing off with regard to race and gender: who was and was not allowed to play or prosper in this coastal territory white Californians were staking out for themselves.

Duke had been the world's fastest swimmer for a decade when he arrived in Los Angeles from Honolulu in the summer of 1922. He had won gold in the 100-meter freestyle at the 1912 Olympics in Stockholm, and then again in the 1920 Olympics in Antwerp. If the 1916 Olympics in Berlin had not been preempted by World War I, there is little doubt he would have taken gold there too. After he captured silver in the 100-meter freestyle behind fellow American Johnny Weissmuller in the 1924 Olympics in Paris, Duke decided to pursue a Hollywood acting career. He already had a couple of films under his belt by the time he pitched camp at Corona del Mar with his surf buddies. In fact, he'd completed work on Hal Roach's comedy *No Father to Guide Him* just the week before. Appropriately enough, he had played the role of a lifeguard.

Duke was a bona fide celebrity in Southern California: acclaimed as a hero for saving lives; celebrated as an Olympic champion; and admired for his handsome features, incredible physique, and inveterate humility. He worked with famous stars and directors during his time in Hollywood—Clara Bow and John Ford, to name two—and yet despite everything he had going for him, he was blocked from achieving fame and fortune on the big screen because of his skin color. The enormous Hollywood success of Johnny Weissmuller stands in stark contrast to Duke's career. After winning Olympic gold medals in swimming at Paris in 1924 and Amsterdam in 1928, Weissmuller also pursued an acting career. He was cast in Metro-Goldwyn-Mayer's *Tarzan the Ape Man,* which premiered in 1932. Weissmuller worked on a dozen *Tarzan* films altogether between 1932 and 1948. Duke biographer David Davis quotes Weissmuller on the role: "It was like stealing money. There was swimming in it, and I didn't have much to say. How can a guy climb trees, say 'Me Tarzan, you Jane,' and make a million?"[5] Duke had been as accomplished as Weissmuller in every respect—and certainly he could have handled the simple dialogue—and yet he had not been given the opportunity for such roles. As Davis writes, "the barrier that Kahanamoku could not overcome in Hollywood was racism."[6] Clarence "Buster" Crabbe offers another contemporaneous example of Hollywood's race-based selection process for leading men. Crabbe, who won gold in the 440-meter freestyle in the 1932 Olympics in Los Angeles, also played *Tarzan* in the 1930s and became famous for his roles in film and television as Buck Rogers and Flash Gordon. Like Duke, Crabbe had grown up in Hawai'i, but Crabbe was light-skinned.[7]

Though Duke was never considered for leading-man roles in Hollywood, he remained atop the marquee of California beach culture throughout the first half of the twentieth century. Duke set the style in every way, from his long, heavy surfboards to the statuesque poses that riders struck as they glided toward shore. Even more, his understated demeanor remains a staple of surf culture today, as captured in this humorous report after the rescues at Corona del Mar:

> The coolness displayed by Duke Kahanamoku, Owen Hale, Gerard Vultee and "Bill" Hurwig, the four hero rescuers, was one of the outstanding features of the rescue. After their work was done, they went to the club house for breakfast. An excited waiter appeared and began telling of the tragedy. The four men pleaded ignorance of the affair and were told in excited terms, all about the drownings and the heroic rescue work. None of the four said a word, and the waiter went away thrilled that he should be the first to tell the story to persons who apparently knew nothing of the disaster.[8]

When a reporter for the *Balboa Times* asked Duke how he had managed to save so many lives, he responded: "I do not know. It was done. That is the main thing. By a few tricks, perhaps."[9] Duke was too gracious to interrupt or correct the waiter at the Corona del Mar bathhouse, and so he let the man enjoy the spotlight. His response to the reporter from the *Balboa Times* follows the same pattern: Duke pleads ignorance as to how he'd managed to save numerous lives ("I do not know") and then uses a passive construction ("It was done") that follows a Native Hawaiian cultural and syntactic sensibility that focuses language not on the subject (Duke himself) but on the action: "It"—the rescue of the twelve men. Duke emphasizes the point for the reporter ("That is the main thing") and again becomes self-effacing: "By a few tricks, perhaps." Duke didn't save those men by "tricks" but by the knowledge and prowess he'd gained from more than thirty years in the ocean. One can imagine the surfers sitting around the breakfast table—tired, hungry, a bit amused perhaps, undoubtedly in shock from hauling live and dead bodies ashore—and following Duke's lead by pleading ignorance and letting the waiter talk. The coolness in the water embodied by Duke became a trait that people who admired and even idolized him emulated on California beaches long after he had returned to Hawai'i.

Lifeguard service continued to develop along Southern California beaches in the 1920s, but Owen Hale's experience rescuing one of the *Thelma* passengers remained typical of lifesaving techniques of the era. As reported in the *Santa Ana Register:* "[Hale] said that one man, an elderly person, dragged him under the water twice before he was able to break the strangle hold the victim had on him. Hale was forced to strike his man in the face before he could save him."[10] Mixed-race Hawaiian George Freeth had set the standard for lifeguarding from Los Angeles to San Diego with his rigorous training methods and invention of lifesaving gear that promoted safe and effective rescues without the need to harm victims. But Freeth had died during the influenza pandemic in 1919, and his methods, though widely admired and effective, were not institutionalized because coastal communities were not yet willing to support a year-round lifeguard service. Newport Beach had a lifeguard crew in place—Antar Deraga was its captain, and one of the guards, Charles Plummer, was involved in the rescue at Corona del Mar. The majority of the dozen lives saved from the *Thelma,* however, fell to the credit of Duke and the other surfers. Lifeguards were simply not trained to perform rescues in large surf. Duke demonstrated what remained true in California for the next several decades: the best surfers made the best lifeguards because of their in-depth knowledge of ocean conditions.

Deraga had been involved in a similar rescue the year before at the Newport Harbor jetty when a set of equally large waves struck the *Adieu* and tossed thirteen people into the water, eight of whom died.[11] On New Year's Day in 1925, again at the jetty, nine people were thrown into the water when their rowboat capsized in a swift current, and three of their party drowned.[12] Deraga was first on the scene in this latter accident, but the other passengers had already reached shore, and Deraga could do little but try and resuscitate the victims. In each case, the deaths were ruled accidental and unavoidable, the blame landing entirely on unpredictable ocean conditions. Duke's quick action at Corona del Mar encapsulates the two foundational activities whose combination had established California beach culture under the guidance of George Freeth—lifeguarding and surfing. But without widespread institutional support, their practice remained fairly random from one city to the next. Beach culture truly began to flourish only in the late 1920s and early 1930s when Los Angeles created critical support structure by funding city and county lifeguard programs.

Along with Duke's presiding influence and a growing interest in developing professional lifeguard service, beach culture in the 1920s benefited from engineering projects that opened up the coast to residence and recreation. To prevent tragedies like the capsizing of the *Adieu* and the *Thelma* from happening again, for example, Newport Beach invested nearly a million dollars in upgrades: dredging the harbor, redirecting the path of the Santa Ana River, and building jetties to protect fishing and pleasure boats as they motored in and out. It's true that the Newport Harbor jetty eventually blocked large swells and ruined Corona del Mar as a premier surfing spot—the sandbars were good for surfing, but not for boat safety. The jetty's eventual completion in 1936, however, created a hydraulic aberration on the jetty's west side—the Wedge—which remains the most famous bodysurfing and bodyboarding wave in California. One core beach-culture activity died because of coastal engineering, yet another was born in its wake. This scenario repeated itself throughout Southern California: famous surfing spots at Dana Point and Long Beach disappeared owing to harbor projects, and others like the Redondo Breakwater were created because of them.

Because of its vast open spaces, no region of the country embraced the novelty of automobiles more than Southern California, and the development of the state's highway system was another engineering project crucial to the growth of beach culture. In 1919 the California legislature authorized the building of a highway that would connect the entire state from the Mexican border to Oregon. Residents of Los Angeles in particular wanted to roam beyond the tracks of Henry Huntington's network of electric trolleys, and automobiles allowed them to do so on their own timetable. Duke himself had arrived in California in 1922 with his convertible Cadillac Phaeton, and he would have traveled the Coast Line Highway from Long Beach to Newport Beach for his camping trip at Corona del Mar.[13] The highway had opened just three months earlier, giving Duke and Angelenos in general direct access to twenty miles of beaches to the south in Orange County: Alamitos Bay; Naples; Seal Beach; Anaheim Landing; Sunset Beach; Los Patos; Huntington Beach; and Newport Beach, which included the Balboa Peninsula and Corona del Mar. The highway would eventually be extended all the way to San Diego, opening up more beaches for recreation and creating a crucial cross-pollination of young people in Southern California. Their common interests in exploring the coastline became the raw ingredients for the growth of beach culture in the mid-1930s at surf spots like San Onofre at the northern edge of San Diego County.

The highway projects—roads built from petroleum byproducts like asphalt and user-financed through gas taxes and motor registration fees—depended on California's oil industry, which boomed in the 1920s and offers yet another example of how engineering impacted beach culture. The discovery of massive pools of oil from Huntington Beach to Ventura County triggered a relentless battle between the petroleum industry and recreationalists, each vying to wrest their vision of California's future from the other's grip. The issue was complex, pitting the city council of Huntington Beach, for example, against its own Chamber of Commerce: the former looking to cash in on oil royalties while the latter planned for the town's future as a recreational area. The recreationalists had Governors Clement C. Young (1927–1931) and James Rolph (1931–1934) in their corner, the latter declaring, "The oil industry has already prostituted itself. Let us not allow it to prostitute our beaches."[14] The petroleum industry also had formidable allies—lobbyists, sympathetic judges, and town councils interested in economic gains, especially during the Great Depression. The issue raged until 1938 when the two sides came to an uneasy compromise: the newly formed State Lands Commission leased coastal properties for drilling but banished rigs from the beaches and earmarked royalties for the development of state beaches and parks. The state's decision to protect coastal Southern California for recreation assured the future growth of beach culture by pulling profits from the lucrative petroleum industry, which continued to extract oil from tidelands and offshore reserves. The state's crude deposits supported beach culture in many ways: the millions of barrels pumped from the ground glutted the market and allowed surfers to travel far and wide on cheap gas, and the gasoline tax that drivers paid (beginning in 1923) pumped millions of dollars annually into the state highway fund, creating more and better roads for easier coastal access.[15]

Beyond the pragmatic goals of easing transportation and boosting the economic prospects of coastal towns, highway development in California aspired to aesthetic concerns, which became important for opening major beach-culture centers like Malibu in northern Los Angeles County. More

Oil derricks on Venice Beach, 1920s. (Courtesy Arthur Verge/Los Angeles County Lifeguard Association.)

details about Malibu come in chapter 8, but we can take a peek at the U.S. Supreme Court's ruling that forced Malibu's owner, May Rindge, to accept the building of a state highway across her seventeen-thousand-acre ranch in 1923: "Public uses are not limited, in the modern view, to matters of mere business necessity and ordinary convenience, but may extend to matters of public health, recreation, and enjoyment."[16] Highways were unveiling all the natural beauty that California had to offer its citizens, and Malibu's undeveloped ranges—its rugged hills and picturesque beaches—gave Californians the opportunity to travel back in time, in a sense, and experience the coastline of a bygone era.

∾

Duke's and the other surfers' presence at Corona del Mar was more than a random camping trip in his sporty Cadillac. Yes, Duke had first surfed the break back in September 1914, and the spot had become his favorite place to ride waves while living in Los Angeles. In an interview for *Surfer* magazine in March 1965, Duke reminisced that he and the others "used to go down just about every weekend."[17] Corona del Mar was a summertime break, so when Duke wasn't working on a film or hitting the golf links, he'd grab his friends on the weekend and drive down to Newport. At the time of the heroic rescue, however, Corona del Mar was marketing itself as an exclusive beach resort. According to Claudine and Paul Burnett, authors of *Surfing Newport Beach:* "Having the surfers at Corona attracted tourists and potential real estate buyers."[18] They note that bathhouse manager Thomas Sheffield, who'd been hired by owner William Sparr the year before, let Duke and the others stow their heavy boards in the bathhouse to make it more convenient for them to surf there. Duke's celebrity surf riding would help draw tourists to the resort and hopefully encourage them to buy up parcels of land. Two months before Duke's rescue, we read the following ad in the *Los Angeles Times* that showcases major elements of 1920s beach culture: "A HAPPY GIRL is planning her vacation days. How she'll pack her hours with the most fun, let nature paint her with a coat of tan and health, ride a tippy surf board and hoist a snow white sail. How she'll bury 'care' with her school books, deep in the sand. You'll meet this happy girl this summer, at Balboa—on the Peninsula."[19] Balboa was tapping into the appealing qualities of California beach culture that have made it so popular over the past century: carefree summer days in the sand, a healthy tan, surfing and sailing—fun, happiness, and the possibility of either meeting this happy girl or becoming her yourself. All you needed to realize this dream was to invest in property.

"Riding a tippy surf board" had been a popular marketing tool in Southern California ever since George Freeth was hired to give exhibitions and attract visitors to beach resorts from Los Angeles to San Diego. Kahanamoku and the other rescuers were noted in the *Santa Ana Register* as being "members of the Corona Del Mar Surf Boat club, originated by Captain Sheffield, and were down for the week-end, to perform surf board stunts."[20] Surfing's development in California between the World Wars is often characterized nostalgically as a grassroots activity, pursued for private pleasure among a small group of hardy individuals. But the sport grew hand in hand with coastal marketing ventures. Sheffield organized what is generally recognized as the first official surf club in California for the financial benefit of William Sparr, the owner and developer of Corona del Mar.[21] The mention of "surf board stunts" in the newspaper likely indicates that Duke and the others were essentially putting on an exhibition for weekend visitors and potential real estate buyers.

Sheffield also used surfing to market Corona del Mar by inaugurating the Pacific Coast Surf Riding Championships (PCSRC) in 1928 and holding them again in 1929.[22] There's more to say about these contests, but for the moment we can simply note that the growth of surfing, and beach culture in general, were inseparable from market considerations.

~

California beach culture was also inseparable from race issues. Two weeks before Duke's rescues and fifty miles north of Corona del Mar, his younger brother, Sam Kahanamoku, was making headlines at the Edgewater Club in Santa Monica by winning a 220-yard "surfboard race"—what we'd call today a paddleboard race.[23] This was the most prominent appearance in Southern California of a new sport that would come to dominate beach culture the following decade. The modern version of paddleboarding had begun as a novelty event during a Honolulu swim meet in 1921, and Sam had taken first place in the 75-yard course.[24] He defended his title the following two years. Sam won a bronze medal in the 100-meter freestyle in the 1924 Olympics in Paris, just behind Duke, and he was in California during the summer of 1925 to compete in various swim meets. The swim instructor at the Edgewater Club, Ben Thrash—himself a diver in the Paris Olympics—had organized the affair and invited Sam to compete in the paddleboard event.

Sam's presence in a private club reinforces how Southern Californians made exceptions for Native Hawaiians like the Kahanamoku brothers that would not be given to the local African American community. The Edgewater's location on the exact spot of a planned African American resort that was blocked by the Santa Monica city council demonstrates that the institutional structures behind the growth of beach culture—private clubs and municipalities—not only restricted access to who would be allowed to participate in certain beach activities, but also actively prevented African Americans from enhancing their own beach-culture traditions. The result of such policies had detrimental long-term consequences for the participation of minorities and women in the two core activities of beach culture: lifeguarding and surfing. John Tabor became the first African American lifeguard in Los Angeles County during World War II.[25] The next African American, Russell D. Walker, wasn't hired until 1965.[26] And female lifeguards didn't appear until 1973.[27] The first organization for African American wave riders—the Black Surfers Association—didn't get up and running until 1975.[28] The land and seascapes so fertile to the development of beach culture in Southern California were nevertheless zoned to exclude women and minorities from fully participating in the growth of these dynamic spaces.

It turns out that the two African Americans who had proposed the resort at the foot of Pico Boulevard in Santa Monica, attorney Charles S. Darden and businessman Norman O. Houston, had the drop on everyone in April 1922. As Alison Rose Jefferson details in *Living the California Dream: African*

John Tabor, the first African American ocean lifeguard in Los Angeles County, 1942. (Courtesy Richard Mark/Los Angeles County Lifeguard Association.)

American Leisure Sites during the Jim Crow Era, Darden and Houston had the idea to cater both to the large African American population in Los Angeles and to attract others from across the country. The men may have considered that inviting thousands of African Americans to Santa Monica would have been received by the city council as having a positive economic impact on the community. But they faced swift and emphatic resistance. The Santa Monica Bay Protective League immediately formed—"A membership of 1,000 Caucasians"—to protest the sale and protect "property values and our bay district as a whole."[29] The league pressed the Santa Monica city council to block construction and cancel the property sale. The council ultimately enforced a zoning ordinance that restricted the area to residential living only. Local businessmen also placed a "Caucasian restriction" on their properties, which prevented "the leasing, occupancy or sale of any property to persons not of the Caucasian race."[30] These were the so-called real estate covenants that had been used throughout Los Angeles to prevent African

Verna Dekard and Arthur Lewis pose in front of the newly installed Casa Del Mar barricade at the segregated section of Santa Monica beach known as the Ink Well, 1924. (Shades of L.A. Collection/Los Angeles Public Library.)

Americans and other minorities from moving into white neighborhoods. So the dream of building a leisure space to enhance an area that African Americans had already been enjoying for more than a decade quickly died.

For African Americans, that is. Darden and Houston's idea of a resort atmosphere suddenly interested the local white population, who had little trouble convincing the city council to award long-term leases for the establishment of private clubs along the coast. The Santa Monica Swimming Club formed in the fall of 1922 and opened the following summer, right next door to another new club, the Santa Monica Beach Club.[31] The Casa Del Mar, the Edgewater Beach Club, and the Santa Monica Athletic Club either organized or opened in 1924, followed by the Breakers, the Gables, the Deauville, the Wave-Crest, and the Jonathan Club.[32] By 1930 eleven private clubs had built their headquarters north and south of the Santa Monica Pier within a three-mile stretch of sand. African Americans, deprived of their own beach club, were relegated to the southern end of the resorts, gathering at a spot near Pico Boulevard sometimes known as the "Ink Well."

The majority of clubs were massive steel and concrete structures, designed to attract wealthy upper-class residents of Los Angeles. The Edgewater Club itself was touted as "the finest recreational center of its kind in the West"

View of Santa Monica private beach clubs south of the municipal pier: the Breakers, Edgewater, and Casa Del Mar. (California Historical Society Collection/University of Southern California Libraries.)

when it was organized in 1924: a seven-story building that straddled an entire city block and cost an estimated 650 thousand dollars to complete (almost ten million dollars today).[33] Membership included use of a heated indoor saltwater pool 120 feet long, a gymnasium, private banquet rooms, game rooms, sleeping quarters for more than two hundred guests, and just over two hundred feet of private beach space. The Edgewater had been accepted into the Amateur Athletic Union in 1924, and Ben Thrash held the club's inaugural swim meet the following May in which Sam Kahanamoku won the paddleboard race.

Racial inequality endured so strongly at the beach partly because Santa Monica's private clubs played such an influential role in the overall growth of beach culture during the 1920s. Much like Waikīkī's Outrigger Canoe Club—also founded on racial restrictions—the clubs created a nexus of support for surfing, paddleboarding, beach volleyball, and lifeguard service.

To take one example, Duke's heroism at Corona del Mar inspired Ben Thrash to begin teaching surfing at the Edgewater. In a *Los Angeles Times* article three days after the rescues—"Tragedy Promotes Surfboard

Riding"—Thrash indicated that the sport "made possible Kahanamoku's sensational rescue" and he intended to include the activity as part of the club's program throughout the summer.[34] Tom Blake, a renaissance figure in surf history for his innovations in board design during the 1930s, began his lifeguarding and surfing career when the Santa Monica Swim Club hired him as a lifeguard in the summer of 1924. Blake made his inaugural trip to Hawai'i later that year and returned to lifeguard for the club in the summer of 1925. This was a critical time in surfing history. Blake began a veritable love affair with Hawai'i that lasted for decades, experiences that were crucial to California's development of a home-grown beach culture in the 1930s. Blake, in many ways, represents the nerve center of California's obsession with Hawaiian culture. His great admiration for Duke and his love of island life not only fueled a deep desire to appropriate all things Hawaiian, but also to forge a dream of actually becoming Hawaiian himself.

Fragments of that dream are visible in the Corona del Mar surf contests, whose dual format of paddleboarding out to a buoy and surfing back to the beach were based on descriptions of traditional Hawaiian surfing that Blake had discovered in an *American Anthropologist* article while doing research at the Bishop Museum in Honolulu. Note the following quotation from that article in Blake's *Hawaiian Surfboard* (1935), followed by his commentary:

> "The riders sometimes also raced to the kulano [i.e. "kūlana nalu"], or starting place. Standing on the boards as they shot in was by no means uncommon. Men and women both took part in this delightful pastime, which is now almost a lost art."
>
> This establishes the fact that some of the races were started from shore, the men paddling, or racing out to the starting of the breakers.[35]

Blake won the inaugural PCSRC at Corona del Mar in 1928. Notices leading up to the contest mentioned that Blake had already won two championships. In fact, Blake had established the contest format in some respects two years earlier, in July 1926, at the Breakers Club, which sat just north of the Edgewater Club in Santa Monica. Not to be outdone by Ben Thrash and the Edgewater, the Breakers inaugurated its own amateur ocean swim meet, and Blake won the 400-yard open surfboard event for men. The *Los Angeles Times* reported that Blake "staged the spectacular performance of the afternoon . . . when he rode the last fifty yards to beach his board standing up, with the field just rounding the turning buoy."[36] Blake's research and the influence of Hawaiians like Sam Kahanamoku had inspired him to combine paddleboarding and surfing in the same contest.[37]

Interest in promoting ocean sports and competition extended to life-guarding as well. In the summer of 1927, about seventy-five lifeguards working for various clubs, bathhouses, and municipalities gathered in Venice on Sunday, June 19, for the "second annual Santa Monica Bay district life guard demonstrations." The guards formed crews and competed in various events: rowboat races, resuscitation drills, and rescues with and without lifeguard "cans" and rowboats. The Los Angeles Department of Playground and Recreation sponsored the event to showcase their safety protocols and to educate the public on the latest lifesaving methods.[38] The founding of the department in 1925 gave an enormous boost to the development of beach culture because the City of Los Angeles began buying up large tracts of coastal property for public recreation and staffing those beaches with lifeguards.

From the mid-1920s to the early 1930s, the lifeguard programs developed by the City of Los Angeles, Los Angeles County, and Santa Monica steadily organized themselves into a professional service where young men had to pass rigorous tests in swimming, diving, rowing, and resuscitation. Those efforts paid off in lives saved. At the end of summer in 1928, Santa Monica mayor Herman Michel praised his city's lifeguard corps for their singular record that season of zero drownings. "Never in the history of Santa Monica," a *Los Angeles Times* article reported, "since the city became a gathering place for thousands of bathers along its shores, has a season passed without fatalities."[39] Among the guards praised was seventeen-year-old Preston "Pete" Peterson, who would become the most decorated lifeguard and surfer of the era.

The *Times* article mentioned that Santa Monica's city lifeguards also worked at the private clubs. Another article from the *Times* in 1932 indicated that the lifeguards, in fact, worked primarily for the private clubs and were given "a nominal sum for serving the city as a sideline to their regular employment at beach clubs."[40] The clubs clearly had better funding than the city of Santa Monica, and the young men benefited from higher wages. This situation alarmed local citizens, who called for a reorganization of the lifeguard service to hire more lifeguards, set them up with the latest equipment, and to have at least the captain and one of his lieutenants on duty year-round. This latter stipulation was a milestone in lifeguard service: understanding that bathers needed protection beyond the normal four-month summer season. The private clubs played a critical role in developing the core lifeguard crews that eventually staffed beaches for Santa Monica, the City of Los Angeles, and Los Angeles County. Beach culture truly took hold among a broad population in Southern California only when its foundational equipment—paddleboards used for rescues and surfing—became a regular part of lifeguard training and service.

Beach culture in San Diego during the 1920s offers a point of contrast to its institutional development up the coast in Los Angeles. Charlie Wright picked up where George Freeth had left off by lifeguarding and surfing in Mission Beach from 1923 to 1927. Like Freeth, Wright worked with the local bathhouse to draw visitors by offering surf lessons, sponsoring contests, starting a surf club, and even regularly "surfing in the New Year" (that is, riding waves at night between December 31 and January 1) as part of the festivities for the Mission Beach Amusement Center.[41] But also like Freeth, when Wright stopped promoting surfing, its momentum quickly stalled. The sport's attraction often depended on a talented and charismatic personality to create interest. For surfing and paddleboarding to continue to grow, municipal agencies like the lifeguard service had to embed the equipment into their rescues and training operations. For Los Angeles, this happened in the early 1930s with the widespread use of Tom Blake's hollow paddleboards.

San Diego County's lifeguard service grew more slowly, establishing itself in 1941.[42] The area had different challenges than Los Angeles: more geographically remote, a population less than 15 percent of its northern counterpart—about seventy-five thousand in 1920 compared to Los Angeles's more than half a million—and a more conservative sensibility. John D. Spreckels was San Diego's patron and owned much of the business and real estate, including Coronado Island and the Mission Beach Amusement Center where Wright lifeguarded. Because of the smaller local and tourist populations, there was less investment in private beach clubs, and less competition among them given Spreckels's monopoly. Competition was the primary motivating factor behind Blake's development of his paddleboards, a craft that became standard gear for lifeguards around the country. Individual towns in San Diego had long-running lifeguard programs—Ocean Beach, for example, which had hired Freeth in May 1918 after thirteen people drowned in one afternoon—but they lacked consistency of standards among the various seasonal crews.[43] Duke visited on a couple of occasions and competed in swim meets—he was even advertised as surfing at Ocean Beach and La Jolla (though it's not clear he ever paddled out)—so there was some cross-pollination of ideas.[44] Surfing and other beach-related activities developed more rapidly in San Diego, however, once highway routes opened up and connected young people to their counterparts in Orange and Los Angeles Counties.

Tom Blake had a lot of Hawaiian dreams. One of them seems to have been imagining that Duke had lifeguarded at the Santa Monica Beach Club in 1925, next door to where Blake worked at the Santa Monica Swim Club. "This meant that he and I were guarding stretches of sand and surf side by side," Blake wrote. "We saw each other every day and became constant surfing and swimming companions. . . . Duke left his lifeguard position at the Beach Club, and I moved up to that position in his place."[45] While Duke saved lives in Southern California—not only at Corona del Mar but also at Catalina Island one day during the filming of *Old Ironsides* when two crew members got entangled among ropes and sails in the water—there's no evidence that he worked as a lifeguard. He acted in two films in the summer of 1925: *No Father To Guide Him* just before his rescues at Corona del Mar in mid-June, and then *The Pony Express,* filmed in Cheyenne, Wyoming, during the month of July. He returned to Los Angeles in August. Blake left for Hawai'i on his honeymoon in mid-August and didn't return until December. Even if Duke had been hired as a lifeguard—doubtful given his studio commitments and celebrity status—there wasn't much time for him and Blake to work together. In the summer of 1924, Duke was competing in the Paris Olympics; in the summer of 1926, he worked on *Old Ironsides* and *Eagle of the Sea,* playing pirates in both films. Again, it's doubtful that Duke had the time or inclination to guard the beach. Blake lived in Hawai'i at various times and got to know Duke well, but the desire to show a close relationship with Duke to establish one's bona fides as a surfer became a theme during the era. As we'll see in chapter 9, Blake positioned himself as Duke's heir apparent in a Hawaiian surfing lineage that stretched back to the ancient *kāhuna* or board builders. Blake's Hawaiian dreams were perhaps consistent with his years of playing bit parts in Hollywood films (much like his idol Duke), an industry fueled by fantasy. In the broader context of settler colonialism, we can relate them to the ongoing process of white settlers assuming indigenous identity for themselves.

Hollywood films became the state's biggest industry by 1926 and had their own enduring impact on California beach culture.[46] During that decade an estimated fifty million Americans were watching films every week, nearly half the nation's population.[47] Duke, once again, is the most obvious connection between the beach and Tinseltown. He worked on at least two dozen films during his eight years in Los Angeles, and he turned water sports like surfing into something of a fad among the Hollywood elite. In 1927 he worked with the cinema's biggest draw, Clara Bow, on the South Seas romance *Hula.* The film tells the story of Hula Calhoun, the daughter of a

Hawaiian planter, who becomes embroiled in a love triangle with a married man. Duke wrote an extended article on the art of bodysurfing for the *Los Angeles Times* while *Hula* was in production. The *Times* reported: "Duke has been spending his spare moments teaching movie stars how the thing is done. Clara Bow was the latest to take lessons from Kahanamoku and she is now an expert."[48] Later that year, Duke played the Hawaiian god Lono in a South Seas adventure, *The Isle of Sunken Gold,* where he rescued the heroine Anita Stewart and got the chance to surf on film. "One moment he is diving from a high cliff into a shark-infested sea," reported the *Pasadena Post,* "another riding the surf board like 'it's nobody's business'."[49]

Duke penned another article that same year for the *Los Angeles Times* on how to surf, stating that women made better "surf board artists" than men: "In my experience as an instructor, this has proven to be true on almost every occasion. While for actual strength and endurance, men are far superior, women, it seems, have a better sense of balance."[50] Duke listed a number of celebrities he had given lessons to during the previous two years: Esther Ralston, Wallace Beery, George Bancroft, Florence Vidor, and Bebe Daniels. "Miss Daniels, by the way," Duke added, "learned more rapidly than any other pupil I have ever encountered. Her sense of balance is perfect." By this time, Angelenos were hearing about a new dance that had originated at a Hollywood party, "The Surf-Board Glide": "This dance is a sort of interpretation of the sport known as surf-board riding. You glide a long step, lean to one side a little and hop to represent the wave crest, and then take another long glide. It is really a very graceful, pretty dance to look at and exhilarating to step."[51]

Some female stars like Betty Compson actually learned to surf for their big-screen roles. Compson played the mixed-race heroine Konia Markham in the South Seas romance *The White Flower,* which was filmed in Honolulu. The *Long Beach Telegram* reported: "Miss Compson is a good swimmer, and indulges in the favorite sport of the Hawaiian Islands, surf board riding, in 'The White Flower.' Numerous spills give her a chance to display her skill in the water."[52] Whether Compson and other stars continued to surf was not as important as their association with the beach. As Elsa Devienne has observed about celebrities like Jackie Coogan, Ron Colman, and Clara Bow, all of whom built homes at Malibu when the private lots first became available in 1926: "By choosing to live at the beach—an unusual choice at the time—stars hoped to elevate their public profiles and benefit from the booming popularity of seaside recreation. Moreover, such a move bestowed an air of eccentricity onto any film star in need of a publicity boost. In the context of Hollywood's rising star system, which pitted actors against one another, living by the beach soon became an essential marker of a true movie star."[53] Both Coogan and Colman had connections to Duke. Coogan arranged to have Duke give a swimming exhibition at the Urban Military Academy where the young star was attending school in 1926.[54] Colman, who built his Malibu home right next door to Coogan's, worked with Duke in the South Seas adventure *The Rescue* in 1928.[55] We'll have more to say about Malibu in chapter 8, but in general, Hollywood lent Southern California beach culture an air of glamour and sex appeal that remains an essential part of its allure today.

The South Seas genre of films—romances and eventually musicals after sound was added in the late 1920s—were a steady moneymaker for the studios during this era. Twenty-three films were made about Hawai'i alone in the 1920s, and another twenty-nine during the 1930s.[56] But they typically disseminated images of islanders living in primitive societies and so reinforced nationalist ideals that justified Western military takeovers and colonial governance. Recall that the Kingdom of Hawai'i was illegally overthrown in 1893 with the help of the U.S. military and subsequently annexed as a territory in 1898 during the Spanish-American War. As Delia Konzett notes in *Hollywood's Hawaii: Race, Nation, and War:* "In an imaginary leap into the past, these fantasies revisit the first encounters of Western Eurocentric culture with nonwhites and non-Europeans in the Pacific and seek to portray European or American imperialism as a benevolent form of uplifting so-called lower civilizations."[57] The prevalence and repetition of negative images of these islanders (and other ethnic groups) reinforced stereotypes of peoples that most Americans had never met. We see the stark contrast between the Hawaiians portrayed in a film like *Hula*—members of a tribal society governed by pagan rituals—and the entirely modern Hawaiian Duke Kahanamoku: Olympic gold medalist, writer of articles for the *Los Angeles Times,* a Cadillac owner who golfed and hobnobbed with Hollywood's elite.

The contrast between actual Hawaiians like Duke living in Los Angeles and those conjured on the silver screen for millions of Americans strikes to the heart of race and identity issues that formed the building blocks of California beach culture. The dream factory of Hollywood spinning out fantasies of whites dominating indigenous peoples for supposedly benevolent reasons—progress and moral advancement—was not so different from young Southern Californians dreaming of, and trying to replicate, a distorted vision of Waikīkī at their clubhouses and local beaches. Both participated in a complex maneuver where violence to native peoples—the taking of their land and appropriation of their cultures—becomes stylized as entertainment or sport that distances the participants from culpability and responsibility for acts of political and cultural aggression. As Shari M.

Hunhdorf has argued in the context of whites adopting Native American heritage, the "primary cultural work" of going native "is the regeneration of racial whiteness and European-American society."[58] Akin to the long history of whites "playing Indian" for purposes of authenticating an original relationship to land and forging a friendly stance toward disenfranchised peoples, surfers and other beach-culture enthusiasts—despite their earnest enthusiasm for all things Hawaiian—were reenacting social paradigms that reinforced the original motives behind political violence and cultural appropriation. In essence, white nationalism.[59]

Hollywood's glamour graced Hawai'i as Waikīkī increasingly became the playground of the rich and famous, and Waikīkī in turn bestowed its own tropical appeal onto Southern California. The critical year in this cross-pollination was 1927, when the Matson Navigation Company completed the Royal Hawaiian Hotel, ushering in an era of five-star resort life at Waikīkī. Hollywood's own royal couple, Douglas Fairbanks Sr. and Mary Pickford, vacationed at the Royal Hawaiian and helped to establish it as the go-to place for film industry personalities. By the summer of 1931, the *Los Angeles Times* was profiling "Hollywood's New Playground." "They think nothing of skipping over to Hawaii for a week-end or short holiday, do the stars of the screen," reported the *Times*, "since the ocean paradise has proven so popular."[60] Among the celebrities pictured in the profile was Bebe Daniels, Duke's surfing protégée, holding onto a surfboard with her husband, Ben Lyon, who later discovered Marilyn Monroe. The Matson Navigation Company purchased the other hotel at Waikīkī, the Moana, in 1932 and cemented its control of both transporting visitors to the islands and lodging them at Waikīkī. The impact on Hawaiian tourism was immediate. The number of visitors jumped from 16,762 in 1926—the year before the Royal Hawaiian was built—to 19,980 in 1928. The number rose again in 1929 to 22,190. Of those visitors, the majority who arrived from the U.S. mainland came from California—no surprise, really, since Matson was based in San Francisco.[61] Matson purchased its closest competitor, the Los Angeles Steamship Company, in 1931, thereby ensuring a monopoly on tourist travel to Hawai'i from the mainland.[62]

The Matson "white ships" themselves were the height of elegance: the fastest, most powerful, most luxurious vessels ever built in the United States when they debuted. The *Malolo*, which made its maiden voyage to Hawai'i in 1927, cost seven million dollars to build and was nearly six hundred feet long.[63] It held 457 passengers in first class, and another 163 in cabin. The ship was essentially a grand hotel that steamed to the islands in five days from California. If you booked one of the eight exclusive Lanai Suites on the *Mariposa*, the *Monterey*, or the *Lurline* in the early 1930s, you enjoyed a

Hollywood celebrities Bebe Daniels and Ben Lyon at Waikīkī. *Los Angeles Times*, July 12, 1931.

private veranda and sitting rooms at the front of the ship, on the A-Deck, for six hundred dollars one-way (more than nine thousand dollars today). A smaller cabin below and astern would run you a hundred and twenty-five (just under two thousand today). Matson understood the benefit of advertising and cultivated a close relationship with the Hollywood studios, even having its ships featured in a number of films. The ships became part of the dream of fantasy vacations. Passengers who frequented the Crystal Club and Veranda Cafe on board were plied with tropical tunes on the way to, and returning from, the islands, highlighting another important influence on the development of California beach culture: Hawaiian music.

Tradition has it that seventeen-year-old Solomon Hoʻopiʻi Kaʻaiʻai—known during his career as Sol Hoʻopiʻi—stowed away aboard the *Matsonia* in 1919 with two other musicians. The U.S. government had commandeered three of Matson's ships to transport troops during World War I, so transportation off-island was scarce and expensive, which led to frequent stowaways. When the three young men were discovered en route, so the story goes, they managed to charm the other passengers so well with their music that these latter took up a collection and paid their fare to San Francisco. By July 1920, the *Honolulu Star-Bulletin* was reporting that Hoʻopiʻi and two brothers—Theo and C. H. Decker—had formed the "Pawaa trio" and were based out of the Hotel Dudley in Los Angeles.[64] C. H. Decker played guitar, Theo Decker the steel guitar, and Hoʻopiʻi the ukulele. Hoʻopiʻi would eventually earn fame as "King of the Steel Guitar" not only for his playing but also for designing his own model that became popular with other musicians. We'll have more to say about Hoʻopiʻi in chapter 4 because he was a central figure on the South Seas club scene in Los Angeles during the 1930s as well as a licensed agent in charge of hiring Hawaiians for the movies. But in terms of beach culture, a strong argument can be made that there would not have been the celebrated surfer parties at San Onofre laced with the sounds of Hawaiian guitar, nor the annual "Hula Luaus" put on by the Palos Verdes Surfing Club, if Hoʻopiʻi and other Native Hawaiians had not saturated Southern California with island music during the 1920s and 1930s.

Hoʻopiʻi had arrived in Los Angeles in the wake of the first mainland craze for Hawaiian song and dance, triggered by two events in California held four years apart. The first was the theatrical production of *The Bird of Paradise*, which debuted in Los Angeles in 1911. The play tells the story of Hawaiian princess Luana, who falls tragically in love with the American Paul Wilson. Because she cannot adjust to his "white ways," she ends up leaping to her death in the volcano Mauna Loa. The story, enhanced by Hawaiian music and hula, created a sensation on Broadway and in touring companies across the country. The play was particularly successful in Los Angeles, which staged performances for thirteen consecutive seasons.[65] The second event was the Panama-Pacific International Exposition—essentially a world's fair—held in San Francisco in 1915. The Royal Hawaiian Quartette introduced Hawaiian music to an estimated nineteen million visitors by performing two shows a day from February to December.[66] They played songs from *The Bird of Paradise* along with originals like "On the Beach at Waikiki," arranged by longtime composer Albert "Sonny" Cunha. Cunha is credited with popularizing *hapa haole* music in the early twentieth century, a genre that mixed Hawaiian and American musical traditions in such hits as "My Waikiki Mermaid" and "My Honolulu Tomboy." The popularity of this music at the exposition—performed as background for *hapa haole* or mixed-raced women handing out slices of pineapple—prompted New York's music capital, Tin Pan Alley, to produce a flood of Hawaiian-themed music to capitalize on the success of "On the Beach at Waikiki." By the time Hoʻopiʻi began performing in Los Angeles in 1920, the key instruments of *hapa haole* music—the steel guitar and ukulele—were already influencing mainland music traditions in jazz, blues, and country.[67]

While mainland USA and other parts of the world enjoyed the sights and sounds of Hawai'i in musical and theatrical performances, the story-lines helped create or reinforce stereotypes of Pacific Islanders that remain in the popular imagination. As Aiko Yamashiro remarks, the influence of *hapa haole* music "solidified and perpetuated U.S. mainland caricatures of Hawai'i as a place of grass shacks, white sandy beaches, lovely hula maidens, and happy dancing natives."[68] These caricatures proliferated at the Panama-Pacific International Exposition in the South Seas Villages exhibit. The *San Francisco Examiner* presented a full-page spread of hula dancers posing in grass skirts: "In their native dances, accompanied by the soft strains of native Hawaiian music, their graceful movements and their happy, smiling faces serve to fix the impressions which most people have received that these members of the great human family in their South Sea home are among the most favored and happiest of mortals."[69] Despite the *Examiner's* assurances that the exhibits were "so faithful in spirit and so accurate in all of their material details," neither the stockings nor the grass skirts of the dancers formed part of traditional Hawaiian hula. The widespread representation of South Sea Islanders as simple people trapped in the past helped justify the ongoing colonial projects of the United States to secure the Hawaiian Islands as part of their political and military expansion in the Pacific. Haunani Kay-Trask, among others, has pointed to the mythic image of Hawai'i reflected in so many lyrics of *hapa haole* songs—"the desire of a male visitor to Hawai'i for a local Hawaiian girl"[70]—as a metaphor for such imperial expansion. "Thus, Hawai'i," Trask states succinctly, "like a lovely woman, is there for the taking."[71]

The legend of the Waikīkī beachboys also played into stereotypes of Native Hawaiian men in the 1920s and served as the most direct antecedent to the kind of beach lifestyle imagined by young Southern Californians in the 1930s. In a 1922 letter to members of the board of harbor commissioners, David Kahanamoku, Duke's younger brother and captain of the Waikiki Beach Patrol, disputed complaints that his men were absent from duty, giving surf lessons, or engaging in indecent conduct. "I would also like to state," he wrote, "insofar as the giving of ukulele and guitar lessons is concerned, that, of the four that now compose the patrol, not one of us are musicians. There are other boys about the beach every day that are musicians. These boys earn their livelihood by giving surfboard and swimming lessons and also take out canoes, and in their leisure hours play their guitars or ukuleles and lie around on the beach, and we are very often blamed for this."[72] Here we have the essence of the beachboy stereotype, later characterized in another Honolulu newspaper as "just one long, long summer of roses and music and moonlight nights, with never a worry, never a care, no responsibility, and no work whatsoever."[73] A member of Kahanamoku's beach patrol reportedly composed the following verses to satirize their situation:

> O stick to the beaches,
> And pass up the peaches,
> Relinquish those long motor drives;
> O teach no more women
> The business of swimmin'—
> Your job is the saving of lives.
>
> Though you may be a dandy
> At surfing, or handy
> At playing the old steel guitar,
> Forget this enjoyment
> Or else your employment
> May find itself chasing a star![74]

Much like lifeguard service in California beach towns, the Waikiki Beach Patrol had begun as a response to beach drownings. In October 1916, two people died near Waikīkī: James A. Mitchell, a soldier at Fort Ruger's 2nd Company Coast Artillery; and Effie Crichton, who worked as a governess in the islands. Calls appeared in the local press to form a beach patrol to protect the rising number of beach visitors. The patrol was eventually funded by the legislature and put under the auspices of the board of harbor commissioners. David Kahanamoku was hired as captain and began patrolling the beach with his crew in October 1917.[75] Except for a stint in the Hawaii National Guard during World War I, Kahanamoku remained captain of the beach patrol until the mid-1920s. His letter to the harbor commissioners distinguishes between the paid lifeguards who worked seven days a week from 7:30 A.M. to 6:30 P.M., and the "gig" workers on the beach—musicians, surfers, unofficial tour guides—who made their living off the growing tourist trade at Waikīkī. It was these latter beachboys who captured the public's imagination as happy-go-lucky beachcombers—part vaudeville clown and part gigolo—and whose imagined carefree lifestyle of sun, surf, and sexuality formed the heart of beach-culture ideals. There is more to say about the development of the Waikīkī beachboy tradition in the next chapter, but we can add here that the beachboys also represented the height of what became known as the waterman tradition: men who excelled at all aquatic activities—surfing, canoeing, diving, water rescue—and set the standard for young people in California.

~

In June 1929 the *Pasadena Post* reported, "Kahanamoku Is Requested To Return To Islands in Legislative Bill."[76] Duke had been living in Los Angeles for seven years by then, and politicians back in Honolulu had passed a resolution announcing in part that "his return and permanent residence here would be an inspiration to the youth of the islands."[77] Of course, there was also tourism to consider. After Duke returned to Hawai'i later that year, he was hired as the custodian of city hall. Mayor-elect William E. Miles, who had proposed Kahanamoku for the position, indicated that "one of the main functions of the office is to conduct tourists through the city hall and pointed out that Duke is admirably suited for this work."[78] Duke, who also oversaw the custodians and groundskeepers, later scoffed that "Superintendent was nothing but official toilet cleaner but at least I was my own boss."[79] He would move on to more notable positions as the sheriff of Honolulu from 1934 to 1959. But this job impacted tourism as well. Fred Siegling, a U.S. Senate candidate in 1934, insisted that "if Duke Kahanamoku was elected sheriff of the city and county it would be worth millions of dollars to the territory in publicity."[80]

By that time—four years into the Great Depression—Hawaiian tourism needed a booster shot. When the legislature had called on Duke in June 1929, no one foresaw the economic collapse on the horizon. Hawaiian tourism had more than doubled during the 1920s, steadily rising from eight thousand visitors in 1921 to more than twenty-two thousand in 1929—these latter contributing the greater part of ten million dollars to the economy. By 1933 the number of visitors and annual tourist revenue had been cut in half: just over ten thousand tourists contributing some four million dollars.[81] Out on the beach in the mid-1930s, Louis "Sally" Hale, captain of the Waikiki Beach Patrol, lamented: "It's not like the good old days though, when a boy considered $15 a day the normal wage, and, if he exerted himself slightly, he could pull down fifty bucks daily with little effort. . . . Those boom days were back in '28 and '29, when people had more money than was good for them and when a fifty dollar tip was expected instead of a fiver. Now the beach looks like it did back in 1920, before tourists began to be attracted here by South Sea island ads."[82] Tourism was the fuel that kept things moving in Hawai'i, and in California it had emerged as one of the state's major industries. In *Material Dreams: Southern California Through the 1920s*, Kevin Starr notes that 250 million dollars had been invested in hotels and other short-term lodging in the Los Angeles area by 1925, catering to the nearly million and a half visitors the city welcomed every year.[83] And for "both tourist and resident alike," Starr adds, "the favorite destination was the beach."[84]

Southern California beach culture of the mid-1930s flourished because the ground had been so well prepared during the 1920s. Duke was indeed chief custodian, lending his knowledge, skill, and relaxed demeanor to a young generation of Southern Californians to imitate and master. He drove the highways that had been built to funnel visitors to the coast, and surfed the famous sandbars at Corona del Mar and Long Beach that would eventually be dredged to make room for more coastal development. He gave swimming and surfing exhibitions throughout the region, including visits to the Santa Monica beach clubs that overlooked his dark skin because of his fame and ability to draw visitors. Local African Americans and other ethnic groups were not so fortunate when it came to enjoying coastal spaces, where they were excluded from working as lifeguards or discouraged from participating in sports like paddleboard racing that fueled the growth of beach culture through competition and camaraderie.

Duke had also brought surfing and bodysurfing directly to Hollywood, which helped glamorize beach life in newspapers, magazines, and theaters around the world. That glamour included Waikīkī as well, frequented by Hollywood stars, where Native Hawaiian, mixed-race, and other local beachboys helped create "an exotic playground where the rich could get away from the pressures and pretensions of their normal lives."[85] Waikīkī represented its own theater, in many respects, where racial norms could be suspended for the price of a cruise ticket and allow well-heeled white women, for example, the freedom to romance (or be romanced by) dark-skinned beachboys. The allure of freedom and romance directly impacted beachwear. As Christine Skwiot notes, "Waikīkī was the first beach where bathing attire went modern, and women adopted bathing suits that revealed necks, arms, legs, and even waistlines and cleavage."[86] Hollywood had its own tradition of "bathing beauties" first exploited by Mack Sennett to spice up his slapstick silent films—"young, pretty, bathing-suit-clad actresses, frolicking on the sand"—and the bolder swimsuit fashions appearing at Waikīkī quickly made their way across the Pacific and into Hollywood films.[87]

By the time Duke arrived home in late December 1929, Tom Blake was in the process of realizing his dream of revolutionizing surfboard design. His new "cigar surfboard"—so called because of its oblong shape—sparked renewed interest in surfboard races and quickly became the centerpiece of California beach culture.[88]

PART I

The Builders

CHAPTER 1

The Dreamer

"[Tom Blake] wasn't the kind of guy to talk
very much. . . . But when he said something,
you had to listen, because it was something
that was, you know, sincere from his heart.
I was very much impressed with Tom, but I
always considered him a dreamer."[1]
—Wally Burton, Santa Monica Lifeguard

Ten days before the stock market crashed and drove the United States into
the Great Depression, the *Honolulu Star-Bulletin* announced that Tom Blake
(1902–1994) "was quietly working on a dream that has now been fulfilled."[2]
The paper explained that he had introduced a new type of surfboard at
Waikīkī—what they called a "cigar board" because of its long slender shape.
Blake had held a practice trial in front of a large crowd at the Natatorium,
Waikīkī's public swimming pool, and shaven several seconds off the Hawaiian record. Surfboard racing season was just beginning in the islands, and
the paper predicted that Blake's invention, created after his assiduous study
of ancient Hawaiian models in the Bishop Museum, would put all the other
contestants on notice. Several weeks later, the same paper reported: "Tom
Blake and his cigar surfboard is causing more comment and discussion than
any other individual or athletic event out at the beach."[3]

Before looking into the particulars of what turned out to be a groundbreaking modification of traditional Hawaiian *olo* surfboards, we can set
the broader context for Tom Blake and the history of beach culture in the
1930s by leaning on Kevin Starr's proposition that Californians of the period
manifested their psychological aspirations through material creations—
buildings, waterways, highways, airplanes, the movie industry, to name a
few. All of these and more had a profound impact on the identity of the
state and its citizens. Starr notes in *Material Dreams: Southern California
Through the 1920s*: "when the stock market crashed in October 1929, an
important new American city had been materialized: a City of Dreams,

Tom Blake with six of his self-shaped surfboards and paddleboards, Waikīkī, late 1929/ early 1930. (The Croul Family Collection.)

its boosters called it; for onto and into its very physical presence . . . was being projected at fast-forward speed a dream of romance and enhanced circumstances testifying in a very American way to the notion that imagination and even illusion not only are the premise and primal stuff of art, they play a role in history as well."[4] "Dreams," Starr adds, "have a way of struggling towards materialization."[5]

Nineteen-year-old Tom Blake came west from his hometown in Wisconsin after a chance meeting with Duke Kahanamoku in a Detroit movie theater as the latter was traveling home from the 1920 Olympics in Antwerp, Belgium.[6] Blake later wrote, "He held out to me his big soft paw of a hand, and gave me a firm, hearty handshake. It made a lasting impression. I felt that somehow he had included an invitation to me to come over to his own Hawaiian Islands."[7] Blake was a sensitive young man; orphaned as a baby, he had spent his childhood and teenage years shifting among extended family members, so perhaps he was looking for a home and a place to belong. One of Duke's unique talents was his ability to make everyone he met feel as if they knew him personally, as if they were old friends. Duke's warm spirit had a lasting influence on Blake, and that handshake sparked the beginning of a journey that would transform Blake and revolutionize California beach culture.

Blake arrived in Los Angeles in 1921 and made it his home base more or less for the next two decades, with lengthy stays in Hawai'i. Blake lived, worked, and dreamed in the City of Dreams. Inspired by Duke to devote himself to swimming, he competed against his idol in the early 1920s as part of the Los Angeles Athletic Club, even snatching an elusive victory from the Hawaiian in the longer distances.[8] Blake became a swimming sensation in his own right, winning the national ten-mile swim in Philadelphia in 1922, but the "Islands still beckoned to me," he wrote.[9] Blake, as we know, also devoted himself to surfing and paddleboard races during his time in Los Angeles, and a strong competitive desire materialized his dreams in the form of lighter, streamlined paddleboards. After he won the half-mile race at Waikīkī's newly opened Ala Wai Canal on his cigar board in January 1930—scorching the record by two minutes and thirteen seconds—and then bested Sam Kahanamoku on a regular surfboard in the hundred-yard event (knocking five seconds off the record), he explained the motivation behind his design after having studied models in Honolulu's Bishop Museum: "my object being to find not a better board to ride, but to find a faster board to use in the annual and popular surf board paddling races held in Southern California each summer. . . . My dream was to introduce, or revive, this type of board in Hawaii where surf board racing and riding is at its best."[10]

Blake went to Hawai'i because he felt called there by Duke, and to realize his dream of building the fastest paddleboards in the world. His romantic visions of Hawai'i, however, soon darkened under the reality of interacting with actual Native Hawaiians. "I discovered too late," he later wrote, "that beating the locals at their own game, in front of their families, could sour relations with my Hawaiian friends."[11] As with many of the Californians who made the trek to Hawai'i—or who tried to re-create Waikīkī on the shores of Southern California—their dream of the islands did not typically include a substantive relationship with Native Hawaiians themselves. This disconnect underlies much of California beach culture in the 1930s and ultimately drove Blake to invent legends of idealized relationships with Native Hawaiians rather than to form actual ones in his day-to-day life.

Blake could not have fulfilled his dream of creating a faster paddleboard if not for the influence of the City of Dreams: the aviation industry in Los Angeles provided the template for the structure of his paddleboards. Blake began with "chambered" racing boards where he cut chunks of wood from

Tom Blake demonstrating the construction of a hollow paddleboard, circa 1939. (The Croul Family Collection.)

solid planks to reduce their weight, but his lightest and most successful hollow board designs followed the pattern of wooden airplane wings being built in area factories. As Peter Westwick and Peter Neushul point out, Blake's fellow competitor at the 1928 Pacific Coast Surf Riding Championships at Corona del Mar, Gerard Vultee, was the chief engineer at Lockheed Aircraft (based in Burbank). Recall that Vultee was one of the surfers who had helped Duke rescue the twelve *Thelma* passengers at Corona del Mar in June 1925. In 1927 Vultee helped design the Lockheed Vega, whose fuselage and wings sported a novel design: long sheets of plywood covering wooden ribs—essentially the same structure as Blake's hollow boards.[12] We don't know if Vultee and Blake exchanged design concepts when the two competed against one another. Blake does credit an anonymous source with inspiring the evolution of his work. "After development of the hollow boards in 1929," he wrote in *Hawaiian Surfboard*, "an acquaintance of mine advised me to have the idea patented. He unwittingly opened up a new field of experiment in the construction of a board of light pieces of lumber, instead of hollowing out of the solid timber."[13] Blake locates this inspiration in 1929, so perhaps it was not Vultee but Abel Gomes, "an expert carpenter" who worked at Honolulu Sash and Door. According to period surfer Wally Froiseth, Gomes was the one who actually built Blake's boards for him at Waikīkī.[14]

Regardless of who might have encouraged Blake, airplane design elements had been inspiring inventors to create their own watercraft in 1920s Los Angeles. In a *Los Angeles Times* article from the summer of 1922—"How To Ride A Surf Board"—we read the following details describing the latest innovation for riding waves:

> One make of board in particular which has been used a great deal at the beaches the last couple of seasons is constructed like the wing of an airplane. They range in size from the small three-foot length for the kiddies to a ten-foot length for the whole family to ride.
> A framework of light but durable wood with the bow, thicker than the midships and stern, forms the hull. The bow bends up slightly. Over the entire framework, several thicknesses of canvas are stitched on. The whole is then painted and varnished.[15]

The design recalls Charles Lindbergh's *Spirit of St. Louis* (built in San Diego in 1927), whose wooden wings were covered in fabric to reduce weight. The *Los Angeles Times* captures a young female bather holding about a four-foot model of the craft in its Sunday edition from June 1924.[16] The article highlights the lightness and buoyancy of the board, which seemed intended for prone riding rather than stand-up surfing. Lorrin "Whitey" Harrison built one of these hollow boards in school in the 1920s and rode waves with it at Laguna Beach with his siblings. "I covered it with canvas tacked on with copper tacks and painted it," he recalled. "We'd ride it till we wore the canvas off, then we'd put new on."[17] Duke Kahanamoku himself refers to hollow boards as early as the summer of 1927. In an article for the *Los Angeles Times,* Duke describes the solid board he used at Corona del Mar—twelve feet long, three inches thick, and two feet wide—and adds: "I do not consider hollow surf-boards practical although many prefer them to the solid wooden ones." Duke may have gotten wind of Blake's experiments with chambered boards, but the idea of hollow boards had been circulating in Southern California from the early 1920s, principally inspired by the growing aviation industry. Blake's originality was to incorporate aviation design elements into models based on Chief Abner Pākī's koa surfboards in the Bishop Museum to create streamlined, "surfable paddleboards."[18] In many ways these boards encapsulate the major elements of 1930s California beach culture: an object inspired by Native Hawaiian culture that combined both surfing and lifesaving, and that was modified, marketed, and mass-produced by Southern California's manufacturing industry.

When Blake wanted to capitalize on his innovation, he left Hawai'i and returned to Los Angeles—not only the City of Dreams, but the city where those dreams materialized in manufacturing. According to historian Robert V. Hine, "Between the wars, Los Angeles rose to become the West's largest industrial center—the nucleus of the nation's oil equipment and service industry, the second largest tire-manufacturing center, and the largest producer of steel, glass, chemicals, aircraft, and automobiles in the West."[19] We can add lumber to the list of resources flowing into the Los Angeles basin. As one of the nation's fastest growing regions—from a population of half a million in 1910 to more than two million in 1930—Los Angeles County imported vast supplies of redwood, oak, and cedar to build houses for all those new residents. More than a billion board feet arrived in Los Angeles alone in 1924, the peak year of construction.[20] Beach culture of the 1930s was literally built in Los Angeles: the surfboards, the paddleboards, the Peterson rescue tube, and all the ancillary gear that individual surfers jerry-rigged in their backyards or shops, from crude surf racks on top of stripped-down cars to "Doc" Ball's surf club posters, photographs, waterproof camera housings, and eventually his book, *California Surfriders*. The culture itself developed and emerged from this hardware, which raced, glided, buoyed, and carried young Southern Californians farther than they could have ever imagined. The 1930s was the era when the collective physical culture of California beach life, while dominated by Hawaiian traditions and ideals, propelled a new generation not only into novel arts and crafts, but also, as Kevin Starr might say, into history.

Blake had arrived in Hawai'i to develop faster paddleboards, but he left the islands in the fall of 1930 with the idea of marketing his hollow boards as lifesaving craft.[21] In what became more or less an automatic gesture for him, Blake associated his innovations with Duke. When Blake introduced his racing boards at Waikīkī, he stated: "The first one to appreciate and use my new board was the famous Duke Kahanamoku."[22] Blake described how Duke liked to take his daily exercise by paddling the board around a fishing barge located three miles offshore. Blake also credited "the gallant surfboard rescue by Duke Kahanamoku and his surfing companions" at Corona del Mar in 1925 for inspiring the idea of using surfboards as rescue craft.[23] In later advertisements for his boards, readers would be told: "At Waikiki Beach, the Great Duke Kahanamoku rides nothing but a Hollow Surfboard."[24] As Duke had stated in his *Los Angeles Times* article quoted above, however, he preferred solid boards that he shaped himself and never rode the hollow boards, which he considered too light.[25]

Blake's logo for the Los Angeles Ladder Company, which produced his hollow boards from 1940 to 1942, is a near twin to Duke's famous poster image for the 1914 Mid-Pacific Carnival: both men balanced on a surfboard and facing the camera, smiling, with arms outstretched. Blake's obsequious deference to Duke seems more than humility: the association worked to Blake's advantage as he marketed his boards and established himself as Duke's heir apparent in surfboard design. We'll have more to say about these matters in chapter 9, but we can note here a photograph appearing in Blake's *Hawaiian Surfboard* that showcases his place in that lineage. The image presents four surfboards standing left to right: Chief Abner Pākī's sixteen-foot *olo* from the Bishop Museum; a twelve-foot board "of ancient *alaia* design"; Duke's ten-foot redwood surfboard; and finally, Blake's own "stream-lined twelve-foot hollow design," the lightest of the bunch. The placement of the boards left-to-right seems clearly designed to show an evolution in board design and Blake's prominent place alongside the Native Hawaiian shapers.[26] Blake's need to be recognized for his personal accomplishments often contributed to his estrangement from others—that had been the case at Waikīkī after his victories in paddleboard racing. He later recalled that, after beating the Hawaiians at their own game, "they began to look at you. There's something we don't like, and that was the end of the real good days."[27] In his personal scrapbook, Blake wrote across the *Honolulu Advertiser* article that had reported his win: "BEAT SAM & SARGENT KAHANAMOKU TO WIN THE MAJOR KING CUP. HOW THEY BURNED UP!!!"[28]

The "real good days" for Blake were the years leading up to his victories in 1930 when he was welcomed at Waikīkī during his annual visits, if treated as an outsider. "You roamed around there," Blake said, "nobody knew you, and it's a wonderful way to live, when you keep a low profile. Like, nobody's shootin' at you, you know?"[29] Blake carried the privilege of his race: leading the life he wanted in and around Waikīkī, an idealized existence where he could stroll into the exclusive Outrigger Canoe Club, change into surf trunks, grab his favorite teak surfboard, and paddle out. On his morning walks to the Outrigger, Blake recorded his observations about race in Hawai'i in the mid-1930s: "I like the opportunity of studying and seeing the great mixture of races gathered here, each one retaining many of their old customs of eating, dress and living. I pick a custom or two from each race to use at my convenience. Perhaps it is the Buddhist religion of the Chinese,—the poi eating and surfriding of the Hawaiians—the raw peanut eating of the Filipinoes [*sic*]—the happiness, enthusiasm and appreciation with which the Japanese meet their daily duties."[30]

As a white man in a U.S. territory, Blake had the advantage of taking or leaving customs at his convenience. These included keeping "one

Tom Blake's presentation of ancient and modern surfboards in his *Hawaiian Surfboard* (1935). "Photo by Hosoka."

hundred percent sun-tan here the year around, rest and sleep for hours in the wonderful sunshine each day."[31] But his idealized vision of race blocked out the tragic 1931 Massie Affair, for example, where five young local men belonging to the ethnic groups he mentions above—Japanese, Chinese, and Native Hawaiian—were accused of raping a white woman, Thalia Massie, the wife of a U.S. naval officer. One of the men, Native Hawaiian Joseph Kahahawai, was murdered in retaliation, even though the five were innocent and the rape itself entirely fabricated. The white men involved in Kahahawai's murder were convicted of manslaughter in April 1932, yet they were set free when the territorial governor, Lawrence M. Judd, commuted their sentences. Racial tensions and bitterness ran high in the local community, but Blake did not see it because he was disconnected from that community and not subjected to the daily realities of racism. His idyllic life as a Waikīkī beachboy clashed with reality only when the locals began to notice him—when they looked back at him—and let Blake know they didn't appreciate him showing them up in front of their families. His ignorance of race issues is perhaps even more glaring when we consider that he formed part of the Waikiki Beach Patrol, a group created expressly as a result of the Massie Affair, as I discuss farther down. Blake's personal disconnect with systemic racism in the islands might have remained a footnote if not for his outsized influence on succeeding generations of young people who imitated his self-described life—"A beach comber from choice, am I,/Content to let the world drift by"—and adopted his romanticized version of Native Hawaiians on beaches throughout Southern California.[32]

Blake's designs spread paddleboarding and surfing from coastal lifeguard crews to the general beach population throughout the 1930s, propelling the growth of beach culture in Southern California, Florida, the eastern United States, and even Australia.[33] Several companies in the Los Angeles area manufactured the boards—Thomas Rogers in Venice (1932–1939), the Los Angeles Ladder Company (1940–1942), and the Catalina Equipment Company in Redondo Beach (1946 to early 1950s)—along with the Robert Mitchell Manufacturing Company in Cincinnati, Ohio (1934–1939), which built boards for the East Coast and Hawai'i.[34] By the fall of 1935, Santa Monica lifeguard captain George Watkins boasted that about 350 surfboards and paddleboards were being used in his city alone.[35] Blake spent significant stretches of time traveling around the United States arranging sales and marketing, giving exhibitions, and working as a lifeguard when he needed the income. By the end of the decade, Blake's boards were a regular part of the Red Cross national aquatic schools program, where instructors taught water safety to coaches, counselors, and camp directors, thus extending paddleboarding to lakes and other inland bodies of water.[36]

Part of the appeal for Depression-era surfers was the do-it-yourself aspect of the boards. Although the higher-end racing models from the Thomas Rogers Company cost up to fifty dollars (almost a thousand dollars today), Blake had published detailed plans in popular magazines so that enthusiasts could build one themselves from cheaper materials.[37] In Blake's how-to article from *Popular Science* in 1939, for example, he presented his template and recommended "white cedar, mahogany, spruce, redwood, or white pine." But one could also supplement "waterproof plywood" for solid wood or "pressed composition wood of tempered quality."[38] Surf photographer and Palos Verdes Surfing Club member Leroy Grannis recalled buying a used paddleboard in 1937 for six dollars. His Hermosa Beach neighbors, Norm Hales and Fred Heidenrich, built their own paddleboards under the brand "H & H Boards" and sold them for twenty dollars.[39] One could also

Santa Monica lifeguards with their Tom Blake hollow paddleboards standing in front of the Casa Del Mar, 1930s. (The Croul Family Collection.)

buy a kit from the Thomas Rogers Company to assemble one of their Blake models—the Beach Boy Square-Tail Board, or the Streamlined Combination Surf and Paddling Board. The various options allowed a wide spectrum of people to own or build a board, which helped spread its popularity, especially among young people.[40]

The rise of surf clubs in the mid-1930s accelerated the use of Blake's designs, especially in the paddleboard contests that cities hosted to attract visitors and stimulate economic growth during the latter years of the Great Depression. The earliest club was "Pete" Peterson's Pacific Coast Paddle and Surfboard Association, founded in 1934 to promote surfing and paddleboarding in area competition.[41] The most famous club—the Palos Verdes Surfing Club (PVSC)—started the next year under the leadership of John "Doc" Ball and Adolph "Adie" Bayer. The Corona Del Mar Surf Club in Orange County had hosted three surfing championships from 1928 to 1932, but jetty enhancements at Newport Harbor blocked incoming

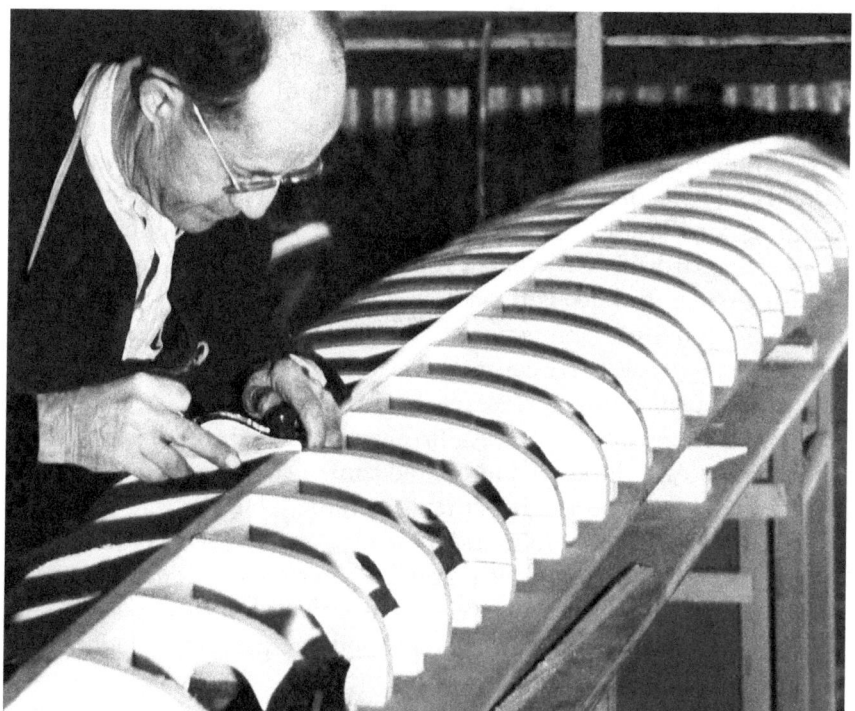

Thomas Rogers building a Tom Blake racing paddleboard in his shop in Venice, California, 1939. (The Croul Family Collection.)

swells and ruined the large waves that Duke had made famous. The surf club scene subsequently shifted north to Los Angeles County, where every beach town seemingly had its own group of young men and women who competed in various surfing, paddleboarding, and even paddleboard water polo events: Long Beach, Cabrillo, Hermosa Beach, Manhattan Beach, Venice, and Santa Monica. There was even a West Coast Paddleboard Association (WCPA) that helped organize and sponsor team paddleboard races from Catalina Island to Santa Monica. According to a letter penned by WCPA president "Adie" Bayer, the association had formed in 1935 and grew to a membership of "five hundred active surf-riders and paddlers" by 1940, comprised of fourteen separate member organizations.[42] These young people were the first wave of enthusiasts other than lifeguards to spread the popularity of Blake's paddleboards.

We know that competition in Southern California and Hawai'i had inspired Blake to design faster paddleboards. The Hawaiian tradition of paddleboarding and surfing in the same event that Blake renewed at the

PCSRC seems to have ended with the Corona del Mar contests; thereafter, paddleboarding and surfing split into separate events, with the former emerging as the dominant competitive sport until World War II. Paddleboarding was more popular because cities could organize races and not have to worry about canceling owing to lack of swell. Surf contests—with the current exception of wave pool events—have always depended on variable factors of swell, wind, and tide. More often than not, surf contests scheduled for any particular day will fail miserably because one can rarely predict consistent swell. Paddleboard races, on the other hand, can be run under almost any conditions; moreover, the judging criteria are straightforward: the paddler who covers the course in the fastest time is the winner. Paddleboarding is open to more contestants because it's easier to learn, and events can be run on a schedule. Surfing involves a much greater investment of time both to learn the sport and to hold contests (with surfers waiting for waves to ride), and the judging criteria are more subjective. Do you judge who has the longest ride? Who rides the most waves? Or who catches the biggest wave? Blake's boards were much lighter than their solid counterparts—his twelve-foot models weighed as little as forty-five pounds—so once you dropped the board in the water and pointed it in the right direction, almost anyone could compete in a race.

And they did. If we consider events reported in Southern California newspapers in 1939—the peak year of paddleboard racing—we get a good sense of Blake's impact on beach culture through the number and variety of contests. Of the dozen or so events reported in the press from May through December that year, we see a broad geographical distribution from San Diego County (Pacific Beach, La Jolla, San Onofre), Orange County (Newport Beach, Seal Beach), and Los Angeles County (San Pedro, Long Beach, Manhattan Beach, Venice, Santa Monica).[43] San Onofre, which had replaced Corona del Mar after 1935 as the most popular summertime surf spot, held two events in 1939: the seventh PCSRC on July 9 won by Lorrin "Whitey" Harrison, and the "first annual surf and paddleboard tourney" on August 27. The surf tourney had to be called off in the afternoon owing to lack of swell, but "Pete" Peterson won both the paddleboard race and the mixed-couples "surfing race" with his wife, Arlene. By 1939 many of the competitions included separate paddleboard categories for women and boys, thus expanding the number and range of participants.

Paddleboarding events had appeared here and there in Southern California after Blake introduced his new designs—usually less than five a year—but the number boomed in 1938, with about ten events that year, followed by another dozen in 1939. Their sudden popularity may have owed to the national recession (within the Depression) that hit the country hard in the last quarter of 1937 and stretched into June 1938. This was "the third-worst recession of the twentieth century," according to Patricia Waiwood, citing statistics from the National Bureau of Economic Research: "Real GDP fell 10 percent. . . . Unemployment, which had declined considerably after 1933, hit 20 percent. Finally, industrial production fell 32 percent."[44] Following the money trail of paddleboard races, in almost every case, individual Chambers of Commerce funded the competitions. In San Pedro, it was for "Harbor Host Days"; in Newport Beach, the second annual "Ocean Frolic"; in Venice, the "Mardi Gras festival." Coastal cities were doing their best to draw visitors out to their communities, and events like paddleboarding, and occasionally surfing, became popular draws.

Municipalities and other organizations funded team paddleboard events as well. In June 1936, five members of the PVSC won a relay race from Catalina to Santa Monica in eight hours and sixteen minutes, besting teams from Santa Monica and the Deauville Club.[45] The event was sponsored by the WCPA, which had connections to Hollywood; film star Virginia Grey presented PVSC member "Adie" Bayer with the first-place trophy as fellow actors Leo Carillo and Johnny Weissmuller looked on. Two years later, the PVSC defended its title with a ten-man team that made the thirty-five-mile crossing in nine hours and forty-two minutes. The club defeated teams from Santa Monica, Venice, Brentwood, and the Deauville Club. Several yachts helped convoy the contestants to and from Catalina, and the winners were escorted the final two miles by *Palama Kai*, the Santa Monica lifeguard boat. The larger number of contestants in the 1938 event—fifty in all—shows the growth in popularity of the sport and reinforces why organizations like the Chamber of Commerce would be interested in supporting it.[46]

Although surf contests were less numerous than paddleboard events for reasons stated above (the PCSRC were held nine times between 1928 and 1941), Blake's boards did help grow the sport because they were lighter than the traditional planks preferred by Duke, and detailed plans published in magazines allowed down-at-heel surfers to build their own models. It's true that hollow boards had certain flaws that made surfing still challenging to learn. Their length and weight made waves easier to catch, but the boxy sides made turning a challenge, and any whitewater that slammed into the boards usually spun them out and dumped the surfer. Blake introduced a low-raked tail fin in 1935 to help stabilize the boards, but the innovation didn't markedly improve maneuverability, and fins didn't catch on until the advent of balsa boards after World War II.[47] Some models included brass plugs at the tail to compensate for expansion and contraction of air, and to drain water that had leaked in. Despite these challenges, young people took to surfing in far greater numbers because of Blake's designs. In an odd way, the difficulty of surfing and its less frequent appearance at beachside carnivals may have increased its prestige. Surf contests were a bit of a unicorn—rare in appearance and always garnering much attention. The riders who won them immediately etched their names into surf lore up and down the coast, even as far as Hawai'i. When Kellar Watson, a relatively unknown surfer who'd won the 1929 PCSRC, arrived in Honolulu, he was surprised to learn that locals already knew his name. "I hope they don't mention it too much at the beach," he told a reporter. "I know the boys out there will probably show me up. So I want them to know I'm here to learn something about it and not to show them anything."[48] Watson was one of two dozen surfers in the Corona del Mar surf club who admired Duke and emulated his humility. No surprise that Watson's gift to himself, after winning the contest, was to do what all California surfers dreamed of doing: boarding a ship to Waikīkī.

Though paddleboard races were more frequent and numerous than surf contests, the growth of the PCSRC paralleled that of paddleboarding in terms of the rising numbers of participants. What the two sports had in common, of course, were the boards themselves, which contestants often used for both activities. If the event that Kellar Watson won in 1929 was like that of the 1928 and 1932 contests at Corona del Mar, they involved twelve to fifteen surfers. The numbers grew steadily as the event transformed into a straight surfing contest held at the hub of Southern California beach culture, San Onofre: thirty to forty contestants in 1936 and 1938, doubling to about eighty contestants in the peak year of 1939. The numbers remained strong the following year, with about seventy-five surfers competing in 1940. The growing numbers of contestants may have been one reason why the PCSRC remained a single event—surfing by itself rather than surfing and paddleboarding. The 1940 championships took over six hours to complete, with Cliff Tucker of the PVSC beating three other surfers in the finals: Jim McGrew, Johnny Gates, and Merle Eyestone.[49]

One exception of note for surf contests outside the PCSRC was at the Flood Control in Long Beach, which hosted the "first annual national surfing and paddleboard championship" in November 1938. The Del Mar Club in Santa Monica had sponsored the PCSRC at San Onofre in July that year, so perhaps the Long Beach junior Chamber of Commerce and the Long Beach Amusement League wanted to offer some friendly competition by sponsoring their own event. The cancellation of the surf contest that day owing to lack of swell shows the dangers of inviting thousands of visitors to the beach, though the paddleboard event continued without a hitch, with "Pete" Peterson, as usual, taking top honors in the men's race, and Mary Ann Hawkins winning on the women's side.[50]

To their credit, the Long Beach organizers persisted with the surfing contest, which was held the following month in December. More than ten thousand visitors reportedly watched Arthur Horner of the Venice Surf Club win the gold cup, with John Campbell and Joe Kerwin of the Manhattan Beach Surf Club following a close second and third. The *Los Angeles Times* reported that one hundred surfers competed in the event.[51] The Flood Control had been growing in popularity with area surfers for several years. Captain Roy Miller of the Long Beach lifeguards told the local press in June 1939 that surfers from Santa Monica often called him on Sunday mornings to get a surf check: "If we tell them the breakers look good . . . in about two hours you'll find anywhere from 40–80 paddleboards dotting the water where this type of sport is most enjoyable."[52] Miller indicated that surfers were primarily interested in two locations: Flood Control and 72nd Street. Miller's comments remind us not only of surfing's great popularity by the end of the decade, but also how much surfers enjoyed riding waves together.

In addition to the influence of Blake's paddleboard and surfboard designs on California beach culture, another player that literally manufactured Waikīkī dreams was Pacific System Homes, the world's largest builder of ready-cut homes during the 1930s. The company produced the raw materials for various models in its south Los Angeles factory—California Ranch House, Mountain Cabin, Waikiki Cottage—and then shipped them across the United States and abroad, where the homes would be assembled onsite. Their influence on mainland and island beach culture began at the start of the Great Depression when Meyers Butte, son of founder William Butte, proposed that the company diversify by building surfboards. Meyers "knew of George Freeth's early exhibitions," reports Craig Stecyk, "and was keen on the Hawaiian sports of paddling and surfing."[53] After developing a saltwater-proof glue to hold the wood together, the company sent its first shipment of six surfboards to Waikīkī in the spring of 1932. The *Honolulu Star-Bulletin* called the boards "the latest thing at Waikiki" and noted their lighter weight and greater buoyancy.[54] A ten-foot board weighed as little as forty-five pounds, making the craft more maneuverable. They were also beautiful to behold, the early models featuring alternating strips of redwood and white pine (later balsa), giving the boards an attractive pinstripe design. California surfboard manufacturer Dale Velzy famously referred to the boards as "droolers": "Everybody had home-mades or hand-me-downs, so people really wanted a Pacific System. There were a lot of them around places where rich guys who had gotten them in Hawaii hung out, like the Bel Air Bay Club, the Jonathan Club, the Balboa Bay Club and the Santa

Portrait of Meyers and Elizabeth Butte, early 1930s. (Courtesy Wilson Butte.)

Monica Swim Club. . . . God, those boards were beautiful. . . . It hurt to look at them because they were so bitchin'."[55]

Meyers Butte originally called the boards "Swastikas" for the symbol's traditional connotations of health and well-being, but he smartly changed the name to "Waikiki Surf-Boards" in 1938 to avoid association with Adolph Hitler and the Nazi *Hakenkreuz.* Velzy's comments about "rich guys" bringing the boards back to their private clubs from Hawai'i points to the company's success in creating a high-end market for its products. Pacific System eventually became the exclusive board builder for Waikīkī's Outrigger Canoe Club, which put the company in the interesting position—very much like Tom Blake—of fabricating a Hawaiian dream through their surfboard models and marketing campaigns. Hawaiians were well aware of the irony. "Waikiki with her surf boards manufactured in Los Angeles," commented the *Honolulu Advertiser,* "will be like Egypt with her scarabs manufactured in Connecticut."[56] The Waikīkī beachboys, who rode and helped advertise the boards, were key to the company's success. The beachboys represented in so many ways the heart of Waikīkī, and winning their approval—including testimonials from Duke Kahanamoku—consolidated Pacific System as a purveyor of Native Hawaiian culture and tradition. To understand the connection between the beachboys and the Outrigger Canoe Club, we must return to the Massie Affair.[57]

In *Waikiki Beachboy,* Grady Timmons summarizes the rumors and negative press that followed the Massie case by quoting a letter written by actress Dorothy Mackaill that appeared in the *Honolulu Star-Bulletin* on January 29, 1932, three weeks after the murder of Joseph Kahahawai. The case had captured the nation's attention, and even the U.S. Congress, fearing civil unrest in a key military outpost, had begun to hold hearings on the matter.[58] Mackaill linked the alleged assault on Thalia Massie to mixed-race men in the islands who witness white women encouraging the advances of Native Hawaiian beachboys:

> What can we expect of these [mixed-raced] people when they see Kanakas openly receiving the attentions of American white women?
> It is little short of disgraceful to see how some white women lie on the beach at Waikiki, in abbreviated bathing suits, and permit the "beach boys" to rub them with cocoanut oil so they will get a good tan.[59]

The letter was little more than a racist rant, and even though all rape charges were dropped against the remaining local men in February 1933, Mackaill wasn't the only one connecting the Massie case to the sexual liberties between dark-skinned beachboys and light-skinned females at Waikīkī. Lorrin P. Thurston, former president of the Outrigger Canoe Club (1929–1930) and publisher of the *Honolulu Advertiser,* believed that Waikīkī had a problem with "beach pests"—men who drank too much, made too much noise, bothered female guests with unwanted attention, and generally annoyed visitors trying to relax and have a good time.[60] William Mullahey, who had been raised in the islands and returned in 1934 after completing his degree at Columbia University, relates that Thurston approached him to help establish a beach patrol. "The reason being," Mullahey said, "that the Massie Case—which was very much in the news—and there were all sorts of rumors about natives jumping out of the bushes—attacking school teachers—and a lot of rumors that were probably untrue but still were—a concern to the beach."[61] Mullahey had lifeguarded for five summers at Jones Beach off Long Island, the last two years serving as captain.[62] Thurston wanted Mullahey to explain to Honolulu's power brokers how the lifeguards were organized at Jones Beach. He then asked the local businessmen for five thousand dollars to buy all the equipment from the beach concessions at Waikīkī—surfboards, canoes, umbrellas—so that the services could be consolidated under one professional group working out of the Outrigger Canoe Club: the Waikiki Beach Patrol.[63]

Tourism was certainly on Thurston's mind when he recruited Louis "Sally" Hale to become captain of the group. Members, wearing matching uniforms and caps, would perform various services for hotel guests—surfing and canoe lessons, or the popular Hawaiian massage *lomilomi*—so they had to be beyond reproach. In Thurston's words, they "would best impress the malihini [newcomer] and adequately serve the kamaaina [old-timers]."[64] They hired Pua Kealoha as one of the first patrol members. He had won gold and silver medals in swimming at the 1920 Olympics and worked as a professional musician along with fellow beachboys Kepoikai "Splash" Lyons and William "Chick" Daniels. Tom Blake himself joined the beach patrol, and he's pictured in a *Honolulu Advertiser* article standing alongside the other members in front of a set of surfboards made by Pacific System Homes. The article, from February 1936, notes that the beach patrol now had forty surfboards.[65]

We see nine of those boards standing tall beside the beachboys, with iconic Diamond Head looming in the background, when Shirley Temple, Hollywood's most famous child actor, arrived in Honolulu in August 1935. "The Little Colonel" was made honorary captain of the beach patrol after chatting with Sally Hale for the news cameras and posing with ten of the members. Such moments crystalized and glamorized the connection between Pacific System surfboards and everything that Californians and the world loved about Hawai'i: surfing, Diamond Head, palm trees, and the beachboys themselves with their catchy nicknames: "Sally" Hale, "Splash" Lyons, "Chick" Daniels, "Panama" Dave Baptiste, "Curly" Cornwall, and "Typhoon" Spencer, among others. Californians like Meyers Butte had tuned into the Hawaiian dream just as they would to *Hawaii Calls*, the radio show that started broadcasting from Hawai'i also in 1935, and they amplified that dream. Pacific System in fact pursued its own programming through photo ops like those with Shirley Temple, or publishing endorsements by beachboys like "Typhoon" Spencer—"I have found much enjoyment in riding my Swastika Hawaiian Surf Board. This board has proved to be perfectly balanced, light and sturdy."[66] The company's letterhead featured a picture of Duke in the margin, and stated boldly across the bottom of the page: "OFFICIAL BOARD OF OUTRIGGER CANOE CLUB."[67]

The company's goal was to capture the Waikīkī dream for those who consumed it most—that is to say, Californians. The West Coast, and Los Angeles in particular, had long been seen as Hawai'i 's target audience for

Shirley Temple being named honorary captain of the Waikiki Beach Patrol, 1935. The beachboys are all outfitted with Pacific System Homes surfboards (the paddleboard at far left a possible exception). (Courtesy Joanne Makalena Takatsugi/Grady Timmons, *Waikiki Beachboy*.)

tourism. Listen to Harry P. Wood, secretary of the Hawaii Promotion Committee—later the Hawaii Tourist Bureau—describe the many possibilities that California had to offer the islands back in October 1906:

> My work on the mainland this year . . . is especially intended to study the conditions existing in Los Angeles, and to plan for the doubling of our efforts in this territory and largely to increase the scope of our work in Southern California.
>
> We realize more than ever the fact that Los Angeles is the great tourist gateway and clearing house of the country. It is here, therefore, that we shall have our recognized center of activity for our tourist propaganda.[68]

Wood had spent fifteen years living in San Diego prior to working for the Hawaii Promotion Committee, and he understood the massive population growth that was happening in Southern California and how that could translate into economic prosperity for the islands. George Freeth's arrival in Southern California in 1907 was part of Wood's "tourist propaganda" efforts, hoping that Freeth's surfboard exhibitions would encourage more

Californians to visit Hawai'i. Twenty years later, of the ten thousand tourists who arrived in the islands aboard ships from the Matson Navigation Company and the Los Angeles Steamship Company, more than half were from California (5,526). The next largest group came from New York (531).[69] California sent ten times more visitors to the islands than any other state. It makes sense: geographical proximity, higher population, and West Coast companies like the Los Angeles Steamship Company (operating direct lines to Honolulu since 1922) and the Matson Navigation Company (headquartered in San Francisco). The Waikiki Beach Patrol also wore matching swim trunks designed by Jantzen Knitting Mills, based in Portland, Oregon. A picture in the *Honolulu Advertiser* in May 1935 captures nine of the members sporting their new "Spring Attire"; in the background, of course, a Pacific System surfboard is leaning against the Royal Hawaiian Hotel.[70] What we see in this collective manufacturing effort is the extent to which West Coast companies materialized Hawaiian dreams primarily for the profit and consumption of those living on the West Coast.

Part of the great success of the Pacific System surfboards—highly expensive and much sought after by collectors today—was their visual appeal: a unique pinstripe look whose outlines belong to the Streamline Moderne movement that has been called "a cultural symbol of the Depression era."[71] Trains, planes, and automobiles of the time all generated this effect: long horizontal lines that connoted speed; rounded noses that cut aerodynamically through wind and water; modern materials that showcased lightness, efficiency, and symmetry. This was an aesthetic of the Machine Age featuring mass production and smooth-surfaced efficiency. Recalling the words of Dave Velzy, "God, those boards were beautiful. . . . It hurt to look at them because they were so bitchin'." Symmetry is a hallmark of Pacific System boards, created through alternating redwood stringers running the length of balsa cores. The company created various sizes and designs, yet each was perfectly symmetrical. Meyers Butte incorporated the aesthetic into the names of his boards—the "Streamlined 'Waikiki' Paddleboard," for example.[72] Thomas Rogers and Robert Mitchell did the same in their respective advertisements for Blake's models: "Streamlined Life Guard Board" and "Streamlined Combination Surf and Paddling Board" for Rogers, and "The New Tom Blake Streamlined Air Chamber Hawaiian Hollow Surfboard" for Mitchell.[73] Tom Blake had pushed the aesthetic himself in *Hawaiian Surfboard* with a caption for one of his paddleboards standing silhouetted in the sand at Waikīkī: " . . . *all nature is stream-lined. . . .* The idea of stream-line is as old as the world. To keep up with life a thing must be that way."[74] While Blake may have understood streamline as an age-old concept based on his studies of Hawaiian *olo* designs, Pacific System was squarely grounded in modern manufacturing as illustrated in their advertisement copy: "Our merchandise has new, scientifically designed stream lines which appreciably increase the speed. . . . [T]he Balsa wood is hand-sorted from finest imported stocks, scientifically kilned, laminated and cabinet finished by expert craftsman under the personal direction of a professional surf-board aquatist."[75] The "professional surf-board aquatists" who worked at Pacific System included the most respected beach-culture influencers of their generation: Santa Monica lifeguards "Pete" Peterson and "Whitey" Harrison. Both men were expert craftsmen, building custom surfboards at the company's factory in Vernon, near downtown Los Angeles, to supplement their incomes.

Los Angeles had several monuments to Streamline Moderne if anyone needed inspiration—the Pan-Pacific Auditorium (1935) in west L.A., for one. But the movement's popularity drew principally from the aviation industry, with surfer-engineer Gerard Vultee playing a significant role in his design of the Lockheed Vega (1927), which Amelia Earhart among others flew to much acclaim. The plane's rounded aerodynamic body and wings, its novel design structure and materials, its lightness and speed—all became elements in the dominant aesthetic of the Great Depression. Surfboards and paddleboards carried that aesthetic to Waikīkī with the first shipment of Pacific System boards in 1932. The relationship between Meyers Butte—president of the Waikiki Surf-Board Company—and the Outrigger Canoe Club looked to grow even stronger in the early 1940s. The *Honolulu Star-Bulletin* reported in March 1941 that Butte was vacationing at the Moana hotel and was considering opening a branch office in Honolulu.[76] The attack on Pearl Harbor later that year shelved those plans. Butte joined the Navy, and Pacific System ceased production of its surfboards.

The boards that Blake had designed at the beginning of the 1930s fulfilled his dream of creating the fastest paddleboards. He also achieved a subsequent goal of using his paddleboards as lifesaving vessels to improve safety in the ocean and other bodies of water. These accomplishments solidified his status as the second most influential surfer in California, right behind his idol, Duke Kahanamoku. Whereas Duke had all of Hawai'i championing his numerous accomplishments over the decades, Blake had to generate his own press. He did this by licensing his surfboard and paddleboard designs, traveling around the country to demonstrate their effectiveness, and sending his writings and photographs to local and national press outlets—newspapers, magazines, and publishing companies. For a younger generation of surfers and lifeguards in Southern California, Blake became the closest thing they could get to achieving a collective dream: living the life of a Waikīkī beachboy. Blake himself had talked up his personal connections to Duke, and he had served on the Waikiki Beach Patrol alongside men who represented a pantheon of lesser gods to California surfers—watermen skilled in every aspect of ocean craft who had carved out a life, according to Blake and popular tradition, of surfing, canoeing, playing music, and romancing women at the most beautiful beach in the world. What young surfer living in Southern California wouldn't want that dream for himself?

Blake and the companies that marketed his designs, or created their own version of them like Pacific System, used Hawai'i to great advantage. In brochures they garnished their "Square-Tail Hawaiian Boards" with pictures of surfers riding waves at Waikīkī. They sold the "Tom Blake Hawaiian Paddle Board" and the "Beach Boy Square-Tail Board." Pacific System secured the exclusive right to furnish surfboards to the storied Outrigger Canoe Club—established in 1908 as the world's first surfboard club—and to the Waikiki Beach Patrol that the Outrigger had organized in 1935. Those striking boards became iconic accessories to the beachboys in mainstream media representations. What we witness over the course of a decade is a campaign that appropriates Hawai'i not just in name and imagery, but the identity of Hawaiians themselves, in this case the Waikīkī beachboys. The association is positive on the surface—praise for their knowledge and skills—and yet the men themselves had to rely mostly on tips to survive. Allan "Turkey" Love dispelled some of the romance of the beachboy life when he recalled that tourism in Hawai'i "only had two seasons, winter and summer. In between there was nothing. And I mean nothing."[77]

The companies that manufactured surfboards in the 1930s formed part of a latter stage of U.S. imperialism in Hawai'i: in addition to usurping land and political power, they appropriated Native Hawaiian cultural identity for profit. Pacific System Homes, the Thomas Rogers Company, and the Los Angles Ladder Company all became popular mediators of Hawaiian culture through surfboards that consumers associated with authentic island life. The designs were based on traditional Native Hawaiian *olo* and *alaia* shapes, but constructed from materials, and aligned with an aesthetic, that emanated from the dynamic manufacturing world of Southern California. It would have been difficult to separate one tradition from the other by simply looking at the Pacific System boards, some of which were inscribed with the names of the beachboys themselves—PUA, or CHIC, or a Hawaiian term like MAKAALA ("vigilant")—all of which can be seen on the boards looming over Shirley Temple. One-time Waikīkī beachboy Tom Blake had inscribed one of his early boards with the Hawaiian word UILA ("LIGHTNING"), a sign of his desire for speed in the language that burnished his dreams.

CHAPTER 2

The Photographer

On the surface, he had everything: a loving,
devoted wife, two wonderful sons, an
education, a profession, and a solid practice.
He had excellent physical health, surfing, and a
circle of faithful friends.

But somehow all of this wasn't enough to quell
the occasional depression and subsequent
suicidal feelings. Part of this was Doc's feeling
about his book, *California Surfriders: 1946*.[1]

—Craig Lockwood, "Granny and Doc"

On January 18, 1931, John Heath "Doc" Ball (1907–2001) opened the Sunday Rotogravure section of the *Los Angeles Times,* and the picture he saw before him changed his life: a moody black and white image of dark clouds hovering over four silhouetted surfers at Waikīkī. The photographer—Tom Blake—had clicked the shutter just as the four men were rising to their feet. It's an imposing visual, filling half the page; the title, streaming across the top of the photograph—"RIDERS OF SUNSET SEAS"—was as dramatic as the four surfers about to steamroll Blake, who had positioned himself directly in their path to capture the action.[2]

The caption beneath the photograph read: "In With The Waves At Waikiki: A copyrighted photo by Tom Blake of Santa Monica, 1930 Hawaiian surf-board champion, and, for three years, Pacific Coast surf-board champion, taken with a waterproof camera of his own devising. Blake snaps the photo from the bucking surf-board, and, if he loses the camera, he just lets it float in with the waves."[3] The description highlighted Blake's accomplishments more than anything else, one of which turned out to be the first known use of a "waterproof camera" in surf photography. In truth, Blake had built a waterproof housing for a 4x5-inch Graflex that he had bought off Duke two years before. Although Blake later referred to the housing as "crude and clumsy"—a two-foot-high wooden box (with controls

Self-portrait by John Heath "Doc" Ball.

on the outside) that fogged up so badly he had to install a wiper blade on the inside to clear the lens—the contraption was indicative of his restless, inventive mind. He always seemed to be tinkering, looking for novel ways to expand his ocean experience and to share it with others.

And to monetize his inventions. Blake later elaborated on the photographs and his life at Waikīkī during this time: "everybody on the beach wanted their picture, because it'd never been done before, except from a speedboat. Instead of giving them all away, I wanted to hoard them myself, and send them into—put them in a book I was writing. So that started creating a little ill will over there. Something that I would avoid if I had to do it over again."[4] Here we see that disconnect again between Blake and the local surfers. They are not named in the caption, only Blake's many accomplishments. Blake is often recognized as a central inspiration for postwar countercultural figures because of his beachcomber fashion and

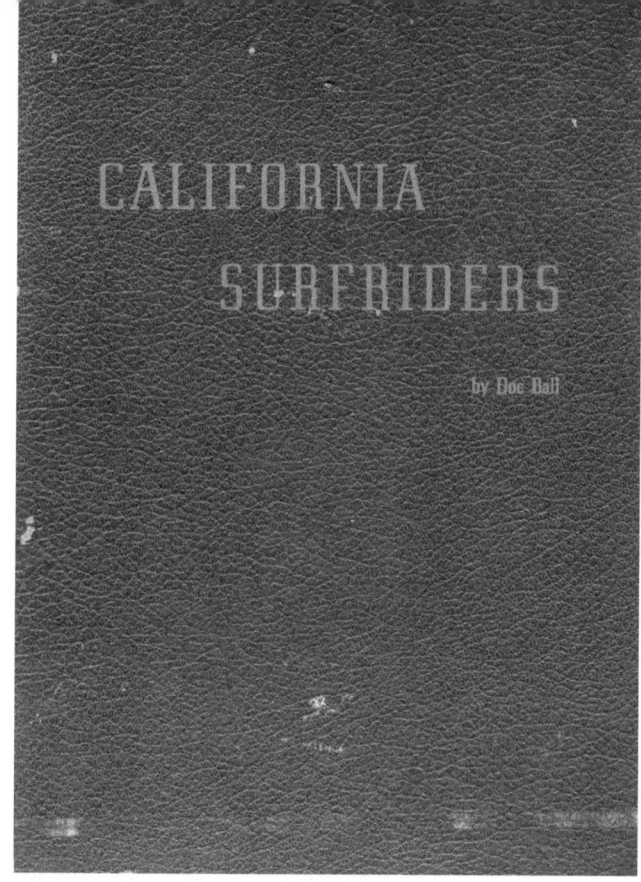

Cover of "Doc" Ball's *California Surfriders* (1946). (Courtesy California Surf Museum.)

proclivity toward leisure rather than the Protestant work ethic. An irregular income-stream, however, forced Blake to become mercenary when the need arose. He sent his Waikīkī pictures, along with a seven-thousand-word article—"Surfriding in Hawaii"—to *National Geographic* in late 1930. The editor ended up offering him a hundred dollars for eleven of the twenty-one photographs and for a scaled-down article. Eight of the images, without the text, eventually appeared in the magazine in May 1935.

Blake turned around and sold one of the photographs to the *Los Angeles Times,* which found its way into the hands of "Doc" Ball. Ball later commented that, when he saw the picture, "I just about flipped my lid. So I cut the things out and I put them under a glass tabletop and look at them every day. . . . Thomas, he was an inspiration to me, the way he lived and the way he was taking those pictures and everything."[5] A second photograph inset on the page, by W. C. Sawyer, captured four bathers wading out toward a swell in front of the Deauville Club—"Out To Buck The Breakers At Santa Monica." Perhaps the proximity of the two photographs gave Ball the idea that Blake's innovation could be applied to local beaches as well. Ball ended up taking some nine hundred photographs between 1931 and 1941, more than 150 of which ended up in his seminal contribution to California beach culture: *California Surfriders: 1946*.

The book, self-published after World War II, remains an artifact of 1930s beach culture because the majority of images were taken and developed before the war. Most importantly, it captures the rise of a regional beach culture distinct from Hawaiian precedents and traditions. Ball caught these young Southern Californians building their Waikīkī dreams with whatever materials that came to hand—homemade surfboards, self-stitched trunks, modified cars, old tires to burn on the beach to ward off winter's chill. The photographs recorded this emerging culture, and because they appeared in such mainstream magazines as *Life* (1938) and *National Geographic* (1944), they helped establish surfing in the popular imagination as a novel and alluring part of California's identity. The surfers in the photographs became the archetype of this new breed of recreationalist: young, white, male, their muscled bodies in full view as they balanced precariously on spear-like boards—or desperately leaped from them to avoid serious injury. When Ball sent Governor Earl Warren a copy of his book (number five of his limited edition of 510), he wrote in his dedication "a plea in behalf of our surfers, that the places described herein be developed for the continuance of this body-building sport."[6] A new pastime was emerging on the West Coast— "Surf-Boarders Capture California" announced the headline above Ball's eight-page spread in *National Geographic*—and the hundred-mile stretch from Malibu to San Onofre was its epicenter.[7]

Blake appeared among Ball's photographs in the *National Geographic* spread, balancing on his hollow board at Bluff Cove off the Palos Verdes Peninsula. He would have been envious of Ball's windfall—eight full pages—but Blake was probably partly responsible for the publication. The same editor who had accepted his photographs back in 1935, Gilbert Grosvenor, was still working at the magazine.[8]

Because of Blake's influence on the "California surfer look" after World War II—the deeply-tanned beachcomber, sporting light pants and tank top, who spends lazy days riding waves and enjoying his freedom—it's easy to overlook his immediate impact on surfers of the 1930s. Beyond Blake's surfboard and paddleboard designs discussed in the previous chapter, it was what Ball described above as "the way he lived" that captured the imagination of his contemporaries. Ball added a subtitle to *California Surfriders*: "A Scrapbook of Surfriding and Beach Stuff." It was this latter subject that Ball had also thought to include in his photographs: cars, clubhouses, gatherings at beaches from San Diego to San Francisco—in essence, *beach culture*—and which Blake had influenced because of his own photographs and how he wrote about his life in Hawai'i. Blake extolled his simple life at Waikīkī in *Hawaiian Surfboard*—the long warm days filled with surfing, canoeing, watching beautiful native women dance the hula, and being initiated into the exclusive Hui Nalu ("Club of the Waves") and "the secrets of spear fishing far out on the coral reefs."[9] Blake also described the natural beauty surrounding him—"coco palms waving in the clean trade winds, the colors of the water on the coral reef"—and added: "It's a great place for a bachelor."[10] No wonder California surfers ached for the islands and did their best to replicate that atmosphere at their local beaches. Ball himself was a little older than his fellow surfers—twenty-eight when *Hawaiian Surfboard* was published in 1935, and a practicing dentist—and he remained a bachelor until 1941. Don James, a budding photographer of the era like Ball, also fell under Blake's spell. "When I saw Tom Blake's surfing photos in National Geographic," he said, "that was it. We'd go to the library and pore over Blake's stuff. My dad had an old Kodak folding camera, and I grabbed it and started taking photos. . . . I began shooting pictures to show our parents and teachers what was going on."[11]

Ball was a student at the University of Redlands in 1926 when his father gave him a Kodak Autographic. Redlands sits in the shadow of the San Bernardino Mountains, about as far from the coast as one could get in the Los Angeles Basin. But the family had a summer house in Hermosa Beach, some seventy miles west, where Ball first became interested in taking pictures of local surfers and in surfing himself.[12]

Ball was athletic. He pole-vaulted in high school and played football at the University of Redlands. His longtime friend and fellow Palos Verdes Surfing Club (PVSC) member, Leroy "Granny" Grannis, described him as "a warm guy, easy to get to know, funny, eccentric—a real screwball."[13] Ball liked to build things, and his eccentricity surfaced in his handiwork: he attached a twenty-foot pipe—the end resting on roller-skate wheels— to a stripped-down Model-T that he'd been given for clearing a friend's backyard. The vehicle had no body, no fenders, and no front tires. He got the thing in working order and drove it around by sitting on the gas tank; he liked to scare his friends by popping the clutch and making the engine backfire out the long tailpipe. He also built a canoe out of orange crates, wooden bicycle rims, and canvas. He paddled the craft through the waterways of Redlands—lakes, rivers, canals—and eventually in the ocean. He carved his first surfboard from a slab of redwood with a hand-held adze and affixed a copper-sheeted shield to the deck. His Hawaiian dreams shone bright with the words "Na Alii" ("The Chiefs") emblazoned across the shield.

After graduating from the University of Redlands in 1929, Ball decided to become a dentist like his father, who had received his training at the University of Michigan. Ball and other influential surfers of the period (Tom Blake, "Pete" Peterson, Mary Ann Hawkins, and "Whitey" Harrison) all share this parental geography: for the most part their fathers and mothers hailed from the Midwest—Michigan, Wisconsin, Illinois, Missouri.[14] All of these influencers were first-generation Californians (stretching a bit for Blake), part of the great migration west that made Los Angeles the fastest growing region in the country in the early twentieth century. This common background may have contributed to the younger generation's attraction to Hawaiian culture, its perceived exoticism a potent remedy for the blandness associated with midwestern values. Perhaps it makes sense that Hawaiian cultural influences—the sports, the music, the dancing, the beach life—boomed first and foremost in Los Angeles, an area whose population migrated predominantly from the Midwest. The successive waves of white settlers during this period reinforced the displacement of indigenous peoples in Southern California and contributed to the enthusiasm that targeted the Hawaiian Islands as fertile ground for continued western expansion.

After Ball completed his first year of dental school at the University of Southern California, he did what every surfer of the period dreamed of doing: he boarded the *City of Los Angeles* at Wilmington and steamed to Honolulu for a summer vacation. His father traveled with him, and the two vacationed for a week in August 1930. Perhaps when Ball saw Blake's photograph in the *Los Angeles Times* the following January, it evoked memories of spending time in the water at Waikīkī. "Doc met Tom right after he came back from his first trip to Hawaii," recounts Grannis, "and I think Blake's camera intrigued him. Doc liked to tinker with stuff, and he was already taking pictures."[15] Ball started surfing at Hermosa Beach with his friend Norman Hales after his trip to Hawai'i; the two roamed south to Bluff Cove on the Palos Verdes Peninsula, a spot they dubbed "Little Waikiki" because of its long rides.[16] On a clear day you can see that cove from the Hermosa Beach pier. Hales later built a fourteen-foot hollow board that Ball purchased and used throughout the 1930s both for riding waves and as a platform from which to take his photographs.

Ball opened his dental practice in 1934, renting an upstairs office in the same building that housed the Regent movie theater on South Vermont Avenue in Los Angeles, near his alma mater, USC. Franklin D. Roosevelt had become president the year before, and his New Deal programs were steadily putting people to work, but money remained tight. Ball couldn't afford to rent a dental office *and* an apartment, so he lived in a small room next door to his office where he also built a darkroom to develop his photographs. He eventually cleared space in an adjacent room, accessed through a trap door, for the weekly meetings of the Palos Verdes Surfing Club, which he and "Adie" Bayer founded in 1935.[17] Ball settled into his dental practice, his photography relegated to a hobby and a labor of love. He experimented with different vantage points for the next several years—taking pictures from cliffs, piers, rocks, and even paddling out on smaller glassy days at Bluff Cove and holding the camera between his teeth to secure an image. A key development came in August 1939 when he was inspired to build a waterproof camera housing that allowed him to capture more fully the action out in the waves, thus giving viewers close-up shots of this novel sport sweeping the California coast.[18]

California Surfriders offers a broad overview of Ball's evolution as a photographer during these years and highlights the raw material from which California beach culture developed. The point may be too obvious to state given Ball's book title, but his collection of photographs emphasized the culture developing in California rather than the Hawaiian traditions that had inspired that culture. It's notable, for example, that Duke doesn't appear at all in the book. Like everyone else at the time, Ball called Duke "one of our heroes" and told stories of meeting him in Southern California and enjoying his company.[19] But unlike Tom Blake, Ball wasn't saturated with Hawaiian culture. His point of reference wasn't Waikīkī but "Little Waikiki"—his own Bluff Cove, where he and surfers of his generation fabricated a distinctly California version and vision of what it meant to be a surfer. The many images in his book are worth considering more closely to track where exactly California beach culture began to separate itself from Hawaiian influences.

After a foreword and epigraph, *California Surfriders* begins with a brief bio and picture of George Freeth, whom Ball called "the Mainland's First Surfboarder." We now know that other Hawaiians had surfed on the mainland before Freeth, but Ball was recording what he believed to be the origins of California surfing.[20] His book, more than simply capturing an era, gestured toward a genesis—a creation myth—that reached back to a solitary figure who brought surfing to the Golden State from across the sea.

Ball then situates the reader geographically by presenting a map of California that covers the broad realm of his surfriders: San Francisco in the north to San Diego in the south. Like many of the artifacts the reader will encounter in the book, including the book itself, the map is DIY ("Do It Yourself"): abbreviated and hand drawn. The hundred or so pages of photographs that follow move north to south, beginning with "Pedro Valley," which captures the Pacifica area just south of San Francisco. Ball presents ten surfing areas in his table of contents. As we might expect, Palos Verdes assumes the lion's share (fifty pictures), followed by Ball's summer vacation spot Hermosa Beach (thirty-four), and then San Onofre (thirty-two), which he calls "Surfers' Mecca." Ball included the work of other photographers to record surf spots that he had either not frequented himself (Shelter Cove, WindanSea) or that had been ruined by coastal development (Corona del Mar). Malibu is represented by only two pictures (taken by John Gates). Any book of California surfing today would probably start with Malibu, or at least devote the bulk of its history to that iconic spot. The pair of photographs is a sign of Malibu's outpost status for surfers of the 1930s. The division of photographs in *California Surfriders* reinforces the outsized influence that the South Bay area of Los Angeles and San Onofre had on the development of early beach culture.

The limned map of California is also notable for what it doesn't include: reference to the geography of migration—the Sacramento and San Joaquin valleys—where the majority of the 300,000 Dust Bowl migrants landed between 1931 and 1934. Another 350,000 migrants came between 1935 and 1940, more than fifty thousand of whom settled in Los Angeles County.[21] The world of Central Valley Hoovervilles, of mass deportation of Mexicans out of Los Angeles during the Great Depression, of the hard-labor camps recommended by the Los Angeles Chamber of Commerce in 1935 to deal with the influx of transients and others falling under the name of Okies— none of these exist on the map or in the book.[22] The points of reference are all coastal, the lens focused on the beaches, the waves, the horizon, not on what was happening inland. The Okies and other Dust Bowl migrants settled primarily in the interior rural areas of Los Angeles County, and so they had little impact on developments at the beach.[23] One would never know by leafing through the pages that the country was experiencing a national tragedy, with millions displaced and unemployed. Ball's book captured young Southern Californians dreaming of life as a Hawaiian beachboy on the shores of 1930s California. Because it was published after the war, the book also represented an act of nostalgia for a life (and a dream) that was never coming back. Ball's son Norman recalled his father's rages and frustration after returning from the Pacific theater—his drinking and verbal abuse—what we would recognize today as symptoms of posttraumatic stress disorder. "He told me that at one time," Norman recounted, "he was actually considering paddling out and never coming back."[24]

Ball married in 1941 and had two sons with his wife Evelyn—Norman (born 1942) and John Jr. (born 1943). After the war, Ball moved his family and dental practice to Hermosa Beach—a place filled with fond memories of surfing and family vacations—and channeled his energy into putting together *California Surfriders*. Grannis said that Ball "wanted to do the best he could with the book and, despite his best efforts, the reproduction, the paper and materials, and the binder turned out to be a lot less than what he'd hoped for."[25] The photographs hadn't reproduced clearly, and the bindings soon broke down. Norman added that "the book began falling apart, and that may have been part of the stimulant of his depression."[26] The war does creep into the book in certain places: a picture of the Santa Cruz Surf Club in March 1944 with visiting surfers who had joined the navy, and a shot of Charles "Doaks" Butler surfing Flood Control in Long Beach; Ball noted that Butler was serving aboard the *U.S.S. Edsall* when it went down in March 1942. The majority of photographs, however, display prewar Southern California, and the language Ball used to describe both the surfers and the surf spots are an early indication of how this group began to separate itself from Hawaiian traditions.

Those traditions are apparent, for example, when Ball titles his photograph of swells capping beyond the Hermosa Beach pier as "Zero Break," a term Blake uses for the outside reef at Waikīkī. Ball writes:

> Perhaps twice a year this remarkable surf will hump up a good half mile offshore and keep all the "malihinis" on the beach.
> Strictly for the "kamaaina," this stuff comes upon one out there with a long steamy hiss, and fills him at first with the apprehensive thought of, "Maybe I better wait for the second one."[27]

Ball's humor comes through in the caption, along with his use of "malihinis" and "kamaaina," which California surfers had picked up from their Hawaiian counterparts and used to connote "beginners" and "experts," respectively.[28] He refers in his book to the favorite hangout of the PVSC—Bluff Cove—as "California's Little Waikiki" and includes a picture of surfers in an outrigger canoe digging into a wave while club member Calvin "Tulie" Clark surfs beside them.[29] The photograph mimics classic tourist images of Waikīkī, with the headland on the south end of Bluff Cove filling in for Diamond Head. Additional photographs from Bluff Cove and San Onofre display various forms of tandem surfing with female partners lying down, standing up, and riding atop the shoulders of a male surfer.[30] Again, classic Hawaiian beachboy images. The caption for the tandem team at San Onofre describes "Benny Merrill and 'Wahini' slicing along as neat as anything."[31] Numerous photographs imitate the Hawaiian beachboys in other ways: groups of men taking off together on a community wave, or lined up at the beach with their surfboards standing tall behind them. Ball has many pictures of surfers wiping out—the fast beach-break waves revealing the

Palos Verdes Surfing Club member "Tulie" Clark surfing alongside an outrigger canoe at Bluff Cove, Palos Verdes. Note the abalone on the nose of the surfboard. (John Heath "Doc" Ball.)

limitations of hollow boards and heavy planks that were designed to ride the longer reef waves at Waikīkī. Although California was the center of surfboard manufacturing during this era, Golden State surfers didn't modify Hawaiian designs to fit local wave conditions until after World War II.

Ball and his friends also imitated the Waikīkī beachboys in their use of nicknames, which Ball calls attention to in *California Surfriders:* "By this time, you'll no doubt have noticed that surfers possess some odd nicknames. We'll quote a few for your pleasure: 'Red Dog,' 'Black Bass,' 'Burhead,' 'Hammerhead,' 'Bird Dog,' 'Button Nose,' 'Gooseneck,' 'Whitey,' 'Scobblenoggin,' and 'Nellie Bly.' 'Ain't they somepin?' "[32] Grannis noted that Ball was "a nicknamer, with a sense of humor," so he derived some pleasure from tagging the younger club members with odd monikers.[33] Also like the Waikīkī beachboys, club members proudly printed their nicknames on the deck of their boards. Ball photographed seventeen members of the PVSC standing with their planks at the annual Long Beach surfing and paddleboarding championship; the nicknames of several of them—"Hoppy" and "Granny," for example—appear stamped above the *Palos Verdes Surfing Club* logo.[34]

For all of Ball's "malihini" and "kamaaina," his "wahini" and "Little Waikiki," the cold-water gear and winter campfires that he captures in his photographs, the remote locations reached by surf wagons, the sleeping bags for overnighters, the tar-stained beaches, the variety of waves and ocean conditions that generated a new vocabulary to describe them—all of these and more reveal a beach culture in the process of creating its own regional identity. Perhaps because it was the Depression and many surfers didn't enjoy excess income, they were forced to rely on DIY skills and ingenuity that opened up possibilities for innovation: surfboard racks on top of cars, bathing caps to keep warm, the hats and hand paddles that Ball describes as being "the surfing gear" for the Cove in 1934.[35] When have we ever seen a picture of a Waikīkī beachboy wearing a hat in the surf?

Fortunately, the ensemble of cowboy hat, hand paddles, and tight canvas trunks did not endure. Much of the surf lingo laced throughout Ball's captions has also faded. A surfer caught inside a wave at the Cove, for example, is about to be "snowed under" by a "smashing creamer."[36] He captures club member Everett J. Oshier and swimming sensation Mary Ann Hawkins at San Onofre "outlined by a big 'Nofre 'snowbank'."[37] Ball had also named the outside break at the Cove "the Mighty Ski Jump" because of the "mountainous height of its seas."[38] While the origin of surf lingo can be hard to trace, the snowy vocabulary describing the white water of large California surf probably does not derive from tropical Waikīkī, but rather from the local mountain range at Big Pines where PVSC members skied.[39]

Ball also describes surfers at San Onofre enjoying "glassy water" and enduring "red hot days when the best of tans will burn to a crisp and noses peel off for weeks."[40] White surfers wore hats during the summer to protect their pale skin, an accessory most island surfers didn't need because of their darker pigmentation. Ball's vocabulary highlights ocean conditions that became prized in California because of its regional wind patterns. Whereas Hawaiian trade winds typically blow offshore all day at Waikīkī during the summer months—and are the dominant wind throughout the year—California's daily wind pattern usually results in onshore winds beginning in the late morning. Occasionally those winds will hold off, resulting in exceptionally calm and "glassy" water, which surfers relish. Although one could certainly have glassy waves at Waikīkī, the term is much more prevalent in California, especially given the local "kelp beds" that Ball describes, whose presence helps smoothen out surface water.[41] The desire to enjoy offshore or glassy conditions probably also encouraged California surfers to sleep on the beach the night before—recall Duke and his friends camping at Corona del Mar in June 1925 to ride the early morning breakers. Because surfers can enjoy offshore surf at Waikīkī all day long, there would be little reason to camp there overnight.

Californians pioneered cold-water surfing (with a nod to Hawaiian George Freeth for his winter exhibitions in Los Angeles and San Diego) and developed a culture around staying warm both in the waves (bathing caps) and after their sessions (campfires). Jack O'Neill eventually developed surfing wetsuits in San Francisco and Santa Cruz during the 1950s to enable surfers to extend their time in cold water. Before the advent of neoprene, however, Ball relied on a more basic rubber product to combat what he eloquently termed "cold butt": he's pictured at the Cove squatting in the center of a burning tire.[42] "A nice warm beach feels plenty good," Ball wrote in his caption for a cliffside perspective of the Cove, "especially after two or three trips to the rocks for your board."[43] The photograph shows more than two dozen surfboards scattered on the rocky shore while as many young people stand or lie on patches of rough ground. No wealthy tourists, no beachside amenities, no glamorous hotels lighting up the beach. Unlike the Waikīkī beachboys and their trademark *lomilomi* for high-end guests, the only massages happening at the Cove were shivering surfers trying to warm themselves before packing their gear. A case in point: Ball captured six surfers sitting around a nighttime campfire after a "Super Surf" in April 1939. His caption reads: "Tired but surf satiated they are seen warming up here prior to carrying their waterlogged planks up the trail."[44] What waited for them up the trail was a beach-culture accessory second only in importance to the surfboard itself: an automobile.

California beach culture, like much of the state itself, depended on automobiles. None of the PVSC members actually lived in the Palos Verdes Estates, so they had to drive to the Cove. There were more than half a million vehicles in Los Angeles County by 1927, about one for every three people, and the automobile itself had become "a radiant source of freedom and pleasure" for residents throughout the state.[45] Surfing, too, is often associated with freedom and pleasure, not to mention speed. Driving and surfing combine most powerfully in the popular imagination with the "woodie"—those Depression-era station wagons whose passenger compartments were made entirely of wood and that postwar surfers bought cheaply and stuffed with surfboards and teenagers. The Beach Boys, and Jan and Dean, glorified the vehicles in such songs as "Surfin' Safari" (1962) and "Surf City" (1963), but surfers of the 1920s and 1930s laid the tracks for those lyrics by rumbling up and down the coast hunting for waves.

A typical San Onofre weekend gathering courtesy of the automobile.
(John Heath "Doc" Ball.)

Access to waves at San Onofre was much easier than negotiating the
precarious cliff at Palos Verdes, where avalanches of dirt and rock regularly
blocked the road leading to Bluff Cove after winter storms. At San Onofre,
surfers drove directly onto the beach and parked in the sand. Many of Ball's
photographs, especially on contest days, show the wide range of cars that
surfers used to reach the remote location in northern San Diego County:
trucks, coupes, station wagons, and convertibles. Double your freedom
and your pleasure by throwing a surfboard on top of your Ford Model
A, your Buick Century, your Hudson Super-Six, your Dodge 5-window
Coupe, and ramble along the coast highway. Elegant steamships floated
many Californians to their Waikīkī dreams during the 1930s, but in their
home state it was often a four-wheeled clunker that did the trick.

Cars often fill the background when Ball photographed beach gatherings—groups of people listening to guitar and ukulele players, or campers
flopped on the sand inside their sleeping bags. If the waves were down, cars
became sources of amusement for surfers. Ball snapped a picture of seven
young men clowning on the roof of a 1925 Hudson in the parking lot at
San Onofre. They're seated in-line, on a stack of surfboards, mugging for
the camera—"Surfing energy being expended on a flat day."[46] During the
1940 Pacific Coast Surf Riding Championships at San Onofre, Ball framed
four separate lineups in one photograph: cars in the foreground facing the

ocean; spectators watching the action from the beach; ten surfers riding an inside wave toward the camera; and numerous competitors sitting like ducks in the distance, waiting for the next set to break the horizon. Ball reported that surfers had driven from "a hundred and fifty mile radius" to compete in the event, indicating how much the biggest surfing event of the year depended on automobiles.[47]

By the fall of 1937, Ball's pictures had begun to gain broad attention for surfing. His jesting brag in *Ye Weekly Super Illustrated Spintail,* a newsletter he wrote for the PVSC—"Ace photo man of the PVSC finally cracks the L.A. Times"—announced his growing commercial success photographing the sport.[48] The *Los Angeles Times* published two of his pictures in their Sunday magazine supplement, along with a long article by Andy Hamilton—"Surfboards, Ahoy!" One can imagine Ball holding the *Times* in his hands and thinking back to the moment six years earlier when he saw Tom Blake's water photographs of surfers at Waikīkī. Hamilton begins his article from the point of view of spectators who drove to the cliffs above Bluff Cove every weekend to enjoy the spectacle: "Watch them from the rocky cliff 300 feet above the restless, green water. Below, perched idly on their surfboards, you'll see perhaps forty-five kamaainas and malahinis . . . a cluster of giant water bugs. They chat and wisecrack in a strange language as they bob up and down on their trim slabs of wood."[49] We recognize terms adapted from the islands—"kamaainas" and "malahinis."[50] But Hamilton includes other expressions in the article that likely derived from the more industrial environment of Los Angeles and the prevalent role that automobiles played in the lives of these young Southern Californians. A used surfboard, for example, is called a "klunker."

Five months later, in February 1938, Ball scored the cover of *Saturday Night* magazine with a picture of PVSC member Kay Murray diving off his board at Hermosa Beach. The corresponding article, "Surf Slaloms" by Bob Sides, included eleven more of Ball's photographs.[51] That same month, Ball landed more photographs in *Life* magazine—"SURF-RIDING IS WINTER SPORT NOW IN CALIFORNIA"[52] The photographs in regional and national media not only strengthened the connection between surfing and Southern California, but the articles also commented on the popularity of Bluff Cove itself as an attraction for Sunday motorists. An editorial in the *Palos Verdes Peninsula News,* ecstatic over the free press in *Life,* boasted that surfing had made Bluff Cove "a national attraction. Thousands of people every Sunday line along the hills of Palos Verdes Drive and enjoy watching the magnificent sport."[53] Automobiles became critical not only for the surfers accessing their favorite breaks, but also for the general public to enjoy watching a sport that was no longer simply a summer pastime in California.

Page Six   LOS ANGELES TIMES SUNDAY MAGAZINE   September 19, 1937

SURFBOARDS, AHOY!

BY ANDY HAMILTON

IT TAKES YEARS TO ACHIEVE THIS NONCHALANCE. LEFT TO RIGHT, TULIE CLARK, E. J. OSHIER AND JIM REYNOLDS

Members of the Palos Verdes Surfing Club gaining regional attention through "Doc" Ball's photographs. *Los Angeles Times,* September 19, 1937.

Thanks to Ball and his PVSC members, participants and spectators could enjoy the novelty year-round.

Surfing, of course, had been covered in the Southern California media for three decades before Ball's pictures appeared in the *Los Angeles Times,* and frequently noted as a fad.[54] But the coverage had been localized to specific beaches—Redondo Beach, Santa Monica, or Corona del Mar—and to the Native Hawaiian influences of George Freeth and Duke Kahanamoku. The surf population had been growing steadily from San Diego to Santa Cruz throughout the 1930s, and the national media was taking note. *Life* observed that though surfing was native to Hawai'i, it had "its greatest number of U.S. devotees in California" where "every week end this winter, on beaches near Los Angeles, groups of surfboard riders have gathered to sport in the waves."[55] The influence of *Life* during this era was tremendous. The publication had quickly become the country's premier photo magazine when its new publisher, Henry Luce, had bought the title in 1936 and focused the content almost exclusively on photographs. The new format more than tripled the magazine's circulation to more than a million readers per week in just four months, and doubled to two million readers per week by 1939.[56] Ball's action shots reached a good number of Americans, especially because *Life* "had what advertising agencies termed the highest

The Photographer   **73**

'pass-along factor' of any mass-circulation magazine."[57] That is to say, by the time photographs of the PCSRC at San Onofre appeared in *Life* in August 1939, surveys indicated that between fourteen and seventeen people read any given copy (or at least thumbed through the pictures) because of how often the magazine was passed along to others.[58] Potentially tens of millions of Americans, then, were being informed that surfing was now a part of what it meant to be Californian.

Part of that identity involved succumbing to what Andy Hamilton terms "the surfing fever" in his *Los Angeles Times* article. He writes that once "the surfing bug bites them, most ordinary, sane citizens go just as goofy over the sport as Dr. Ball. Lawyers abandon their cases, doctors leave their patients and husbands desert their wives when the 'grapevine' reports that the big waves are running."[59] *Life* ran with this idea in their description of surfers at San Onofre as "surfboard addicts" who usually "arrive late Saturday afternoon, stay up half the night singing, dancing and having fun. Then they roll up in blankets, sleep on the sand. At 4 a.m. they begin their surfboarding."[60] The image makes for good copy, and precedents exist for Native Hawaiians abandoning work and family responsibilities, even risking their lives, to feed their obsession with surfing.[61] For the most part, however, riding waves remained a weekend activity for California surfers during this era. Hamilton reinforces the point when he writes: "From dawn to dusk almost any weekend, you can find enthusiastic surfers along the Southern California coast." Both *Life* articles make the same observation. When Ball lists specific dates for surf sessions in his *California Surfriders,* most are Saturdays or Sundays, with the occasional holiday thrown in.[62] The majority of surfing and paddleboard contests were also weekend affairs, intended to draw tourists out to coastal cities. Ball later reflected that his dental business could be slow during the Depression, which prompted a surf safari north or south.[63] But professionals like Ball generally worked during the week, the younger crowd went to school, and both groups played at being Hawaiian beachboys on the weekend.[64]

We can add that this division of play and labor marks a significant difference between surfers in California and those in Hawai'i. The Waikīkī beachboys did not have the luxury of surfing merely for pleasure. They drew no regular salary, so riding waves became part of their bread and butter, earning income from the surfing lessons and other services they provided during the two main tourist seasons: summer and winter. This is not to say Hawaiians didn't enjoy surfing or surf on their own time, only that mainlanders tended to follow a Protestant work-ethic calendar and relegated their sporting activities to the weekends. The possibility of someone living to surf, and surfing to live, was not open to surfers of the era—even Tom Blake couldn't pull it off—and it would have seemed a bizarre idea to pursue, even under the influence of "the surfing fever." The very concept is a Hollywood creation—the Big Kahuna in the 1959 film *Gidget* comes to mind. It wouldn't be until the 1960s, when surfers began to earn sponsorship and contest money, that select surfers could actually make a modest living by riding waves. Only when surfers themselves began to sell their lifestyle in the 1950s and 1960s—surfboards, magazines, films, apparel—did they realize a dream of making a living out of what they loved to do. That dream, too, started in Southern California.

～

The July 1939 contest at San Onofre covered by *Life* was the most successful of the PCSRC in terms of numbers of contestants, with some eighty surfers battling in the waves (compared to thirty-six the year before).[65] "Whitey" Harrison grabbed top honors in front of at least two thousand spectators, also an increase from the fifteen hundred reported the previous year. The San Clemente Chamber of Commerce took note of the event's popularity (and widespread press) and contacted Ball, asking him if he would organize a similar event at San Onofre for the end of August. Ball complied. Knowing that surf was difficult to predict, even at bountiful San Onofre, he devised a combination paddleboard/surfing tournament in case the swell died.

It was a good thing he did. Ball recounts in his PVSC newsletter that the "first annual surf and paddleboard tourney" received great publicity in the papers leading up to contest day—Sunday, August 27—"then—as usually happens—at the nofre duck pond—no surf appears."[66]

Ball goes on to explain: "but this did not stop that mad Dentist for he had some races all arranged—to be run over a triangular course: paddle around the angles and slide back down the soupy hypotenuse—the first guy across the finish line—the winner." The only "hitch" Ball mentions was that Santa Monica lifeguard "Pete" Peterson and his wife Arlene "copped both first places" in the single and tandem paddleboard events. Peterson was not a member of the PVSC, so Ball played up some gripes for the sake of his club: "He is tops on the coast no doubt but he wins too dam much—too much of a business with him."

On the second page of the newsletter, Ball glued a photograph of Jim Bailey taking off on a wave at San Onofre while his cocker spaniel (named "Rusty") crouched on the nose of the board. (Bailey had caught the wave in the morning on contest day, before the surf died.) The *Los Angeles Times* had published the picture the day after the contest—a terrific action shot that captured Bailey's statuesque poise as he towered over the soaking wet dog, the pup staring cutely at the camera.[67] The photograph set a fire under

Jim Bailey and his cocker spaniel "Rusty" at San Onofre. This is the photo that inspired "Doc" Ball to develop his water camera housing for close-up action shots in the surf. (Ted Hurley/*Los Angeles Times*, August 28, 1939.)

Ball. He wrote in the newsletter: "JBHall purchases yet another graflex—this one to be built into a new super water-kodak. It will see use in the near future—at the cove and elsewhere. Hope some killer dillers arrive within the fortnight. Never again will this MCE ['Master of the Candid Eye'] get scooped by Times er otherwise."[68] ("JBHall" was Ball's playful term for himself, the initials of his middle and last names transposed.) For years Ball had been taking pictures of surfers out in the water, but none were as eye-catching or close to the action as the shot of Bailey and his dog. Ball rolled up his sleeves and got to work on a waterproof camera housing that became not only a prime artifact of built beach culture, but also a critical mechanism for proliferating that culture through hundreds of subsequent photographs.

Ball was excited enough about his handiwork to give PVSC members an update on the camera housing two weeks later. "Have you heard???" he

"Doc" Ball's water camera housing. (Courtesy California Surf Museum.)

announced in the newsletter, "JBHall's new invention nears completion—a rebuilt Graflex all water tite n everything—when finished—nobody will ever come near scoopin old JBHall again. . . ."[69] He had built a plywood box about the size and shape of a large toaster to fit around the camera.[70] He screwed a stainless-steel viewfinder on top of the box. He cut a square hole on one side so he could change film, and a small round opening at the end for the lens to look out; each had a small door that could be quickly opened and closed in the surf. He fitted the box with brass screws and sealed it with rubber gaskets and marine glue. Ball's son Norman believes that his father may have gone to the nearby Pacific System Homes factory (where his friend "Whitey" Harrison worked) to use tools and waterproof glue to complete the housing.[71] Ball also used his own dental tools to refit the front end of the camera. He attached a heavy brass handle on one end of the box so he could hang onto the thing if he had to bail off his board to dodge a loose surfboard or an oncoming wave. He could take twelve black and white pictures with the camera, one at a time, before having to change the film magazine.[72] The whole process took expert timing to set the shutter speed, focus the lens, take the picture, then shut the camera housing up tight before the wave rolled into him. Ball brushed multiple coats of varnish over the plywood on the outside, and covered the camera on the inside with paraffin to protect it from any saltwater that leaked in.

The camera housing was ready for a dry run (so to speak) by mid-October 1939. Ball hauled it out to Bluff Cove and the Flood Control (in Long Beach), allowing him, for the first time, to capture close-up action shots of surfers riding large waves. Up until then, his photographs either had to be taken at a distance (so he didn't ruin his camera) or on small-wave days that allowed him to maneuver his board around in the surf. Another swell hit the coast in early November, giving Ball his first real test of how the camera would survive getting rolled in the surf. He details the outcome in his newsletter for November 8, 1939:

> Ye ace fotog while attempting some tandem shots did verily get the royal works. It all happened when the big set came and the water was thick with boards, guys, and churning soup—four planks—having slid as far as the cracker [i.e., "big wave"] permitted—suddenly left their respective pilots and then crashed into some malahini—the whole mass of debris heads for JBH—right for that fat gut—sooo the foto-hound deserted deck and dove for the depths—taking the camera marvel below. . . . When everything blasted by—ye doc came up using the foto box for a life raft. After getting beneath 2 more grinders the box was sent to deep water and JBH swims for his board. Indeed—what a stinkin mess, but—nary a drap [sic] of salt water was found inside that super water box.[73]

Doc had also invested in a Big Bertha lens for the camera that cost him the princely sum of 120 dollars (more than two thousand dollars today), his goal being "TO SUCK UP THE SURFING VARMINTS RIGHT INTO THE BLOOMIN BOX."[74]

The new water housing and lens energized Ball, opening up a new dimension for his surf photography. He could now paddle viewers out to the lineup, as it were, into what he called "Honolulu type of surf," meaning the towering waves that broke every so often on the outside reef at Waikīkī.[75] When the "Mighty Ski Jump" broke at Bluff Cove on December 22, 1940, Ball was there with his waterproof camera to record PVSC members swooping down the massive breakers.[76] Ball later noted for an article in *Modern Photography* that surfers loved to see pictures of themselves riding with other surfers because they could all compare riding techniques, and newspapers favored publishing such "mass action" shots.[77] Ball also managed to capture with his new camera some of the most iconic images of Tom Blake surfing—at Bluff Cove and Hermosa Beach—which helped reframe the Hawaiian pastime that Blake himself had championed so strongly into a Southern California tradition.[78] Blake returned the favor and ducked behind the lens, capturing in his turn a gorgeous shot of Ball dropping

![Surfing photograph]

An example of "Doc" Ball's typical surfing photograph before the development of his water camera housing: a long-distance shot in calm conditions. (John Heath "Doc" Ball.)

down the face of an outside set at Bluff Cove. Ball included the picture in his newsletter and wrote: "Finally after ten years of collectings and neg shooting ye doc finally gets one of his own hide—and on one of the super waves of the day."[79] He continued to refine his innovation, building a collection of photographs that both captured and created the most powerful images we have of what it meant to be a surfer in California in the years leading up to World War II.

In *The American Surfer: Radical Culture and Capitalism,* Kristen Lawler makes a strong case for including surfers of the 1930s in the larger dynamic of the dream factory that has pushed images of surfers onto American consumers since the nineteenth century. The popularity of such images— appearing in magazines, books, newspapers, advertising, and Hollywood film—has endured, she argues, "because they tap into our deepest, most 'primitive' desires for freedom and connection."[80] She adds that in our modern, alienated world of work responsibilities and repressed adult identity,

"Doc" Ball's innovative water camera housing allowed him to take close-up action shots of club members like Hal Landes in large surf. (John Heath "Doc" Ball.)

surfer images from Hawaiʻi and California draw our desires toward a fantasy life of leisure, forbidden sexuality, and close connection to nature. In particular, Lawler presents Freud's concept of the "oceanic feeling" and our deep-seated urge to recapture a lost paradise of complete plenitude for the self. "Unconsciously," she writes, "we all continue to be driven by this memory, this desire to return to what is symbolized so powerfully by the ocean."[81] Understanding that Ball's traumatic war experiences likely prompted him to gather a number of his photographs and publish them in *California Surfriders,* we can add a more topical layer to his desires and connect them to the life he was probably hearkening back to as he selected, arranged, and captioned his photographs, which in themselves were already an act of longing for a distant paradise.

In one of the last issues of the newsletter for 1940, Ball includes a picture of what he calls (playing the grumpy editor) "THAT LOUSY MOB AT YE COVE LAST SUNDAY."[82] The photograph only partially frames the lineup, but about two dozen surfers are floating on their boards. It's the most crowded day that Ball had probably ever photographed at the Cove. He couldn't have seen it coming, but "Doc" Ball was the original perpetrator and victim of the surf photographer's curse: the shutterbug, driven to publish images for renown or money, who exposes a surfing spot to the public, thereby inviting crowds that inevitably ruin his paradise. Ball's gift of media attention for himself and his pals was a dubious one. Waikīkī had already achieved photographic fame by the time Blake published his images, so he merely added fuel to a well-tended fire.

But not so for the waves of Palos Verdes, Malibu, or San Onofre. *California Surfriders* served as the sport's first guidebook to California surf spots, its images idealizing a coastal life of freedom, excitement, and camaraderie. His photographs could not help but attract attention, which invited more young people out into the waves. Ball's photographs had already changed the beaches that his book sought to preserve; its publication was partly intended as his personal pathway back to a paradise long gone because he had helped opened it up, a paradise as elusive as the Hawaiian ideals on which it was based. The fleeting nature of his desires became manifest in the book's blurred images, its flawed paper, its broken spines. His dream couldn't hold. Similar to his mentor, Tom Blake, who eventually abandoned island life, Ball moved out of Southern California in the early 1950s and placed his faith in God.

CHAPTER 3

The Waterman

"If you ever needed a job done, you called
Pete. . . . Once Pete set his mind to something,
he did it, no matter how tough it was."[1]
—Versal Schuler

On September 7, 1932, Santa Monica's *Evening Outlook* announced that lifeguard lieutenant Preston "Pete" Peterson (1911–1983) planned on paddling from the mainland to Santa Catalina Island later that month, a twenty-six-mile journey he would undertake by himself.[2] Peterson had recently made a seven-mile trial run up the coast in less than three hours, so he figured he could reach Catalina in about eight hours. Peterson was likely selected because of his expertise on the craft, compiling "a fine record in saving lives through use of the hollow, air-chambered board."[3] This was Tom Blake's design, of course, now being manufactured in neighboring Venice by local carpenter Thomas Rogers.[4] Santa Monica lifeguard captain George Watkins had recently purchased a set of the hollow boards for his crew of fifteen men.[5] When he'd been appointed five months earlier, Watkins had asserted that "no other municipality on the Pacific Coast will have superior equipment or personnel."[6] Blake's boards came just at the right time for Watkins to fulfill that promise. He intended for Peterson's crossing "to prove the efficiency of the paddle-board in life-saving work."[7] A little positive press for both Rogers and the newly reorganized lifeguard service wouldn't hurt either. The *Evening Outlook* reported that members of the Santa Monica lifeguard service committee who had come up with the idea of the crossing "said that the feat, if successful, would be of inestimable benefit to Santa Monica through the publicity given the newly created lifeguard service and the city."[8]

Watkins was working within a historical nexus of initiatives by city, county, and state agencies to protect citizens at the beaches and to preserve the coastline for future generations. This combined effort, which included organizing year-round, 24/7 lifeguard service in select cities, was

"Pete" Peterson shaping Don James's first surfboard in his garage on 17th street in Santa Monica, 1938. (Don James.)

absolutely crucial to the development of California beach culture. Owing to a massive population surge in Los Angeles—more than doubling from 1920 (576,673) to 1930 (1,238,048)—the city took the lead in creating agencies that established long-term support for beach services like life-guarding.[9] The city of Los Angeles established a charter in 1925 that created the Department of Playground and Recreation and provided a budget to acquire property. Beaches were of prime interest, especially Venice (the closest beach to downtown Los Angeles), which had an estimated fourteen million visits during the fiscal year 1927–1928 (July 1 to June 30).[10] The department superintendent, George Hjelte, wrote in his annual report for that year that the beaches had become "the most popular of all recreation places in Southern California. The lure of the sea has proven more powerful than the attraction of the mountains or the various play fields and parks located within the city."[11] He gave three reasons for this popularity: "vastly improved transportation, increasing congestion of city areas and growing population."[12] By 1932 the city of Los Angeles employed approximately thirty-five lifeguards working at Venice, Cabrillo Beach in San Pedro, and Terminal Island just east of San Pedro.[13] Los Angeles was also hosting the summer Olympics that year and so had added incentive to ensure beach safety for the world's athletes and visitors.

The county of Los Angeles created its own Department of Recreation Camps and Playgrounds in 1929 under the leadership of superintendent Fred Wadsworth. In addition to acquiring numerous coastal properties, Wadsworth oversaw beach enhancements in the form of volleyball courts, fire rings, slides, swings, and seesaws—amenities that encouraged even more families to visit the beaches. By 1932 the county employed about fifteen full-time lifeguards and protected eight beaches from Santa Monica to Long Beach. During the summer months and holidays, of course, many seasonal guards were hired to help supplement the full-time crew. The county estimated about eight million visits on its beaches in fiscal year 1931–1932.[14] Some lifeguards remained in their position year-round, and two of the beaches at Santa Monica and Manhattan Beach maintained twenty-four-hour lifeguard service in case of emergencies—a stark contrast to the long tradition of releasing all lifeguards at the end of the summer season.[15] The California legislature created the state park system in 1927, and though the state owned several beaches in Los Angeles, lifeguard service was contracted out to either the county or individual municipalities.[16]

What were the daily responsibilities of a lifeguard during this era? If you worked for Los Angeles County, for example, you had an entire checklist to perform beyond ocean rescues, resuscitation, and first aid. You ensured that organized games, surfing included, remained in designated areas; you kept an eye out for unauthorized peddlers trying to drum up business at the beach; you watched for any "unseemly conduct" by male or female visitors, which might include getting dressed (or undressed) on the beach or in a parked car; you checked that motion picture companies had secured the correct permits; and you inspected rubber tubes, rafts, and life preservers for seaworthiness, and prevented homemade skiffs or canoes from entering the surf zone. You also coordinated rescue efforts with various municipalities and county departments: forestry, sheriff, surveyor, flood control, and the coroner.[17]

The lifeguards also coordinated with the influx of welfare workers who gained employment during the Depression as support staff for general maintenance. At Redondo Beach, for example, where a kelp cutter working the offshore beds had littered the sand with hundreds of tons of seaweed, workers helped clear the mess, which had stacked two and three feet high along the shoreline. Workers also improved service roads, built retaining walls, and performed general landscaping to make the beaches more attractive and accessible for visitors.[18] Because the guards were at the beach every day, they also helped keep records of who came and went. The following figures appear in the 1931–1932 annual report for the Department of Recreation Camps and Playgrounds: 8,379,958 bathers and spectators at seven beaches (along with Alamitos Bay and Puddingstone Dam in the San Gabriel Valley); 863,778 cars parked; 21,233 tables used; 7,399 fire circles used; 430 rescues; 18 boat distress calls; 9 corpses recovered; 1,128 first-aid cases: 6 false alarms; and 18 resuscitation cases. Finally, the guards were responsible for inspecting the beach and swimming areas, along with making daily records of tides and water temperatures.[19] They were a busy group, more often than not, and their collective efforts greatly increased the safety and enjoyment of the county's beaches.

The Santa Monica city council, under public pressure to equal or excel the level of lifeguarding at neighboring city and county beaches—Venice to the south and Santa Monica Canyon to the north—reorganized their part-time service in the spring of 1932.[20] The council hired Watkins, who supervised lifeguard tests and eventually hired more than a dozen men, including Peterson as one of his lieutenants. Peterson had grown up in Santa Monica—his parents co-owned two bathhouses on the boardwalk in the Ocean Park neighborhood, as well as the Rendezvous dance pavilion—and he had lifeguarded for Watson since at least the age of seventeen.[21] He was twenty-one years old in 1932—tall and blond, with rangy arms—and his offer to paddle solo to Catalina had piqued the interest of his fellow life-guards.[22] Wally Burton, also a lieutenant in the Santa Monica lifeguards, and Chauncey Granstrom, who lifeguarded at Santa Monica Canyon State Beach, soon decided to join Peterson. Tom Blake got wind of these events, and by 4:05 A.M. on Sunday morning, October 2, the crossing had turned into a race.

While Blake started paddling several hours every day to prepare for the crossing, the three lifeguards decided to train by entering the third PCSRC at Corona del Mar, to be held on Sunday, September 25, one week before the Catalina event.[23] On that day, Peterson showcased the skills that would make him the most dominant waterman in California during the 1930s. Not only could he perform every ocean-related activity—swimming, surf-ing, diving, rowing, paddleboarding—but he was the best at all of them. He won the surfing contest at Corona del Mar from a field of fourteen contestants. He also won both the hundred-yard and the half-mile paddle-board races. Granstrom and Burton came in second and third, respectively, in the paddleboard events. There was also a women's surfing contest (won by Helen Hoffman) and a bodysurfing event (won by Ted Sizemore).[24]

The following Sunday, Burton, Peterson, and Blake (Granstrom had scratched) left Point Vicente, at the western edge of the Palos Verdes Peninsula, and headed due south on their paddleboards, the three men staying together. The ocean remained calm until about five miles short of Catalina, when the wind suddenly kicked up and caused Burton to become seasick.

Tom Blake, "Pete" Peterson, and Wally Burton at the conclusion of their race to Catalina Island, October 1932. (The Croul Family Collection.)

Peterson hung back to make sure his fellow lifeguard was okay. Blake asked the two men if they wouldn't mind if he paddled ahead, which he did and won the race. Blake completed the run in just under six hours. Peterson stroked in half an hour behind Blake, and Burton brought up the rear.[25] It was a small but telling gesture on Blake's part, which Burton later characterized as "opportunistic, and a little headline-grabbing."[26] As for Peterson, he was "the kinda guy who kept any personal things to himself," recounted surfboard builder Dale Velzy. "He didn't put other people down, no matter what he might have thought about them."[27] Blake biographers Gary Lynch and Malcolm Gault-Williams relate that when the convoy boat *Gloria H.* returned the three paddlers to Santa Monica, "Tom could not find a ride back home and had to walk back."[28] Whether that had to do with Blake's singular focus on winning is up for debate, but Blake was a loner, highly competitive, and he worked to promote himself throughout his life. The photograph commemorating the awards ceremony at Avalon Harbor captures a fundamental contrast between Blake and Peterson: the former looking eagerly at his trophy—a blue urn—the latter standing patiently with his head bowed. It's a common gesture to observe in pictures of Peterson, even after he had won a contest—his shy glance away from the camera, a sign of reserve and humility. Blake, a veteran Hollywood performer, invariably struck a pose in pictures, ever drawn to fame and recognition.

"Blake respected Peterson," Wally Burton later recalled, "but he never gave him an outright compliment . . . he'd always watch him and incorporate his thoughts (designs) into his [own]."[29] Recall the description of Blake that "Doc" Ball had read in the *Los Angeles Times* the year before, the former taking photographs of surfers at Waikīkī "from the bucking surf-board."[30] To pursue the analogy: if California beach culture were a western—not too far-fetched considering its many connections to Hollywood—Blake would be the young rodeo star spurring for the limelight and golden trophy, wowing the crowd with his novelty and daring. Peterson would be the sheriff: terse, rock solid, the guy you turned to when you needed help.

Two months after the Catalina crossing, Peterson made his first trip to Hawai'i, arriving on December 2, 1932.[31] He tells the story of working at his parents' bathhouse as an enterprising nine-year-old (in 1920): he allowed visiting Hawaiians to swim for free in exchange for use of their surfboards, which they had brought to ride the local waves.[32] The boards had piqued his interest, and he wanted to try them out. That same curiosity surfaced at Waikīkī when Peterson encountered surfboards made from balsa. They were much lighter than the standard redwood boards—only about twenty pounds. He liked how they worked, and so he started shaping them when he returned to California in the spring of 1933.[33] Here we see an instance of the broader dynamic by which California beach culture progressed in the 1930s: a cross-pollination of ideas from Hawai'i to California that developed into a product line manufactured in Los Angeles and marketed to the world. In this case, Peterson and "Whitey" Harrison (they shared a room at Waikīkī during this trip) later worked for Pacific System Homes and crafted the innovative balsa and redwood surfboards that became so strongly identified with Hawai'i and the Waikīkī beachboys.[34]

While renting a room at Waikīkī, Peterson established a routine every morning of paddling some eight miles toward Diamond Head and back, trying out the various surf breaks along the way.[35] He simply continued the kind of workout he had begun in Santa Monica on Blake's paddleboard, heading up and down the coast to stay in shape and explore wave-riding possibilities. The Waikīkī surfers noticed his dedication; his interest in the novel balsa material also told them that he was a craftsman and knew about board design. Most important, they noticed how he carried himself: quietly, respectfully, without fanfare or self-promotion. George Downing, one of the most influential big-wave surfers in Hawai'i after World War II, commented that locals at Waikīkī during the 1930s "were a pretty selective group. They didn't just accept anyone. But Pete was not only accepted, he was respected."[36] It's not uncommon for years to pass before visiting mainland surfers are accepted by their island counterparts; some are never accepted at all. Peterson slipped into that fellowship as smoothly as a paddleboard cutting through the ocean on a warm, glassy morning. He adopted the ocean skills of the Hawaiians in every respect. As a child at his parents' bathhouse—Peterson and Smith baths—he had not only been interested in the Hawaiians' surfboards, but also in what he called the islanders' "watermanship."[37] Their ease and expertise in the ocean made a strong impression on him at a formative age. It's no stretch to call Peterson the very first, and the very best, homegrown beachboy in California. As a lifeguard who was raised at the beach and made it his source of work and pleasure throughout his life, Peterson embodied the core values for which island watermen like George Freeth, Duke Kahanamoku, and certainly the Waikīkī beachboys were admired and emulated throughout California.

During his first trip to Hawai'i, Peterson also continued the process of mainlanders influencing Hawaiian surfing, following in the steps of Tom Blake. Peterson and Harrison decided to take a three-day journey to the north shore of O'ahu after locals told them about the large waves that broke on that side of the island during the wintertime. That stretch of coastline would eventually become known as the seven-mile miracle, a clutch of world-class surfing breaks—Hale'iwa, Waimea Bay, Pipeline, Sunset Beach—where surfers came to establish their reputations and to test their limits on some of the planet's most exciting and dangerous waves. Peterson and Harrison hitchhiked and walked across the island, as the story goes, eventually landing on the beach at Pipeline during a large swell. Numerous people have died surfing Pipeline over the years, and the two watermen would have immediately recognized its inherent dangers. But Peterson knew if they didn't at least swim out—which they did—they'd always regret it.[38] The two Californians modeled the sense of adventure and exploration that epitomized surfing back home: the willingness, and often necessity, to get on the road—even if that meant hoofing it along Oahu Railroad's train tracks—to score bigger and better waves.

Peterson happened to be on the beach at Waikīkī during the next major design innovation after the introduction of balsa surfboards, though this particular idea failed miserably in California surf. He arrived in the islands during the last week of October 1937, just as local surfers Fran Heath, John Kelly, and Wallace Froiseth were experimenting with narrow tails to prevent their surfboards from spinning out—what they called "sliding ass"—when they turned them across the face of the wave.[39] The heavy, finless boards of the time caught swells easily and rode smoothly as long as surfers stayed ahead of the breaking white water. Unlike today, most surfers of the 1930s stayed as far away from the curl as possible, especially in large waves; any contact with the plunging lip resulted in precarious wipeouts that normally meant long swims to the beach and possible injury from crashing surfboards. Heath, Kelly, and Froiseth changed all that. Their design innovation, begun the day that Kelly took an axe to the tail of Fran Heath's surfboard, finally allowed the board to hug the face of a steep wave—what Froiseth called staying in "the hot curl," a name by which the design innovation is still known.

Froiseth later recalled that Peterson and Harrison, once they had seen what the Hawaiian boards could do in big waves, "cut their tails down— right there on goddamn Waikiki Beach!"[40] Both Peterson and Harrison had been working at Pacific System Homes by that point, so they knew what they were doing.[41] They may have even had a hand in building the board whose tail Kelly had hacked since the board's owner, Fran Heath, had custom-ordered it from Pacific System.[42] But Peterson and Harrison soon discovered that the boards, specifically designed to ride big waves breaking off Hawai'i's coral reefs, did not perform well in California's milder surf. The boards needed the push from powerful swells, and most mainland waves simply did not have the juice to get the boards moving. Be that as it may, Peterson and Harrison remained crucial pollinators of Hawaiian culture in California. They established, for their own generation and those that followed, the standards and rituals of what it meant to be a California surfer. One of the most important rituals was simply traveling to Waikīkī and surfing its venerated waves. Such were the tangible benefits for white mainlanders of the decades-long colonial process that had begun in earnest in 1893 with the takeover of the Hawaiian monarchy, with the help of U.S. Marines, followed by the annexation of Hawai'i in 1898. California surfers especially enjoyed greater access to Hawai'i as a U.S. territory, riding the coattails of military expansion into the Pacific.

What did period surfers think about Native Hawaiian loss of sovereignty? The lack of commentary on the subject in their written records makes it hard to determine one way or the other. In *Waves of Resistance: Surfing and*

History in Twentieth-Century Hawai'i, Isaiah Helekunihi Walker writes eloquently about the special impact colonialism had on Waikīkī, and how local surfers established a zone of resistance and autonomy—"ka po'ina nalu (the surf zone)"—where Native Hawaiian men contested and subverted emasculating colonial discourses.[43] The California influencers who spent the most time in Waikīkī during the 1930s—Blake, Peterson, and Harrison—each had to negotiate this zone in ways that may be indicative of their general sympathies (or lack of sympathy) with the day-to-day realities of colonialism.

Blake, for example, leveraged his relationship with Duke to maintain a privileged place among the Waikīkī beachboys. Without the protection of Duke—oldest of the Kahanamoku brothers and the most revered figure at Waikīkī—it's likely Blake would have taken a lot of beatings and, despite his myriad skills and accomplishments as a waterman, been driven from the surf zone by local men who didn't appreciate his desire for center-stage attention.[44] Hawaiians would have considered Blake's actions not only as disrespectful but also, as Walker points out, as a failure to understand the historical impact of colonialism on the local community.[45] Peterson, as George Downing mentions above, was respected by Waikīkī locals for his waterman skills; more important, they accepted him into their ranks because of his deference to their position atop the beach hierarchy, displayed quite naturally enough for Peterson through his self-effacing personality. Harrison gained acceptance among the Waikīkī beachboys through his own waterman skills and enthusiasm for all things Hawaiian, and also because his sister, Ethel, married into a local Hawaiian family in 1936. Although Blake, Peterson, and Harrison all carried the privilege of their race to Waikīkī, the stronger acceptance of the latter two among the locals may be an indication at least of their awareness of a colonial situation and their desire to mitigate its effects among people they greatly admired.

As Peterson and Harrison were much influenced by their trips to Waikīkī, so too was Hawaiian beach culture influenced by the two surfers' work at Pacific System. Harrison recounts that while he was shaping for the company in the summer of 1936, they "were shipping sixty boards a month to Hawaii."[46] That same year, Pacific System had selected the Outrigger Canoe Club as its sole distributor of the "Swastika" models in the islands.[47] Those beautiful, glossy surfboards inundated the Hawaiian market. The *Honolulu Star-Bulletin* announced that the boards were "the proud possessions of the patrol boys. To make the scene more resplendent the names are painted on the boards in bright red or blue letter."[48] Some of the beachboys opted to be even more flamboyant: Charles "Panama Dave" Baptiste painted "Scotch and Soda" on the deck of his board, while Joe Minor named his

"Betty B." in honor of a college student.[49] Pacific System created a mark of prestige on the beach, enhancing the Waikīkī dream with some California marketing and manufacturing.

When Peterson returned to Santa Monica in the spring of 1933 after his first Hawaiian adventure, Waikīkī stayed on his mind.[50] He sent a letter to the islands in October that got picked up by the *Honolulu Star-Bulletin*. The details highlighted a particularly Californian surfer experience—Peterson's discovery of a new surf break—and his attempts to replicate Hawaiian traditions at Los Angeles beaches:

> Comes word from Preston Peterson, lieutenant of the Santa Monica lifeguards, who was here this spring enjoying the surf at Waikiki, that he has found a new place to surf.
>
> "All the fellows around here have been surfing down past Redondo way, at Palos Verdes, they call it,' he writes. "No one knew this surf was there until lately. I had stopped and watched it several times but never tried it until the other day. You get quite a long ride."
>
> He further stated that he and another fellow bought an outrigger canoe that used to be at Topango [*sic*] Canyon.
>
> "The scene at Palos Verdes, with the canoe and surfboard riders reminds me of the islands," he said.[51]

Peterson was chasing his Hawaiian dream in typical Californian fashion, exploring up and down the coast for new waves to ride. "Doc" Ball indicates that he had started surfing Bluff Cove at Palos Verdes after his own trip to Hawai'i in 1930, but news of the break didn't hit the general radar, at least according to Peterson, until the fall of 1933.[52] Ball's catalogue of photographs actually includes a shot of Peterson riding a wave at Bluff Cove in his outrigger canoe. Another action shot of Peterson manning the stern of the same (or similar) craft, guiding three friends through the surf at Santa Monica, appeared in the *Los Angeles Times* on December 3, 1933, under the title "Hawaii-Style."[53] The canoe looks a bit wonky: the outrigger is roped awkwardly to the bow and stern, and the paddle blades are thin and rectangular. The overall impression is one of rough imitation: the outrigger on a Hawaiian canoe would be securely lashed at the booms, and the paddles would be traditionally oval-shaped to catch more water with each stroke. The discrepancies don't seem to bother the riders, however, who appear perfectly content to simulate a Waikīkī thrill with Peterson playing the role of Hawaiian beachboy.

Peterson explored the northern points of the Santa Monica Bay as well, landing at Malibu for the Pacific Coast Paddleboard and Surfboard championships, held on September 9, 1934.[54] Part of building beach culture in

SOUTHLAND SEASIDE SCENES

"Pete" Peterson in the stern bringing his enthusiasm for Waikīkī to Santa Monica in a local version of a Native Hawaiian outrigger canoe. *Los Angeles Times*, December 3, 1933.

California included founding organizations that promoted use of the material objects, in this case paddleboards and surfboards. Peterson was at the forefront of this movement. He was the first president of the Pacific Coast Paddle and Surfboard Association (PCPSA), which formed in July 1934.[55] Owing to the growing popularity of surfing and paddleboarding, the group organized to sanction and officiate various contests, including the one at Malibu. Santa Monica's *Evening Outlook* reported in advance of the contest: "Surf conditions at Malibu are said to be similar to those in the Hawaiian islands. Spectacular riding can be done there and an unobstructed view of the race may be had from the highway."[56] Although the state highway now cut through the Malibu Ranch—it had officially opened to the public in 1929—most of the land remained private property, including what came to be known as Surfrider Beach. As Craig Lockwood tells the story, Willie

Grigsby, a lifeguard friend of Peterson, had a connection with the Adamson family, who owned the ranch—Rhoda Adamson was the daughter of Frederick and May Rindge—and Grigsby arranged for the newly formed paddleboard club to hold the contest at Malibu.[57]

In terms of Peterson's influence on both his contemporaries and the growth of California beach culture, it's important to note that although the Palos Verdes Surfing Club has generally been recognized as the first surfing club in the Los Angeles area (founded in 1935), Peterson had already established his association and was sponsoring contests as early as the summer of 1934.[58] The first took place on August 8: a mile-long race around the Santa Monica pier (won by "Whitey" Harrison) to celebrate the dedication of the new harbor.[59] The second was the contest at Malibu on September 9. The organization continued the following spring by sponsoring paddleboard races at Santa Monica and Huntington Beach.[60]

The founding of the PCPSA also reinforces the direct connection between Tom Blake's hollow boards and the growth of beach culture through city and county lifeguards. The lifeguards were the first group to be trained on the boards; they then helped spread paddleboarding and surfing throughout Southern California. The experience of Don James, an early surf photographer and protégé of "Doc" Ball, encapsulates this process in the mid-1930s. "When I was a kid," James recollected about his childhood in Santa Monica, "I used to go hang around the lifeguards because I was interested in surfing, and I learned from them about surfing. And I learned what kind of board to get. . . . They had a great influence on my life."[61] W. W. Madge, secretary of the PCPSA (a former Venice lifeguard and beach supervisor for the Los Angeles Department of Playgrounds and Recreation), traced the association's founding to Blake's paddleboard victories in Hawai'i. "He brought back the story of his success," Madge stated, "and soon such boards were being built from San Diego to Santa Barbara."[62] Madge included a list of thirty-six members who belonged to the PCPSA, part of his estimated two hundred "surf and paddle board enthusiasts" in the region. He added that the membership represented "nearly all the life guards on Southern California beaches."[63]

Peterson's new organization also likely inspired the formation of the West Coast Paddleboard Association (WCPA), founded in 1935. The two groups had essentially the same purpose: to promote paddling and surfing, and to sanction competitions. A review of newspaper reports on the two groups indicates that the WCPA superseded the PCPSA: the last mention of Peterson's group is in July 1935 when they helped sponsor the paddleboard races for an aquatic sports day at Huntington Beach; the first mention of the WCPA is in December of that same year when the organization's first president, Gene Hornbeck, announced plans to hold a team race from Catalina Island to Santa Monica.[64] The WCPA became an influential umbrella organization from 1935 to 1941, encouraging the formation of various surf clubs and their participation in paddleboard events, surfing contests, and even several seasons of paddleboard water polo (played in area pools).[65]

One example of the WCPA's influence on supporting the growth of paddleboard racing in Southern California is an April 1940 letter from the organization's president, "Adie" Bayer, to Harry Welch, secretary of the Newport Harbor Chamber of Commerce. Bayer introduced his association and offered to organize races for the city's celebration of the new Balboa pier on July 7, 1940. Bayer stated that his membership had grown to "five hundred active surf-riders and paddlers in the past five years" and included a list of fourteen clubs from Santa Monica to Long Beach, including two women's surfing clubs.[66] Although it's common to read that there were no more than two hundred surfers in California before World War II, Bayer's letter, along with a general headcount of surfers who belonged to area clubs—in addition to those who had formed clubs from Santa Cruz in the north to San Diego in the south—confirms that the total number of surfers was more than double that amount.[67]

Peterson was busy or otherwise occupied the day of the Balboa paddleboard contest, which left the door open for members of the Palos Verdes Surfing Club to take top honors. "Doc" Ball crowed in the first club newsletter following the event, "We scooped 'em one and all."[68] Leroy Grannis had won both the quarter-mile and the novelty race, and Ball himself captured the novice event—"OLD JB (YA CANT CALL ME AN OLD MAN NOW) DID TRIM THE WHISKERS OFF A FIELD OF SIX TO GET OUT OF THE NOVICE CLASS."[69] Competition was good for the growth of California beach culture. And though Peterson missed a chance to add another trophy to his shiny collection, his influence cast such a long shadow across Southern California that every paddler competed against him whether he was present or not.

Don James, who eventually became a Santa Monica lifeguard himself, described Peterson as a "neat freak who never used any wax on the surface of his board for traction because he felt it violated the pristine look he so admired."[70] His description speaks to Peterson's careful craftsmanship; some of the boards he built included five coats of varnish both to protect the wood and to provide the highest quality finish for the customer. James remembered standing in Peterson's garage at 17th Street in Santa Monica, watching him run a planer down the rails of a board that Peterson was finishing for James:

eleven feet long, eighty pounds of balsa and redwood. James, seventeen years old at the time—with a year of work ahead of him acting as Peterson's "lawn boy, babysitter, and aide-de-camp" to pay for the board—recalled urging Peterson, "Pete, can't you please get it ready for tomorrow?"[71] James' impatience to surf the brand-new plank met the headwinds of Peterson's exacting standards of excellence in everything he did, whether shaping surfboards, training for a competition, or even riding a wave.

Though Peterson might have made a business out of winning surfing and paddleboard contests, following "Doc" Ball, his real business was saving lives. His expertise extended to manufacturing innovative lifeguard equipment, which allowed him and other lifeguards to do their jobs better. He and Santa Monica lifeguard captain George Watkins developed a galvanized metal rescue can that followed models used by Roy "Dutch" Miller and his crew of lifeguards at Long Beach. It's worth taking a moment to track the development of this important device before it landed on Peterson's workbench. This history includes a tribute to Long Beach, which had the foresight to develop a municipal lifeguard service under the Public Safety Department as early as 1911—fifteen years before any other city in Los Angeles County. Hans Vockeroh and Gus Gillette began working at Golden and Linden Avenues that summer, though they and other guards, following tradition, were let go at the end of the summer season.[72] "Dutch" Miller became captain of the lifeguards in 1922 and supervised a corps of eleven full-time men. Long Beach made a groundbreaking decision at the end of the season that year: to retain Miller as a policeman who would respond to all lifeguard calls during the winter. In essence, Miller became the first year-round lifeguard in Los Angeles County, a position he maintained for more than forty years.[73]

Captain Miller inherited a version of the "torpedo tube" that George Freeth had introduced to Los Angeles beaches back in 1912. Lifeguards swam the hollow metal tube out to struggling swimmers who could grasp one end and be pulled into shore. But the devices were comparatively big and heavy—Freeth's version was over three feet long and made of copper. Miller worked with a local manufacturer in Long Beach, Willie's Tin Shop, to reduce the weight and size. They first began making the rescue cans out of steel, then eventually developed an aluminum model.[74] Watkins and Peterson developed their own version of the rescue can, but the pointed metal ends, though made of light metal, could still inflict injuries to either swimmer or lifeguard. And if a victim happened to be unconscious, he or she would not be able to grab hold of the device to be towed into shore.

Watkins and Peterson are credited with the idea of using an inflatable rubber tube to replace the metal rescue can.[75] The softer material would

Captain George Watkins and Santa Monica lifeguard with the "Pete" Peterson rescue tube. (Los Angeles County Lifeguard Association.)

have the benefit of reducing injuries during a rescue, and if a victim were unconscious, the lifeguard could wrap the tube around the swimmer and tow him or her into shore. The roughly cigar-shaped device had the added benefit of being easy to swim out through the waves. The descendant of that tube—a solid foam version sealed with liquid rubber—remains standard gear for lifeguards around the world today. Peterson began to manufacture the devices in his workshop in 1934 under his "Pete Peterson Company" label and sold them for about eleven dollars apiece.[76] They became known as the "Peterson Rescue Tube" and were built much like his surfboards: one at a time with the highest possible craftsmanship. The raw materials were close at hand: the strong presence of rubber companies in Los Angeles by 1930—including Goodyear, Goodrich, and Firestone—made the city the second largest tire production center in the United States.[77] Certainly that industrial environment, with its ready supply of rubber, established critical support for the design and manufacture of the new rescue device.

Pacific Coast Surf Riding Championships, San Onofre, 1941. Left to right: Eddie McBride, Vincent "Klotz" Lindberg, Don Okey, Dorian Paskowitz, Lloyd Baker, "Whitey" Harrison, Tom Blake (trophy presenter), "Pete" Peterson (winner), Walter "Slim" Van Blom, unknown. (Courtesy California Surf Museum.)

Peterson even trained his Scottish terrier "Hughie" to wear the tube and leap into the ocean to rescue swimmers. Captain Watkins, ever the showman, ceremoniously pinned a medal on Hughie after one such rescue, awarding him official status as a Santa Monica city lifeguard.[78] The same summer that Peterson began manufacturing the rescue tubes, he had to undergo the Pasteur treatment after protecting children on the beach who had been attacked by a rabid dog.[79] Peterson managed to capture the animal, though it bit him on the hand in the process. The treatment didn't slow him down. He helped form the PCPSA the following week and began preparations to hold their first paddleboard race the week after that, the one-mile event around the Santa Monica pier won by "Whitey" Harrison.[80]

Peterson did in fact lose paddleboard races and surfing contests in the 1930s. It just didn't seem like it. He entered the PCSRC seven times between 1932 and 1941, and he won four of them (1932, 1936, 1938, 1941). He won the Pacific coast dory rowing championships twice at Hermosa Beach (1933 and 1934), and the Santa Monica lifeguard swimming competition four out of five years between 1932 and 1936; after his third win in this latter event, they simply gave him the E. C. Segar trophy and let him take it home.

When various coastal cities decided to inaugurate annual championships, Peterson swooped down and cleaned up first prize: the first annual national surfing and paddleboard competition in Long Beach (November 1938), the first annual surf and paddleboard tourney at San Onofre (August 1939), and the first international paddleboard meet at La Ballona lagoon in Venice (December 1939). He schooled every paddler in three counties at distances from one hundred yards to seven miles. Venice held two Pacific Coast lifeguard championships in 1939 and 1941. Guess who smoked the competition in the individual lifeguard events? The same guy who won the inaugural all-around waterman's title in 1941—the top lifeguard on the Pacific Coast—by beating all comers in an ocean triathlon: swimming, canoeing, and paddleboarding.

Beyond all the surfing, paddleboard, and lifeguard contests, which pushed design innovation and drew people out to the coast, the enormous increase in yearly beach visits in Los Angeles County during the Great Depression indicates how ordinary people turned to the beach in hard economic times. Beaches were free and readily accessible to the white majority population. L.A. County lifeguards recorded just under two million visits on four beaches in 1929–1930; during the first full year of the Great Depression (1930–1931), that number rose dramatically to more than eight million visits on six beaches. By the end of the decade (1939–1940), more than thirty-one million visits were recorded on nine beaches, an increase of almost 300 percent from 1930 to 1931.[81] By comparison, the population of Los Angeles County rose just over 25 percent during that same decade.[82] People had less expendable income, and the beach became a source of cheap leisure every year for millions of Angelenos. For all of Peterson's accomplishments shaping surfboards, starting surf clubs, innovating lifesaving gear, setting the bar at surf and paddleboard competitions, and generally spreading enthusiasm for Hawaiian traditions by embodying the skills of a Waikīkī beachboy, his impact on the daily beach-goer came down to this: if you got into trouble around the Santa Monica Bay, and you could choose one person to come save you, his name would be "Pete" Peterson.

CHAPTER 4

The Waterwoman

Woman Among Aspirants For Beach Patrol Jobs: The routine tests of endurance swims, ocean rescues and first-aid technique were varied by the unofficial entry of one girl swimmer, Mary Ann Hawkins, amateur aquatic star. Miss Hawkins's performances, on a par with the swimming prowess of the regular contenders, were hailed by James K. Reid, superintendent of the Los Angeles County Department of Recreation, as possibly winning her a place on the corps of women life guards for work at pools and beaches.
—*Los Angeles Times,* May 25, 1938

Mary Ann Hawkins (1919–1993) was fifteen years old when she ran into Gene "Tarzan" Smith for the first time at Corona del Mar. "Pretty Mary Ann Hawkins," as the *Los Angeles Evening Post* had called her, a "tall, slender" swimmer for the Los Angeles Athletic Club, had won the national junior championship in the 880 freestyle in 1933. She'd been competing in her hometown of Pasadena since the age of ten. Hawkins had seen Duke Kahanamoku give an exhibition there in the late 1920s, and he became one of her heroes.[1] Her mother, Beulah, "was very ambitious for me," stated Hawkins, so in 1934 they moved from Pasadena (about twenty-five miles from the Pacific Ocean) to Costa Mesa, just inland from Corona del Mar, so that Hawkins could build her endurance for the ocean swims she had recently discovered.[2] Over the July 4th weekend in 1933, Hawkins had swum in two "rough-water" events at Venice and Hermosa Beach, the latter a two-mile race between the Manhattan Beach and Hermosa Beach piers. She came in second and fourth place, respectively, in those races, and quickly fell in love with ocean swimming. Once they arrived in Costa Mesa, Beulah started looking for someone who could teach her daughter how to bodysurf so that Hawkins could improve her swim times.

Mary Ann Hawkins at Bluff Cove. (Bob Wallace/*Life* magazine, February 7, 1938.)

"Tarzan" Smith was twenty-three years old in 1934, a boozer and a brawler: six-foot-two, about two hundred pounds. When he was seven and living in the San Francisco Bay area, his mother, Goldie Rose, died suddenly in a horse-riding accident. Smith spent the rest of his childhood and adolescence in foster homes, with extended family, or moving about the country with an abusive father and a stepmother "who didn't want anything to do" with him and his younger sister, Phyllis.[3] Smith learned how to fight to survive—to protect himself and his sister. He ended up in reform school, and eventually ran away from home to work in lumber camps in Oregon. Santa Monica lifeguard and long-distance paddler Tommy Zahn relates that "Pete" Peterson had told him in the early 1930s that Smith was living in a cave at Corona del Mar with his dog:

> he had one suit of clothes and one pair of shoes. And, on Saturday night, his big kick was to go down to the Rendezvous Ballroom—the Balboa Ballroom. And to get across the channel at Corona del Mar, he'd get on his paddleboard, with his suit on, tie his shoes around his neck, roll up his pant legs and sleeves and just paddle across the channel and go down to the ballroom.

Gene "Tarzan" Smith, Corona del Mar, early to mid-1930s. (Courtesy Stephen F. Foster.)

Smith was a really aggressive guy and he was never happy unless he got into a big fight down there. He'd usually take on 2 or 3 guys. Like [Tom] Blake says, he's broken the jaws of 6 guys he knows in the Islands. And, so, he'd be this totally thrashed-out, worked guy.

. . . he'd come back down to the channel and he'd just jump on the board and lie down and paddle across, suit and all. Monday morning, the suit would go back to the cleaners and then hang in the cave until the next Saturday night![4]

Smith was working as a lifeguard at Corona del Mar when he spotted Hawkins training in the ocean, and bodysurfing. He'd had his first taste of Hawai'i in January of that year, following in the wake of Tom Blake, "Whitey" Harrison, and "Pete" Peterson, all of them soaking in the traditions of Waikīkī like deep-sea sponges.[5] Smith decided to try a little Hawaiian-style tandem surfing at Corona del Mar, and there was pretty Mary Ann Hawkins. She recalled:

My mother had taken me down there early, and dropped me off, so I could [body]surf, and be on the beach all day. But we were far out past the jetty, riding tandem, when this wave came along. . . . I'll never forget when we caught that wave. I know that wave had to be 30 feet high, because I've been on 30 foot high platforms, diving platforms, and knew what 30 feet looked like.

I would not have fallen off that board for the world. I was sticking out there in front of Gene, and looking straight down. It was just like looking straight down off a diving platform. And we rode. He made me get up. We rode across that jetty, and he pulled out. We had no problem.[6]

Hawkins was seventy years old when she described that wave. She said, "the most thrilling and exhilarating thing that ever happened to me was riding tandem with Gene Smith."[7]

Smith became the greatest long-distance paddler of his generation, the first one in the modern era to "chain" the Hawaiian islands by completing solo journeys on a hollow surfboard between Moloka'i and O'ahu (forty miles in eight hours, at night), between O'ahu and Kaua'i (about ninety miles in thirty hours), and between Hawai'i and Maui (forty miles in twelve and a half hours).[8] In between these treks, he was one of the few who managed to beat "Pete" Peterson in several shorter-distance races.[9] Smith was one of the young Californians who followed his dreams to Waikīkī. He moved to the islands in the mid-1930s and lived there for more than three decades, working variously as a beachboy and police officer while devoting himself, much like Tom Blake, to the life of a Hawaiian waterman. Although he led a hard life, punctuated with bouts of violence, he maintained a correspondence with Hawkins, who drew out his softer side. In one letter from Hawai'i in December 1939, while Smith was working for the Waikiki Beach Patrol, he reminisced about the "old days" at Corona del Mar and the Thanksgiving in 1934 when Hawkins' family had taken him in. He encouraged her to come over to the islands where she could train and compete against Hawaiian women. Like many other Californians of the period, he adopted the habit of sprinkling his writing with Hawaiian terms, beginning and ending his letter to Hawkins with "aloha nui" ("much love" or "much affection").

Hawkins also met twenty-one-year-old "Whitey" Harrison at Corona del Mar in the summer of 1934. He wrote her letters as well—from the Waikiki Tavern and Inn on Christmas of that same year after stowing away aboard a Matson steamer. He called her "the best tandem rider I ever had because I could do all kinds of tricks when we were sliding waves together."[10] The lonely surfer, waxing romantic in the land of romance, added: "Gee, you really don't know how much I love you. I even dream of you sometimes and imagine thinking I'm riding a wave with you on my shoulders; gee and it sure seems real, only when I wake up I find I'm over here. Then I always wish you were here to go tandem with me."[11] Harrison evokes the sensuality of men and women sharing a wave together, which has a rich tradition in Hawaiian lore. As John Clark notes in his *Hawaiian Surfing:* "When men and women shared this experience in the same place, on the same wave, or even on the same board, it was stimulating for everyone and sometimes led to romantic interludes."[12] Recall Mary Kawena Pukui's examples of such incidents in *Hawaiian Proverbs and Poetical Sayings:* "O ka papa heʻe nalu kēia, paheʻe i ka nalu haʻi o Makaiwa (*This is the surfboard that will glide on the rolling surf of Makaiwa*—A woman's boast. Her beautiful body is like the surfboard on which her mate 'glides over the rolling surf')."[13] The young Californians learned about tandem surfing from watching the Waikīkī beachboys take female tourists out in the waves, and they eagerly carried that tradition back to mainland beaches.[14]

Hawkins noted one particular tandem experience with Harrison at Corona del Mar, though it was hardly romantic:

> Suddenly, we saw this huge gigantic wave coming up far beyond the bell buoy, and Lorrin told me to get off the board, and get far from him. . . . So I did, and, of course, he told me to dive, or else I knew to dive as deep as I could . . . and that wave was so gigantic that it caught me, and turned me around, seemingly forever. And when it passed, and everything was quiet, it was pitch dark. I didn't know which way was up, so I just started drifting, and eventually the water lightened, and I thought I was near the surface because I certainly was almost completely out of air. But . . . I had only drifted up to where it became light. I don't know how much further I had to go until I actually reached the surface. When I did pop up, Lorrin was sitting there on his board looking all over, and I think he thanked God, but I do know that he said, 'I thought we'd lost you!'[15]

The giant waves at Corona del Mar had taken many lives—recall Duke's heroic rescue there in 1925—but Harrison needn't have worried so much. Although only fifteen years old at the time, Hawkins was already showing the strength, endurance, and ocean skills that would make her the top waterwoman on the California coast.

The Hawkins family moved from Costa Mesa to Santa Monica the following year, in 1935, probably so that Mary Ann could be closer to the Los Angeles Athletic Club. She remarked that her mother's idea to move her nearer the ocean to improve her swim times "actually backfired, because right away I started learning to body surf and then started going tandem as I met the surfing boys. And I fell so much in love with surfing and body

Mary Ann Hawkins at Bluff Cove with E. J. Oshier. (John Heath "Doc" Ball/California Surf Museum, E. J. Oshier Collection.)

surfing that I really never did my best in swimming from that time on."[16] When Hawkins said she never did her best, she was referring to pool competition. She began a string of victories in "rough-water" or ocean swims over the next four years that cemented her reputation as the top female ocean swimmer in the Southland. She won events at every distance, from eight hundred yards to one mile, in three different counties: San Diego, Los Angeles, and Santa Barbara. She won the annual breakwater swim in Venice three years in a row (1936–1938). Like "Pete" Peterson, she often compounded her victories: the same day that she won the 1938 breakwater swim in Venice, she also captured the women's half-mile paddleboard race. There's a nice picture of her in the Santa Monica *Evening Outlook* standing front and center among the winners that day, which included two members of the Palos Verdes Surfing Club with whom she had been romantically linked the previous year: Calvin "Tulie" Clark, winner of the mile paddleboard race, and Everett "E. J." Oshier, winner of the half-mile paddleboard race.[17] Standing directly behind her is "Pete" Peterson—gaze turned to the side—with a rare second-place showing behind Clark. Hawkins had won the very first women's paddleboard race in California two years earlier—dubbed the Pacific coast paddleboard championship—held on September 12, 1936 at the Santa Monica breakwater.[18] A student at Santa Monica High School at the time, she bested Peterson's wife, Arlene, and Patty Godsave in the 150-yard sprint.

There were very few surfing contests for women during the 1930s. The 1932 PCSRC at Corona del Mar offered a women's category: Helen Hoffman of Newport Beach beat four other women, including Ethel Harrison, Lorrin Harrison's sister, to win the prize. The next major contest to include women was the 1938 national surfing and paddleboard championship in Long Beach. Although Hawkins won the quarter-mile paddleboard event that day, the surfing contest had to be postponed owing to lack of swell. She and the second-place winner of the paddleboard race, Dorothy Fincannon (Long Beach Surf Club), surfed the following month in chilly fifty-two-degree water; the newspapers, however, make no mention of any prizes awarded to the women.[19] Those two surfing contests represent the sum total for women during the decade. Of the first five major paddleboard races held for women during the 1930s, Hawkins won three of them, including the national championship at Long Beach.[20] She married Thomas "Bud" Morrissey in April 1939 and did not compete in the Long Beach women's championship in December of that year, won by Mary Riehl of the Hermosa-Manhattan Surfing Club.[21]

Hawkins had started surfing on her own board when the family moved to Santa Monica in 1935. She didn't recall seeing many other women surfing around her in those days, save Ethel Harrison down at Corona del Mar. The lack of opportunity for women in surfing and paddleboard contests was undoubtedly a factor of the general sexism they faced in the water. Hawkins described one formative incident when she was sixteen and had paddled her board out at Santa Monica State Beach: "this young kid, he was probably 14, felt I'd gotten in his way, and started swearing, and said that girls didn't belong in the surf. That really put a damper on me, as far as my own surfing went, because from then on I always tried to stay out of the way of the boys . . . I just didn't get in there and fight. I tried to stay out of the way. If I had it to do over again it would be a little bit different."[22] Given the large and cumbersome boards of the period, surfers getting in the way of one another was simply par for the course. But being a young woman in the lineup made Hawkins a target for verbal abuse simply because of her sex. Her spirits dampened, she nevertheless overcame such obstacles and found a supportive group of young men who surfed at Bluff Cove and encouraged her progress. She starts to appear in Ball's photographs in *Ye*

Members of the Palos Verdes Surfing Club with Mary Ann Hawkins. (John Heath "Doc" Ball.)

Weekly Super Illustrated Spintail beginning in January 1936.[23] Ball calls her "the Santa Monica beauty" and praises her for paddling out at the Cove on one of the biggest days he had ever seen ridden there.[24] She surfed Bluff Cove regularly, attended PVSC social functions, dated two of the members, and eventually married club associate and surfboard shaper "Bud" Morrissey.

Young women may have been discouraged from surfing by some, but that didn't stop them from participating in the development of beach culture, which included banding together to form their own surf and paddleboard clubs. The San Onofre Surfing Wahines (SOSW)—also known as the "Pilikia Wahines" (literally "Trouble Women")—formed in May 1938.[25] The initial group included Mary Jo Best, Eleanor Roach, Jean Olsen, Irene and Marion Chovan, Helen Hughes, Dorothy Hackett, Ruth Sizemore, and Ruth Gates. Within several months the club had more than a dozen members, the majority of them linked socially to members of the male surf clubs. They all partied, surfed, and competed in contests together, and a number of them married one another. SOSW member Ruth Sizemore wed PVSC member Jimmie Reynolds on October 15, 1938 in what was called "a real surfers wedding" because the entire wedding party frequented the

Palos Verdes Surfing Club member Jimmie Reynolds and San Onofre Surfing Wahines member Ruth Sizemore at San Onofre after their engagement announcement, May 1938. (Courtesy The Huntington Beach International Surfing Museum.)

beaches together.[26] Ruth's sister, Kate (also a SOSW member), was one of her bridesmaids, and PVSC member Leroy Grannis was an usher; "Katie" and "Granny" announced their own engagement the following year.[27] Eleanor "Auntie" Roach, who later served as president of the SOSW and often performed hula dances at PVSC gatherings, married Vincent "Klotz" Lindberg, a fisherman who surfed regularly at San Onofre. Irene Chovan, who also danced the hula at PVSC parties, married Bruce Duncan, a member of the Del Mar Surfing Club.[28]

"Doc" Ball had announced the formation of the women's club in his newsletter for June 15, 1938: "New Paddlers Form Club: And now come the—Nofre Paddle Club nee Pilikia Wahines—and rite off the bat they crash out with a great big super-dance at the Hollywood Riviera club house—that's the one down near the cove—the bids are 1.25 and the entertainment

San Onofre Surfing Wahines member Irene Chovan dancing at the home of E. J. Oshier. (John Heath "Doc" Ball.)

will be lavish and it's Fri Nite the first of July—whatcha waitin for."[29] This event was the "Okole Maluna" dance (named after a Hawaiian drinking song—literally "bottoms up") where guests were greeted at the door with colorful leis that the female club members had made; two of the members, Eleanor Roach and Irene Chovan, performed hula dances for the guests as a floor show, backed by surfer/musicians Barney Wilkes, Bruce Duncan, and E. J. Oshier.[30] The gathering was typical of the social atmosphere of the men's and women's surfing clubs during this era, which celebrated their Hawaiian ideals in dance, music, dress, and language.

The women also formed part of the literal building of beach culture in their efforts to lend a touch of civilization by constructing a shack on the beach at San Onofre in August 1938. The beach was barren of all basic amenities (surfers defecated in a spot they called "Kukae" canyon, borrowing the Hawaiian word for "excrement"). The women dubbed their shack "The Hawaiian Hut." One of the club members commented: "We started that bodacious grass shack which the boys so enthusiastically helped us with (between surfing periods)."[31] The women probably wanted a place simply to change clothes or to sleep (five of the club members were spending a week

San Onofre Surfing Wahines member building the first San Onofre shack on the beach, August 1938. (Courtesy The Huntington Beach International Surfing Museum.)

The San Onofre Shack Completed, August 1938. (Courtesy The Huntington Beach International Surfing Museum.)

there), but their desires took the form of a South Seas dream—a grass shack to match the grass skirts that members Eleanor Roach and Irene Chovan often wore as part of their hula outfits when they danced at interclub parties. Some of the women also formed part of the larger manufacturing industry in Southern California as the country geared up for war. Jean Olsen worked at the Douglas Aircraft Company, as did Jane Waterman (president of the Santa Monica women's paddleboard club), who had to take "an indefinite leave of absence" from her position when she started working night shifts.[32]

The Santa Monica group formed in January 1939 as a "women's auxiliary" to the Santa Monica Paddle Club. The *Evening Outlook* reported that the group was "headed by Mary Ann Hawkins, champion woman paddler as well as one of Southern Cal's expert swimmers."[33] When Jane Waterman later became president of the club and took the job at Douglas, she asked Hawkins (vice president at the time) to run the next meeting for her on

January 8, 1940, and to represent the club at an upcoming West Coast Paddleboard Association gathering at "Doc" Ball's office in Los Angeles. Other members of the club included Jean Francis, Marjorie Jorgensen, Dorothy Lane, Monica Roche, and Doris Wyman.

Much like the San Onofre Surfing Wahines, the Santa Monica group included working women and college students who liked to surf, travel, and party with members of the male surf clubs. The *Evening Outlook* noted on April 18, 1939 that the men's paddle club had left Saturday morning for San Onofre: "Following close at their heels were the members of the girls Surfing Club, who left Sunday morning to join the boys."[34] A surf report in Ball's newsletter the previous week noted that San Onofre was "the only spot it humped in the whole sea."[35] One of the larger waves—"a veritable grinder"—dumped him off his board, and he had to spend nearly ten hours rebuilding his camera after it got soaked. He also reported that the water was a "warm" sixty degrees, so perhaps the San Monica Paddle Club had gotten wind of the spring swell and temperate conditions and decided to take a road trip. San Onofre had just started charging surfers twenty-five cents to park there. Ball, a little outraged at the expense, commented: "The only way to be rid of this evil—is to enter late at nite, stay out on the planks all day and depart in the middle of the nite again."[36] Beyond the camp's owner seeing an opportunity for profit, the growing popularity of San Onofre as a surfing destination testified to the evolving nature of California beach culture. Male and female surfers were discovering that good waves broke at San Onofre well beyond the summer—not unlike Waikīkī—so they could pursue their Hawaiian dreams there year-round. As one of the SOSW members commented, "Nofre season never ends for some of the varmints."[37]

But summertime, of course, was the most popular season to spend weekends (or entire weeks) at San Onofre, and because beach nights were chilly, the SOSW introduced the fashion of surf hoodies to stay warm. A member noted on July 2, 1938, "we came out in our Sweat Shirts. They were quite effective, and greatly add to ou[r] comfort at the beach."[38] The matching white hoodies all had the women's individual names sewed onto the front, following the style of sweat suits worn by the PVSC members. Like the men, the women competed in various paddleboard contests up and down the coast, along with two seasons of paddleboard water polo. Also like the men, they shared quarts of Aztec beer, nursed morning hangovers, played beach volleyball, surfed solo and tandem, participated in abalone and spaghetti feeds to celebrate birthdays and holidays, and even went lobster diving at Bluff Cove.[39]

Members of the San Onofre Surfing Wahines posing with their new hoodies. Left to right: Eleanor Roach, Jean Olsen, Mary Jo Best, Marion Chovan, Irene Chovan, Dorothy Hackett, unknown, Ruth Sizemore, Helen Hughes. (Courtesy The Huntington Beach International Surfing Museum.)

But the women also highlighted different aspects of their shared lives, according to a period scrapbook created by one of the SOSW members: engagements, linen showers, wedding invitations and photographs, and who had announced a pregnancy. The following entry for February 9, 1940 is typical:

> Marian and Dot Sizemore were the belles of the ball, at the association dance at "Zucca's." We hear you are now giving lessons in necking. How about it? The same night Bet and Dot L. left with Little Joe, in Dutchy's car for Nofre. Say did you ever hear about the time we went to Nofre in the mud??!! In the cold, cold mud? You should of been there. Dot Clark showed up at Nofre Sunday, and the kids dropped by her place for sandwiches and beverages, spelled with a capital *B*.
>
> Ruth got a super tan skiing at Magee Creek.
>
> Jean went to Rosarito Beach, Mexico. She remembers only the beer, which, she says, was plenty all right.

Irene had a party and Addy Bayer proceeded to initiate the house. Eleanor and Klotz went for a trip on their newly painted boat.

A shower for Jean Foote was held at Eleanor's. She received some lovely gifts, and the 6th present to be opened was Bette's. Well she will be the next married, and Dot L. the next engaged, and Eleanor will have to work fast to beat Irene, and have the next off-spring.

The week-end of the 17th, Irene and Eleanor were at Nofre. We hear there was a super brawl Saturday night. Dot L. went down Sunday morning with a tale of drunkenness proceeding her. What a surprise when she was sober.[40]

Along with the parties (*that is,* "brawls") and travel to places like San Onofre, the scrapbook detailed who was dating whom, and kept close track of married and single members. After an engagement announcement in March 1939, the anonymous author of the scrapbook wrote, "Six down and three to go now."[41] As the longer entry above details, Eleanor Roach (Lindberg) and Irene Chovan (Duncan) continued to frequent San Onofre in the wintertime though both were married and the latter was pregnant. The scrapbook mentions SOSW members taking the Santa Fe bus down to San Clemente—the closest town to San Onofre—and staying at the Travel Inn, which also served as the location of Irene Duncan's baby shower in April 1940.[42] So it may be that the women sometimes opted out of camping on the beach in favor of nearby motel amenities.

Mary Ann Hawkins gets a mention in the scrapbook when the author reviews the results of the national paddleboard championships held in Long Beach in November 1938: "The girls race was won by Mary Ann Hawkins, enabling her to keep her title of surfing queen, although she was given a good race by Dorothy Fincannon, with Camille Bayer getting third place honors."[43] Hawkins reported that she had been among the first group of surfers to "discover" San Onofre in the summer of 1934 when Corona del Mar faded as the premier summer surfing spot owing to continuing harbor construction at Newport Beach, so SOSW club members would have seen her there from time to time.[44]

The Long Beach paddleboard contest in 1938 capped off a banner year for Hawkins. In February the eighteen-year-old had appeared in *Life* magazine shouldering a balsa surfboard into the water at Bluff Cove, knee-paddling out to the waves, and then riding one into shore standing up.[45] In May she was the sole woman to compete among 150 candidates for a Los Angeles County lifeguard job. Although her "achievements were considered on a par with those of the regular contenders," she was not offered a position because women were not allowed to be lifeguards.[46] In June she won the half-mile

George Watkins and Frank Holborow, Casa Del Mar, Santa Monica, late 1920s. (PhotCL_555_06_1141/The Huntington Library, San Marino, California.)

paddleboard race in Venice, along with the rough-water ocean swim (her third year in a row).[47] In August she entered the forty-four-mile aquaplane race from Catalina Island to Hermosa Beach (her boat driver was pioneer aviator Bernadine Lewis King). The winner of the event, county lifeguard Frank Rodecker, had to be admitted to the hospital after the grueling race; Jack Burrud, who won the inaugural race in 1935, also had to be admitted to the hospital and failed to finish, along with three other teams. The *Los Angeles Times* reported: "Probably the calmest contestant at the finish was Mary Ann Hawkins, lone woman entrant, who came across the line in fourteenth place. Miss Hawkins, making her first attempt in a contest that has defeated some of the strongest men, rode a beautiful race. She fell twice, but was not injured. She said that her feet became numb about the middle of the grind and that her body ached terribly but that she knew all the time that she could make it."[48] Hawkins bagged another photograph in *Life* magazine that month, which was covering the race.[49]

"Pete" Peterson also entered the aquaplane race that year and came in fourth. He and Hawkins both competed for the Casa Del Mar club in Santa Monica, which had been training swimmers and sponsoring competition since its formal opening in 1926.[50] The club's longtime swim instructor, Frank Holborow, offered Peterson and Hawkins a link to California's original waterman, Hawaiian George Freeth, who had often competed against Holborow and later trained him to surf, lifeguard, and play water polo.[51] Holborow worked with Hawkins when she first moved to Santa Monica in 1935, running her through workouts every Monday night in the club pool.[52]

Hawkins had started out 1938 in fine fashion as well, representing Palos Verdes in the Pasadena Rose Parade on New Year's Day. The *Palos Verdes Peninsula News* reported that Hawkins had been selected "from 75 surf riders who make use of the Palos Verdes Cove."[53] The newspaper went on to extoll her many accomplishments: "Miss Hawkins, the surfboard rider, won the swimming Junior National's in Pasadena in 1933 breaking the one-half mile record. She holds over 25 cups and trophies won in swimming and diving contests. She is the Southern California Paddle Board Champion and probably outstanding girl surfboard rider in California."[54] Hawkins's mother had come up with the theme for the float—"California's Little Waikiki." Her daughter appeared in a white, one-piece silk bathing suit "riding a white chrysanthemum surfboard on a wave made of blue delphinium and stevia into a sandy beach made of dusty miller. On the beach were three bronzed surf-board riders playing Hawaiian music on two guitars and a ukulele for Eleanor Roach who danced interpretive native Hawaiian dances."[55] Six of the PVSC members, including "Doc" Ball, walked beside the float in white silk trunks.[56] Pacific System donated the balsa "Waikiki" model surfboard on which Hawkins stood, and West Coast–Manchester Mills, makers of Hollywood Swim Suits, donated all the silk suits and trunks.[57]

The float encapsulates, in many ways, both the general Native Hawaiian influence on California beach culture by 1938 and how Californians appropriated that culture to their own ends. The Native Hawaiian traditions of surfing, music, and dance were all marshalled in the service of marketing Palos Verdes (whose Chamber of Commerce sponsored the float) and of enacting the Rose Parade theme that year—"Fantasy Playland." That theme could well have represented California beach culture itself in terms of the surfers' understanding of the Native Hawaiian traditions that inspired their recreational activities. The *Palos Verdes Peninsula News* went to some pains to legitimize the Native Hawaiian look and the cultural knowledge of the young people involved. The men were described as "bronzed Palos Verdians"—an unlikely appearance in the wintertime, even in Southern California.[58] The paper also reported, "All participants will be expert surfboard riders. Eleanor Roach, who formerly lived in Hawaii will be the hula dancer."[59] Roach, however, had only visited Hawai'i once (the previous summer); during her month-long stay, she took surfing lessons from Hawaiian paddleboard champion Tommy Kiakona and presumably picked up some

Pasadena Rose Parade, 1938. Eleanor Roach (dancing the hula) and Mary Ann Hawkins (riding tandem) surrounded by members of the Palos Verdes Surfing Club. (The Croul Family Collection.)

hula technique.[60] A sense of the cultural disconnect that permeated the era's California beach culture can be drawn from islander Benet Costa's weekly column in the *Honolulu Advertiser,* "Hawaii in Hollywood":

> To us who have awakened early New Year's day (to become part of a million and half crowd) the 49th annual Pasadena Tournament of Roses parade with its 60 huge flower floats, was a breathless thrill . . . with but a single disappointment. The disappointing note being the Palos Verdes entry, entitled "Little Waikiki."
>
> The float itself was a dream of flowers—a white chrysanthemum surf board in a heather sea dashing in toward a beach of marigolds. But the decorative athletes, a pert, blond surf-rider, three Jewish-looking fellas strumming sour notes on guitars and ukes, while a jerkey-limbed haole gal faked an Hawaiian hula—it was too much for your reporter.
>
> And think this: 1,500,000 eager-eyed people saw the darn thing! How much nicer 'twould have been if the real thing were offered 'em. Maybe then "Little Waikiki" would not have been judged last choice in its particular class by tournament officials![61]

Costa flashes antisemitism in his review, but his observation of offering spectators "the real thing" directs us to the Native Hawaiian community of professional musicians, dancers, and actors who lived in Los Angeles at the time. As an aside, we can explain that the simplest reason why Native Hawaiians had not been hired for the float was the serious financial straits experienced by the Palos Verdes Estates during the Great Depression. Owners had defaulted on payments in the small unincorporated community, and by 1938 the homeowners' association owed some $50,000 in back taxes to the state.[62] Float chairman Reg. F. Dupuy commented that "the float was built at a lower cost than any other entry and that proportionately for the money expended the local and national publicity will exceed that of any other float."[63] After the parade, Dupuy took out a large ad in the *Palos Verdes Peninsula News* thanking the many volunteers who had donated their time and expertise in the design, construction, and decoration of the float, along with the many private financial contributors.[64]

We can leave Mary Ann Hawkins poised on her chrysanthemum surfboard, for the moment, and pause Eleanor Roach in her hula dancing, and the PVSC members walking along the eight-mile parade route ("What a day," Ball commented in his newsletter, "and what dead dogs at the end of that super grind") to broaden the context of Hawaiian cultural influences in Los Angeles during the 1930s.[65] The great wave of Hawaiian music, dance, and South Seas films that inundated the region spurred the dreams of California surfers toward Waikīkī and energized their efforts to re-create that dream at home. What gets erased in the process is what Benet Costa would call "the real thing"—the traditions and cultural identity of a people who had been disenfranchised in their own land.

An appropriate time and date to begin is 9:30 P.M. on Monday, November 18, 1935—the first broadcast of *Hawaii Calls* in Los Angeles on radio station KHJ.[66] The program, begun the previous month, originated from the Royal Hawaiian hotel in Waikīkī. The territorial legislature had awarded the Hawaii Tourist Bureau $25,000 to support radio broadcasting.[67] *Hawaii Calls* was the result of that investment, a weekly half-hour "Hawaiian Luau (musical feast)" that featured Harry Owens and the Royal Hawaiian Orchestra. On alternate Mondays, the show broadcast from the roof garden of the Alexander Young hotel in downtown Honolulu and featured Del Courtney's orchestra. After complaints about excessive noise from guests at the Royal Hawaiian, the show moved down the beach to the Moana Hotel, where host Webley Edwards began the program with the sound of waves breaking on the shore.[68] Accompanied by the melody of what has become the iconic sound of Hawaiian music—a steel guitar—the typical Edwards greeting went like this: "And here we meet again beneath the mighty Moana banyan tree beside the sea, the great panorama of Waikiki beach before us; old Diamond Head at one end, surfboards and outrigger canoes catching waves out there; many colors along the shore, a bright and beautiful picture."[69] The program, featuring local musicians and singers, ran for forty years and was carried by 750 stations around the world at its height.[70] To prime the pump before the first show on October 7, 1935, the Hawaii Tourist Bureau sent out seven thousand announcement cards to daily newspapers and travel agents throughout the United States and Canada.[71]

The program had the precise impact sought by the Hawaii Tourist Bureau. PVSC member Calvin "Tulie" Clark recalled: "We had ukes and guitars, and one fella had a trumpet, and we used to have big luaus. After we'd surf, we'd go back to the beach and just eat, then we'd play Hawaiian songs till midnight or so. Just Hawaiian music because that's all we liked. We used to listen to this radio program called *Hawaii Calls,* it was broadcast out of Waikiki, and we'd all dream about going to Hawaii."[72] As the *Los Angeles Times* reported in their review of the show, "they succeed in transmitting the atmosphere of the magic islands over the air waves in delightful fashion."[73] To have live music emanating across the Pacific from Waikīkī, with the actual sound of waves breaking on shore, must have saturated the aural senses of the young beachgoers, fueling their desires to emulate what they heard by playing music themselves. Their tropical dreams burned all the brighter as they hunkered around smoking tires on wintry nights, thawing their bodies from bone-chilling surf sessions at Bluff Cove. They showed the same mentality as those midwesterners who packed the Sunset Theater in Wichita, Kansas, for two weeks in 1966, in the middle of winter, to see the national test-market debut of Bruce Brown's surfing documentary, *The Endless Summer.* Prominent in both broadcasts was distinctive guitar playing: the relaxed, plaintive sound of steel guitar in *Hawaii Calls* that has become a staple of island music everywhere; and the mellow instrumental by the Sandals—"Theme from the Endless Summer"—that highlights a similarly wistful melody by electric guitarist John Blakeley.[74] The music, in both cases, helped transport the listeners to distant shores that existed, for the most part, in the realm of imagination. Beyond providing the mainland with Hawaiian tunes, *Hawaii Calls* also showcased island musicians playing their own versions of popular American dance numbers.[75] The program boosted the profile of many local artists, and a number of them signed lucrative contracts with mainland record companies. On the first anniversary of the show, Herbert Ira Rosenthal of the Columbia Broadcasting System (CBS) reported that it was "the most popular sustaining program on the network."[76]

Hawaiians living in Los Angeles also tuned into the radio show, according to Georgia Stiffler, Hollywood columnist for the *Honolulu Star-Bulletin*. "It is such a pleasure to hear the broadcasts from Honolulu," she wrote. "All the Hawaiian colony here listen in . . . and thrill."[77] The "Hawaiian colony" consisted primarily of island musicians, singers, dancers, and actors (and their children) who worked in the entertainment industry. The numbers in the community fluctuated depending on work, but anywhere from seventy-five to 150 people were probably present at any given time during the mid-1930s.[78] As mentioned in the introduction, Stiffler was the spouse of Sol Hoʻopiʻi, "King of the Steel Guitar," who had arrived in Los Angeles around 1920. He became influential in Hollywood not only through his expert musicianship, which placed him in the swankiest clubs in town, but also because he was the only Hawaiian who was a "licensed and bonded employment agent," which meant that he could hire Hawaiians (and others) to work in the film industry.[79] So Sol and Georgia Hoʻopiʻi were very much at the center of the Hawaiian colony, a perfect opportunity for Georgia, who also composed and sang in Hawaiian, to inform folks back home about all the doings in Tinseltown. She captured in her weekly Saturday column, which ran from August 1935 to February 1938, the explosion of the Hawaiian nightclub scene in Los Angeles. *Hawaii Calls* and the clubs were part of what Stiffler called in January 1936 the "South Sea craze . . . sweeping Hollywood like a kona storm":

> There are cafes all over town savoring of the tropics. Hawaiian musicians and hula dancers are kept busy (much to their financial delight), and such names are appearing in Neon lights as: Tropical Hut, Hawaiian Hut, Little Grass Shack, Seven Seas, The Beachcombers, The Tropics, and the Aloha Buffet. And maybe a few others that I've missed. And talk about their cockeyed conception of Hawaiian decorations! Whew!!! Some of them would make your great-grandmother shiver in her grass skirt. One place has oil paintings of supposedly seductive South Sea belles attired in nothing but flowers in their hair! Hotcha![80]

Stiffler chronicled the beginning of what later became known as "Tiki culture," anchored famously by Don the Beachcomber's (founded in Hollywood in 1934), an establishment that served up tropical drinks, food, and décor for mainlanders seeking to imbibe a little exoticism into their lives at the end of Prohibition (1920–1933).[81] Stiffler, a mainlander herself married to a Native Hawaiian, often tracked the disconnect between what she knew of Hawaiian culture and the one being displayed in the growing number of tropical-themed Hollywood clubs. "Each of these cafes," she wrote, "employs a Hawaiian orchestra and hula girls (you'll notice I said 'hula girls' instead of 'Hawaiian girls,' because some of them are decidedly pseudo!)."[82] By September 1937, Stiffler listed a dozen South Seas clubs that were hiring Hawaiian musicians and dancers, and another dozen with "South Sea atmosphere" that couldn't "feature Hawaiian music because there isn't any more to be hired."[83] Even if the residents of Palos Verdes had wanted to hire actual Hawaiian musicians for their Rose Parade float several months later, they might have had a hard time landing them because of their high demand and busy work schedules.

Stiffler marked 1934 as a milestone year for the South Seas fad, when several clubs joined what she called "the grand-daddy of all the South Sea cafes, Gene's Hawaiian village" (opened in 1932 by Eugene Long), which had given many Hawaiian musicians and dancers their start. These new clubs included the Hawaiian Hut (opened by two Honoluluans, Tony Guerrero and "Whistling Willie" Ornellas), and Ray Haller's Seven Seas on Hollywood Boulevard, "credited with the original idea of creating thunder, rain and lightning, against a pale lighted tropical scene, behind the bar—a captivating illusion—a keen idea until half a dozen other cafes copied it."[84] Stiffler's column itself, "Hawaiians at Hollywood," was a sign of how popular island culture had become in the Los Angeles area.[85] The *Honolulu Advertiser*—rival to Stiffler's *Honolulu Star-Bulletin*—eventually started its own Sunday column in July 1937, "Hawaiians in Hollywood," authored by Benet Costa.[86]

The fad truly erupted in 1937 as Hollywood perfected its South Seas genre of films. As Stiffler wrote in her January 2 column that year, "Things are beginning to pop!" She related that every major studio had a South Seas film in various stages of production: *Waikiki Wedding* (Paramount), *Hurricane* (Samuel Goldwyn Productions), *Volcano* (R.K.O.), *Wings Over Honolulu* (Universal), "and Walt Disney is making a very clever Silly Symphony [i.e. *Hawaiian Holiday*] with Donald Duck riding a surfboard and Mickey Mouse playing the steel-guitar while a group of mousey hula-dancers strut their stuff."[87] By April, Stiffler reported that two more films were in production, *Honolulu Honeymoon* (Grand National), and *Paradise Island* (Talisman Studio). She enthused, "The Hawaiians are in the movies, and how! Every kane ["man"], wahine ["woman"], and all the little keikis ["children"] in this colony are working at one or another of the studios."[88] Bing Crosby's version of "Sweet Leilani," performed in *Waikiki Wedding*, won an Oscar for the Best Song category of 1937, helping to popularize the fad even more. Composed by Harry Owens and performed with Lani McIntire and his Hawaiians, "Sweet Leilani" offered a rich dose of the steel guitar that musicians like Sol Hoʻopiʻi—who had recorded the song himself in 1935—had been playing in Hollywood for more than a decade.[89] "Sweet

Leilani" stayed on the charts for six months, over a third of that time at the number one spot. It became Bing Crosby's first gold record and helped make *Waikiki Wedding* the third top-grossing movie of the year. The sheet music for "Sweet Leilani" eventually sold fifty-four million copies.[90]

California beach culture, then, blossomed in the winds of the South Seas fad. The most influential surfers of the period—Blake, Ball, Peterson, Hawkins, and Harrison—had a head start on Hawai'i mania through their love of surfing. But the founding of surf clubs in the Los Angeles area; the rise of surfing and paddleboard contests; the enthusiasm for beach luaus, hula dancing, and playing Hawaiian music—all of those aspects of beach culture developed under, and alongside, the influence of Hawaiian sounds and images flowing across the region from the radio, movie screens, and dozens of South Seas nightclubs. Southern California's beach culture was unique from its Hawaiian origins in this respect, fueled by the power of Hollywood to broadcast images and ideals of the South Seas cultures that lent beach culture much of its allure.

There were moments of direct contact between members of the Hawaiian colony and the Los Angeles surfers. The PVSC hired Dick McIntire's Harmony Hawaiians to play at their first "Hula Luau" on March 19, 1937.[91] The club held these annual dances to have fun and raise money. McIntire—brother of Lani McIntire, who performed "Sweet Leilani" with Bing Crosby that year in *Waikiki Wedding*—had his own successful career as a steel guitar player and band leader, eventually recording more than three hundred songs with the top singers of the period, including Bing Crosby. Dick McIntire had a regular summer gig in the mid-1930s at the Miramar Hotel on the beachfront in Santa Monica, so his performances were within easy earshot of many surfers who lived and worked in this important beach-culture center.[92]

For the most part, however, the surfers and Hawaiians didn't seem to mix that much. Hawkins stated, for example, that Joseph Kukea, who married Ethel Harrison ("Whitey" Harrison's sister) in September 1936, was "the first Hawaiian I ever got to know very well."[93] Kukea had left Hawai'i on the *Lurline* with "Whitey" Harrison in March 1935 and stayed in Southern California until August of that year.[94] Many of the Southern California surfers idolized Duke, of course, including Hawkins, but for all of their enthusiasm about Waikīkī, they seemed less interested in establishing substantive relationships with Native Hawaiians themselves. Beyond the ability of the Palos Verdes Chamber of Commerce to hire Native Hawaiian performers for their New Year's Day float, I'll argue that the young Californians were not actually interested in "the real thing." What they wanted was to perform as Native Hawaiians themselves: to dress and dance and play (in multiple senses of that word) the part of people whom they romanticized and exoticized.

Philip J. Deloria's *Playing Indian* outlines the complex dynamics of white Americans who adopted Native American dress and customs through the centuries, a practice that he connects to the construction of both national and individual identity. Native Americans and Native Hawaiians have distinct histories concerning their experiences with white colonial aggression, but Deloria's study illustrates patterns that apply well to Californians' appropriation of Native Hawaiian dance, music, and language.[95] The young surfers—typically first-generation Californians—were in the process of creating an identity for themselves and their generation that revolved around beach recreation. Unaware of indigenous cultural traditions (the Chumash, Tongva, or Kumeyaay, for example), they adopted those of Hawai'i to establish their difference from the mainstream values of their parents, who were largely conservative Protestant midwesterners. At the same time, their mildly subversive behavior actually reinforced the status quo not in terms of cultural content but in terms of hegemonic process: they adopted Hawaiian customs to suit their own needs and interests without more than a passing regard for the cultural knowledge behind those customs.

We see specific examples of this process in such names as the PVSC's "Hula Luau" or the SOSW's "Pilikia Wahines." *Hula* and *lū'au* are distinct terms for a Native Hawaiian dance (or song) and a Native Hawaiian feast, respectively. One will not find either word modifying the other, in any way, in the *Hawaiian Dictionary*. The same is true for *pilikia* ("trouble" or "problem") and *wahine* (a "woman"—the plural is *wāhine*). The point is not to correct the Californians' use of Hawaiian, but to see in their mash-up of Hawaiian terms a disregard for the cultural meanings and traditions they had taken as their own. Among the aspects lost in Eleanor Roach's hula dancing (during the parade or at many of the club parties), for example, were the sacred traditions, the poetry of the music, the physical act of storytelling, and the fact that Native Hawaiian men performed the hula as well. What largely remained were the sensual aspects of the dance—the men along the parade route, described by "Doc" Ball, "craning their respective necks to get a last look at our fair Eleanor and her wiggling hips."[96]

Deloria reminds us in his study that the appropriation of identity is ever connected to the appropriation of land.[97] In the late 1930s, the United States was in the process of establishing permanent control over the Hawaiian Islands: annexed as a territory in 1898, and finally admitted to the union as the fiftieth state in 1959. On the one hand, we might see the surf club members and their acquaintances as far removed from the larger geopolitical maneuvers of the time: they were young people simply having fun and pulled toward the exciting image of Waikīkī and all it had to offer—sandy beaches, swaying palms, warm waves, and the sensual beauty of hula dancers and beachboys. All of that was undoubtedly true. Their appropriation of Hawaiian language, dress, and customs (actual or invented), however, formed part of a broader social pattern. Circe Sturm's *Becoming Indian: The Struggle over Cherokee Identity in the Twenty-first Century* characterizes this phenomenon as "a form of cultural cross-dressing in which whites selectively try on a nonwhite cultural identity without compromising their white identities or white racial privilege."[98] She adds that "white society has a tendency to commodify and then absorb the symbolic and material aspects of nonwhite society that it finds most desirable. Yet, at the end of this process, race is a barrier that is actively maintained by those with white privilege."[99] The racial barrier between Native Hawaiians and white Californians was embedded in state law of the time. Ethel Harrison, for example, had to travel to Hawai'i to marry Joseph Kukea because Native Hawaiians were classified as Malayans and thus not allowed to marry white people. The category was added to the state's anti-miscegenation law in 1933, which also prevented African Americans or Asian Americans from marrying white people.[100]

The cultural disconnect between white Southern Californians and Hawaiians surfaces in two responses to the Palos Verdes float. "Doc" Ball complained about his tired feet afterward, but overall he saw the day as a success that might help the PVSC glean a few favors from the Palos Verdes homeowners' association: "All in all me lads we done noble and the publicity obtained was widely broadcast."[101] Islander Benet Costa, however, was truly offended by the sight—"it was too much for your reporter"—which came across in his acerbic descriptions of the musicians' "sour notes" and the "jerky-limbed haole gal" faking a hula.

After being featured in national magazines and celebrated on beaches throughout Southern California for her many swimming and paddleboard victories in 1938, Hawkins culminated her competitive career by turning her sights toward Hawai'i. She decided to visit the islands for the first time during the Pacific Aquatic Carnival in July 1939. Organizers arranged to have her compete in seven swimming races altogether at various venues: the War Memorial natatorium at Waikīkī (an outdoor pool), Honolulu's Punahou High School (an indoor pool), and the Ala Moana ocean channel. She became something of a media darling even before the races began. Referred to as the "Los Angeles backstroke swimming star," Hawkins, clad in a bathing suit, posed for the *Honolulu Star-Bulletin* in the arms of two husky wrestlers performing at the carnival, the threesome captioned as "Beauty and Brawn."[102]

She received more attention when she started winning races. The first day of competition, she won the 100-meter freestyle at the natatorium, and captured second place in both the 100-meter backstroke and the 300-meter individual medley. The second day she won the 200-meter freestyle, again at the natatorium (establishing a new Hawaiian record); the third day she won the half-mile ocean swim at the Ala Moana channel. She rounded out her trip with two second places on the fourth day at Punahou in the 100-meter and 220-meter freestyle.[103] Her photograph appeared in the Hawaiian papers half a dozen times during the month of the aquatic carnival, including a picture of her modeling the latest sportswear outfit for local designer Branfleet—a mini-skirt and top (bare midriff) with bobby socks and saddle shoes.

Branfleet was the same company that had signed Duke Kahanamoku to a five-year contract (beginning in 1937) to use his name in their clothing lines of shorts and aloha shirts.[104] Hawkins had appeared in a local newspaper with Duke early in July—posed in her bathing suit, looking excited to be meeting her girlhood hero. Perhaps that encounter had led to the modeling shoot later in the month. Duke was forty-eight years old by then, in his third term as sheriff of Honolulu. Half a century later, Hawkins stated, "I'll never forget the first time I saw [Duke]." She was living in Pasadena, eight or ten years old. Duke had arrived in town to give a swimming exhibition. She recalled, "this big beautiful Hawaiian man was in the pool, making loud bubbling noises with his mouth. He fascinated me."[105] Ten or twelve years later, she got the chance to meet him in Honolulu, and to shake his hand. "I treasure that picture," she said.[106]

For Hawkins and the rest of the California surfers, and so many other visitors to the islands, Duke remained their touchstone for the Hawaiian experience. Recall the handshake from Duke in a Detroit movie theater that set Tom Blake on his path. Hawkins also reminisced about being chosen by Duke: "the Australians came over to compete against Duke [in the aquatic carnival] . . . and he and his brother, and I were a team together. He picked me to team with him, to surf against the Australians. But unfortunately, there was no surf for the meet, and it was canceled."[107] Hawkins also recalled during her trip that Duke "helped me every day. He'd always have me get to his right, he'd coach me. . . . I surfed with him daily."[108] Duke's charisma made everyone he met feel special, feel as if they had a personal connection to him, and, by extension, to Hawai'i itself. Duke's grace and aloha perhaps obviated the need for most mainland surfers to establish relationships with other Native Hawaiians, or with the indigenous culture itself, because they

Duke Kahanamoku greeting Mary Ann Hawkins in Hawai'i. *Honolulu Star-Bulletin*, July 4, 1939.

saw in their connection to him (real or imagined), and in their devotion to surfing, a bridge that spanned racial and cultural differences. As noted in previous chapters, however, the broader political reality of the ongoing colonization of Hawai'i would have placed the visiting surfers and Native Hawaiians at odds. The strong desire by so many mainlanders to connect with Duke may have been the outward symptom of either a general ignorance about the colonial situation on the ground—in itself a position of privilege—or a deep denial that refused to acknowledge the injustice taking place against Duke and all Native Hawaiians.

~

The national and regional exposure that Hawkins received in the media opened up opportunities for her in Hollywood. Similar to Tom Blake and "Pete" Peterson, she found stunt work in a number of South Seas films because of her expertise in swimming and diving. She doubled for Dorothy Lamour in Paramount's *Aloma of the South Seas* (1941) and *Beyond the Blue Horizon* (1942). She recalled being asked to double for Judy Garland, but then "they said I was too fat. So they made me lose some weight and put me in a film called 'Washington Melodrama'."[109] Hawkins ended up performing in the film's aquacade sequence. Her stints in Hollywood, especially in the South Seas films, would have been a good opportunity for her to establish contact with members of the Hawaiian colony, who worked in many such films. One thing that Hawkins had in common with the women of the Hawaiian colony was the constant pressure to lose weight. Georgia Stiffler writes about the experience of Mamo Clark, perhaps the biggest success in the Hawaiian colony—she starred opposite Clark Gable in *Mutiny on the Bounty* (1935). Mamo Clark lost opportunities for roles after that film because she had gained weight. Stiffler wrote, "until she's sliced off a few chunks here-a and there-a, the roles will go to the more sylphlike creatures. Stoo bad!"[110] The hula dancers in the night clubs faced similar pressure. Stiffler reported on the Maui dancer Audrey Robinson, who performed at the Hawaiian Hut: "that gal has brought her weight down from 155 pounds to 116 pounds in exactly six weeks. And is this gang envious? Everybody in town is trying to find out how she did it! Audrey is becoming quite an accomplished and graceful dancer too, since she worked in Waikiki Wedding, and the customers clamor for her."[111]

Hawkins spoke about the sexism that she also faced in the surf, experiences that initially discouraged her from catching more waves when she was first learning in Santa Monica. But after several years of riding waves at Bluff Cove, San Onofre, and Waikīkī, she had a very different reaction to such behavior. She recounted the day at Malibu when a beginning surfer paddled out and "started griping because a female was in the surf."[112] He didn't know who she was, so she decided to show him. She caught the biggest wave she'd ever ridden on her own—"the best wave that I've ever had in my life . . . I rode over near to the pier on this particular wave. All because I knew he couldn't surf very well. . . . And I had a thrilling ride, so I'm actually glad it happened."[113]

Malibu ended up being her favorite place to surf in California, the screen on which she rose to become, by competitive record and general consensus, the "surfing queen" and most versatile waterwoman of her generation.

CHAPTER 5

The Traveler

Stowaway Pair Here on Jackson: After stowing away on the Oceanic liner Monterey only to be discovered in time to be returned to San Francisco on the Manukai, Lorrin Harrison, 19, of Garden Grove, California and Henry Valentine, 25, of Belgium, boarded the President Jackson and succeeded in reaching Honolulu today aboard that vessel.

They left the ship in the custody of the police.
—*Honolulu Star-Bulletin,* October 13, 1932

The Matson Navigation Company was having a problem with stowaways. The San Francisco–based company, begun in 1882 by Captain William Matson with a three-masted schooner, had invested more than twenty-five million dollars in the late 1920s to build three luxurious steamships for their Hawaiian routes—the *Mariposa,* the *Monterey,* and the *Lurline.* In 1927 they spent four million dollars to build the Royal Hawaiian hotel. In 1931 they absorbed their closest rival, the Los Angeles Steamship Company, to monopolize tourist travel to Hawai'i from the West Coast.[1] And in 1932 they spent another million and a half dollars to acquire the Moana Hotel. But the ongoing Depression was throwing a wrench into their growth plans. Five and a half million fewer tourists visited the islands in 1932 than in 1931 (10,370,000 compared to 15,779,000), a total that was almost twelve million fewer than in 1929 (22,190,000).[2] The tourist pipeline to Hawai'i had ruptured, and high unemployment in California was driving many to seek jobs wherever they could find them. Stowing away aboard a passenger steamship, or even a freighter, held low risks and modest rewards for the desperate. Rumors spread of good jobs in the islands, and the territory could not prosecute stowaways because the act fell under maritime law, governed by the U.S. Congress. As long as stowaways were not wanted on a warrant in their home port, the Honolulu police had to release them after forty-eight hours.

Lorrin "Whitey" Harrison. (Courtesy California Surf Museum/Harrison family.)

The financial burden to mitigate the problem dropped into Matson's lap. "We are doing everything we can to stop this stowaway nuisance," stated Randolph Sevier, representing Matson through his employer Castle & Cooke, "in spite of the fact that each time we transfer stowaways it means a heavy expense to the company."[3] Sevier listed the costs, which included stopping the inbound ship three miles off Koko Head and hiring a tugboat to transfer the stowaways and guard them until the outgoing ship arrived to pick them up. In the case of Lorrin "Whitey" Harrison (1913–1993) and Henry Valentine, Sevier also had to hire an extra radio operator on the San Francisco–bound *Manukai* because the two stowaways pushed the number of people aboard to more than fifty, which required the ship to carry another operator. Sevier estimated that as many as fifteen stowaways arrived in Honolulu each month, and he complained about the lack of laws to either deport the unwanted passengers or to prosecute them once they landed.[4]

Harrison had climbed aboard the *Monterey* at Los Angeles harbor on September 23, 1932. He had finished high school and was living with his parents in Santa Ana Canyon in Orange County. His mother, a school-teacher, told him that he needed either to go to school or to get a job. So, he enrolled in classes at Fullerton Junior College. "But every time I'd show up at the beach," Harrison recalled, "Will[ie] Grigsby would be there just back from Hawaii and he'd tell me, 'God, Whitey, you've gotta go over there, you won't believe it. The warmest water, you can stay in all day. It's paradise!'"[5] Grigsby was the Santa Monica lifeguard who would arrange, through his connections with the Adamson family, to hold the Pacific Coast Paddleboard and Surfboard championships at Malibu in September 1934. Following Grigsby's advice, Harrison quit school and started hitchhiking up to San Pedro to find work on a ship headed to the islands. Every day for two months he made the thirty-mile trek looking for work. "To get there," he said, "we'd hop bumpers on the back of cars with the big spare tire and big rear bumper. The cops would be blowin' whistles runnin' after us. . . . There were lines of able-bodied seamen trying to get a job, so they weren't going to hire any kid out of high school."[6] Tired of his fruitless efforts, Harrison stole aboard the *Monterey* and slept on a deck chair until he was discovered early the next morning. They put him in the brig, along with three other stowaways. "Everyone was either riding freights or stow-ing away," Harrison said, "that was the only way to get anywhere."[7] Four days later, on September 28, the Matson company had the *Monterey* stop off Koko Head about 11:30 A.M. and transfer the four men onto a tugboat. The outgoing freighter *Manukai* then picked them up shortly after noon, and the stowaways, within tantalizing sight of Oʻahu and Waikīkī Beach, headed back to San Francisco.[8]

Once the four of them landed in San Francisco on October 5, Harrison recalled the judge telling them, "You guys are from L.A., we don't like your type up here. I give you twenty-four hours to get out of town or we'll really get you."[9]

Henry Valentine, from Belgium, looked in the papers and saw that the *President Jackson,* owned by the Dollar Steamship Company, was departing for Japan from Pier 42 at 4 P.M. on October 7, with a stopover in Hono-lulu.[10] He told Harrison that he had already sent all of his clothes over to Hawaiʻi, so he was going to be on that ship. Harrison replied, "Well, if you are, I'm going too."[11] Harrison recalled, "all that time my mom was thinking I must have gotten a job 'cause I didn't show up."[12]

Harrison and Valentine got caught again aboard the *President Jackson.* Harrison had hidden in a lifeboat for a couple of days, but thirst and hunger finally drove him out. When a crewman spotted him and asked

4 Stowaways Transferred Off Diamond Head Today

Within three miles of Oahu, their destination after having stowed away on the Oceanic liner Monterey, four men were taken off the liner at 11:30 a. m. today to a Young Bros. tug and picked up shortly after noon by the San Francisco bound Matson freighter Manukai for return to the coast. The stowaways were kept on the tug until the Manukai, which sailed from Honolulu at noon, took them aboard.

According to Castle & Cooke, Ltd., local Matson and Oceanic agent, this transfer of the stowaways within sight of Oahu was another attempt to stem the influx into Honolulu of stowaways from the mainland.

The four stowaways were Henri Valentine, 25; Herman Mathews, 23; Lorrin Harrison, 19, and Joseph Geier, 18. All of them, according to officers of the Monterey, were seeking employment in Honolulu.

"We are doing everything we can to stop this stowaway nuisance, in spite of the fact that each time we transfer stowaways it means a heavy expense to the company," Randolph Sevier, acting manager of the steamship department of Castle & Cooke, Ltd., said today.

"In this case it means the expense of stopping two ships, hiring a tug and hiring men to guard the stowaways on the tug while waiting for the Manukai," he said. "In addition, we had to hire an extra radio operator for the Manukai, as taking aboard the stowaways raised the ship's complement to more than 50 souls; a ship with more than 50 aboard must have two operators.

"But we are willing to stand this expense to discourage this annoying practice. We are having as many as 15 stowaways a month coming into this port, and once they land we cannot send them back; neither is there any law by which they can be prosecuted here.

"This company is willing to take stowaways from ships of other lines as well as from our own."

Lorrin "Whitey" Harrison risking arrest to achieve his Waikīkī dreams. *Honolulu Star-Bulletin,* September 28, 1932.

who he was, Harrison replied, "I'm a surprise!"[13] Back in the brig he went for the remainder of the trip, with nothing but bread and water on the menu, a selection shipping companies typically served to discourage future attempts. They found Valentine a day before arrival, hiding in one of the ship's ventilators. The *President Coolidge* departed Honolulu at 6:00 P.M. on Wednesday, October 12, passing the *President Jackson* in the night without taking on the stowaways. So, the next morning at 6:30 A.M., the *President Jackson* docked in Honolulu Harbor at Pier 8. Harrison and Valentine were the first ones to debark, in handcuffs, along with forty-seven passengers and 574 sacks of mail.[14] Perhaps because the *President Jackson* and the *President Coolidge* belonged to a rival shipping company, Matson decided not to incur the extra expense of transferring the stowaways. Or perhaps, as Harrison later recalled, "the sea was too rough" to transport the two men.[15] At any rate, Harrison had finally arrived. He said the Honolulu police "were great. I ate six breakfasts, ham and eggs, everything! They made us stay at the station till the boats left. When I walked out I was able to find a job for four dollars a day pressing clothes."[16] He also found a room at Waikīkī for under eight dollars a month and settled in for the winter.

Harrison traveled regularly to Hawai'i for the remainder of the decade, usually arriving in late fall and staying through the winter. He married his first wife, Muriel Lambert, in Honolulu on Christmas Eve in 1935; his sister,

Ethel, who married Joseph Kukea in Honolulu the following September, acted as a witness. Harrison was working as a watchman at a beach hotel that winter, taking whatever job he could find to support his prolonged stays in the islands.[17] He was in the process of creating the prototype of the California surfer who based his life around the beach. Harrison took various jobs throughout his adult years—lifeguard, surfboard shaper, mechanic, abalone diver—so that he could prioritize spending his days riding waves and enjoying the ocean. His numerous trips to Hawai'i in the wintertime were his way of enacting an endless summer before Bruce Brown popularized the idea in 1964. After surfing through California's summer season, Harrison would travel to Honolulu, where he could continue to catch warm waves. Much like Tom Blake, who won the twenty-six-mile paddleboard race to Catalina while Harrison sat in the brig on the *Manukai,* Harrison demonstrated that, with enough persistence, one could actually materialize those Waikīkī dreams. His extended winters in Hawai'i came at a formative time in his life, and the lessons he learned determined its future course. "The Hawaiian beach boys," he said, "taught us to love their music and instruments as well as their waves."[18] More so than "Pete" Peterson, who devoted himself to a lifeguard career from a young age, Harrison decided that the dream came first, and he cobbled together whatever opportunity came his way to realize that dream in Southern California.

Travel became as necessary to the development of surfing in California as surfboards themselves, and nobody took to the road more than Harrison. When there wasn't a road, he walked. Such was the case when he was twelve years old. You couldn't drive from Laguna Beach, where his parents owned a beach house, to Corona del Mar in the early 1920s, so he and his siblings walked two hours north to get there. Harrison didn't own a surfboard at the time, so he used the ones stored at the bathhouse in Corona del Mar. This was around the time period when Duke and his surfing friends from Los Angeles frequented the resort. Harrison mentions other surfers that he saw there, including Wally Burton, the Santa Monica lifeguard who paddled to Catalina with Blake and Peterson; Delbert "Bud" Higgins, a Huntington Beach lifeguard; and Keller Watson, who won the Pacific Coast Surf Riding Championships at Corona del Mar in 1929.[19] Duke had made Corona del Mar the most popular surf spot in all of California, so surfers from across the Southland traveled to ride its waves. Surfers who gained the most respect during this era did so not only because of their contest results, but also because they were well traveled and had surfed the most famous waves, Waikīkī topping the list. California surfers were looking for waves that most resembled those at Waikīkī—the long breakers that offered smooth rides for hundreds of yards—and they often had to drive for hours to find them: Corona del Mar, Palos Verdes, San Onofre, Dana Point, and Malibu. Because beach roads could be as sketchy as the vehicles traveling over them, these trips required time and effort—with frequent breakdowns—so surfers often camped for multiple days, or entire weeks, once they arrived. To fill the time if the waves were down, they played music, they built surf shacks, they dove for lobster and abalone, and they partied together. These activities broadened the appeal of going to the beach and helped to develop a culture around the act of riding waves. As for surfing itself, travel became a part of its DNA, an essential building block spiraling toward the primordial dream of Waikīkī.

What happened when a surfer arrived at the source of that dream? If you were Harrison, you kept going. Recall that he and "Pete" Peterson took a walking/hitchhiking tour to the North Shore in search of waves during their first trip to Waikīkī in 1932, about a forty-mile trek one way. The two brought their California surfing experience to Hawai'i, which is to say they got on the road and explored what the island had to offer. Waikīkī was the hub of Hawaiian tourism in the 1930s. If you were a beachboy trying to make a living, or you simply loved to surf, there was little incentive to roam beyond the sea between Diamond Head and the mouth of the Ala Wai Canal. All the action was at Waikīkī—a beautiful setting, plentiful waves, the most innovative surfing, and a strip of ocean where Hawaiians had likely been enjoying themselves for more than a thousand years. Why go anywhere else?

Because there might be a bigger wave around the bend. And how would you know unless you looked? That seemed to be Harrison's philosophy. He ran afoul of the law once more after returning to the mainland in the spring of 1933.[20] He and two friends—Charles Wood and Vincent "Klotz" Lindberg (future husband of San Onofre Surfing Wahine Eleanor Roach)—were arrested for siphoning twenty gallons of gas from several cars. They were fined ten dollars each and had to pay for the fuel they stole.[21] No surprise that Harrison's transgression involved travel. One can't help but think the three were trying to get to some surf spot. When Harrison returned from his third winter trip to Hawai'i in 1936, newly married, he lived at Dana Point and started working as a commercial fisherman, harvesting abalone in the local coves. To supplement his income that summer, he took a job shaping surfboards at the Pacific System Homes factory in Vernon, making the sixty-mile trek on a motorcycle.[22] He always seemed to be on the go, and if he wasn't building surfboards, he was making outrigger canoes like the ones he had learned to paddle in Hawai'i.[23] Harrison's enthusiasm for travel landed him in the driver's seat of one of the most famous trips in surf history: the day he and a group of friends took the highway south from Corona del Mar and stumbled into the true Waikīkī of California, San Onofre.

The story has become something of a legend in the surfing community, partly because the hope of discovering new waves has supercharged surf travel for the past half century, ever since Bruce Brown's national release of *Endless Summer* (1966) tapped into the dream of travel, exploration, and finding the perfect wave. As Scott Laderman has admirably shown in *Empire in Waves: A Political History of Surfing,* discovery and pleasure may be two hallmarks of modern surfing, but the sport became a child of American Empire and colonization in the early twentieth century.[24] The verve for "discovering" new waves that began in earnest in the 1930s because of surfing's growing popularity in California continued overseas in subsequent decades along with the nation's global political ambitions. Harrison and his friends may have been simply seeking an alternative to Corona del Mar's fading waves, but their romp down the coast was not so much a discovery, as we note in chapter 7, but the reenactment of paradigms that seek to erase the history of peoples and events that predated the arrival of so-called pioneers.

Harrison was hanging out at Corona del Mar with his siblings and surf buddies in the summer of 1934 when Bob Sides pulled up.[25] Sides is an interesting figure, an example of the broad social community that surfing attracted. He couldn't have been more different from Harrison, the son of an orange-tree farmer. Sides was about ten years older than Harrison. He came from a moneyed family in Hollywood and graduated from the University of Southern California with an engineering degree. His parents were longtime Santa Monica Beach Club members, and Sides moved in circles with socialites and Los Angeles power brokers. He could surf, too, at least well enough to win a contest in Huntington Beach in the summer of 1935.[26] Blake cited him in *Hawaiian Surfboard* as one of the best of the "new crop of boys from California" along with Peterson, Harrison, "Tarzan" Smith, Chauncey Granstrom, and Wally Burton.[27] Sides was a bit like Santa Monica lifeguard Willie Grigsby—a "wave hunter, who liked to surf different breaks."[28] In an article for the Los Angeles magazine *Saturday Night*—"Surf Slaloms"—Sides commented that he had surfed all the top breaks in Southern California except for the "magnificent combers" at Point Loma lighthouse at San Diego Bay, which were accessible only by boat (or by crossing the military base).[29] Like his peers, Sides had his connection to Duke, who, he said, had taught him and Gardner Lippincott how to surf in the 1920s. Sides followed up the lesson with a trip to Hawai'i in 1929, and then again for a five-week honeymoon in early 1934.[30] He chased the Waikīkī dream along with many surfers of the era, but his tickets were always first class. In "Surf Slaloms," which includes nearly a dozen of "Doc" Ball's photographs of PVSC members in action, Sides waxed poetic about the surfing experience: "The thrill of conquering these white-maned stallions, to go fairly flying down the slick silk backs, to feel the wind and spray whip past your face and the intense electric-like vibration from your board go pulsating through your body, gives one a mystic god-like feeling."[31] His prose soars like the best of Jack London. Then again, Sides *did* give his second wife the unusual wedding present of a brand-new surfboard.[32]

"Hey Whitey," Harrison recalled Sides telling him at Corona del Mar, "there's this neat spot down south where the waves break way out."[33] Sides often traveled between San Diego and Orange County, and he did what all surfers do when driving along the coast: they keep an eye out for waves breaking across rocks, reefs, and sandbars. Or piers, cliffs, and shipwrecks, for that matter. It's a hope that springs eternal, if not for spotting a new wave, then at least for spying signs of a rising swell. Sides told Harrison, referring to Corona del Mar, "They're wrecking this place."[34]

And they were, at least for the surfers. Since the days of Duke's heroic rescue in June 1925, the city of Newport had been working hard to dredge the harbor channel to make boating safer. Harrison remembered surfing there during the two-million-dollar construction project: "They had cables going across the break out to the dredge. We'd be riding and we'd have to jump the cable or lay down on our back to go under it."[35] Newport finally completed the work in 1936. The summer before, the *Santa Ana Register* had offered the headline, "Harbor Improvement Just 'Pain In Neck' To Riders Of Surf; Ruins Sport Here."[36] The newspaper provided a fine eulogy for the break: "the huge rollers which once swept in at the beach and were such a peril to yachts and small pleasure craft and such a boon to surfboarders are tamed at last by the dredgers and long jettys. The riders of the foam-flecked surf will be seen no more at Corona Del Mar."[37] The paper interviewed Gene "Tarzan" Smith, who compared the break favorably to Waikīkī. He commented that, although the rides were shorter than those at Waikīkī, the waves at Corona del Mar were bigger and broke more quickly. The paper even interviewed visiting Waikīkī surfer Joseph Kukea, who had arrived with Harrison several months before. Kukea lauded San Onofre as the only comparable break in California to Corona del Mar.[38] San Onofre, then, had quickly inherited the illustrious mantle of Corona del Mar and become Southern California's go-to spot for summer surf. The Pacific Coast Surf Riding Championships, inaugurated at Corona del Mar in 1928, transferred to San Onofre in 1936 and remained there until the final contest of 1941.

Another surfer might have simply nodded his head at Bob Sides and gone back to staring "wistfully out towards sea" at the steam derrick—what surfers had been doing throughout the summer of 1934, according to the *Santa Ana Register*—"hoping that the extension of the jetty might improve the breaker situation."[39] But Harrison wasn't just another surfer. He was twenty-one years old that year, much younger than Sides and without the latter's social connections and clout. Harrison, however, embodied adventure. Not only was he a top surfer at Corona del Mar, but he was one of those people who absolutely lived in the moment, and he was up for anything. He was the guy who had told Belgian Henry Valentine on Pier 42 in San Francisco, *If you're getting on that ship, I'm going too.* Everyone at Corona del Mar would have heard that story. He was the same guy who traveled up to Santa Monica in August 1934 and captured the one-mile paddleboard race in Peterson's backyard, at the inaugural competition of Peterson's own Pacific Coast Paddle and Surfboard Association. Surfboard shaping pioneer Joe Quigg, growing up in Santa Monica in the early 1930s, recalled fishing off the pier and noting the difference in surfing styles between Peterson and Harrison, one that spoke to divergent personalities. "He was so perfectly controlled," Quigg said about Peterson, "every thread in place, his hair all combed, and he just stood there [on his surfboard] so smoothly. . . . Lorrin Harrison would come up to see Peterson. He was a little wilder in his mannerisms and his personality—the way he surfed. He'd wave and jump and tear all around; when he was young he was quite a wild guy."[40] If you pulled up in front of Harrison and told him, "there's this neat spot down south where the waves break way out," you just knew he was going down there. And because he was Lorrin Harrison, you'd want to go with him.

Harrison didn't really know any other way. He had been traveling to the beach since he was a baby. His dad had built a big house for the family in Santa Ana Canyon, about thirty miles from the coast. Harrison recounted: "Our family's had a place in Laguna ever since I was one year old, right at Sleepy Hollow. My mom and dad would take us down there on a horse and wagon back when you had to go through Aliso Canyon to get to Laguna. It took days for us to get there. They'd stop to visit friends along the way."[41] Harrison, his two brothers Vern and Winfred, and his sister Ethel, roamed the beaches around Sleepy Hollow, located about seven miles down the coast from Corona del Mar. They learned to bodysurf and ride waves prone on redwood bodyboards. Harrison eventually made a hollow board in school and covered it with canvas, which he painted; they'd ride the thing until the canvas wore out, then he'd tack on a new one. In high school, Harrison used the family horse to sneak out in the middle of the night and ride over to his girlfriend's house. Corona del Mar surfer Ned Leutzinger explained,

"She was asleep on the back porch, so he just tied up the horse and climbed into bed with her."[42]

In another escapade, Harrison and Leutzinger got a ride out to Laguna Beach on the day of Harrison's high school graduation, thinking they would have plenty of time to get back for the ceremony. They went fishing for barracuda on Winfred Harrison's boat, caught a big one, and headed back in so they could hitchhike home. They walked for hours before someone finally picked them up. Harrison missed the ceremony, but he accepted his diploma backstage, one hand gripping the barracuda wrapped in newspaper.[43] If there was anything to catch in the ocean—below the surface or breaking across the top of it—Harrison was all in. Twenty years after his first trip to Laguna Beach with his family, Harrison described climbing into the Great Depression's equivalent of a horse and wagon—touring cars—with "a whole bunch of people . . . and went down there and tried it out."[44]

There wasn't much to speak of at San Onofre in 1934. The village sat on the northern border of San Diego County, about twenty-six miles down the highway from Corona del Mar. Fewer than two hundred people lived there, mostly Hispanic, Anglo, and Japanese agricultural workers.[45] The whole region was farmland, part of the vast holdings of the Rancho Santa Margarita, an old Mexican land grant that spread over two hundred thousand acres in San Diego and Orange counties. The Roosevelt Highway, completed in 1929, cut through the Rancho along the coast, so Harrison's troupe would have had little trouble getting there. Immediately preceding San Onofre, they would have passed the towns of Dana Point, Capistrano Beach, and San Clemente, all founded during the real estate boom of the 1920s but each struggling to survive during the Great Depression.

The San Onofre service station, owned by local rancher Charles Page, would catch travelers heading south from San Clemente, or driving north from Oceanside. Although the two-lane highway was new, there wasn't much of a shoulder in the early days. E. Raymond Cato, chief of the California Highway Patrol, recorded twenty-four deaths and 334 injuries on the stretch of road between Oceanside and San Onofre from 1930 to 1935, mostly owing to the sharp drop-offs (ten inches in places) between the asphalt and the dirt.[46] Cato was arguing for funds to widen the highway, which would eventually happen toward the end of the decade. Harrison and his crew would have negotiated the narrow strip until they reached the Santa Fe train depot, built in 1888 to ship livestock and crops off the Rancho. During the early 1930s, the depot saw a dramatic drop in business—no surprise given Californians' love affair with the automobile—and could only afford to pay a part-time worker. The surfers turned right off the highway, crossed the railroad tracks, and followed the dirt road down

"Whitey" Harrison and crew on inaugural trip to San Onofre, circa 1934. (Courtesy *The Surfer's Journal*/Harrison family.)

to the beach. "We went clear down to where the atomic plant is now and surfed that spot," Harrison said. "Then we came back up the beach and tried it right where the main shack is now. That's where we found it was always steadiest. The surf was always up pretty good. In one day we surfed all the different breaks."[47]

Harrison recalled that a Hollywood film company had built a palm-thatched hut on the beach for a production, and the group spent their first night in there. San Onofre had been known for years, in fact, as a popular place to camp, take family outings, and catch a good number of fish. Its remote locale would have been ideal to try and replicate a South Seas beach setting. The presence of the beach hut anticipates the future work of the San Onofre Surfing Wahines, who built their own "Hawaiian Hut" on the beach in August 1938.

Although the presence of a Hollywood film company setting the stage for surfers seeking an exotic dream resonates strongly with the fantasist nature of re-creating Waikīkī on the shores of Southern California, the decisive connection to Waikīkī for the surfers lay in what Harrison called "all the different breaks." Waikīkī is what we might call a wave field—multiple breaks spread over a wide area that provide a variety of conditions for board riders of every skill level. Whether you are the local longboard champion or a novice paddling into your first wave, you will find the right conditions to sate your stoke at Waikīkī. Like Waikīkī, San Onofre is the most democratic surf spot in all of California, frequented by the greenest gremmies, the greyest granddads, and every walk of surfer in between. The vibe is vacation-friendly, the waves break all year round, and the beach is a great place to relax with friends and family. The feeling you get from surfing San Onofre is so good that not even the shadow of a nuclear power plant (currently inactive) can mar the pleasure. The same is true for the steel and cement backstop of hotels at Waikīkī: the palm trees, the trade winds, and the surf remain a potent balm against the blight of overdevelopment.

San Onofre wasn't ever going to replace Waikīkī. But it was, as Matt Warshaw aptly notes in *The History of Surfing,* with reference to a 1969 Beach Boys tune, "The Nearest Faraway Place."[48] The beach was raw, wide open, and the surfers had it all to themselves, save for occasional campers or local fishermen. They could play out Waikīkī dreams to their hearts' content. "Doc" Ball noted in his weekly newsletter that everybody had gone down to San Onofre the last weekend of May 1937 for the christening of the outrigger canoe Harrison had built after returning from Hawai'i the previous year. Ball snapped a picture of Harrison and three others paddling near shore, with a young woman sitting in the bow. The easy-breaking rollers were ideal for those staples of Waikīkī—canoe surfing and tandem riding. San Onofre had other advantages over a place like Bluff Cove, for example: it was a larger beach with easy access and ample parking right in front of the waves. Though Ball eventually warmed up to San Onofre, his early comments about the beach capture a little territorialism for his beloved Bluff Cove: "Half the club goes off to Nofre last Saturday nite only to return early Sunday morn to PV where THEY'RE ALWAYS HUMPIN."[49] But even a Palos Verdes diehard couldn't resist the many charms of San Onofre. Harrison and his carloads of friends couldn't have foreseen the genie they were letting out of the bottle by crossing those train tracks on the Rancho Santa Margarita. What they found that day was not the hallowed hearth of California beach culture, just an expansive lot where it could be built.

Before departing San Onofre—treated in more detail in chapter 7—we might give a quick shout-out to Ethel Harrison. Had she not left California in the mid-1930s to marry Joseph Kukea, she would have been a worthy contender for Mary Ann Hawkins's title, "Queen of the Surf." Ethel Harrison was five years older than Hawkins and had grown up at the beach alongside her brothers—bodysurfing, riding waves on wooden boards, and helping to build a raft every year that they'd drag out to the kelp bed in front of their house. "We floated an old wood burning stove out there," "Whitey" Harrison recalled, "sunk it, filled it with rocks and anchored the raft to it with cable. We'd go fishin' out there. I can remember my mom getting so mad at me for getting my sister to swim out there. And I said, 'Well, Jesus, if she can swim to her surfboard she can swim out there.'"[50]

Ethel and "Whitey" Harrison traveling to Hawai'i, 1935. (Courtesy Surfing Heritage and Cultural Center/Harrison family.)

Ethel proved her ocean chops when she was eighteen years old and captured second place in the women's surfing event at the 1932 Pacific Coast Surf Riding Championships at Corona del Mar. She made the trek to Corona del Mar regularly with her brothers—the only other woman that Hawkins saw surfing there—and she was part of the gang that visited San Onofre in 1934. A brief look into the future confirms her ocean talents: she was the most dominant woman at the Makaha International Surfing Championships during the mid- and late-1950s, winning either first or second place in the surfing and paddleboard events from 1954 to 1959. The first year that women were allowed to compete (1954), she took first place in the women's paddleboard event; in 1955 she defended her paddling title and

Ethel Kukea looking graceful as she angles left at Waikīkī. *Honolulu Advertiser*, September 7, 1958. (Courtesy Surfing Heritage and Cultural Center/Clarence Maki.)

also won the surfing event. She was forty-one years old that year and the mother of three children.

~

"I'd never seen anybody ride standing up until about 1920," Harrison said, recalling his first experience watching surfers when he was seven years old, "when my dad took us to Redondo Beach in the car. We parked up on a hill and ate lunch there and I looked down and saw these guys riding surfboards. That was where [George] Freeth had started surfing."[51] Freeth had died in San Diego the year before in the influenza pandemic, so Harrison never got a chance to meet the Hawaiian who popularized surfing on the mainland. Freeth never had children himself, but those surfers in Redondo were his progeny nonetheless: the first generation of California surfers whom Freeth taught and encouraged to see the many possibilities for pleasure available to them in ocean waves.[52] The same year that Harrison perched on that hill in Redondo, nine-year-old "Pete" Peterson was working at his parents' bathhouse up the coast in Santa Monica, letting Hawaiians in for free so that he could try out the surfboards he had seen them riding. Harrison and Peterson had a love for the beach from a young age. What the Hawaiians gave them, and so many other Californians, was the dream that they could build a life around what they loved, and that this would be a life worth pursuing. Perhaps more than any of his contemporaries, Harrison absorbed that gift and served as a model to others in the way he lived and the craft he built.

"He had a dream," Harrison's daughter wrote about her father building a canoe. "We drove back into the valley from San Onofre. He had looked at the old sycamore tree for a long time imagining how the natural bow in it would shape into the perfect surfing canoe much like the ancient Polynesian Koa wood outriggers. The 'Nofre gang accompanied us with saws, ropes, and chains, everyone ready to lend a hand to bring down the old sycamore for Lorrin."[53] She added that once they felled the tree, it "was revered, covered and cared for while curing for several years. Well, it should have been five years of curing but Lorrin was impatient to begin the work."[54] One can't help but think of the Native Hawaiian traditions that surrounded the important task of canoe building, which included dreams of the canoe maker and various religious offerings and chants. This was not Harrison's first canoe, which he'd built out of planks in the mid-1930s, but his first "dugout"—one constructed entirely from a single tree trunk, following Native Hawaiian tradition.[55] Harrison probably had the closest relationship to Native Hawaiians of all his contemporaries, based on his connection to the Kukea family through his sister Ethel and his frequent trips to the islands. He may have learned of canoe-making traditions from his conversations with Native Hawaiians, or have gleaned them from various written sources.[56] Clark's account of her father's state of mind at least gives the strong impression that he was doing his best to imitate the process of building a canoe according to traditional Native Hawaiian methods.

Other projects that Harrison likely propagated from Waikīkī to California were the surf racks he built on the beach at Dana Point after returning from Hawai'i in 1936. Alexander Hume Ford had written about surf racks at the Outrigger Canoe Club back in 1909; in Harrison's era, the Royal Hawaiian Hotel (like other hotels at Waikīkī) offered surf racks for the convenience of beachboys giving lessons.[57] "There was no way anybody was gonna take one of those boards by carrying it outta there!," Harrison said, referencing the great weight of a redwood plank in the rack at Dana Point. "It might float away before anybody was gonna carry it out."[58] Like his contemporaries during the Great Depression—and even in the years following World War II—Harrison built most everything he needed for work and pleasure at the beach himself: surfboards, canoes, boats, lobster traps, even woolen bathing suits for his growing daughters. Rose Harrison Clark writes, "he would haunt the Army/Navy stores for old woolen underwear, sweaters and uniforms. He cut black wool trunks for us out of sailor suits. They were laced on the sides with heavy cotton cord used for fish line."[59]

Much of what Harrison fabricated was inspired by his formative experiences at Waikīkī, and the life of simplicity that he associated with the Hawaiian beachboys, much like his friend Tom Blake. Harrison's daughter relates that her father "subscribed to the school 'If you can dream it, you can do it,' or rather in his case, build it."[60] Again recalling Blake, the dream became manifest not only in watercraft associated with ideals of Pacific Islanders, but also—and especially relevant for Harrison—in the cultural artifacts used for pleasure and travel.

PART II

The Beaches

Palos Verdes

Landslide Closes Cove: A landslide of several tons of dirt and rock across the road leading down to Bluff Cove has practically closed this famous surfboarding mecca for the summer. Surfers are driving to San Onofre or frequenting Hermosa and Manhattan Beaches rather than carry their heavy boards up and down the quarter-mile incline.

Known all over the southern coast by surfers as "Little Waikiki," the Palos Verdes aquatic playground has drawn thousands of persons in years past to watch and participate in the paddleboard sport.

Members of the Palos Verdes Surfing Club today are striving to find some solution whereby money might be raised to clear the road.
—*Palos Verdes News,* August 15, 1941

The road to Bluff Cove had to be cleared every time a storm broke another ton of dirt and rock off the cliff face at Palos Verdes Estates. At least if the surfers wanted to drive their heavy wooden boards down to the beach rather than carry them a quarter mile on their shoulders—and then haul them back up the cliff after a long, cold session, their thighs burning with every step. It would be exhausting even for the hardiest, most surf-fevered of the young men. So when the storms came in January 1936 and wrecked the road, "Doc" Ball used his newsletter to rally the troops: "FLASH—International news—Local flood inflicts serious damage to Cove arterial. However, the young stalwarts of the Club are rapidly restoring order out of chaos."[1] He included a picture with the caption—"Local huskies labor unceasingly to restore Cove road to former glory"—and added underneath, "'Clear the road by sundown' is the cry, will they, can they do it? NO, NO, HELL, NO!

"Tulie" Clark and Palos Verdes Surfing Club members clearing the road to Bluff Cove. (John Heath "Doc" Ball.)

The Dxxx thing is still impassable."[2] Pictured is nineteen-year-old Calvin "Tulie" Clark posed on top of a Fresno scraper chained to the bumper of a Ford coupe. Ball's humorously overwrought language nevertheless hints at the importance of the road for him and all the surfers. The "Cove arterial" was the aorta of their dreams, bearing the very lifeblood of desires down to rocky shores and cold water. The powerful influence of Waikīkī can be measured by the monumental physical labor that surfers undertook not only by building surfboards, paddleboards, and outrigger canoes, but also in the tons of dirt, rock, and sand that had to be hauled around Bluff Cove in a communal effort to realize their Hawaiian dreams.

Ball had put those dreams on the map for the Palos Verdes Estates through his articles and photographs—the *Palos Verdes Peninsula News* eventually used one of his surfing images as a regular embellishment on its front page, along with the slogan: "Bluff Cove in Palos Verdes Estates—'Little Waikiki of America'."[3] The Palos Verdes Homes Association returned the favor by putting surfing on its map of the Palos Verdes Estates in a 1936 advertising booklet—*Judging Palos Verdes as a Place to Live.*[4] Bluff Cove sits at the center bottom of the two-page illustration, with bronzed surfers riding waves and lounging on the beach under a palm tree. The next page includes a photograph (undoubtedly Ball's) of three surfers riding a wave at

"Tulie" Clark helping to grade the road to Bluff Cove. (John Heath "Doc" Ball.)

Bluff Cove, with the description, "Surfboard riding in Bluff Cove is said to be the best along the whole coast, rivalling Waikiki."[5] The booklet is divided into nine sections, each one highlighting an attribute of the "ideal California home." Section seven is called "Desirable Neighbors." The description reads: "Nothing will spoil a home more quickly than undesirable neighbors. We should be careful to choose a district that will be permanently settled by substantial people."[6]

The booklet is glossy and upbeat, filled with photographs of beautiful vistas, wholesome (white) families having fun, and luxurious amenities—golf

Surfers at center bottom boosting the image of Bluff Cove as "Little Waikiki." (Courtesy Palos Verdes Library District/Local Library Collection.)

club, swimming pool, horseback riding, beaches—all surrounded by architectural marvels. Palos Verdes Estates had been planned by the most prestigious landscaping firm in the country, Olmsted Brothers, beginning in 1914.[7] After several financial setbacks and a change of ownership, the Palos Verdes Estates opened to the public in 1923. Robert M. Fogelson's *Bourgeois Nightmares: Suburbia, 1870–1930* (which uses a subdivision plan of Palos Verdes as the book's cover), presents much of the history behind Palos Verdes, from Spanish and Mexican land grants in the nineteenth century to the early twentieth-century eastern financiers who purchased the agricultural land to establish a suburban utopia. Fogelson fills in the legal details of the "protective restrictions" that defined what it meant to be a "Desirable Neighbor" in this community. The restrictions "forbade an owner to sell or rent a lot or house to anyone 'not of the white or Caucasian race'."[8] He goes on to explain that "an owner was even forbidden to permit an African- or Asian-American to use or occupy the property" unless they were hired help and lived on the premises.[9] "Far from being thought repugnant," Fogelson writes, "these restrictions were central to [promoter E. G.] Lewis's vision that Palos Verdes would bring together 'the cream of the manhood and womanhood of the greatest nation that has ever lived, the greatest race that has ever lived, the Caucasian race and the American nation.'"[10]

Ball stated that he preferred his club remain "unaffiliated" with the Palos Verdes Estates, but ultimately, we cannot separate surfing from the places where surfing happens.[11] The sport is too entrenched in specific locations. The Palos Verdes Homes Association warmed up to surfing enough to use the sport as an advertisement for a community built on racial, economic, and other social exclusions. In this sense, the PVSC remained tightly connected to Palos Verdes and the broader Los Angeles community that practiced racial covenants as a matter of course. The PVSC constitution, though formally excluding only women, mirrored other social restrictions of the period that were often implied rather than overtly stated. The dream of Waikīkī, as it turned out, was fashioned in the narrowest of molds, an ideal built to reinforce notions of white racial superiority. It can be no accident that the Palos Verdes peninsula remains today one of the most renowned areas of surfer territorialism, where outsiders are threatened with violence as a matter of course. This dynamic is an extension of the settler-colonial mentality that persisted into the 1930s ("We should be careful to choose a district that will be permanently settled by substantial people") and that depended upon racial exclusion.[12]

Ball had first visited Bluff Cove as a ten-year-old, rambling south along the shore from Hermosa Beach, where his parents owned a summer house. Listen as he recounts the importance of that memory after returning home from his first trip to Hawai'i in 1930, when he was twenty-three:

> I found myself very much engrossed in learning the art of riding surf on the top side of a 12 foot plank. The majority of this process took place at Hermosa Beach, so having graduated from the "malahini," or beginner class, my chum, Norman Hales, who learned with me, suggested the possibilities of bigger and better surf in other places. It was then I recalled the cove at Palos Verdes and for many weeks as the surfing fever waxed hotter, so did the trips to Palos Verdes. A most extraordinary spot—that cove. It is geologically set so that its floor creates the long rolling swells which build up on a "big day" and roll in for nearly 700 yards (we measured it with a big tuna reel.) Because of the similarity to Hawaii's Waikiki we christened it "Little Waikiki" and the name still sticks.[13]

Because Ball and the Cove had a history together that reached back to his childhood, we begin to understand his devotion to the place. We nod when we read that he is writing his newsletter from Bluff Cove in January 1939, watching "feathers" or large waves crash over two abalone divers— "Can hear them yelling clear up on the top of the cliff."[14] We get it when he describes spending summer nights there watching for signs of a swell, and complaining of red ants—"the dirty sons-a botches do plague my brows all nite."[15] Undeterred, he asks his PVSC brethren, "Who wants to go there to sleep tonite?????"[16] Ball surfed there, slept there, wrote there, photographed and filmed there; he dove for abalone and lobster, named a surf club after the place, and tried to understand its many moods so he could predict when the biggest waves would crash off the outside rocks. It was common for him and other members to ring in the New Year with a midnight surf session.[17] The "surfing fever" waxed hottest for Ball at Bluff Cove, part of the reason why he chose to have his ashes spread there after his death in 2001.[18] This, too, is the influence of Waikīkī, which serves not only as the altar of surf culture, but also its hallowed graveyard because the cremains of beachboys and other expert surfers have been scattered there by tradition since the early twentieth century.[19]

That dirt road dropping across the face of a three-hundred-foot cliff was not just any road, then, leading to just any surf spot. "The Cove at Palos Verdes," wrote C. P. L. Nicholls in 1936 for *Westways* magazine, "is perhaps the best location at the present time for the practice of surfing."[20] Nicholls worked for the city of Los Angeles as the supervisor of aquatics, so he may have shown some bias toward a surf break in his own county. In the summer of 1936, however, Corona del Mar had already been subdued, Malibu had yet to reveal its true potential, and San Onofre was just starting to bloom—but all the way down in San Diego County. Moreover, Nicholls became an "honorary member" of the PVSC owing to his work on behalf of the club to prod the Palos Verdes Homes Association into helping repair the road. Or as Ball whooped in a November 1937 newsletter, "HONORY MEMBER GETS HOT ON HUMP."[21] Nicholls had written a letter to C. E. Watt, who sat on the highway and transportation committee for the Palos Verdes Estates Chamber of Commerce and who also supervised area contracts for the Public Works Administration (PWA), an agency that formed part of President Franklin Roosevelt's New Deal. Watt had met with Ball in late September 1937 and was impressed with all the publicity the PVSC had generated. (Andy Hamilton's expansive "Surfboards, Ahoy!" article in the Sunday edition of the *Los Angeles Times* had appeared two weeks earlier.) Ball wrote: "[Watt] assured ye Ed that he would do all in his power to get those dumb PWA gravel-scratchers to dig where the diggin is needed."[22] Ball was hopeful that Watt's influence would remedy what he called "the demon hump" (i.e., the landslide across the road) once and for all.[23] Since Andy Hamilton's article had come out, Ball had also noticed a "change of attitude shown by the officials around the estates. They are just beginning to realize the value of surfing as a gross factor in publicising their project. So me lads, we may expect bigger and better things in the near future."[24] By mid-November no progress had been made on the road by Watts, so Nicholls penned his letter to the Palos Verdes Homes Association.

The letter seemed to work. Ball understood that the association would provide the trucks and asphalt to resurface the road if the PVSC provided the manpower. "PAVEMENT at and to the cove???" Ball wrote, "Wow and Horny [PVSC member Gene Hornbeck] says that OC Fields will back us in our attempt to fix up all the comforts of home on the beach."[25] Fields was an influential oil man with property on the peninsula. Ball noted that the pavement would be in by the following month—mid-December 1937.[26]

Needless to say, no asphalting took place. The road down to Bluff Cove remains a dirt and rock path to this day. The PWA was probably not the right agency to complete the work. The PWA offered loans and grants to create employment on a broad scale across the nation. The agency, for example, helped fund the renovation of the entire Los Angeles County school system—536 schools.[27] Given the agency's broad scope, it's unlikely one "demon hump" would attract its attention.

Even if the PWA had been interested, Palos Verdes Estates could not have provided matching funds. In response to Nicholls's letter, the *Palos Verdes Peninsula News* printed an editorial in November 1937 stating that "Palos Verdes cannot undertake to finance the building of the road or the improving of the beach with the erection of comfort stations and other necessities."[28] The Palos Verdes Estates Land Company remained in significant debt for unpaid property taxes since 1932; the community eventually incorporated into Los Angeles County in 1939 to settle its financial debt.[29] Although the editorial acknowledged the unique contribution that Bluff Cove and surfing had made to generate interest in the community, the Palos Verdes Estates board of supervisors argued that Los Angeles County should pay for the road repairs considering people from all over came to "enjoy their surf-board riding."[30] It was a fair point, one that many cities had made with regard to splitting the costs of lifeguard service, for example, between city and county budgets.[31] Generally speaking, however, Palos Verdes Estates did not want the liability of people driving down the side of a cliff. The editorial explained: "The road that leads to the beach of Bluff Cove along and under the cliff has been practically built by the enthusiasts of that sport [i.e., surfers] themselves. All the signs and fences to prevent them from using Bluff Cove are of no avail. Finally, the idea of stopping them was given up as a hopeless attempt. The reason that Palos Verdes Estates did attempt to stop surf-board riders was because of the dangers in which the riders are placed when rolling down the hill with their cars."[32]

The dangers were real. In his newsletter for August 16, 1939, Ball described helping rescue a crash victim at Bluff Cove. Ball "was sleeping up top side in his favorite roost" when the car threw its rider into the brush and then "smear[ed] its livin guts out all the rest of the way down—landing in a worthless heap on the waters edge."[33] Ball helped the driver up the cliff and eventually into an ambulance. He graced page one of his newsletter with a photograph of the mangled vehicle. The previous Christmas, heavy rains had washed out the road once again, stranding the 1927 Model-T Ford roadster that teenaged Bob "Hammerhead" Gravage had bought for fifteen dollars. When he and sixteen-year-old Jim "Burrhead" Drever came back the following weekend to salvage what they could, they discovered that "unknown locals" had pushed it over the edge down onto the rocks, where it sat and rusted for years afterward.[34]

Winter storms, then, weren't the only obstacle for surfers trying to get down to the waves. In February 1940 Ball announced, "Those road blockers are at it again."[35] Someone in the Palos Verdes Estates had set wooden posts into concrete at the top of the road "to keep out the stinkin tourists and fishermen."[36] But Ball remarked that "they left a slit wide enuf for any surf hound to get thru."[37] He admitted that the "crack between the posts can dam well scrape off plenty paint from the well known fenders," but he didn't seem to mind the idea that "few visitors are going to risk the rubbing just to clog up our surfing grounds."[38] By 1940 the Cove was getting quite popular, partly a result of Ball's photographs and boosterism. He was growing territorial about the place as well, calling Bluff Cove "our surfing grounds." Things heated up the following month when someone used roofing nails to try and stop the surfers from driving down. Ball complained in his newsletter: "Some stinker got the bright idea to strew roofing tacks all over the cove road—down at the bottom. . . . There has already been several tire casualties and there will be more if that bastard is not stopped—or at least his dam tacks picked up."[39]

Such annoyances didn't deter the surfers in the least. They were more than willing to sacrifice a little paint or a punctured tire to enjoy the long rides that evoked Waikīkī. When storms battered the road, the surfers arrived with picks and shovels to clear it again. After the great downpour that marooned Gravage's roadster at the bottom of the cliff, Ball wrangled a bulldozer to come and clear the landslide. "Everybody should be at the cove this weekend," he wrote in his newsletter for January 18, 1939. They needed PVSC members to loosen the dirt so that the bulldozer could scoop it away.[40] Unfortunately the bulldozer got stuck in the mud, which offered Ball a nice photo-op for his newsletter the following week.[41] "Grave concern must have been felt by the pilot of that most unfortunate contraption," Ball

Homemade beach at Bluff Cove strewn with planks and Blake-style hollow boards. (John Heath "Doc" Ball/The Croul Family Collection.)

wrote, "when the dam thing came down the steepest part of the hump and straight way nosed for the brink of the beetling cliff."[42]

The PVSC members even built their own sandy beach amid the rocks on shore. When big storms or excessive high tides washed the beach away, they built another one. Ball graced a March 1939 newsletter with a photograph of the club's latest "engineering feat"—"the luxury of a super sandy beach" enjoyed by a dozen young people relaxing on towels and soaking up the sun. Ball challenged members to name the beach, offering "Surfers Roost" or "Table Beach" as two possibilities.[43] Ball and club members did everything in their limited power to create amenities for themselves at Bluff Cove. They may have had Waikīkī in mind, but the geography of Palos Verdes determined to a great extent the particular form of their beach culture. Bluff Cove required an automobile, a cache of old tires to burn on the more frigid days, a sleeping bag and basic camping gear to catch those early morning glassy conditions, and a knowledge of tides, which have larger swings in California, to avoid cracking surfboards on offshore rocks. As old-time San Onofre surfer George "Peanuts" Larson remarked in 1980, "You gotta remember that in those days nobody knew anything about surfing except the Hawaiians. We had to make it up."[44] Ball's self-described "surfing fever" kept him and the others energized enough to rise early on winter mornings and drive out to the coast, to grab sun-bleached spars and use them as levers to pry boulders out of the way, to attack "the demon hump" with picks and shovels every winter because it stood in the way of their dreams.

And what was that dream exactly? "Words are lacking and inadequate," Ball wrote, "to describe the emotions one feels while riding the foaming brine atop a 12 foot board on a big day."[45] The wave-riding experience is famously ineffable among surfers. So, we must look to deeds to sound the emotions that Ball was trying to express. Above the newsletter photograph of the club's new beach at Bluff Cove, Ball posted an action shot of Long Beach Surfing Club member John Lind, who had driven 498 miles from San Francisco to Bluff Cove for a two-hour surf session. Ball explained:

> It took nine and a half hours getting down and the schedule called for an early return—all of which gave our good fran [friend] a short two hours of good old brining. Would you do it ?????
> So would I.[46]

We're in the realm of Jack Kerouac and Neal Cassady bombing down the highway for the sheer pleasure of reaching a destination that may or may not result in a sublime experience. The travel time and assorted hurdles along the way are always an important part of the story because they define a surfer's desire. The farther the trip, the higher the commitment. Ball's "So would I" implicitly echoes his readers' willingness to make the same run and recalls the verve of Lorrin Harrison as he stood on the edge of the continent looking toward Hawai'i ("Well, if you are, I'm going too"). Lind's nineteen-hour road trip demonstrated the high commitment for surfing that Ball encouraged in all PVSC members and expressed, far better than words, how Lind felt about the sport.

Ball himself was quite the roadrunner. He often traveled the coast during storms to capture big waves on film. He made a Lind-like haul up to Santa Cruz, about seventy-five miles south of San Francisco, the last weekend of May 1940 with PVSC members E. J. Oshier and Lewis "Hoppy" Swarts. Earlier that month in the newsletter, Ball had printed a photograph of Oshier with "some of his new pal[s] at the Santa Cruz Surfing hole."[47] Doc suggested, "How about some of us whipping up there to surf some week-end?"[48] Oshier had moved to Oakland, along the eastern shore of the San Francisco Bay, in 1939 and began traveling the seventy-five miles southwest to Santa Cruz for weekend surfs. He met a group of Angelenos attending San Jose State University who also surfed; they mingled with the Santa Cruz locals, some of whom had been surfing Cowell's Beach regularly since 1936 on Blake-style hollow boards.[49] Hopping onto the Hawaiian

Santa Cruz Surfing Club members (left to right) Harry Murray, Harry Mayo, Don Patterson, and Norm Handley carrying their homemade hollow boards from the barn to Cowell's beach, Summer 1941. (Ed Webber/Covello and Covello Photography Archives.)

fad sweeping the mainland, the *Santa Cruz Sentinel* called Cowell's the "Waikiki of western America."[50]

The Santa Cruz Surfing Club had gotten a boost in July 1938 when Duke Kahanamoku arrived in town and gave a swimming exhibition and paddled his surfboard in the pool before a crowd of fifteen hundred people.[51] The following summer, through the efforts of the junior Chamber of Commerce, local surfers scored a shed for their surfboards at the wharf fronting Cowell's Beach.[52] Before that, they'd had to haul their boards from the nearby barn of Santa Cruz Surfing Club member David "Buster" Steward. The barn was where Oshier and other visiting surfers slept during their weekend surf trips. The Palos Verdes crew would have felt right at home in Santa Cruz. The sixty-two-degree water, the long paddles out, the heavy kelp beds, the shoreline rocks guarding a raw coastline, spectators watching from nearby cliffs—all of it would have reminded them of surfing Bluff Cove. "That stuff was so good in fact," Ball crowed in his newsletter the week after they returned, "that ye crew had nary a wink of sleep in 36 hours."[53] The three surfers switched back and forth between riding waves at Cowell's and Natural Bridges ("we surfed out our livin eyeballs until the wind came in").[54] The Santa Cruz Surfing Club had nearly forty members by the time Ball, Oshier, and Swarts arrived—twenty-five men and a dozen women—so the surfing craze sweeping Southern California in the late 1930s had definitely invaded the wave-rich region of Santa Cruz.[55]

It's worth noting that Santa Cruz probably has the longest continual tradition of surfing in California. The San Lorenzo River mouth holds the distinction of being the first recorded location of surfing in the state—when the three Hawaiian brothers David Kawānanakoa, Jonah Kūhiō Kalanianaʻole, and Edward Keliʻiahonui paddled out on a Sunday afternoon in July 1885.[56] The break remained the center of Santa Cruz surfing from then on, receiving occasional mention in local newspapers from the 1890s through the 1930s.[57] In the summer of 1913, for example, Hawaiians returned to Santa Cruz when Duke Kahanamoku gave his first swimming exhibition there and his friend, Bobby Kaawa, paddled out and rode waves for the crowd.[58] As Duke would later do during his trip to Australia in 1914, Kaawa "presented his surf board as a souvenir of the tournament to Manager Wilson of the Casino."[59] A decade later, the *Santa Cruz Evening News* reported continued interest in the sport among locals: "The bay has been unusually rough for the past two days as a result of the large ground swells that have prevailed. As a result the breakers have been unusually large, much to the enjoyment of those who like to indulge in surf-board riding."[60] A typical mention from the early 1930s comes from the *Santa Cruz Sentinel:* "The surf board riders generally gather at the mouth of the river, close to San Lorenzo point, where the breakers are higher."[61] In the summer of 1940, floodwaters pushed sand west from the river mouth toward Lighthouse Point and refocused wave riding toward Cowell's Beach, where Ball's crew had surfed so hard—an area he called "Paradise Point" in his *California Surfriders*. Reporting on the floods, the *Santa Cruz Sentinel* captured well the sentiments that sustained the growth of California beach culture, even as far north as Santa Cruz: "The shifting of the sand has made it possible to wade out 60 or 70 yards from shore. When waves are running it is the answer to a surf rider's dream."[62]

The same summer that the San Lorenzo River mouth was flooding in Santa Cruz, Los Angeles County completed a "Master Plan of Shoreline Development" that recommended, among other things, purchasing the area around Bluff Cove because it provided good waves for surfing.[63] The county supervisors had ordered the plan in February 1938 to designate coastal areas in Los Angeles that could be acquired and/or improved for public benefit. At that time, the county owned just under 30 percent of the coast (eighteen out of sixty-six miles of beach frontage) and was looking to invest in beach recreation. The county estimated that between five and six hundred thousand people visited the beaches multiple times a year (more than 20 percent of the population), a proportion that, according to its report, "probably exceeds the number of participants in any other sport, the users of any other tax-supported recreation, unless the use of highways can still be counted as a recreation."[64] The beaches were one of the cheapest forms of recreation supported by the county, working out to less than a dollar a year per person who used the beaches.[65] The master plan represented the combined efforts of city, county, and state agencies; C. P. L. Nicholls, honorary member of the PVSC, provided his input for the city of Los Angeles, which is probably why Bluff Cove and the mouth of Malibu Creek landed in the "First Priority" of acquisitions (number six and eleven, respectively).[66] The plan proposed to purchase from the Palos Verdes Homes Association just over sixty-five hundred feet of ocean frontage for about fifty thousand dollars. Improvements would be minimal: "a better road down the face of the cliff, the levelling of sufficient space below for auto parking for participants, a simple shelter, toilets and perhaps stone fireplaces."[67] The county also suggested improving the expansive lot on top of the cliff for spectator parking.

Ball would have appreciated help shoring up the road to Bluff Cove, but improvements would have lured even more people to the break. By early 1940, crowded lineups had pushed him to scout neighboring coves, which is how he discovered Lunada Bay—perhaps the most infamous surf spot in all of California today for its territorialism. Ball wrote in a February newsletter that year, "Lunada bay may prove to be a suitable relief come summer and the five thousand varmints who always clutter up the Cove waterways."[68] A week earlier, Ball had recorded about forty surfers riding two-foot waves at the Cove—"plunks and clunks did beboggle even the wary kamaaina—[Hal] Pearson came closest to getting the final works when about ten planks in boiling soup came flying by."[69] It was just as well that Palos Verdes Estates held onto its coastline; incorporating into Los Angeles in December 1939 had resolved the issue of back-taxes, so the residents weren't tempted to sell off Bluff Cove to the county.

The whole proposition of purchasing the shoreline around Bluff Cove would have been a moot point had the Pacific Coast Yacht Club been allowed to occupy the site thirteen years earlier. The *Palos Verdes Bulletin* for January 1927 announced the venture, along with attractive architectural

Proposed model of the Pacific Coast Yacht Club. *Palos Verdes Bulletin,* February 1927. (Courtesy the Palos Verdes Library District.)

models.[70] Francis B. "Dry-Dock" Smith, a mining engineer based in San Francisco, had inspected the entire coastline of the Santa Monica Bay and decided that Bluff Cove was the ideal location for a new yacht club. Two months later, the state corporation commissioner granted the Pacific Coast Yacht Club permission to sell thirteen hundred memberships to raise a total of $1,250,000: $100,000 to purchase the site; $300,000 to build a Mediterranean-style clubhouse on the bluff; $500,000 to build a break-water; $75,000 to construct a sea wall; and the rest for general equipment and additional expenses. Passenger and freight elevators would carry people and supplies from the clubhouse to the beach below. They envisioned a waterfront promenade along with mooring space for four hundred yachts in the sixty-six acres of water around Bluff Cove, eventually increasing to a capacity of sixteen hundred vessels.[71] Work was set to begin in the summer of 1927. Everything seemed to be on track for the new club, "more complete in its facilities than anything yet built on this coast, and having a harbor for pleasure craft whose waters will be safe and clean."[72]

The plans were quickly dropped. One particular incident probably didn't help matters go forward. The yacht club members had organized a two-day regatta off Palos Verdes for the weekend of June 25—sloops, schooners, and yawls—to show off their new home. Owen P. Churchill, member of the Board of Governors of the Pacific Coast Yacht Club and commodore of the Catalina Island Yacht Club, arrived early Saturday morning off the coast of Palos Verdes to race his new R-class sloop, *Galliano IV*. The vessel had been anchored in one of the coves in anticipation of an early start the next morning. The *Los Angeles Times* reported: "When Churchill arrived on his power boat yesterday morning to prepare for the race he found his racing craft high and dry on the rocks with her starboard side stove in in several places."[73] Later that day "a heavy surf smashed the yacht so badly it stove her whole right side in below the waterline and she began to sink."[74] Apparently, the sloop had slipped its mooring line during the night. The newspaper reported that the ten-thousand-dollar vessel, in its first season of racing, was uninsured.

The combination of heavy swells that roll into Bluff Cove, and the unstable cliff face above—culprit of endless pick and shovel parties for Ball and his friends—probably would have doomed the new yacht club fairly quickly. Bluff Cove would not suffer the fate of Corona del Mar, Killer Dana, and the Long Beach Flood Control as far as harbor construction wrecking another surf spot. The smashed yacht didn't faze Owen Churchill. He simply ordered a new one and kept on racing. Churchill is a well-known figure in sailing circles. By all accounts he was the primary booster of yachting in Southern California during this era, even leading the United States to a gold medal in the sport at the 1932 Olympic games in Los Angeles. Like so many others, Churchill fell under the South Seas spell in the late 1930s, taking several extended vacations to Tahiti with his family.[75] His trip over the winter of 1937–1938 resulted in the development of molded rubber swim fins, a design he based either on local Tahitians that he had seen "weaving small mats from palm fronds and dipping them into a tub of hot tar," or on models patented by Louis de Corlieu in 1937 (or perhaps both).[76] For our purposes, we can cite Churchill as a further example of how the foundational artifacts of California beach culture flowed from the South Pacific to the manufacturing center of Los Angeles.

Churchill secured permission to license Corlieu's fins in the United States, but he had the idea to improve upon the design. Corlieu's fins contained metal reinforcements and were constructed from eighteen separate pieces. As Churchill described in his patent application from September 1940 (granted in 1943): "Another object of my invention is to provide in a swim-fin of the character described a symmetrical stream-lined molded rubber device which is relatively simple and inexpensive to manufacture and which can be molded and manufactured in one piece."[77] Churchill manufactured his first set of fins in his hometown of Los Angeles in 1938 and gifted them to the local lifeguard service in Santa Monica. His idea was to have the lifeguards test-pilot the invention, which he argued would benefit numerous water activities—swimming, lifeguarding, sport diving, and even riding surfboards because of the fins' flexibility.[78] Interest in the fins increased after the U.S. Navy used them during World War II as part of their Underwater Demolition Teams (precursors to the Navy SEAL teams). The fins became a staple of numerous beach activities before and after the war, from lifeguarding and body surfing to boogie and bodyboarding. Much like "Pete" Peterson developing his rubber rescue tube, Churchill didn't have far to go to access the raw ingredients for his fins because Los Angeles was only second to Akron, Ohio, as the largest producer of automobile tires in the United States. The connection between tire companies and companies that developed beach gear can be seen in the career of William J. Voit (1880–1946). Voit worked for many years in the tire industry in Los Angeles before forming the W. J. Voit Rubber Company in 1928 and securing a patent for the inflatable rubber ball in 1932.[79] Voit's company produced beach balls, volleyballs, and, beginning in 1947, an updated version of the Churchill swim fins.[80]

Another beach-related innovation that became critical to Allied success in World War II—swell forecasting—first caught the attention of "Doc" Ball in September 1939 because a storm running up the Mexican coast produced no waves at Bluff Cove.[81] In his newsletter for September 27, 1939, Ball listed the south-facing beaches that had been hit with giant waves—San Onofre ("too dam big to ride"), Dana Point ("This giant Dana stuff really took ye doc by storm"), and Malibu ("really the nuts").[82] "Amazing as it seems," Ball reflected, "ye cove did not intercept any of that fine Mexican storm and no surf was seen either at PV or at Hermosa."[83] It's clear to surfers today why Bluff Cove was entirely flat: the bulk of the Palos Verdes peninsula, looming to the south of Bluff Cove, completely blocked the swell. Bluff Cove breaks best on swells punching from the west—where the mouth of the cove faces; any waves marching up the coast from the south will bounce off the Palos Verdes headland. San Clemente and Santa Catalina islands, lying to the southwest of Palos Verdes, form a double barrier to swells emanating from that direction. Hermosa Beach, as Ball noted in his newsletter, was also flat because its coastline sits in the shadow of those two islands. An illustration that appeared in the *Los Angeles Times* on September 7, 1934 provides a helpful visual of the phenomenon and gives us insight into the state of swell forecasting at the time.

The illustration attempted to explain why waves had battered certain cities between Newport Beach and Malibu the previous two days. The Rainbow Pier in Long Beach had a forty-foot hole in its structure because of the swell, and the five-hundred-foot Pine Avenue Pier had been completely demolished. Residents in Newport Beach and Malibu were sandbagging the shore to save their homes.[84] The illustration, though rather crowded,

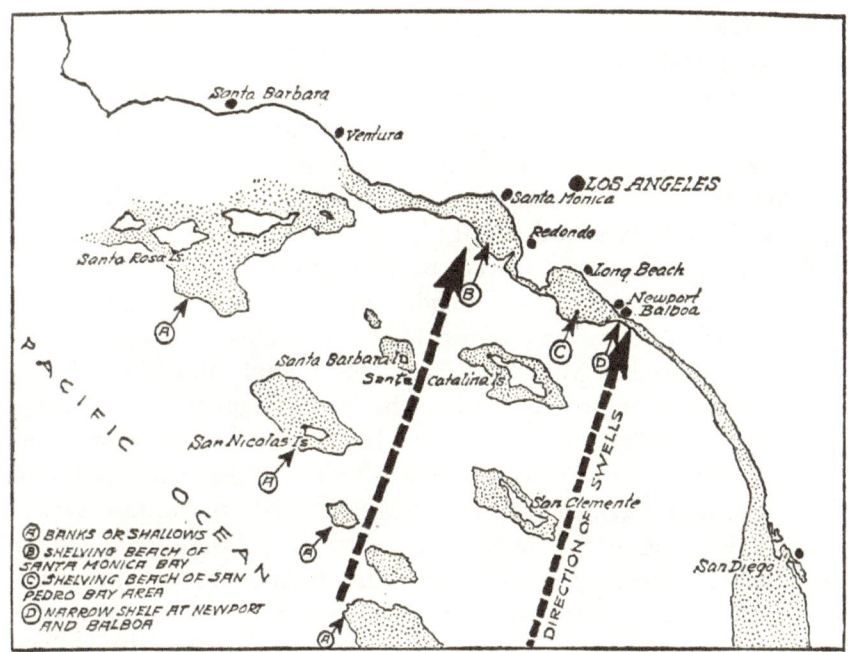

Map indicating swell directions from a South Seas storm hitting California. Staff artist Charles H. Owens/*Los Angeles Times*, September 7, 1934.

uses two arrows to show that ocean swells flowing from specific directions have a straight path toward beaches that sit in what surfers call a "swell window." Unimpeded swells (that is, those not blocked by offshore islands) will hit with greater force. Scientists understood the dynamics of wave action pretty well, but they were less sure of the causes. The illustration presents Harry Leypoldt's theory of "tidal oscillations" to explain the gigantic surf (Leypoldt was an engineer with the Los Angeles Harbor Department). Dr. T. W. McEwen, president of the Scripps Institute in San Diego (later the home of Dr. Walter Munk, who pioneered the field of swell forecasting during World War II), proposed three theories for the waves: a large storm some thousand miles away at sea, an "oscillating barometric disturbance" equally far away, or disturbances on the ocean floor (like an earthquake). The newspaper article also reported the opinion of Dr. Beno Gutenberg, a geophysicist at the California Institute of Technology: "the devastating ocean assault on the Southern California beach area is due to a heavy storm in the less-frequented areas of the Pacific Ocean."[85]

Dr. Gutenberg and others were correct about distant storms causing large waves. Dr. Walter Munk ultimately proved this theory by tracking the ten-thousand-mile journey of waves born in storms off Antarctica and dying along the beaches of Alaska.[86] Ball's first exposure to swell forecasting came in September 1937 after a visit from Tom Blake. Ball writes: "He suggests keeping a record of all the good surf then making a chart and plotting a curve. So by scrutinizing the chart after a years work ye may there-by predict when the humpers will be humping and everybody is happy."[87] In his inimitable way, Ball started recording his observations of Bluff Cove: "Sunday 9/26/37 Flattest day in the history of the annals of surfing."[88]

Blake learned the record-keeping technique from A. E. "Toots" Minville Jr., an island-born engineer and longtime member of the Outrigger Canoe Club. Minville had started tracking the surf at Waikīkī in 1930 so that he could predict swells.[89] Minville observed, for example, that "Zero Break," where the largest waves appeared on the most distant reef, broke about three days a year; "First Break," the reef that produced waves up to twenty feet, broke about twenty-eight days a year.[90] Although Minville understood that ocean storms caused surf, Blake himself stated, "the wind has nothing to do with big surf."[91] He believed that the largest waves resulted from earthquakes: "Great swells are started from the place of the earthquakes and travel just as ripples travel to the edge of a pond when a stone is cast in. In the ocean these reach shore in the form of ground swells."[92] Blake wasn't wrong—earthquakes do cause waves—but, as his response shows, the cause of long-period swells was up to much guesswork before Dr. Munk provided the data.

Ball eventually did get more scientific about his swell forecasting. The week after his observations about Bluff Cove being flat during the Mexican storm, he reported in his newsletter:

CHUBASCO DEL SURF

Its still 15 hundred miles south—but—the results will be felt on most of the southern beaches—Nofre to Flood control should be collossal. And now with the ever growing Lake Mead casting off its vapor pressure—who knows—this may become the super storm area—with the highs and lows getting all squeezed up—over Southern California—. All of which points to a tropical spot with bigger n' better giant surf—. What a stinkin bonanza.

Old Oggle swoggle boggle [that is, Ball himself] got to messin around with his prediction metre and has not been seen since early this AM—so ye sheet [that is, the newsletter] may take a swipe at this week-ends stuff and forecast heavy surf.[93]

Ball had keyed into this second tropical storm (or "chubasco") off the Mexican coast, focusing his predictions on the south-facing beaches. His descriptions tell us that he has started to dissect meteorological data to help him forecast surf. He announced two months later, in mid-December 1939:

JBHALL OFFICIAL SURF PREDICTOR
SIGNS FOR GOVT WEATHER MAPS

Yea man the first one is in today and from minute study of same it looks like big stuff in the offing. Another pair of lows appear in the Alaskan Gulf area—

Should they hook up into one big low or move farther south—we cash in—

The maps are issued every day except Sundays and holidays—see your official forecaster Oggleswoggleboggle.[94]

By the end of January 1940, Ball was in full weather-map mode: "NEW STORM ON THE WAY with a 993 center and a fifty mph wind (gale) at the fringes—a new blast is heading towards the coast in full velocity—Its below parallel 35 and is only about 800 miles offshore. Ye oggleswoggleboggle hereby forcasts a giant zero break—probably before the weekend."[95] On Valentine's Day of 1940, Ball's new love was surf forecasting; he developed what he called a "Surf-Metre" that he unveiled at the PVSC weekly meeting, "designed to aid in the mapping of surf in the south bay area."[96] He predicted, "By next year old Oggleswoggleboggle the surf forecaster will be supplanted by this new system—and the varmints will look to the current surf charts to see if they should go Nofre or not."[97]

We don't have more information about Ball's "surf-metre" or how exactly it functioned. His forecasting, like everybody else's at the time, was hit or miss. But the various details of his surf predictions interest us because they illustrate the importance of place in Ball's life—Palos Verdes in general, and Bluff Cove in particular. We know the time and effort he devoted to maintaining the road to Bluff Cove and building sandy beaches at the bottom. When the surf was flat, he combed the cove for abalone and lobster. Bluff Cove was the primary testing ground for his waterproof camera housings and thus the development of his surf photography. Ball developed an intimate relationship with Bluff Cove; he spent days and nights there studying its rocks, tides, and moods to better understand why and how it produced quality waves. A seminal moment in the history of California beach culture occurred in May 1935 when Ball decided to formalize his relationship with Bluff Cove and establish (with "Adie" Bayer) the Palos Verdes Surfing Club.[98]

The PVSC was a fraternal, formal affair: constitution, bylaws, elected officers, initiation rituals, fines, penalty swats, candlelight ceremonies, club wristlets, monthly dues, and the recitation of the following creed at each Wednesday night meeting (7:30 p.m. sharp, or risk a five-cent fine): "I as a Member of the Palos Verdes Surfing Club do solemnly swear to be ever steadfast in my allegiance to the Club and its members. To respect and adhere to the aims and ideals set forth in its Constitution. To cheerfully meet and accept my responsibilities hereby incurred and to at all times strive to conduct myself in a manner becoming a Club member and a gentleman, so help me God."[99] The members gathered at Ball's suite of rooms above the Regent Theatre on Vermont Avenue in Los Angeles. The club began with seven charter members, eventually growing to a roster of thirty-one.[100] According to the club constitution, members had to be male, own their own surfboard, and be able to ride it "satisfactorily."[101] Each member also had to obtain two pictures of himself: one action shot and one "standing in front of his board."[102] Ball used the portraits to decorate a clubhouse wall; the majority of them were taken at Bluff Cove, reinforcing the importance of their home surfing spot. The photographs also evoked a collective Waikīkī dream since the typical pose of the surfers, with the southern edge of the cove descending in the background, recalls classic images of Waikīkī beachboys gripping their surfboards on the beach, with Diamond Head looming in the distance.[103]

Ball relates that when he and Bayer were forming the club (circa May 1935), the latter suggested naming it the "Palos Verdes Paddleboard Club," but Ball insisted on using the word "surfing."[104] Bayer was probably influenced by two clubs that had already been established in the area—Peterson's Pacific Coast Paddle and Surfboard Association and the Santa Monica Paddleboard Club—as well as the contemporaneous West Coast Paddleboard Association. Ball's usage caught on, however, and new clubs borrowed the term: the Del Mar Surfing Club (1936), the Venice Surfing Club (1938), the San Onofre Surfing Wahines (1938), the Manhattan Beach Surfing Club (1938), the Long Beach Surfing Club (1939), the Hermosa Beach Surfing Club (1939), and the Cabrillo Beach Surfing Club (1939).[105] All the clubs competed in paddleboard events, but both the term and the idea of "surfing" seemed to resonate more with the young people. Because surfing became more popular than paddleboarding after World War II, surfers look back to the founding of the PVSC as an important event in the crystallization of their sport and the ideal of prioritizing surfing rather than paddleboarding.

The PVSC was different from the other clubs in more than name: it was better organized and more team oriented. Members wore matching chain wristlets and jackets with club patches, and all were required to have the club name stenciled on their surfboards.[106] Ball made it a point to remind members why their club was special. After "Granny" Grannis had been elected president in June 1939, following the six-month term of "Hoppy" Swarts, Ball encouraged members to acknowledge Granny's hard work:

and we can show it in no better way than getting behind Granny and shoving ahead—WE are the oldest and strongest club on the coast—DO WE WANT TO STAY THAT WAY????
    WE DO.....[107]

Ball reported in February 1940 that the Hermosa Beach Surfing Club had celebrated its one-year anniversary "with eats, cake and all the trimmings. Several big shots were there from the city council and the speeches were many."[108] He then took the opportunity to crow a bit about his own club: "Ye ed is still glad however that we are an unaffiliated outfit—in spite of all the gew gaw etc etc Ye HB club can still not quite come up to the PVSC organization. We just got sumpin nobody else has got."[109] Hermosa Beach city council members attended the banquet because they had voted the year before to allow the Hermosa Beach Surfing Club use of a room on the pier vacated by county lifeguards.[110] In a similar move, the Manhattan Beach Surf Club had secured seventy-five dollars from its own city council in March 1939 to remodel club quarters on the pier.[111] Although Ball's comment about remaining "an unaffiliated outfit" may have been a case of making a virtue out of necessity because the Palos Verdes Homes Association really had no money to offer, he clearly took pride in the PVSC funding its own activities. Members raised money through monthly dues (one dollar), initiation fees (six dollars, which included the wristlet), various fines, and the annual "Hula Luau."[112]

The weekly newsletter itself stands as one of the most important examples of how the PVSC differed from other surfing clubs. Ball created the newsletter with the intent "of stimulating club interest and activity."[113] He typed most of the copy, glued photographs to the pages, eventually formatted the newsletters on a printer, and shared them with members at the weekly meetings. The newsletter, more than any other artifact associated with the PVSC, carries Ball's personal stamp on the development of California beach culture. The physical labor of writing and assembling the newsletter surpassed any work he did clearing the road to Bluff Cove. As an opus, the five years' worth of weekly publications tracks the evolution of beach culture from the material to the social: above all, Ball's newsletter built the one thing absolutely necessary for the growth of California beach culture: community.

Craig Lockwood has called *Ye Weekly Super Illustrated Spintail* "surfing's primary periodical."[114] The newsletter began in late December 1935 and ran through December 1940.[115] One finds much information within its pages reminiscent of a surf magazine: photographs, wave reports, editorials, competition results, descriptions of notable surf sessions, columns devoted to social gatherings and technical innovations, along with updates on who surfed where, when, and with whom. Much of this information focused, of course, on Ball's beloved Bluff Cove. His passion and purpose for the club come through in the newsletter as both founding father and mother hen, head cheerleader and sergeant at arms, captain of the ship and its cruise director. When Ball threw a party at the clubhouse on a Saturday night in January 1936, and new members Bob Westbrook, George Feister, and Bill Pierce were no-shows, he jabbed, "What in Hell did they join us for if they don't get in on the fun or come to meetings? How about it boys, lets get behind things."[116] After E. J. Oshier had moved to Santa Cruz in 1939, Ball encouraged the other members to write him letters: "And so you see me frans—those notes are really appreciated—lets keep them rolling."[117] Ball described new pledge Art "Gooseneck" Alsten as one of the "shining lights" interested in the club; but when Alsten brought a date to movie night, and she was wearing his wristlet (Bylaw 6: "Absolutely no one but club members shall be permitted to wear the official club wristlet"), Ball reported that "old JBH did warn the good Alsten that he better get it back before the good dame decided she liked it sorta permanent."[118] Ball was the head nicknamer and taskmaster, and he considered it his duty to bring any member's shortcomings, including his own, to the club's attention.

As a whole, the newsletter codified the values and traditions that formed the basis of surf culture, and by extension beach culture, in the 1930s. Members became associated with a home break—Bluff Cove—which they watched over and tended to. They learned about other well-known surf spots, when they broke, and who rode them best. They absorbed Hawaiian tradition not only through club parties (clothing and music) but also Ball's sprinkling of Hawaiian words and phrases throughout the newsletter—a "malahini," "kamaaina," or "pau hana" ("work is finished").[119] The newsletter reinforced the everyday surfing vocabulary that described their world, from surfboards ("slanchwise") and waves ("feathers") to ocean conditions ("minus tide") and an occasional use of Spanish ("oleadas" for "waves"). These terms marked a diversion from island influences, one that would play a larger part in surf culture especially as post–World War II surfers explored Baja California and the Mexican mainland. Members saw photographs and read descriptions of activities that happened around riding waves—the cars, the camping, the competitions, the parties, the wrecked boards, and all of the responsibilities or hurdles in life that prevented their fellow surfers from scoring waves when mother nature delivered a gorgeous swell: jobs, injuries, relationships, or fear for life and limb. Most every week for five years, Ball produced a powerful bonding agent that roused and strengthened his community of surfers.

The stronger the community, of course, the more thorough the exclusion of those on the outside looking in. The club's constitution limited membership to males; the de facto requirements restricted participation to those who were young, white, heterosexual, and able-bodied.[120] There are few explicit references to race or ethnicity in the newsletter; one occurred in October 1939 when Cliff Tucker, winner of the 1940 Pacific Coast Surf Riding Championships, was pledging. Ball wrote, "ARE WE GOING TO HAVE A JEW IN THE PVC? Its all right if his name is Tucker."[121] Tucker seemed to fall right in with the other members. In a later post, Ball reached out to the PVSC community to secure rides for him: "Youse varmints whoever you are—as enjoyed Tuckers hospitality and free rides to the briny—please notice—Tucker has no car available now and craves to get to humpin once in a while—PV varmints taking quick trips to the briny—stop and pick up our only 'Hardbutt Tucker' and transport him to the promised waters."[122] One finds the occasional disparaging reference or joke about effeminate men—how the Cove water in December was "Colder'n Hell. . . . No place for the sissy boys."[123]

For all of its originality at the time, the PVSC, along with the majority of surfing clubs so strongly influenced by Ball's organization, could not escape the racial and gender biases woven deeply into the social fabric; they wore them as everyday attire, unaware perhaps of how much the material itself, like the heavy wooden surfboards on which the surfers stood, restricted the movements and freedom of everyone.

CHAPTER 7

San Onofre

The real 'Nofre guys didn't care about a
club. They went there to get away from
that. They didn't want organization, rules,
bylaws, meetings, and such . . . There,
['Nofre] everybody was a member, or
nobody was a member, because nobody
cared. You just wanted to catch another
wave, play another Hawaiian song, and
for some, have another sip of wine.[1]
—E. J. Oshier

San Onofre has had a reputation since the 1930s of accepting a broad mix
of people, at least in terms of age, sex, and social status. As Oshier's words
above indicate, the surfers who frequented San Onofre didn't seem to care
who came and went. Their focus stayed on riding waves, and the partying
and other activities that surrounded surf sessions were simply a way for
the young people to fill time until the waves came up again. This spirit of
accessibility may have been encouraged by the location itself. Recall that the
Pacific Coast Paddleboard and Surfboard championships held at Malibu in
1934 required permission from the Adamson family since Surfrider Beach,
as it would come to be known, rested on private property. And though Bluff
Cove was described by Los Angeles County as "quasi-public" because of the
number of people who frequented the place, legal restrictions of many kinds
were deeply embedded in the community.[2] It's hard not to connect those
restrictions to the occasional animosity that greeted surfers driving down to
Bluff Cove, either in the form of signs and gates or, in at least one instance,
roofing nails strewn at the bottom of the road where surfers parked.

The thin strip of beach at San Onofre, however, was remote enough
that excluding people probably seemed unnecessary by the mid-1930s. The
area formed part of the sprawling Santa Margarita ranch in San Diego and
Orange counties. Chapparal-covered sandstone bluffs, a hundred feet high,

Pacific Coast Surf Riding Championships, San Onofre, 1938. Left to right: "Pete" Peterson (winner), "Whitey" Harrison, "Adie" Bayer, Joe Parsons, McClure "Duke" Hughes, Dexter Wood, "Hoppy" Swarts, Marold Eyestone, Bob Sides. (Courtesy California Surf Museum.)

overlook the denser cobblestones that spread from shore and give shape to the incoming waves. Farming and cattle-raising occupied the land during the Spanish and Mexican periods (1769–1848), owned in this latter era by Pío Pico (1801–1894), the last governor of Alta California. The Acjachemen people had lived in the region for more than ten thousand years when Spanish Franciscan missionary Junípero Serra arrived in 1776 to establish the mission at San Juan Capistrano, about a dozen miles north of San Onofre. The Acjachemen had developed a hunter-gatherer society over millennia, which likely included fishing the local waterways, along with the ocean on calmer days, in the workhorse of the coastal California Indian community, the tule balsa. Serra colonized the Acjachemen (renamed Juaneños), who represented about five thousand people inhabiting fifteen villages or so in a territory of approximately five hundred square miles.[3] Serra tried to convert the Acjachemen to Catholicism and relied on forced labor, as did other mission priests, to build the twenty-one missions that eventually stretched from San Diego to San Francisco. The sacred site Panhe, about four miles inland from San Onofre state beach, remains a vital gathering place for descendants of the Acjachemen today.[4]

A brief look into the American period after the Mexican-American war (1846–1848) reveals how historical exclusion of native peoples in the San

Onofre area, who had their land stolen from them, prepared the ground for future surfers to enjoy their sense of freedom. As Southern California passed from Mexican control under the 1848 Treaty of Guadalupe Hidalgo, Mexican citizens residing in California, which included Native Americans, became American citizens with all the rights of land ownership.[5] In 1851 Congress passed the "Act to Ascertain and Settle the Private Land Claims in the State of California," empowering federal commissioners to determine ownership of land that had belonged to Mexican citizens. According to Florence Connolly Shipek in *Pushed into the Rocks: Southern California Indian Land Tenure, 1769–1986*, the commissioners, who had evidence of land ownership by the San Juan Capistrano Indians, for example, basically didn't do their jobs and "ignored all the evidence."[6] Without federal recognition, those lands became public and were open to settlement. By 1865, as Southern California became increasingly inundated with settlers looking for farmland, reservations were created to gather the entire population of Native Americans onto inland townships. Shipek writes, "much of this reserved land was rocky and rugged, not particularly good even for grazing, much less as farmland for *all* the Indians of Southern California."[7]

This is the same time period (1864) when the Santa Margarita ranch passes ownership from Pico to his son-in-law, John Forster, "under mysterious circumstances."[8] Looking to turn a profit, "Forster began a plan to sell off ranch land and create housing subdivisions."[9] After Forster died in 1882, the land passed to the Flood and O'Neil families who continued the farming and cattle operations through leases; the O'Neil property lines included the beach at San Onofre, which they leased to Frank Ulrich in 1937. The bountiful fishing grounds that helped sustain the Acjachemen for thousands of years became popular with local sportsmen in the 1920s and 1930s. One reads the following report, for example, from a Los Angeles newspaper in July 1926: "Plenty of Sport for L. A. Anglers: Corbina, yellowfin, croaker and bass are being caught in large numbers at San Onofre, according to Elmer Latz and Ben Dear, local sportsmen, who returned yesterday from a fishing trip. The corbina are averaging about two pounds each."[10] Such announcements undoubtedly encouraged adventurous Angelenos to head south and try their luck in the waters off San Onofre. We also read frequent reports in Orange County papers of area families gathering together and driving to San Onofre for "weiner bakes" and weekend camping trips.[11] "Doc" Ball mentions in April 1939 that surfers had started being charged twenty-five cents as a day-use fee at San Onofre (about five dollars today). Before that time, the beach was presumably cost-free and open to all.[12]

Palos Verdes club member E. J. Oshier—also a San Onofre *habitué*—provided more details about the difference between surfers who frequented San Onofre and those of the PVSC. These latter, he said, "were 'straighter' . . . They just didn't care for—you know—like Barney Wilkes. Some of those guys would get real falling-down drunk. I wouldn't go that far, but I'd get pretty loaded, myself, in the course of an evening. And it would get wild and loud. Nobody got hurt or anything. It was just a noisy, friendly, happy party time. Doc Ball and those guys just didn't care for that."[13] "Tulie" Clark corroborated the idea of PVSC parties being fairly tame: "Nobody ever got too sauced or boozed up. We just played the ukes and the guitars and had a good time. Doc Ball would set up the camera and show his motion pictures from down at the Cove and that would go on for an hour or so. It was just a nice group of guys and gals. Nobody ever got out of hand, everybody was courteous, we were nice to each other."[14] Oshier explained that San Onofre surfers "liked it just free as a breeze and no commitments."[15] He added that whereas the PVSC organized gatherings like the annual "Hula Luau," the "San Onofre group would never do anything like that cuz they didn't want to act as a group . . .—they were all independent spirits and they didn't want any part of an association type thing."[16]

Being a PVSC member, of course, was primarily about "association" and commitment both to the club and to the other members. Article Three of the club constitution reads in part: "It shall be the purpose of the Club and its members to create an active interest in the art of surfing by elevating and maintaining the moral[e] of those concerned and by promoting the good fellowship of all concerned."[17] Ball created the "ceremony of Candlelight" to help this process and to edify the young men.[18] PVSC member Johnny Gates revealed the details of the ceremony: "a member would stand & the others would, in turn, offer him friendly criticism. The member was not to respond in defense."[19] Amendment Nine to the constitution indicates that the ceremony "shall be held every two months."[20] Ball reminded club members of the purpose behind the ceremony in his 1938 Christmas newsletter:

Are you afraid of criticism? If so, why? If the critic is honest in his criticism, it is for your good. He may be honest and still be wrong. In case he is right you have a chance to improve, to change your manner, your thought or whatever it may be. On the other hand when the critic is wrong you have also benefited because it strengthens your position.

We are inclined to fear criticism. Some people will use criticism as an excuse for omitting duties, or will refrain from doing things because they have been or will be criticised [sic]. Thus they place their own fears and feelings above principle.

Criticism should be an inspiration to the attainment of that which is better and higher. We should never falter at the critic's arrow. It may be a means of keeping us from many pitfalls.

Error is the thing we should fear, and whatever may steer us from its path is a blessing.[21]

Built into the PVSC, then, was an obligation to survey one's actions and those of others for the benefit of all. This process supported the goal of developing the three major principles on which the club was founded, as listed in Article Three of the constitution: "COURAGE, HONOR, and SERVICE."[22]

The gang at San Onofre, following Oshier, was a wilder group. His observations provide context for Ball's occasional newsletter-gloating about the superiority of PVSC members, as when Cliff Tucker won the 1940 Pacific Coast Surf Riding Championships at San Onofre. Several weeks before, Ball had described one of Tucker's practice sessions at San Onofre on his new square-tailed ("slanchie") board: "Tucker did give those Nofre varmints a severe lesson in surf riding."[23] After Tucker won the contest, Ball explained away criticism that two PVSC members in the final heat (Johnny Gates and "Hoppy" Swarts) had run interference for Tucker: "Heard from another source that the PV lads really did sew up the deal by putting in some boggle men to pave the way for a feller member—so what??? All for one and one for all says ye sheet—a dam good demonstration that ye PV mob is a real sticktogether outfit."[24]

Oshier's comments about the distinction between PVSC members and the "independent spirits" who frequented San Onofre indicate that the surfer population in Southern California had grown large enough for surf spots to begin developing what we might call distinct "personalities." These attributes were partly a function of the breaks themselves. San Onofre is a more "forgiving" wave, so to speak. Multiple take-off zones—The Point, Old Man's, Dogpatch—offer more options for surfers of all levels, and the slow-rolling breakers mean less chance of serious injury or board damage than at a place like Bluff Cove, which is surrounded by rocks. Dealing with a board that "wound up on the rocks" was a constant concern at Bluff Cove during big swells.[25] Mary Ann Hawkins, no slouch in the water, nevertheless recounts this memorable scare at Bluff Cove: "There was one frightening day at Palos Verdes when I lost my board, the waves were very, very large, and a thick fog came in. I was being swept toward the rocks. My board had already gone to the rocks. And I was absolutely terrified. And, sure I screamed like a maniac, and my husband, Bud Morrissey, finally came and got me just in time, before I was swept onto the rocks."[26] The fact that San Onofre offers more rideable waves year-round than Bluff Cove, holds a larger number of surfers on its various reefs, hits its peak during the warmest months of the year (rather than in winter), and offers more coastline on which to spread out and enjoy the beach—all of these elements help to make San Onofre a more appealing break to a broader range of surfers.

Although "the real 'Nofre guys" might not have cared about a club, the real 'Nofre gals did, and the accepting spirt of the place allowed for this range of freedom. As we know, the San Onofre Surfing Wahines started their club in May 1938, and they eventually built their "Hawaiian Hut" with help from the young men. If you didn't want to be in a club at San Onofre, that was fine. If you wanted to start a surf club there, that was fine too. San Onofre was able to contain various groups of surfers because they all shared a common love of riding waves. Frank Ulrich, who ran the gas station and cafe off the highway, and leased the beach property, was a bit more welcoming than the Palos Verdes homeowners. The San Onofre Surfing Wahines scrapbook editor noted how he received surfers over Labor Day weekend in 1939: "A real luau was put on by Frank Ulrich. (sorta house warming for the fixing up of the shack) Every one sang, danced, and was merry (what a booming business for Alka Selzer the next morning) Ruth Gates and Irene were the first of the club girls to get square tailed outside of Eleanor and her Keoki—see you in the soup girls."[27] Ulrich had incentive to be a good host since he was making money from day-use fees (not to mention beer sales).[28] His "luau" took place a week after the paddleboard contest sponsored by the San Clemente chamber of commerce (organized by "Doc" Ball) that had attracted two thousand spectators, so perhaps Ulrich was showing his appreciation to the surfers for all the business they were drumming up.[29]

The biggest single tribute to San Onofre not only as the epicenter of Southern California beach culture during this era, but also its presiding atmosphere of laissez-faire, was its selection from 1936 to 1941 as the home of the PCSRC. The beach absorbed all comers—independent spirits, club members, and contest organizers. There was no bigger tournament that celebrated surfing than the coast championships, and the event allowed California to establish its own coterie of heroes along the lines of the Waikīkī beachboys. The first mention of San Onofre as a surf destination, in fact, comes in connection to the PCSRC at Corona del Mar. In May 1930, the *Santa Ana Register* reported that a group of college students planned to hold a practice session at San Onofre in preparation for the surfing

Local Surfboard Experts In Meet

With two of its members slated to ride in the Pacific Coast championships in July, the Russian club of Santa Ana junior college purchased five new surfboards for their practices at Newport Beach.

The new boards are 16 feet long and weight 150 pounds each, according to Carol Bertolet, president and stellar surfboard rider. Bertolet set a record last week of a paddle ride of four miles on one of the new boards. The Russians will meet the Redondo Surfboard Kings in a practice meet at San Onofre May 3. There are eight expert riders on the Redondo team.

Mertolet and Herman Reinau will enter the coast championships from the local club.

San Onofre was known as a surfing beach as early as 1930. *Santa Ana Register*, May 1, 1930.

contest. The Russian Club at Santa Ana Junior College had purchased five new surfboards—sixteen feet long, a hundred and fifty pounds each. The paper stated that the club's president, Carol Bertolet (a "stellar surfboard rider"), had "set a record last week of a paddle ride of four miles on one of the new boards. The Russians will meet the Redondo Surfboard Kings in a practice meet at San Onofre May 3. There are eight expert riders on the Redondo team."[30]

There is no further information about the "Redondo Surfboard Kings" or whether this practice meet ever took place. The paper related that Bertolet and club member Herman Reinau planned to enter the PCSRC that year at Corona del Mar, but the event wasn't organized again until 1932. Bertolet was better known in surfing circles as "Laholio"—a combination of Hawaiian words that surfers of the time translated as "horse balls."[31] Bertolet later worked with Harrison and "Tulie" Clark shaping surfboards at Pacific System Homes and received the occasional mention in Ball's newsletter ("Again we say, remember not to forget the DMC-PVSC luau on the first Tuesday of December, come everyone and see Laho Liho crowned the mayor of Kukai Canyon").[32] Ball's reference was intended as a joke since surfers defecated in the canyon, but it does connect Bertolet to San Onofre in a distinguished (if dubious) way. Bertolet was reported as a member of the Corona del Mar surfboard club in December 1931 when he went surfing at night with his younger brother, Wallie, and Gene "Tarzan" Smith. Wallie almost drowned when he wiped out in storm waves and lost his board; the other surfers found him in the darkness and hauled him to shore unconscious. The local lifesaving crew finally resuscitated him after several hours.[33] The various reports situate Bertolet amid an active crew of surfers in Orange County who at least knew about the potential of good surf at San Onofre as early as the spring of 1930. It may be, then, that some of them had frequented the place for several years before Harrison landed there circa 1934 with his carloads of siblings and friends.[34]

As we know, the PCSRC had begun in 1928 as a combination paddleboard-surfing event organized by Tom Blake. By the time San Onofre hosted the contest on September 7, 1936 (Labor Day), the meet was strictly surfing. This was in fact the first stand-alone surfing event of the 1930s. The few previous contests that included surfing had also staged separate paddleboarding events.[35] Although "Doc" Ball also included paddleboarding when he organized his contest at San Onofre in August 1939, this seems to have been partly as a backup in case (as happened) the surf went flat.[36] The remaining championships at San Onofre, held every year from 1938 to 1941, were limited to surfing. These circumstances helped to codify San Onofre as *the* surfing break par excellence in California prior to World War II. As Matt Warshaw aptly states in *The History of Surfing*, "Over the course of three or four hundred Depression-era weekends at San Onofre, surfing socialized itself."[37] The sport had assumed the crown of California beach culture, and San Onofre shone as its most precious jewel.

The Santa Monica *Evening Outlook*, interviewing lifeguard captain George Watkins on the location of the 1936 PCSRC, stated that San Onofre "was chosen as the scene for the contest because it has the long-rolling surf essential to successful surfboard riding."[38] The comment offers subtle but important context for the organization of the PCSRC, directing our attention not to the differences between PVSC members and the "real 'Nofre guys," but to the broader power structures in society that reinforced their similarities. Although the contests were staged at San Onofre, the organizers and top contenders managed affairs primarily from Santa Monica. The top three finishers in 1936, for example, were all members of Santa Monica's Casa Del Mar Surfing Club (Peterson, George "Nelly Bly" Brignell, and

"Whitey" Harrison).[39] The club had also sent members Carol "Laholio" Bertolet, Alfred "Barney" Wilkes, and Dexter Wood to compete along with four members of the Santa Monica lifeguard service (double-counting Peterson). The Del Mar Surfing Club sponsored the subsequent meet in 1938, and five of the top ten finishers came from its ranks, including winner Peterson (former club president), runner-up "Whitey" Harrison, and "Barney" Wilkes (eighth place and actual club president).[40] George Watkins served as a "finishing" judge that year. Watkins had strong connections to the Casa Del Mar club, where he had worked as a swimming instructor and lifeguard for six years prior to being hired as captain of the Santa Monica lifeguards in 1932. Under Watkins, the Santa Monica Life Saving Station, operational center for lifeguards working south of the pier, sat on the grounds of the Casa Del Mar.[41] The West Coast Paddleboard Association (WCPA), which sanctioned the 1938 event, was essentially housed in Santa Monica's Deauville Club just north of the municipal pier; "Adie" Bayer (third-place finisher in 1938 and three-time president of the WCPA) was a swimming instructor at the Deauville and used the club as his office headquarters.[42]

Part of the growing success and visibility of the PCSRC was due to the organizational efforts coming out of Santa Monica. In February 1938, for example, fifty-five members of the Santa Monica Paddle Board Club, the Del Mar Surfing Club, and the PVSC gathered at Sam and Fat's cafe (in Santa Monica) to plan a calendar of events for the year. They were joined by the presidents of the Santa Monica chamber of commerce and the junior chamber of commerce, local sportsmen, and C. P. L. Nicholls, supervisor of aquatics for the Los Angeles Department of Playgrounds and Recreation. "Of primary interest," reported the *Evening Outlook*, "were plans for the big annual Catalina-to-Santa Monica paddleboard race, which will be held in June. Nation-wide publicity through the medium of newspapers, magazines and news-reel together with a broadcast of the 40-mile grind are planned to make the event a real Santa Monica celebration."[43] "Doc" Ball reported on that same meeting in his newsletter: "The Jr. and Sr. chamber of commerce Presidents are hot to get the publicity for the coming race under way . . They want it advertised and how—and they will be backing us plenty when it comes to the gruesome details as to officials trophies Etc."[44] Ball's PVSC ten-man team won the race that year in June, beating out four other teams in nine hours and forty-two minutes, with each member paddling in fifteen-minute intervals.[45] Not surprisingly, part of the entertainment for the meeting at Sam and Fat's was "hula girls" and a "Hawaiian string band."[46] A similar publicity push for the 1938 PCSRC, held two weeks after the Catalina race, made the contest the most successful coast championships to

Pacific Coast Surf Riding Championships, San Onofre, 1940. Left to right: Marold Eyestone, Jim McGrew, Cliff Tucker (winner), Johnny Gates, Hoppy Swarts. (Courtesy California Surf Museum.)

date, hosting between thirty-six and forty-eight competitors and welcoming fifteen hundred fans to San Onofre.[47]

The PCSRC grew steadily in popularity, with the number of contestants growing to approximately eighty in 1939 and 1940.[48] This latter contest required six hours to complete whereas the 1938 contest had lasted only two hours because of the fewer number of contestants.[49] The WCPA sponsored the 1940 contest ("Adie" Bayer had returned as president), and we get a sense of the careful planning that went into the program by reviewing the format and judging. *The Los Angeles Times* reported: "The meet will be staged over a course of approximately a quarter of a mile. Each contestant must catch his wave at the left of the starting buoy, stand erect on his board and cross over to the right of the buoy marking the course limit, approximately 440 yards from the start. Points will be awarded each performer according to the distance he travels after passing the last buoy marking the foul line."[50] The winner of the contest would earn the most points by riding the farthest, working his way diagonally from the starting buoy on the outside of the surf line to the finishing buoy near the beach (riding south to north). A good-size swell would be needed to consistently generate waves that broke that distance, which is probably why the contest had been put on hold for a month until the right conditions prevailed.[51] To get a sense of the point totals, Peterson took the prize in 1938 with seventy points, followed by Harrison (fifty-five), "Adie" Bayer (forty-nine), Joe "Bush" Parsons (forty-five), and Del Mar Surfing Club member McClure Hughes rounding out the top five with thirty-nine points.[52] Peterson's dominance in the event, winning three out of the five times it was held at San Onofre (1936, 1938, 1941), was a testament to his paddling endurance, his wave knowledge and selection, and his ability to maneuver through a dozen or more surfers riding on the same wave.

Newspapers and other sources provide incomplete information for sponsorship, club affiliation, and sanctioning for the PCSRC events, but it's probable that the WCPA sanctioned all of them from 1936 through 1941. The organization was active during those years, sanctioning numerous races in Orange, San Diego, and Los Angeles counties. "Adie" Bayer mentions that by April 1940, the association had grown to five hundred members. Dues were minimal (fifty cents a year), so broad participation was easily secured. All surfing and paddleboard events had to be sanctioned by the WCPA for its members to participate, and members were subject to dismissal if they entered an event not sanctioned by the WCPA.[53] These requirements, and the large membership, meant that the association had a hand in organizing all of the major paddleboard and surfing events from 1935 through 1941. Of the eighteen or so events held in 1936 and 1937, for example, the WCPA likely sanctioned fourteen of them, or about eighty percent.[54] In 1938, the number of contests grew to about a dozen, with the WCPA probably sanctioning half of them.[55] The one year that neither "Adie" Bayer nor Gene Hornbeck served as president of the WCPA—1939—those responsibilities fell to Trevor Povah, two-time president of the Santa Monica Paddle Board Club.[56] Given the presiding influence of Santa Monica groups and the PVSC in helping to organize, sponsor, or sanction the San Onofre contests, we can say that, at least in terms of competition, San Onofre represented exactly the same values as the clubs stretched along the Santa Monica Bay.

As we also consider the participation of Del Mar Surfing Club members "Barney" Wilkes, Carol "Laholio" Bertolet, and George "Nellie Bly" Brignell in various paddling events and the San Onofre contests, we can refine Oshier's distinctions between the "real 'Nofre guys" (Oshier placed all three surfers above in that category) and the "straighter" types of the PVSC.[57] It seems to have come down mostly to the heavy drinking that PVSC members "Doc" Ball and "Hoppy" Swarts disapproved of.[58] Since

Wilkes served as president of the Del Mar Surfing Club the year it sponsored the 1938 PCSRC, he would at least nominally have believed in meetings, organization, and bylaws. He had also been a member of Delta Sigma Delta (a professional dental fraternity) while attending the University of Southern California dental school (graduating in 1936, three years after Ball). Like Ball, Wilkes' father had been a dentist. Dr. Alfred Wilkes and "Barney" had planned to share a practice when the latter graduated, but in July 1935 Dr. Wilkes drowned in a harrowing accident off Catalina Island.[59] Father and son had left San Pedro an hour before sunset in a small boat, which ran out of gas along the way and capsized, throwing both men into the water. The two were discovered the next morning in the channel about eight miles off Catalina, their bodies "sprawled across the hull."[60] As the *Los Angeles Times* reported, young Wilkes "was clinging with one hand to the bottom of the boat, with his other arm around the body of his father." Alfred Wilkes had drowned during the night, and "Barney" had hung onto him. Rescuers transported the latter to a hospital on Catalina where he recovered from a case of severe exposure. The following year, "Barney" started his practice in the same building on Wilshire Boulevard where his father had worked. One wonders what went through his mind as he stroked across the Catalina channel in July 1937, on his way to Santa Monica and victory for the Del Mar Surfing Club.[61]

The dénouement of the Santa Monica-San Onofre connection extends beyond the boundaries of this study, but we can briefly project to April 1952 and the founding of the San Onofre Surfing Club by none other than "Barney" Wilkes, who became the club's first president. In 1957 the club assumed the lease and controlled all access to the break, transforming San Onofre into a private beach club. "The next 15 years were the club's glory days," reported the *Los Angeles Times* in 1992, on the club's fortieth anniversary. The club boasted about five hundred members, a roster that grew to a thousand by the late 1960s, with another two thousand names on the waiting list.[62] San Onofre *is* a precious jewel, and it was always going to reflect the power structure that set it in place. In the 1930s, that power flowed from the Santa Monica Bay and private clubs, or municipal organizations like the Santa Monica lifeguards, that formed their identity by excluding others, either women or ethnic minorities (or both). What I'll suggest is that a similar mentality girding Santa Monica's clubs in the 1920s and 1930s landed at San Onofre in the 1950s and created an anachronistic community, a white preserve that maintained the Waikīkī dreams of an earlier era even as the region's minority population blossomed and society at large progressed beyond racial covenants and de facto segregation to the daily realities of civil rights.

The most direct connection between the two eras was "Barney" Wilkes, one-time president of the Del Mar Surfing Club and later organizer and president of the San Onofre Surfing Club. Recall that the Casa Del Mar had been established in 1924 at the foot of Pico Boulevard after Charles S. Darden and Norman O. Houston had attempted to create an African American resort there but had been blocked by the hastily-formed Santa Monica Bay Protective League (self-described as a group of "1,000 Caucasians").[63] Membership restrictions defined the Casa Del Mar as much as its opulent facilities and two hundred and ten feet of fenced-off beach frontage. A decade after the club's founding, president T. D. Harter reminded members, "As you know, ineligibles are rigidly excluded. Our spirit of courtesy and gracious entertaining is a treasure to be guarded. We have the right people, and these are drawing in their chosen companions. A roster of brilliance and charm is the result."[64] The wording reminds one of the 1936 booklet *Judging Palos Verdes as a Place to Live* with its reference to "undesirable neighbors" and the warning: "We should be careful to choose a district that will be permanently settled by substantial people."[65] If you wanted to frequent Casa Del Mar or the Palos Verdes Estates, you had to be the "right people." In most cases, that usually meant being the "white people."

Being white was essentially a base requirement for membership in the San Onofre Surfing Club, although no one probably expressed this directly. As Belinda Wheaton notes, "Surfing participants often claim—indeed believe—that surfing culture is inclusive of all, and that race and gender do not matter."[66] When David F. Matuszak was researching his comprehensive history, *San Onofre: Memories of a Legendary Surfing Beach* (2018), he commented that, in forty years of surfing the break, he "had seen less than a dozen African American surfers."[67] This time frame places him at San Onofre in the 1970s, the same decade that the state of California assumed control of the beach and transformed it into a state park. Matuszak relates that beach elder Wally Duesler had not seen a female African American surfer at the break in the sixty-plus years that he had been going there, which would date from 1957, the year the San Onofre Surfing Club purchased the lease from the U. S. military for an annual fee of one dollar.[68] The situation at San Onofre is not a personal indictment of "Barney" Wilkes any more than the realities of surfing at the Palos Verdes Estates is an indictment of "Doc" Ball. Ball did not live in the Palos Verdes Estates, with its myriad restrictions, and though Wilkes surfed for the Club Del Mar, there is nothing to suggest he was a regular member of the organization. Nevertheless, the policies of the PVSC, like the member roster of the San Onofre Surfing Club, speak for themselves: women were not permitted in Ball's surf club, and African Americans and other people of color were long excluded from the "glory days" of the San Onofre Surfing Club.[69]

As a general rule, women were excluded from all of the Southern California surfing clubs in the 1930s.[70] If they wanted to be part of a surfing club, they had to form their own. There were also no people of color in the clubs as far as I have been able to determine. Surfing may have been a relatively novel sport in the 1930s, practiced mostly by young people who appropriated Native Hawaiian cultural practices to help distinguish their generation from their parents' Midwestern values. But the surfing clubs reinforced mainstream attitudes by embracing all of the same exclusions regarding sex and race. Notwithstanding the "independent spirits" who frequented San Onofre, when it came to organizing, funding, or promoting contests and clubs—that is to say, weaving surfing into the region's social fabric—the sport fell in line with the established gender and color norms holding sway.

Surfing in California remains a bastion of whiteness, in both actuality and imagination.[71] This state of affairs can be traced back to settlers who populated the coastal areas in the nineteenth century, taking advantage of public domain laws that dispossessed Native Americans of their ancestral lands. Institutions that developed the foundations of surfing in the 1920s and 1930s played their part by continuing policies or practices of racial exclusion for decades after World War II. The Santa Monica Beach clubs, so important for developing surfing, lifeguarding, paddleboarding, and beach volleyball, were themselves bastions of whiteness that prided themselves on excluding people of color and other "ineligibles" (oftentimes Jews). The organization of city and county lifeguard services, so critical to the spread of surfing and beach culture in general, remained all-white until 1965 (with the exception of John Tabor during World War II), and all-male until 1973. The San Onofre Surfing Club, the largest surfing club in the state from its founding in 1952 until California assumed control of San Onofre in 1971, remained private and essentially all-white. Other factors certainly contributed to the homogeneity of California surf culture—economic, demographic, and cultural—but the core institutions that developed surfing and disseminated the beach-culture ideal throughout Southern California maintained the same racial exclusions into the 1960s that had cemented their foundations in the 1920s.

We touched on beach volleyball above, but the sport quickly became part of California beach culture in the mid-1920s, so it deserves our attention. Beach volleyball followed the same path of so many other Southern California beach activities: traveling from Waikīkī, where it was first played in 1915 at the Outrigger Canoe Club, to Santa Monica, where the private beach clubs developed it through recreation and competition.[72] Six players on a side were the norm until Paul "Pablo" Johnson experimented with two-player teams in 1930 at the Santa Monica Athletic Club, a novel format (arrived at through necessity due to a lack of players) that eventually became the standard in beach volleyball competition.[73] The sport arrived in the earliest days of the Santa Monica beach clubs. The *Los Angeles Times*, reporting in July 1925 on the clubs' sudden popularity, and the millions of dollars being invested in them, noted that the Edgewater had already set up a volleyball court for members to enjoy even though the club building itself was still missing the top two floors.[74] Johnson recalled that volleyball at the Edgewater and other clubs "caught on fast because it was the only game that was suited to the beach . . . You could cool off when you wanted by jumping into the ocean, or when you were tired get a hot dog, or just stretch in the sun. Best of all, you didn't have to wear shoes."[75] Clubs were in heavy competition to attract new members, and beach volleyball was a strong selling point for recreation and fitness. As the clubs got up and running, interclub competition helped drive more interest in the sport.[76]

The annual reports of the Department of Recreation Camps and Playgrounds for Los Angeles County indicate that the popularity of beach volleyball extended well beyond the private clubs. The 1929 report, for example, included expenses for building and maintaining volleyball courts. "It was found that properly located facilities for volley ball and other beach games," the report stated, "attracted more people than any other single feature. The volley ball courts being in constant use."[77] County beaches at this time comprised Alamitos Bay, Manhattan Beach, Redondo Beach, and Santa Monica Canyon Beach (also known as "State Beach"). Two-player volleyball began at State Beach during the early 1930s, according to Johnson, where guys who played on the single public court were influenced by what they saw at the private clubs. Although the two groups didn't mix socially—"We had our places to hang out and they had theirs," Johnson said, "and nobody thought much about it one way or another"—when the club members grew bored of playing one another, they challenged the best teams from the public court, oftentimes with small bets on the line (fifty cents a game).[78] Johnson provides the following glimpse of what a typical day at the beach might look like for a young, sports-minded club member during the Depression:

> There were no jobs to be found in town at all, so most of us either went to work for our parents or waited it out. My dad had a ranch in the San

Fernando Valley, and I was in charge of the men. I would get up early, and give them their chores. After they had gone on their way, I would go to the beach and play volleyball almost all day. I made sure I was back at the ranch by four o'clock, just before they returned from the fields. It was like that for most of us at the clubs—whenever we weren't needed, we would head for the beach.[79]

Compare Johnson's experiences with those of Doug Batt, who played on the public court in Santa Monica. Sinjin Smith and Neil Feinemen write in *Kings of the Beach: The Story of Beach Volleyball*:

> The guys on the public beach didn't have regular jobs either and, for the most part, also lived with their parents. While most did not have to come up with rent money, the public beach boys did have to find ways to support their beach habit.
>
> Some, such as Doug Batt, worked as beach boys at the clubs during lunch and, on busy days, through the afternoon. Others waited tables, parked cars, bartended at night or took occasional odd jobs. 'You didn't need much,' says Batt . . . 'If you made a few bucks during the day, you could get a French dip and milkshake at a popular Santa Monica hangout called Weiss's, and still have enough left over to go to a movie and take the Red Car home' [an electric trolley].[80]

Although Johnson and Batt came from different social classes, their stories show the impact of the Great Depression on the development of beach culture in the Los Angeles area. The lack of regular jobs allowed certain young people to arrange their lives around spending time at the beach and to develop sports like volleyball (or surfing). A similar mindset preoccupying a new generation after World War II—*How can I spend as much time as possible at the beach and still get by?*—served as the driving force behind the development of the surf industry during the 1950s.[81]

Because San Onofre has large open spaces along shore, volleyball became a particular favorite when the waves were down. Matuszak reports, "Far and away the most enduring activity that San Onofre surfers have participated in while out of the water has been volleyball."[82] An entry in the San Onofre Surfing Wahines scrapbook from 1938 reinforces his point: "AHAH! GOOD OLE 'NOFRE AGAIN. October 8—Quite the same gang showed up. Volley ball WAS IT, this week-end. Most of the club girls were present."[83] Beach volleyball could be played by everyone who was allowed at the beach, of all ages, at private clubs or public courts, which helped the sport grow rapidly on beaches throughout California and around the world.

Hollywood actor John Leslie "Jackie" Coogan became affiliated with the Del Mar Surfing Club in 1937, and the WCPA announced in June of that year that he would be joining "Pete" Peterson, "Whitey" Harrison, "Barney" Wilkes and other team members in the paddleboard race from Catalina to Santa Monica.[84] Coogan did not end up competing that year for unknown reasons, although he was an avid San Onofre surfer. He had been discovered as a child by Charlie Chaplin and cast as an orphan sidekick in *The Kid* (1921), which catapulted him to national fame. Five years and a dozen films later, as a student at Hollywood's Urban Military Academy, Coogan celebrated his twelfth birthday by arranging to have Duke Kahanamoku put on a swimming exhibition for his classmates.[85] He started dating Betty Grable, "The Girl with the Million Dollar Legs," in 1935, the same year he survived a car wreck that killed his father, his best friend, and two others as they were returning home from a hunting trip in Mexico. His mother said that "swimming and surf board riding" were his favorite hobbies that year.[86] In 1936, Coogan entered the PCSRC at San Onofre, the year Peterson and his two Del Mar Surfing Club teammates took top honors. Betty Grable—Coogan's fiancée now—attended, and the *Santa Ana Register* reported that Fox Movie-tone Newsreel cameramen had come down and filmed Coogan and the other contestants.[87] It's not hard to imagine the media company arriving on scene due to the promotional efforts of Santa Monica lifeguard captain George Watkins, who was well connected to Hollywood celebrities. "Doc" Ball mentions seeing Coogan and Grable at San Onofre in April of 1937, and Coogan graced the front page of Ball's newsletter the following month sliding down a wave at Bluff Cove.[88] Coogan and Grable married later that year in November.[89]

Don James—Santa Monica lifeguard, photographer, and another surfing dentist—captured much of the California beach scene on film in the late 1930s, inspired by the efforts of Tom Blake and "Doc" Ball. His work includes pictures of Coogan, whom he got to know while lifeguarding in Santa Monica and surfing at San Onofre. James recollected: "Jackie used to bring his wife, Betty Grable, with him to San Onofre, and she would complain constantly, saying things like 'get me off this filthy beach'." To consider the place from her perspective, for a moment, San Onofre did not have much to recommend it if you weren't a surfer: little shade, lots of rocks, and few basic amenities. You certainly wouldn't have wanted to go wandering barefoot in kukai canyon. Frank Ulrich did install bathrooms at some point, something probably akin to an outhouse. There just wasn't

Jackie Coogan, John McMahon, and Bob Butt at San Onofre, 1937.
(Don James/Courtesy Tom Adler.)

much to do at San Onofre if you weren't surfing, or waiting for the surf to come up. It's one of the reasons why volleyball took hold so strongly there.

To stay with Grable: what beach might she have imagined for comparison? Somewhere closer to the couple's Westwood home, perhaps—more private, more upscale, less rustic than a fish camp. Maybe a half-mile stretch of white sandy beach with cottages lining the shore leased by the likes of Bing Crosby, Gary Cooper, Delores Del Rio, and Jackie Coogan. A place frequented by the kind of people who "blend in with the seascape, being in much the same key," following James M. Cain, author of the hard-boiled crime novel *The Postman Always Rings Twice*; "they too are dazzling, a little wearisome, and more than a little unreal; they too have that quality, that suggestion of having stepped out of somebody's fever dream, that goes with the Pacific Ocean and no other ocean."[90]

A beach like that might have appealed much more to Grable than San Onofre. And as it so happened, James noted, Coogan's house at the Malibu Colony "was just a couple of hundred feet from the best waves in the world."[91]

CHAPTER 8

Malibu

> We were never sure what reception might
> await us when we walked through the couple's
> Malibu Colony house on our way to Surfrider
> Beach. One day Coogan had sold all of
> Grable's furniture without her permission and
> then used the proceeds to purchase a new
> Mercury convertible. Jackie's transgression
> instigated a tremendous argument. He came
> out in the water to surf and said, "Well, boys,
> it looks like I'm going to have some extra
> time on my hands; I think I'll chrome my new
> motor." I never saw Betty again except as a
> pin-up on other sailors' foot lockers.[1]
>
> —Don James

Betty Grable divorced "Jackie" Coogan in October 1939 after less than two years of marriage, a raucous period for Coogan, who remained "relatively philosophical," according to Don James, about recovering from his mother and stepfather only a small portion of the vast fortune he had earned as a child star.[2] Coogan had been one of the earliest residents at the Malibu Colony and retained his lease on the beach cottage through the lawsuit and divorce. Despite all of his personal turmoil, Coogan still "considered himself to be extremely fortunate" because he lived so close to such an amazing surf spot.[3] It's the kind of remark only a surfer would make. Surfrider Beach—the stretch of coast between the Colony and Malibu pier—was itself fortunate to bask in the glow of Hollywood's aura, a serendipity that accented the break like a beauty mark, lending it star appeal perhaps only matched among beach resorts by the dreamlike mirage of Waikīkī.

California beach culture had begun as a tourist attraction in the early twentieth century. Resorts and bathhouses attracted tens of thousands of people who populated the beaches in the summer, cooled off in the breakers

Motion Picture Colony at Malibu, 1930s. (PhotCL_555_06_2006/The Huntington Library, San Marino, California.)

with the help of lifelines and lifeguards, and watched hired professionals like George Freeth and Charlie Wright perform surfing exhibitions. The younger and sportier visitors tried their hand at riding waves themselves. During the 1920s, private clubs along Santa Monica Bay added prestige to beach culture. They sponsored various sports—surfing, paddleboarding, swimming, volleyball—and provided a training ground for the young men who formed the nucleus of city and county lifeguard services that both spread the popularity of beach sports and ensured the safety of those who participated in them. During the 1930s, a dozen surfing and paddleboard clubs amplified beach culture through competition and social gatherings, enthused by ideals of Native Hawaiian culture that became part and parcel of coastal recreation at places like Palos Verdes and San Onofre. Malibu added the glamour of Hollywood to California beach culture, a sheen that persists even today. That radiance, begun in the mid-1920s with the opening of the Malibu Colony, went supernova in the late 1950s and early 1960s with films like *Gidget* and *Beach Party* that fused two ideals in the popular imagination: Hollywood and Southern California beaches. Malibu's combination of point-break perfection and proximity to silver-screen icons outshone even the exotic allure of Waikīkī and soon shifted the axis of beach culture away from the Hawaiian Islands to the shores of Southern California.

Hollywood stars had helped popularize Waikīkī as a romantic destination, especially after the opening of the Royal Hawaiian Hotel in 1927, so it's no surprise that they did the same for Malibu. But many of the era's biggest stars actually *lived* at Malibu; they weren't just tourists on vacation. One had the feeling, from glossy magazine photographs and newspaper profiles, that you might actually run into Clara Bow or Delores del Rio tanning their toes if you could only squeeze around that privacy fence.[4] Hollywood celebrities were among the first to be offered leases when Malibu's owner, May Rindge, decided to open ten miles of coastline to pay off legal debts acquired from a dozen-year battle to keep the Roosevelt Highway from blighting her property. Her case made it all the way to the U.S. Supreme Court, where she lost, and the highway formally opened to much fanfare on June 29, 1929. Hollywood stars had begun arriving several years earlier, and though Angelenos could now motor through the Malibu Ranch up to Ventura at their leisure, what became known as the "motion picture colony" remained private property, leased to Tinseltowners who paid thirty dollars a month (less than five hundred dollars today) for thirty feet of beach frontage.

It's worth noting that surfing, and beach life in general, returned the favor and buffed the image of Hollywood stars through the 1920s and 1930s. Malibu was not the only location to provide these benefits—Waikīkī remained a favorite playground for actors and directors—but a quick pose with a surfboard at the beach, or reference to an exciting afternoon of riding waves, helped promote the vigor and sensuality of any rising star ("Miss [Virginia] Corbin . . . is an excellent athlete, her favorite sports being swimming and surf-board riding") or established studio veteran ("Cary Grant boasts a better California tan than the local Waikiki beachers—he has been doing some fancy surfing").[5] In *American Tan: Modernism, Eugenics, and the Transformation of Whiteness,* Patricia Lee Daigle credits Hollywood star and Malibu regular Joan Crawford with popularizing suntanning in the United States. Daigle maintains that Crawford, along with husband Douglas Fairbanks Jr., "fortified the notion that suntans conveyed health, prestige, and sex appeal, and spread the practice of sunbathing to every corner of the U.S. through their films as well as their widely publicized lifestyle."[6] Daigle traces this trend back to late nineteenth and early twentieth century beliefs in heliotherapy, eugenics, and Progressive movements that connected a healthy body to a healthy society. In ways that align with and deepen our discussion from chapter 4 of surfers' appropriation of Native Hawaiian culture, Daigle argues that suntanning reflected a "racialized embodiment" among the era's Anglo Americans—a deeper desire to appropriate indigenous identity than merely adopting native dress or customs.[7] This appropriation left ideals of white racial supremacy intact because darkened skin was only temporary for Anglo Americans, a "coat of tan," in the parlance of the times, that could be donned or shed at the discretion of the vacationer.

Like a magnificent crystal, the Malibu Colony gathered all of the idyllic qualities attributed to Southern California—health, sunshine, leisure, happiness—and refracted them through the lens of Hollywood, creating a beacon for the rest of the world to admire and emulate. By the late 1930s, for example, one could read in a heartland newspaper like the *Detroit Free Press* what it meant to be a Hollywood star now that summer had come to California: "From now on, the entire colony will go in for sun tan, bathing suits, play suits, slacks and shorts. Everybody will take on an Indian hue and life will be a continuous performance of swimming, surf-riding and boating."[8] The commentary is intentionally glib, but the image had already been cast: Hollywood had taken up residence by the sea, and California beach culture, from then on, was lifted toward the stars.

Surf history is filled with discovery tales, popular narratives laced with colonialist desires that play on nostalgic longing for uncrowded waves. Malibu is no exception. In fact, it probably represents the archetype of the genre. Sam Reid offered his retrospective account of Malibu's first-contact moment:

> Visualize, if you can, a beautiful fall day in California, September, 1927. On this day the first wave was ridden at what was then the Malibu Ranch, stretching from Las Flores Canyon to Oxnard, and owned by Samuel K. Rindge.[9]
>
> The coast highway was then a two lane road, dirt most of the way, and Tom Blake had stopped by the Santa Monica Swimming Club to pick me up and we decided to try out a new surfing spot. . . . In those days cowboys, with guns and rifles, still rode the Malibu Rancho, and the gate at Las Flores Canyon had a forbidding "No Trespassing" sign on it. But we took our ten foot redwoods out of the Essex rumble-seat

and paddled the mile to a beautiful white crescent-shaped beach that didn't have a footprint on it, and no building of any kind. Needless to say, there was no pier there in those days![10]

Reid added that he and Blake shared "a beautiful eight foot swell" for the first wave: "it was perfection in its sheer classic beauty, and I still remember that ride as if it were only yesterday: the blue water, the majestic mountains stretching to the sea, the clean air, the perfect white beach!"[11] One gets the sense from Reid's narrative of a remote western outpost, an island-like utopia devoid of human existence save the vague threat of armed cowboys on their horses. But Reid and Blake would have paddled by the recently opened Malibu Potteries near the mouth of Malibu Canyon, a five-hundred-foot building that stretched along the beach and employed more than fifty workers.[12] The completion of that manufacturing plant represented something of a dream for May Rindge, who had long wanted to use the natural clay deposits on the ranch to create decorative floor and wall tiles. The Malibu Potteries was located just east of the Malibu Pier; this latter structure was built in 1905 to export agricultural products off the ranch and import various commodities for the livelihood of the Rindges. Blake and Reid would have paddled right past that pier to reach the break. Reid's willful erasure of the Malibu Potteries building, the Malibu Pier, and the Roosevelt Highway (the dirt road from Santa Monica had been paved years earlier) speaks to the strong desire to plant an explorer's flag on a given territory and claim it as our own.[13] The imagined absence of humans on shore ("a beautiful white crescent-shaped beach that didn't have a footprint on it") creates the comforting illusion that the land was uninhabited and simply there for any purpose suiting the pioneer. In this case, a stealthy surf session.

Here is Tom Blake's pared-down version of the session, which his biographers date to 1926 (a year before Reid's recollection): "the Malibu Ranch had recently opened-up. Sam and I drove up there. The road was black topped. I had previously noted surf there. The day we arrived, the waves were about 3' high. The area was deserted except for seagulls and pelicans and the Rindge house. To be the first to ride it, I caught a 3-foot wave. We played around in it for an hour or so. Real exclusive riding."[14] The Malibu Ranch had formally opened for one day in 1926—Sunday, September 19— an invitation for the public to peruse the coastline that was coming up for lease. The *Los Angeles Times* mentioned a "steady parade of cars over the new state highway was reported by officials of the Harold G. Ferguson company, who are leasing agents."[15] Twenty-five thousand people were estimated to have visited the Malibu Ranch that day.[16] Perhaps Blake had been one of them—an opportunity for him to spy waves at Surfrider Beach. If 1926 is

Malibu Potteries plant, Malibu, California. (Courtesy Malibu Adamson House Foundation.)

the correct year, he and Reid must have motored up toward Malibu later that month. Although the highway through Malibu Ranch—known today as Pacific Coast Highway or PCH—had been legally open to the public since the U.S. Supreme Court ruled against May Rindge in June 1923, the surrounding property remained private. Blake and Reid would have been able to drive past Surfrider Beach, but not to park there or to trespass on the beach to reach the waves.[17] So they stopped at Las Flores Inn, which sat on the eastern border of the ranch about ten miles north of Santa Monica, walked past the picnic tables behind the inn with their surfboards, and paddled the two miles or so up the coast to Surfrider Beach.

Blake mentions seeing "the Rindge house," which is probably a miscue since the Mediterranean-style residence that sits right on the beach, now known as the Adamson house and world-famous for its decorative tile, was not built until 1929.[18] Blake is unapologetic about his desire to be the first to ride a wave—similar to his request to Peterson and Burton in October 1931 to continue paddling so he could be the first to land at Catalina—and summed up the experience as "real exclusive riding." If the date is accurate for this first foray to Surfrider Beach, then Blake would be correct because the Malibu Ranch had only begun to offer leases that same month and year, and the Malibu Colony would not get up and running until the summer of 1927.[19] After thirty-one years of ownership, the Rindges were forced to open their property so that California could complete a Mexico-to-Oregon highway for the pleasure, profit, and convenience of countless citizens and travelers. Blake and Reid's trip up the coast, much like Duke Kahanamoku's jaunt to Corona del Mar in June 1925, serves as another reminder of how the growth of California beach culture depended upon the development of the state's highway system.

May and Frederick Rindge had battled to fend off, and to fence off, their 13,315 acres from anyone who might encroach on their earthly paradise. Frederick Rindge, a wealthy and devout easterner who had moved to Los Angeles with May in 1887 and purchased the Malibu Ranch five years later, not only thanked the Almighty for his good fortune ("God, in his goodness, had brought me to just my ideal farm"), but considered himself the absolute master of his domain. "Behold, these hills are mine in trust," he wrote in *Happy Days in Southern California* (1898), "none, save my country, disputes my right to yonder ocean; through Christ the sky is mine. Yes, I am a monarch of all I survey."[20] He, and later May in his memory (Frederick died in 1905), felt a divine calling to safeguard the last of the great Mexican land grants in California. As with San Onofre, the Rancho Topanga Malibu Sequit had passed through various owners during the Spanish and Mexican periods (José Bartolome Tapia, a Spanish colonist; Leon Victor Prudhomme, a young Frenchman who married Tapia's granddaughter) before its acquisition in 1857 by Matthew Keller, an Irish businessman, whose descendants sold it to the Rindges.[21]

Also like San Onofre, the area had been populated by Native Americans for thousands of years before the arrival of the Spanish in 1542, principally the Chumash, who thrived from present-day Topanga Canyon (the eastern border of the Malibu Ranch) up to San Luis Obispo, inland to the San Joaquin Valley and out to the northern Santa Barbara Channel Islands. The Chumash who lived at *Humaliwo* (literally, "the surf sounds loudly"), the settlement from which Malibu derives its name, formed part of a network of about twenty thousand Indians whose economic and political center spread from the Santa Barbara region and its offshore islands.[22] The Chumash colony near the Malibu Lagoon, approximately twenty-five hundred years old according to archeological digs, would have been an ideal location for the hunter-gatherers, giving them access to both fresh water and the ocean for fishing, travel, and trade. Their large domed houses were nestled near a south-facing shoreline; this allowed easy departure and landing much of the year for their tule balsas, or for the sturdier *tomols* (plank canoes) used for sea-hunts and voyages, the redwood planks sealed using the natural deposits of tar native to the region.[23]

Archeologist Lynn H. Gamble argues that many of the Chumash from Malibu and the surrounding area probably worked on Spanish ranchos after Gaspar de Portolá arrived in California in 1769. This work would have continued until at least 1803 when 118 individuals at *Humaliwo* were baptized at the two nearest missions, San Buenaventura (in present-day

Ventura, founded in 1782) and San Fernando Rey (in present-day Mission Hills, founded in 1797). As Gamble reports, "once Indians were baptized at these missions, they lived there until they died or until mission secularization, which occurred between 1832 and 1835."[24] Before 1803, the Chumash would have been a natural choice to work for ranchers like Tapia because they knew the region intimately.

Gamble's description of the excavation of a historic Chumash cemetery at *Humaliwo* reveals a time when some of the cowboys were actually Indians: buried in the graves alongside traditional Chumash artifacts (glass beads, plank canoes) were metal items linked to the Spanish *vaqueros*—various saddle and bridle ornaments, and part of an iron spur.[25] The Chumash adapted to the Spanish colonizers and learned how to ride horses and herd cattle, among other skills. One can't help but think of Sam Reid's description of cowboys riding the Malibu Ranch, his vision of an impediment rather than a cultural continuity of those who had lived on the land and had, for thousands of years, crossed the same waves that he and Blake would surf in the fall of 1926. Blake himself described the area as "deserted," a notion that Frederick Rindge had intimated when he described his family's arrival at Malibu: "You must know that we have given our own names to the places around us, because it was un-named ground."[26] The colonial narratives of Reid, Blake, and Rindge serve as cautionary tales to seek out the names of our predecessors. Malibu, for many reasons, holds an important place in the history of California beach culture. *Humaliwo* held an equally important place for the Chumash long before California's name ever appeared on a map.[27]

Malibu's mystique in the early decades of the twentieth century derived not from its Native American traditions, which were little understood, but from its standing as the last of the great Spanish ranchos where notorious, even violent, confrontations occurred between the wealthy Rindges and their hardscrabble neighbors—a cluster of homesteaders who lived back in the canyons and fought tooth and nail to preserve their right to cross ranch property on supply trips into Santa Monica.[28] Residents like Marion Decker, who preceded the Rindges by half a dozen years, saved himself a day and a half of rough travel by horseback and wagon through steep mountain passes and thorny chaparral if he cut across the ranch and skirted the coastline into town, a route that had to be planned around low tides so that Decker didn't get trapped by the surf. A years-long chess game ensued between Rindge, who really didn't want anybody crossing his land, and the homesteaders, who threatened at one point to ask the county to build a road through Malibu if Rindge didn't remove the locked gates he had installed on the eastern and western borders to keep the public out. Rindge placated Decker and the others by removing the locks (but keeping the gates), all the while secretly pursuing a plan of buying out as many of the homesteaders as possible to build a buffer around his immense landholding.

In early December 1903, a brush fire ripped through the Malibu Ranch, charring thousands of acres over three days and destroying the Rindge family house. As David K. Randall writes in *The King and Queen of Malibu: The True Story for the Battle of Paradise,* May Rindge "saw a conspiracy" in the fire, which had started close to the Rindge home, "a plan on the part of the men she viewed as barely able to survive their squalid existence to rob her own family of its happiness."[29] She suspected frontier justice—a desperate act of revenge on the part of the homesteaders to burn out the Rindges. After Frederick Rindge died two years later from complications related to diabetes, the battle between a resolute May and the homesteaders became the stuff of a Hollywood screenplay. She built gates along the coastal wagon trail, and her ranch hands discovered them torn down. She lobbied the White House—President Theodore Roosevelt was an old classmate of Frederick Rindge—to convert seventy thousand acres abutting her property into a national forest, trying to use the federal government to oust the homesteaders permanently. When a federal judge handed her a legal victory in 1913 that reaffirmed the homesteaders' paths as Rindge property, she ordered the paths dynamited to block travel routes. Randall writes: "When new paths began appearing in their place, she mounted a horse and rode into the hills alongside Darlington [her chief engineer]. There, she took up a shovel and, next to a team of bodyguards, began filling them in herself."[30] When the state supreme court decided in 1917 that the coastal route was also Rindge property—after a ten-year battle that had kept it open to public travel—she locked down her ranch. Later that fall, more than two hundred sheep on the ranch died from suspected poisoning.[31] In retaliation, May dynamited two canyon passes to prevent the homesteaders from bringing their products to market, forcing them to take the longer route through the San Fernando Valley. The feud finally erupted into a pitched gun battle between the homesteaders and the Rindges, though few details and no clear victor emerged when the dust settled.

May Rindge fought on multiple fronts. She spent millions to build a private railroad across fifteen miles of her property to keep the Southern Pacific from constructing its own line. She endured a lawsuit from her eldest son, Samuel, who believed she was squandering the family fortune. And she squared off against the county of Los Angeles, the state of California, and eventually the U.S. Supreme Court in a desperate attempt to keep her property barricaded against hordes of motorists and other undesirables. The drama, the mystery, the history—plus the glamour of Hollywood—it was all too much to pass up for a journalist like James M. Cain, who had moved to Hollywood to make his mark on the big screen. And what better way to do that than to write about something that May Rindge would come to understand intimately: the failed American Dream.

Cain added an important element to California beach culture of the 1930s: a counterpoint to the popular images of Malibu as a beacon of sun and glamour. His writings worked like a photographic negative, capturing nightmarish strains that haunted the City of Dreams. He brought grit, violence, and desperation to the beach, a tradition that continues today in the surf-noir novels of Kem Nunn, among others.[32]

Cain was a hitchhiker on the road to fame in the summer of 1933. He'd arrived in Hollywood in November 1931 as a screenwriter for Paramount Studios, flaunting a paycheck of four hundred dollars a week after working as the managing editor for the *New Yorker*.[33] His screenwriting gig ended after six months, so Cain fell back on journalism and writing short stories to pay the bills. He penned "The Widow's Mite, or Queen of the Rancho" for the August 1933 issue of *Vanity Fair*, a profile of Malibu and its eccentric owner, May Rindge. The story continued the process for Cain—begun earlier that year with his first novel *The Postman Always Rings Twice*—of dragging Malibu into the jaded world of Los Angeles crime fiction. "Whatever else may be said of Malibu," Cain began his article, "the place where the movie queens grow their sunburn, there is one thing that you have to hand it: it is probably the finest beach ever created by God."[34] Favoring sunburns to suntans, Cain already flags the wry bent of the narrative. Before noting the dream-like quality of the stars who reside there, the cost of a beachside lot (twelve thousand dollars), and Rindge's legal troubles ("In the end, the State of California won the war, and built the road, and Mrs. Rindge didn't like it much, as she is a woman rather inclined to have her own way"), Cain holds the reader's attention with a detailed description of the surf, which he can't help but describe in terms an actor would appreciate:

> Far out a swell appears, and breaks into a curling lip. This spreads, until there is a wall of water a quarter of a mile long, which comes in slowly, and gets higher as it comes. Then it smashes down, and sends a smother of foam sliding up the sands. This recedes, and for a minute or more there is quiet, with the ocean still as a pond. Then the sea stirs again, there is another swell, and the performance is repeated. Each swell gives a strictly solo number, with entrance, build-up, punch-line, and tag all complete. While it is on, no other swells appear to crab its act.[35]

The solitary wave that Cain describes is the one that breaks around the point from Surfrider Beach, out in front of the Malibu Colony, where the bottom contour causes the swell to rise up and break all at once over the sand—nothing a surfer would be interested in. The more famous wave that breaks across First Point, directly in front of the Adamson House, rolls steadily around the point toward the pier, offering surfers a long wall to glide down, carve up, and race across. And yet, technically speaking, they are two parts of the same wave: the former barging straight onto shore while the latter takes its time curling around the point, releasing its energy the way a model moves down the runway—all flow and precision, the cut and pace of a surfer's dream.

It's no accident that Cain had chosen the Malibu area for the murder scene of *The Postman Always Rings Twice* (1934), which followed such hard-boiled tales as Dashiell Hammett's *The Maltese Falcon* (1930) and preceded Raymond Chandler's *The Big Sleep* (1939). Malibu allowed Cain to shadow Hollywood's limelight, to bust the Southland's boom in the figures of Frank Chambers, a young drifter, and Cora Papadakis, the beautiful wife of Nick Papadakis whom Cora and Frank murder in the steep mountain passes leading to the Malibu Colony. We join the novel in progress as Frank explains why Cora decided to exit the 101 Freeway on "Malibu Lake Road," which leads to Decker Canyon Road (named after the clan of our homesteader, Marion Decker):

> the idea was, she had never seen Malibu Beach, where the movie stars live, and she wanted to cut over on this road to the ocean, so she could drop down a couple of miles and look at it, and then turn around and keep right on up to Santa Barbara. The real idea was that this connection is about the worst piece of road in Los Angeles County, and an accident there wouldn't surprise anybody, not even a cop. It's dark, and has no traffic on it hardly, and no houses or anything, and suited us for what we had to do.[36]

What they had to do, of course, was make Nick's murder look like an accident. Cain grabs the romance of visiting beachside movie stars and rams it down "about the worst piece of road in Los Angeles County." The automobile, the highway system, the Malibu hills, the colony itself—all of it takes a Depression-era detour from the California Dream through the dregs of the down-and-out, the reckless lives of desperate men and women whose dream came up short.[37]

Grit suddenly became the new glam for Cain and Hollywood—the film rights for the best-selling novel sold quickly for twenty-five thousand dollars (more than half a million dollars today). The beach, long associated with the healthy fun of summer sports, the prestige of private clubs, and the glitter of screen stars, now included darker strains of human depravity. Cain plays on the shifting image of the beach in his novel. Early on, during their first trip to the ocean, Frank describes Cora in terms of innocence—"a little girl" in her yellow bathing suit and red cap.[38] "It was the first time I ever really saw how young she was," he says. "We played in the sand, and then we went way out and let the swells rock us."[39] Ten chapters later—after getting away with Nick's murder and landing a ten-thousand-dollar insurance policy—Frank and Cora are married, and Cora is pregnant. They head to Santa Monica State Beach and swim out:

> A big [swell] raised us up, and she put her hand to her breasts, to show how it lifted them. "I love it. Are they big, Frank?"
> "I'll tell you tonight."
> "They feel big. I didn't tell you about that. It's not only knowing you're going to make another life. It's what it does to you. My breasts feel so big, and I want you to kiss them. Pretty soon my belly is going to get big, and I'll love that, and want everybody to see it. It's life. I can feel it in me. It's a new life for us both, Frank."[40]

The two are on the verge of realizing the California Dream. Frank swims down in the ocean, which he believes cleanses him: "it seemed to me that all the devilment, and meanness, and shiftlessness, and no-account stuff in my life had been pressed out and washed off, and I was ready to start out with her again clean, and do like she said, have a new life."[41]

He comes up only to see Cora coughing and feeling "funny inside."[42] She remarks, "Wouldn't that be awful? I've heard of women that had a miscarriage. From straining theirself."[43] Frank plays the lifeguard and tows her in. He disparages the real one on shore—overturning the normally positive, even heroic figure lifeguards play in the public eye—after Cora suggests calling him: "Christ no. That egg will want to pump your legs up an down."[44] Rather than a new life for the couple and their baby, Cora dies in a horrible wreck on Pacific Coast Highway as Frank rushes her to a hospital, a death the court construes as murder, which lands Frank in San Quentin waiting to be executed. The ocean swells in which Cora strained herself keeping her head up, and the beach itself, are no longer the stuff of youth and innocence, but just another site of love gone wrong, of senseless tragedy and death.

Dreams denied make for compelling stories, and Hollywood seized on the beach as an ideal place for the California Dream to unravel. In the adaptation of Cain's novel *Mildred Pierce* (1941)—suntan influencer Joan Crawford won an Oscar in the title role—the beach is the site of the plot's greatest violence and treachery: where Mildred discovers her husband's affair with her own daughter, Veda, and where her husband is murdered. The location of the beach house? Malibu, of course, just up the road from the colony. Hollywood's biggest female stars played the lead roles in Cain's stories—Lana Turner, for example, as the sultry Cora Papadakis—adding unbridled lust to Malibu's dreamy reputation, which only made it more forbidding, and thus more appealing as a destination.

Malibu didn't hit its stride as a popular surf destination until after World War II. This partly owed to the difficulty of accessing the break. Santa Monica surfer Jack Quigg described the obstacles involved in sneaking over the "high block wall" that protected the property around the Adamson House:

> We knew [it] was risky but we'd toss our boards over the wall, scale it and nestle out of sight in the small dunes. There we'd bask while playing Hawaiian songs on our windup portable record player. . . . Out on the waves, we were visible. A couple of times the folks in the mansion, apparently called the sheriff as a deputy pulled up and began hollering and waving us in. We pretended not to notice. But when we got back to our car the distributor cap was gone. Dead engine. To reclaim it we had to hoof it to the substation and listen to a lecture.[45]

A young surfer might only get so many warnings before more serious consequences ensued. After Peterson's failed attempt to run a surf contest at Malibu in September 1934, no one else tried to repeat the experiment. Even if you *could* get permission from May Rindge's daughter and son-in-law, Rhoda and Merritt Adamson, who lived in the house on Surfrider Beach, the break was too fickle. Good waves roll off the point only under a specific (and rather narrow) combination of circumstances, and though Malibu was much closer to surfers in the Los Angeles area than San Onofre, this latter break remained infinitely more reliable and accessible. In surfing's stable of wave-rich beaches, San Onofre worked like a quarter horse: dependable, friendly, easy to ride. Malibu acted the thoroughbred—sleek and spectacular when it ran, but it scratched more often than not.

The circumstances surrounding Peterson's contest provide a case in point. Waves had pounded south-facing beaches from Newport to Malibu for several days before the contest, ripping into piers, houses, railroad tracks, and the coast highway. The *Los Angeles Times* reported that "a score of screen notables" in the Malibu colony, alarmed that storm waves had destroyed their fencing, "hurriedly joined a crew of workmen" to build a barrier of sandbags.[46] But come Sunday, September 9, the ocean had calmed once again, resulting in a no-go for the surfing championships. Recall that of the nine hundred or so photographs in the "Doc" Ball opus, none are of Malibu. Only two pictures of the break appear in his *California Surfriders*,

Adamson House, Malibu, California. (PhotCL_555_06_2010/The Huntington Library, San Marino, California.)

both taken by PVSC member John Gates. Malibu doesn't appear in the PVSC newsletter until very late—September 1939, when "Pete" Peterson "got a smoker clear across the end of the Malibu pier."[47] Word of the swell got out, because two weeks later, Ball mentioned ten of the PVSC members trekking up the coast. He added, "Hear that this new Malibu spot is a honey—Fast bein the name for it."[48] It's telling that he calls Malibu a "new spot," an indication that few people rode it throughout the 1930s. May Rindge lost control of the Malibu Ranch in June 1938—a result of more than ten million dollars owed in federal taxes. It's likely that Rindge's financial woes favored greater access to Surfrider Beach, with more opportunities for surfers to enjoy the break without fear of being prosecuted for trespassing.[49]

Once the PVSC members got a taste of Malibu's potential, however, they—like everyone else who has had the pleasure of racing down one of those walls—were hooked. Ball wrote in *California Surfriders:* "Waves here are fast and track down [toward the pier] like dynamite."[50] An apt description given the explosive history between the Rindges and the homesteaders. "Granny" Grannis and "Hoppy" Swarts returned to Malibu the following month, in October 1939, for a late summer swell, and again in December after leaving Bluff Cove in search of smaller conditions.[51] Malibu stayed

A Board and Lots of Room

SP🔫RTS

Los Angeles Times

Gardner Lippencott, Bill Dillehunt, and "Pete" Peterson practicing for the Pacific Coast Paddleboard and Surfboard Championships, Malibu. *Los Angeles Times*, September 5, 1934.

on their minds through the spring of 1940. Guest editing the newsletter, Swarts wrote: "When is Malibu going to hump? Our Granny has got to have his sleep, so hump up you Malibu."[52]

One good wave at Malibu stays on your mind, pulls you back up the coast highway looking for that scarce combination of factors that create long, exciting rides. It's part of what makes the place special. Long rides were the determining factor for the best surf spots and the best surfers in the pre–World War II era. Duke Kahanamoku and Tom Blake made headlines gliding on mile-long waves at Waikīkī, displaying their skill at selecting and navigating the largest waves that broke on the distant reef known as Kalehuawehe or Castle's.[53] The winners at the Pacific Coast Surf Riding Championships scored the most points by riding the longest waves between contest buoys. The favorite breaks of the 1920s and 1930s—Corona del Mar, San Onofre, Flood Control, Bluff Cove—all offered longer rides than the more common surf spots known as "beach breaks"—Manhattan Beach, Hermosa Beach, and Santa Monica are all good examples—whose waves break off shifting sandbars (rather than reefs or cobblestones) and offer rides usually lasting only a few seconds. Beach breaks were much more difficult to ride on the longer, heavier boards, and usually more dangerous because they broke closer to shore.

Because of Malibu's coastal position and bathymetry (the depth and shape of its seabed), the wave breaks quickly right to left if you're watching from the sand—from the top of the point down toward the pier. It's not a wave you can ride straight in toward the beach, as you often can at Waikīkī or San Onofre, using momentum to glide on the swell as it passes over deeper water before it begins to re-form on the shallow reef or cobblestones. Surfing Waikīkī or San Onofre is oftentimes an exercise in milking a wave—turning left, right, or moving straight ahead, trying to adapt to the breaking water and gliding for the longest possible distance. Malibu, as Ball wrote, is fast, compared to San Onofre or Waikīkī. If you're not up on your board and racing toward the pier, the wave will leave you behind.

In addition to speed, which makes surfing there a thrilling experience, Malibu has that quality that James M. Cain nailed in his profile for *Vanity Fair:* "Each swell gives a strictly solo number, with entrance, build-up, punch-line, and tag all complete. While it is on, no other swells appear to crab its act."[54] We can state directly what Cain implies: the wave at Malibu, above all, rewards performance. Matt Warshaw follows a similar stage direction in *The History of Surfing:* "Malibu wasn't so much a surfing location as it was a small, intimate, well-designed surfing theater."[55] As Cain began his career checking readers into a back room at the Motel California, he inadvertently captured the essence of surfing Malibu. The aura of Hollywood spilled over to the break around the point, providing a venue where every surfer can feel like a star. The wave breaks close to shore—running across the beach rather than straight in—one at a time, in full view of everybody parked on the sand and every surfer paddling up the point. If you bungle the take-off and wipe out, everybody knows it. If you pull the most amazing maneuver of your life, everyone sees that too. Surfers watch each other; they pay attention to who does what in the surf. No wave in California shone with a brighter spotlight than Malibu.

But we are getting ahead of ourselves. The era of Blake, Ball, Peterson, Hawkins, Harrison, and so many others in California followed the Hawaiian tradition of surfing as a communal sport. The "solo number" Cain describes would not fully materialize until after World War II, when surfboards became lighter and more maneuverable. The widespread use of fiberglass not only to seal balsa boards but also to attach fins securely to the tail, and thus make them more maneuverable, ushered in an era when the solo surfer reigned supreme on the wave, allowing Malibu to reach its full potential as surfing's biggest stage in California.

PART III

The Dream

CHAPTER 9

Hawaiian Surfboard and the Writing of Surf History

"Hawaiian Surfboard" is the ideal aloha gift
and should be of keen interest to the tourist.

The author has incorporated into his pages
the ancient Hawaiian legends of surf-riding.
Many of them are new to us.
—E. B. L., *The Honolulu Advertiser,* June 9, 1935

Tom Blake's *Hawaiian Surfboard* (1935) has long been regarded as a semi-nal work in surf culture, hailed as the first book to treat the sport's history from its Polynesian origins through the early decades of the twentieth cen-tury. The four chapters cover in turn ancient Hawaiian legends of surfing, observations of the sport (primarily Western) from Captain James Cook's arrival in 1778 to 1896, "modern surfriding" in Hawaiʻi and California, and finally a how-to manual for Blake's new hollow surfboard. Complement-ing the four chapters are four groupings of black and white photographs (some taken by Blake) illustrating Waikīkī and its various water sports, primarily surfing and canoeing. Blake mixes memoir into the historical record—his own experiences living at Waikīkī and developing the hollow surfboard—and includes excerpts from articles he had published on surf-ing in the *Mid-Pacific Magazine* and *Paradise of the Pacific* magazine. He cites various historical writers throughout the book—Abraham Fornander, David Malo, Nathaniel Emerson—using their knowledge to lend authority to his own account. For our purposes, *Hawaiian Surfboard* works as the ideal capstone for a study that tracks the development of California beach culture during the 1930s through the lens of physical objects—surfboards, cameras, lifesaving gear, surf shacks, outrigger canoes, among others. The objects materialized a dream of Waikīkī and Native Hawaiian culture, fol-lowing our reading of Kevin Starr, while reinforcing colonial attitudes about Native Hawaiians themselves. Starr writes that Los Angeles, after the stock

Tom Blake's *Hawaiian Surfboard*, 1935. (The Croul Family Collection.)

market crash of 1929, illustrated "in a very American way . . . the notion that imagination and even illusion not only are the premise and primal stuff of art, they play a role in history as well."[1] *Hawaiian Surfboard,* an object whose content is saturated with Blake's idealization of island culture, becomes the vehicle where imagination and illusion project him into Native Hawaiian history as the hero of a surfing romance. In the end, this fictional fantasy might be considered nothing more than a white man's self-indulgence except for the significant influence that *Hawaiian Surfboard* exerted on later histories of surfing.

Blake begins his first chapter, "Ancient Hawaiian Legends of Surfriding," by establishing his authority for the reader, one gleaned not from any particular historical writer, but directly from the ancient Hawaiian surfboards themselves, which hung on the walls of the Bishop Museum in Honolulu. "Although radically different from the modern surfboard," Blake writes, "these old time models tell me their story, by their length, shape, thickness and weight, as clearly as though I were living in the past."[2] He then channels that story by conjuring a young chief named Kealoha, who paddles out to Kalehuawehe, the farthest break at Waikīkī, to catch one of the twenty-five footers breaking across the reef.[3] The fictional scenario, occurring a thousand years ago, allows Blake to introduce the various surf spots at Waikīkī and to illustrate their timelessness. Once Kealoha has completed his ride, Blake spends a dozen pages or so introducing famous Hawaiian legends, mostly derived from Abraham Fornander's *An Account of the Polynesian Race: Its Origins and Migrations* (1878–1885), and his *Fornander Collection of Hawaiian Antiquities and Folk-Lore* (1916–1920): Kelea, Umi, Moikeha, Lonoikamakahiki, Kawelo, Pamano, and Keaka, among others. The tale at the center of the chapter, however—eight pages, nearly three times longer than any of the legends—centers around two lovers, Moloa and Nani, which Blake has entirely fabricated. Moreover, Moloa—"a chief in his own right"—is based on Blake himself.[4]

Blake precedes the story by quoting two authorities on Hawaiian burial customs, David Malo and Nathaniel Emerson. He has devoted almost fifteen pages to establishing his knowledge of Native Hawaiian history based on his study of these authors and others in the Bishop Museum library. It's true that Blake calls his narrative a "story" rather than a "legend"; he uses this latter term consistently for the actual legends. But it's disingenuous. The Hawaiian names of the two main characters, following the most well-known Hawaiian surfing legends, in a chapter titled "Ancient Hawaiian Legends of Surfing"—and no disclaimer that he's suddenly shifting from historical figures to fictional ones—it all feels like sleight of hand. He concludes the tale with an authentic sounding, "So ends the story of two lovers of old Hawaii."[5] As we read their adventures, and slowly realize the parallels between Blake's life and that of Moloa, we have to wonder: *What is Tom Blake up to?*

Like Blake, Moloa grew up sporting in the mountains, which gave him "a sturdy body," and he "journeyed across the waters to Oahu, to live at Waikiki."[6] Blake then sets the stage for his hero's apotheosis:

After five years Moloa rode the biggest surfs with the greatest surfriders of the day. He became known throughout the island as the one who became a favorite of the king, and made a chief, because of his surfriding and the winning of surf races.

Thus Moloa lived a charmed existence, he being supplied with the needs of life by the king who was himself a famous surfrider in his youth.

Moloa became a great authority on surfboards, and sacred rights [sic] followed in their making and was called upon by the careful people who were making boards and wanted the best in design, and the best of luck with their boards by observing the necessary rituals.[7]

At this point, it almost feels like Blake is writing an advertisement for his shaping services. But the timeline parallels his own experiences traveling to Hawai'i for the first time in 1924, his research and development of surfboards over the next five years, his growing friendship with Duke Kahanamoku and his brothers ("the greatest surfriders of the day"), and his triumph winning paddleboard races in late 1929 and early 1930. The story proceeds to a surf contest that culminates in two champions going head-to-head: Koea (from Kaua'i) and Moloa; this latter wins in classic Blake fashion by cruising to victory as others tend to the fallen (one thinks of Blake's victory in the 1932 Catalina race as Peterson stopped to help a seasick Burton): "Koea was unconscious with fatigue. Moloa signaled the outside judges to care for Koea, and catching a huge wave in the fading light, rode to the shore the winner of the surf race, the sixteen war canoes for his king and great honor for the Island of Oahu."[8]

Nani then makes her appearance in the story. Blake lifted elements from the most legendary of Hawaiian surfers, Kelea, for his heroine: both arrive on O'ahu from a distant island, borrow a surfboard to ride the waves at Waikīkī, and boast "clear skin, sparkling eyes."[9] Moloa and Nani fall in love in the surf. They travel to the forest to select a tree from which Moloa will shape a surfboard for Nani, who has become Moloa's soul mate. Blake describes her as his "apt and willing pupil to learn the teachings of the kahunas of his boyhood. He also found Nani eager to learn the laws of life, thereby rounding out a mutual understanding for which Moloa praised the gods for his good luck."[10] What Blake seems to be up to is recasting his negative experiences at Waikīkī into positive ones. Nani is a stand-in for Blake's wife Francis Cunningham, a young Native American from Oklahoma whose father worked in the film industry.[11] They honeymooned in Hawai'i from late August to early December in 1925 (he was twenty-three; she was eighteen) but divorced upon returning to the mainland.[12] In the story, Moloa tells the king of his plan to take Nani away from the islands and raise a family: "He asked the king to honor their children who would some day seek the pleasures of surfriding at Waikiki."[13] Blake "had few regrets" in life, according to his biographers. But Blake's protégé Tommy Zahn revealed an important one: "I think his *only* regret—and it was keen—[was] not

Francis Cunningham and Tom Blake on their honeymoon at the Outrigger Canoe Club, Waikīkī, 1925. (The Croul Family Collection.)

having a son."[14] Santa Monica lifeguard Wally Burton added, "For their honeymoon—[Blake] told me this himself—on the honeymoon they went over there and she saw very little of Tom. He was surfing all the time."[15] Blake shaped a board for Francis, but she refused to paddle it out. In Nani, Blake was able to rescue a failed marriage and transform Francis into a life partner who shared his love of the waves and provided children to continue his surfing legacy: "For there came to Moloa with full force a desire to have this beautiful girl, this surfrider, bear him children who could also enjoy the fine things of life he had shared so fully."[16]

Blake was also able to triumph over the local surfers who didn't appreciate him showing them up in the Waikīkī races after the development of his hollow surfboard. Moloa "loved the sea," Blake wrote, "but not the life of the court. After all he was a stranger from another land and only by the king's special favor was he tolerated by some of the alii (nobility)." One can't help but imagine Duke as the king in the story, and his brothers and friends cast as nobility. In chapter 3 of his book, Blake describes Duke as embodying the qualities of King Kamehameha I (ruled 1795–1819): "Because I am so familiar with the deeds of Kamehameha I described in old literature and because I have had the opportunity of closely studying Duke, I see a parallel of character and physical make-up between the two, that would, in my mind, allow Kamehameha to beat the world at sport and Duke to rule the islands."[17] Blake escapes the typical beatings that other mainland surfers often endured (like Gene "Tarzan" Smith) because of his close connection to Duke, who wrote the Introduction to *Hawaiian Surfboard*. Blake detailed Moloa's situation at court: "There existed among some of the alii, always an undercurrent of hatred and jealousy. Twice his food had been poisoned by kahunas working in the interest of those who found Moloa's place in the court life detrimental to their own ends. Especially his success in the races prompted these attempts upon his life."[18] In terms of linking the court nobility to Duke's brothers, recall what Blake wrote in his personal scrapbook across the *Honolulu Advertiser* article that had reported his win in 1930: "BEAT SAM & SARGENT KAHANAMOKU TO WIN THE MAJOR KING CUP. HOW THEY BURNED UP!!!"[19]

Luckily, Moloa was able to escape death through his cleverness: "Moloa, being of high intelligence, was able to interpret this work of the kahuna and moreover had a name for it. He called it poisoning, thereby exposing the cult of praying to death as a most easily understood game of where one pays the kahuna enough and he poisons the enemy and makes it look like death from natural causes thereby fooling the people and saving his own neck."[20] According to Tommy Zahn and Santa Monica lifeguard Chauncey Granstrom, Blake fixated on the idea that Waikīkī locals were out to get him.[21] Moloa provided Blake a belated opportunity to show that he had outsmarted his enemies and foiled their plans.

Blake established other similarities between himself and Moloa, but his motivations seem clear. A regular performer on Hollywood sets for more than two decades, Blake sketches his early experiences at Waikīkī as the plot of a South Seas Adventure: the hero breezes in, overcomes all challengers, grabs the prize, wins the girl, and sails off into the sunset ("When the night was on and the full moon new in the sky, Nani and Moloa sailed quietly past the Kalahuewehe surf and into the open sea").[22] Blake is "playing Indian" to the extreme here: appropriating Native Hawaiian identity and inserting himself into Hawaiian history alongside legendary figures.

Before charting the influence of *Hawaiian Surfboard* on later surf histories, it's worth referring to the quotation that opens this chapter, excerpted from a period book review ("'Hawaiian Surfboard' is the ideal aloha gift and should be of keen interest to the tourist"). The review praises the illustrations (nearly fifty of them), many of which were supplied by two agencies centered on tourism: the Pan-Pacific Press Bureau and the Hawaii Tourist Bureau.[23] The opening photograph in *Hawaiian Surfboard*—a portrait of teenaged hula dancer Pualani Mossman—sets the tone in many ways for the rest of the book. Mossman is smiling, extending a lei to welcome the reader as if we were arriving in Hawai'i. She's on her knees, arms and shoulders bare: young, attractive, sensual, inviting. She had starred in *Song of the Islands* the year before (1934), an early color film that showcased the beauty and romance of Hawai'i through the tradition of throwing a lei into the ocean as one departs the islands, a promise to return someday. In 1937 Mossman became the "Matson Girl" when the steamship company hired her to promote its cruise lines. "For more than 50 years," reported the *Honolulu Star-Bulletin* in her 2006 obituary, "Pualani Mossman (Avon) epitomized the image of a Hawaiian hula dancer as the original poster girl for Matson cruises and the Hawaii Visitors Bureau."[24] Mossman's photograph and the book review alert us that *Hawaiian Surfboard* presents more than surfing history and the promotion of Blake's hollow surfboards: we are entering the realm of tourism. The publisher, Paradise of the Pacific, began as a periodical in 1888 with a slogan boosting tourism and investment: "Hawaii for Health, Pleasure and Profit."[25] Blake's content plays to the American tourist and evokes a mindset similar to the one that had justified arguments for U.S. annexation of the Hawaiian Islands.

That mindset expresses itself in narratives where mainlanders like Blake arrive in the islands and show their superiority to the natives. A figure like Moloa becomes "more native" than the indigenous people through his study of local history and tradition, and triumphs over them in their own cultural practices (like surfing). Essentially, the visitor "knows better" than the native, and this knowledge precipitates justification for taking control of everything from cultural artifacts to land and government. Here is Blake's story of restoring Abner Pākī's surfboards in the Bishop Museum:

> For twenty years or more they had been hanging or tied with wire against the stone wall on the outside of the museum, covered with some old reddish paint and rather neglected.
>
> My inquiries into the art of surfriding disclosed to me the true value of these two old koa boards. They are the only two ancient surfboards of authentic olo design known to be in existence.[26]

Blake tells us that his study revealed "the true value" of the surfboards, and he eventually convinces the museum's board members to allow him to restore them, and they promise to give the boards a more prominent location. In this scenario, the visitor knows island traditions better than the islanders themselves, and he succeeds in establishing the correct value system.

Chapters 1 and 2 of this study mention Blake's great influence on both his contemporaries and the generation of young surfers after World War II. Here we can jump ahead to the late 1950s for Blake's influence on the writing of surf history itself—Ben R. Finney's master's thesis in anthropology at the University of Hawai'i at Mānoa, "Hawaiian Surfing, A Study of Cultural Change" (1959). Finney's research—published the following decade with James D. Houston as *Surfing: The Sport of Hawaiian Kings* (1966)—represents the first academic scholarship on surfing and has long been the starting point for Western histories of the sport. Finney's central argument springs from Ernest Beaglehole's theory of "cultural peaks," which Finney applies to Hawaiian surfing: "In Hawaii a cultural peak developed in regard to surfing; i.e., Hawaiian surfing is a complex that was selected from an Oceanic pattern of body-board surfing and given formal elaboration."[27] In other words, as Finney and Houston later state in *Surfing: The Sport of Hawaiian Kings,* "throughout the Pacific no island group developed surfing to the level of sophistication attained in Hawaii in pre-European times."[28] Tom Blake states precisely the same idea on the first page of *Hawaiian Surfboard:* "The first migrators from the South Seas probably brought the idea of surfriding on boards with them. I feel, however, that the art reached its highest development in Hawaii."[29] Influence casts a tricky shadow. It's not clear if Finney was directly influenced by Blake here, but the coincidence encourages us to look for further correlations.

Hawaiian Surfboard offered Finney a helpful list of sources, one of which was George Washington Bates, whose five-paragraph description of an idyllic Waikīkī in the 1850s (quoted in *Hawaiian Surfboard*) spurred Blake to write, "This is a very pretty picture of Waikiki beach. I would give my best surfboard to find it like that again some bright morning when I come down from Kaimuki."[30] Two pages later, he adds: "Aside from the charm of Bates' description of old Waikiki it establishes the fact that under those conditions, surfriding was, indeed a lost art. I feel, however, that there was always surfriding at Waikiki beach, on some kind of a board. Waikiki's condition in 1854 indicates that the great popularity of the national pastime, surfriding, was but a memory."[31]

Bates becomes one of Finney's sources for his master's thesis argument that surfing nearly died out in the nineteenth century, and that "the first impetus in the revival of surfing came from Caucasians," principally Alexander Hume Ford, who spearheaded the founding of the Outrigger Canoe Club at Waikīkī in 1908.[32] Finney likely drew this information from Blake, who gave Ford primary credit for leading "the true revival of the sport."[33] Although Blake also mentions a number of Native Hawaiians who preceded Ford, Finney nevertheless sticks with his race-based conclusion: "The revival of surfing nowhere occurred among the natives until the Caucasian's interest in the sport in Hawaii."[34] Finney tones down the assertion in his book with Houston by mentioning the contributions of mixed-race Hawaiian George Freeth, but his point basically remains the same: "Also prominent in the new movement was Alexander Hume Ford, an adventurous mainlander who was so enamored with the sport that he took it upon himself to personally boost its revival and popularization."[35] Crediting Ford for pulling the sport back from the brink of extinction—which in itself is a myth, considering surfing in fact endured throughout the nineteenth century—is essentially the same narrative that Blake proffers in the figure of Moloa and in his account of restoring Abner Pākī's surfboards: the newcomer to the islands who understands indigenous cultural practices better than the natives and shows them what it's worth.[36] In Ford's case, following Finney's narrative, that meant recognizing the importance of surfing and organizing a largely whites-only club to preserve it.[37]

George Washington Bates arrived in the islands himself in early 1853, a "roving correspondent" for a San Francisco newspaper.[38] Blake appreciated the romantic description of Waikīkī in Bates' book, *Sandwich Island Notes* (1854), and the following statement of surfing is what informed Blake's reference to the sport as "a lost art": "Of the numerous national games and amusements formerly practiced by the Hawaiians, surf-bathing [i.e., surfing] is about the only one which has not become extinct. Lahaina is the only place on the group where it is maintained with any degree of enthusiasm, and even there it is rapidly passing out of existence."[39] Bates's primary purpose for visiting the islands, however, was to promote annexation by the United States. He and others feared that England or France would annex the islands first, thus securing dominance in the Pacific. Bates argued: "The Hawaiians, as a race, are physically and morally doomed to pass away. . . . The probability is, that, if brought exclusively under the fostering care of the American people, a wreck of the people may be saved; otherwise, no legislation, civil or religious, can long perpetuate their existence."[40] If Bates had actually witnessed a surf session in the islands, he would not have taken it as a sign of cultural endurance. He was too committed to the prospect, and the ensuing commercial profit, of annexation. It was a foregone conclusion even before he left San Francisco on the *Sovereign of the Seas* that the Hawaiian Islands needed saving from the Hawaiian people.[41]

Bates's narrative of surfing and Hawaiian culture dying out—biased by his political goal of annexation—was picked up and repeated by Blake, and later informed Finney's assertion that Caucasians had recognized the importance of surfing and saved the sport from near extinction. The mindset behind Bates's claim that the Hawaiian people could only be saved if they were "brought exclusively under the fostering care of the American people" is the same one that justified Blake's restoration of ancient surfboards, or Finney's insistence on the role of Caucasians at Waikīkī in 1908. They are rescue narratives, as illusory as any Hollywood adventure film and cast with white heroes.

Here is James Jackson Jarves, for example—quoted by Blake in *Hawaiian Surfboard* and later appearing in Finney's history—describing the demise of Native Hawaiian sports like surfing and the salutary work of the missionaries, who had arrived in Hawai'i in 1820: "In 1847 the scene has greatly changed. Christianity has provided schools, medical science and churches. Moral stimulation is at work to elevate, preserve and arrest the obliteration of the Hawaiian race from the earth and give a pass port to fut[u]rity."[42] Here is missionary child Nathaniel B. Emerson, a significant resource for Finney (also referenced in Blake), in his "Causes of Decline of Ancient Hawaiian Sports" (1892): "But [surf-riding] too has felt the touch of the new civilization, and to-day it is hard to find a surf-board outside of our museums and private collections."[43] Here is Jack London, nearly twenty-five years later, relying on the same narrative in his description of how surfing could be used to boost tourism and populate the islands with (white) residents: "Not only did the Hawaii-born not talk about it, but they forgot about it. Just as the sport was at its dying gasp, along came one Alexander Hume Ford from the mainland."[44] Finney relied on this same narrative, and his history of surfing became the most respected academic source on the sport well into the twenty-first century.

Historians have offered helpful readings within the past decade on the complex relationship between whites and Native Hawaiians in early twentieth-century Hawai'i, especially in the context of U.S. imperialism and the sport of surfing. Isaiah Helekunihi Walker, evoking Houston Wood's *Displacing Natives: The Rhetorical Production of Hawai'i,* speaks to the "kama'āina anti-conquest," a usage of the Hawaiian term *kama'āina* (literally, "child of the land") that positioned whites as benevolent curators of indigenous Hawaiian traditions and artifacts (like surfboards) in ways that conveniently obscured the whites' responsibilities for the eradication of those traditions.[45] Similarly, Scott Laderman, drawing on Gary Okihiro's *Island World: A History of Hawai'i and the United States,* cites the "racialized burden" whites took upon themselves to bring Western Civilization to the islands; Laderman offers a comprehensive analysis of Alexander Hume Ford's role in this process and his use of surfing to consolidate imperial power "in the interests of whites."[46]

Tom Blake certainly falls into the role of Wood's *kama'āina* as he spied the *olo* boards at the Bishop Museum, acting the part of those "enlightened moderns who sometimes kindly serve as curators for exotic Native artifacts that the Natives themselves cannot properly take care of."[47] Ford explicitly referred to himself as "kamaaina" after living in the islands for a month and testing the waves ("for I have learned to ride your native surf-board, and in memory of that victory and the toils and pains that accompanied it, I believe I may be fairly inscribed as one who has suffered sufficiently on your islands to love them and sympathize with them").[48] Ford might as well be George Washington Bates here—Ford was a strong proponent for Hawai'i's statehood—his love and sympathy bestowed not upon the native people but rather upon the true target of annexation and statehood: the islands themselves.[49] Overall, the rescue narratives work as a blanket justification for appropriating cultural traditions and assuming political control of the land and its people. In this context, we have to wonder if the narrative itself—running from Bates and Emerson through Ford, London, Blake, and Finney—endures precisely because it's a story that, at heart, many white people really want to believe in.

Hawaiian Surfboard, then, is not so much a history as it is a powerful discourse that marshals a mainlander's Anglocentric view of surfing's past and guides readers to the conclusion that surfing's future lies with Western innovation. The book works as an extended eulogy, praising Native Hawaiians and simultaneously marking them as obsolete. Blake writes that the islanders who first came into contact with Captain James Cook in the 1780s were "as primitive as the world has ever known, yet were as wise as any the world knows today."[50] Jane C. Desmond has argued in *Staging Tourism: Bodies on Display from Waikiki to Sea World,* that representations of islanders at the turn of the twentieth century "actively constructed an image of Native Hawaiians as primitives living in the past," which ultimately helped serve as a foil for Euro-Americans' emerging sense of modernity.[51] Blake's words and illustrations consistently follow this pattern, framing Native Hawaiians as relics that Blake himself, along with other whites, have superseded.[52] His sense of modernity connected strongly to technological innovation, which he credited for his wins in the hundred-yard and quarter-mile races at Waikīkī: "as is true in yacht and other similar racing, I won because I had a superior board."[53] We have already referenced a visual parallel of this idea in chapter 1, where Blake positioned his hollow surfboard as the evolutionary culmination of Hawaiian surfboard shaping. *Hawaiian Surfboard* as a whole pursues this same progression; its four chapters are essentially divided into two parts in the table of contents: the "Ancient Hawaiian Legends" and "Early Hawaiian Historical Period" of surfriding, followed by "Modern Surfriding" and "How to Use the New Hollow Surfboard."[54] The sequence and rhetoric of his chapter titles lead the reader from past to present, from Native Hawaiian traditions to the self-appointed heir of those traditions—author and champion surfer, Tom Blake.

Beyond the influence of *Hawaiian Surfboard* on subsequent histories of surfing, the great impact that Blake had on future generations was not his hollow surfboard, whose design fell quickly out of favor after World War II owing to innovations in foam and fiberglass, but his concept of recreation and leisure, which he learned from Native Hawaiians and developed in some detail in his book:

> I have learned much from these people.
>
> Acquaintances in the States have asked me why I bury myself in the Hawaiian Islands. The reason is because I like it. It fits my nature, it is life's compensation for such a nature as mine. I like it because I can live simple and quietly here. I can live well, without the social life. I can dress as I please, for comfort, usually it's a pair of canvas sneakers, light trousers and a sleeveless polo shirt with swimming trunks all day. I like the Islands because I can keep one hundred percent sun-tan here the year around, rest and sleep for hours in the wonderful sunshine each day.[55]

Blake modeled this ideal in his everyday life as much as possible. He never held a permanent job, and he tried to organize his life around spending time at the beach. He did not feel the need to apologize for this lifestyle. On the contrary, he embraced it openly. The only precursor we might point to in California who lived a similar life was George Freeth, who also chose to live by the beach whenever possible, from Los Angeles to San Diego, and preferred the precarious vocation of lifeguarding—mostly a seasonal job—to more established occupations that he resorted to in times of financial necessity.[56] But Freeth was no apologist for his life, as Blake was, and Blake knew little about his predecessor.[57]

We gain a sense of Blake's antiestablishment attitude when he describes mainland friends who inquire about his life ("Acquaintances in the States have asked me why I bury myself in the Hawaiian Islands"). Blake was writing in the heart of the Depression, of course, a time when most people were eagerly seeking work, not trying to escape it. The Depression's great gift to California beach culture was forced leisure time. As Paul Johnson mentions in his account of how he became interested in beach volleyball: "There were no jobs to be found in town at all, so most of us either went to work for our parents or waited it out."[58] Johnson was a club member and more fortunate than most, but even those less fortunate had to rely on patching together jobs to get by (with the national unemployment rate

Tom Blake striking a pose and setting an early standard for casual beachwear. Malibu, 1928. (The Croul Family Collection.)

soaring to nearly 25 percent by 1933).[59] Surfing requires a great deal of time to learn the basic skills, and even more time to understand and take advantage of ideal surfing conditions in the ocean. One often has to travel great distances, and even then, riding waves becomes a waiting game—for the swell to arrive, for the wind to cooperate, for the tide to rise or drop, and for that single wave to break in your direction. Blake benefitted from a number of privileges at Waikīkī, but money was not one of them. He idealized the life of a Hawaiian beachboy, and though he ultimately could not sustain that life on the beaches of Hawaiʻi or California (or Florida or New York, for that matter), his simple, occasionally poetic prose celebrated it as a goal well worth pursuing. His ideals appealed to Californians of the 1930s who, as Kevin Starr notes, represented "the emergence of a pleasure-seeking, leisure-oriented society that contained within itself the formula for post-war America."[60]

Before leaving *Hawaiian Surfboard,* we should mention bodysurfing, a sport that Blake touches upon and whose influence on beach culture we have not yet charted. In a reference that sends us back to our prologue and the influence of Duke Kahanamoku, Blake calls Duke "the world's outstanding body-surfer" and notes that the sport has a long Hawaiian tradition. Duke, in fact, had given readers of the *Los Angeles Times* a quick tutorial on the sport in August 1927 while he was filming *Hula* with Clara Bow, to whom he was giving lessons. He called it *ho'o pae umauma* ("to surf on the chest") and described the importance of judging waves, timing the take-off, positioning the head and body correctly, and riding on a cushion of water ahead of the breaker. Underneath a dynamic picture of Duke in full swan-dive mode—head up, arms spread, bursting ahead of an ocean wave—he mentions that the sport of bodysurfing in Hawai'i was "just about as popular as that of riding the surfboard."[61] Duke seems to have bodysurfed wherever he traveled when given the opportunity—France, New Jersey, Australia—and the same was true for his trips to California.[62] His first time in Los Angeles—visiting George Freeth in the summer of 1913—Duke had to beach his board in Redondo when the waves didn't cooperate, but he and Bobby Kaawa salvaged the day by "shooting the surf without boards."[63] Freeth bodysurfed himself, and, like Duke, made a practice of offering free instruction as part of his lifeguard duties.[64]

Bodysurfing undoubtedly arose with coastal communities around the world, the only requisite skills being a knowledge of both swimming and ocean waves. Native Hawaiians like Freeth and Duke actively practiced the sport in California and gave instruction through the teens and twenties, but bodysurfing remained the stepchild to surfing and paddleboarding in the rise of California beach culture—perhaps because bodysurfing needed no equipment, and so there was little to develop, refine, or market. In 1931, Los Angeles city lifeguard Ron Drummond could write in his introduction to *The Art of Wave Riding*—a twenty-six-page booklet that served as an instruction manual—that "few people" were familiar with bodysurfing, a sport he considered to be "in its initial stages of development."[65] Olympic swimmer Wally O'Connor provided this testimonial for Drummond's publication: "A great deal of publicity has been given the Hawaiian swimmers on riding waves with surfboards. Without a doubt it is a great sport, but in my estimation it cannot compare with the thrills, pleasure, and exercise of body surfing."[66] Bodysurfing had its fierce supporters, but, as O'Connor indicates, it couldn't match the publicity of surfing. One could theoretically bodysurf at any beach in the world where waves broke a reasonable distance off shore. Surfing, however, was first marketed as a sport unique to the Hawaiian Islands. Recall Alexander Hume Ford's pitch from 1908: "Anyone can learn to ride the surf-board at Waikiki. It is doubtful if the beginner would ever learn in any other surf in the world."[67] Even in the 1930s, after two decades of surfing in the Golden State, the allure of riding Waikīkī's waves captivated every surfer in California. Bodysurfing wasn't

The Art of Wave Riding, by Ron Drummond, 1931. (The Croul Family Collection.)

able to generate that same romance, and so it remained a fun yet generic beach activity in Southern California.

The sport also didn't attract dedicated photographers like Tom Blake, "Doc" Ball, or Don James who could promote its excitement and danger. Drummond included a dozen action shots of waves and bodysurfing in *The Art of Wave Riding*, but the swimmer (mostly Drummond himself) is often difficult to discern in the distance. There's little to get excited about visually, and the writing favors technical instruction over artistic expression. Bodysurfing did maintain a presence in contests here and there throughout the 1930s. Long Beach lifeguard Ted Sizemore (his stepsister, Katie, married PVSC member Leroy Grannis) won the bodysurfing event at the 1932 PCSRC in Corona del Mar.[68] Huntington Beach maintained bodysurfing events in its annual Black and Gold Days through the end of the 1930s, but the only listing of a club that might have helped to promote the sport along the lines of the PVSC occurred in San Diego county's Del Mar, where a group of men in their twenties held contests and issued prizes.[69]

In its issue for August 26, 1940, *Life* ran a short blurb on bodysurfing, accompanied by five action photographs—"Surf Riding On California Beach Is A Favorite Summertime Sport." The profile used a handful of bodysurfers at Santa Monica to represent beaches across the state: "There ["California beaches"] almost every boy and girl is an expert surf rider. After school, after work, over a weekend, or just any time at all they trek down to the beach, spend hour after hour playing in the waves, swallowing water, scraping stomachs on the sand, occasionally getting a long, spectacular ride which leaves them belly-down, high and dry on the beach."[70] The article described the popularity of bodysurfing, but *Life*'s coverage of stand-up surfing at Palos Verdes two years earlier (February 7, 1938) shows how much more publicity this latter sport typically received: nine photographs in all—four by "Doc" Ball and five of Mary Ann Hawkins at Bluff Cove.[71] The photographs embellished the dangers of surfing (Kay Murray diving from his board at Hermosa Beach) and its sensual side (Mary Ann Hawkins poised on a wave in her white bathing suit), aspects that were hard to reproduce in pictures of bodysurfing.

Beyond bolstering California's image as a summertime haven of sand and surf, the bodysurfing article in *Life* registered how far California beach culture had come since the days of seasonal lifeguards, chronic drownings, and beachgoers in Victorian bathing suits clutching at lifelines when waves pushed through. The youngest generation of Californians was as comfortable at the beach as they were on roller skates or bicycles, and their ease in the waves built the foundation for an emerging lifestyle that the rest of the nation wanted to emulate. Hawai'i maintained its attraction for mainlanders, of course, but California beaches had firmly established their own distinctive allure for health, sport, and sex appeal.

California Beach Culture during World War II

Hawaiian music and dance were extremely popular at our surfing beaches in the thirties and forties. Everyone wanted to go to the islands and experience the culture firsthand. Ironically, the war sent many to the tropics, but the net results were a bit different than the dreamers had anticipated.[1]

—Don James

More than eight hundred thousand Californians served in World War II, and about a million soldiers and defense workers passed through the Hawaiian Islands during the four-year conflict, influencing the future growth of both Hawaiian tourism and California beach culture.[2] That influence began, of course, the morning of December 7, 1941, when Japanese airplanes attacked Pearl Harbor and triggered U.S. entry into the war. It was one of those dates inscribed on public memory. Everybody knew exactly where they were.

Twenty-year-old Don James and two friends, Ed Fearon and Jack Quigg, were relaxing on the beach at Topanga, just down the coast from Malibu. "It was a balmy Sunday," James recalled, "and the news about the Japanese attack upon Pearl Harbor was coming in over the radio. We were paying sixty dollars a month for rent, which was split three ways, and life was good. Suddenly, everything had changed. We all knew we were going off to war."[3] Twenty-four-year-old PVSC member Leroy Grannis related: "We were in the water off Hermosa Pier with a pretty good winter swell running, when someone paddled out to shout the news that Pearl Harbor had been bombed and the Pacific Fleet sunk."[4] Grannis said that the next day, he and "Doc" Ball were by the pier collecting redwood that had floated in on the tide, "talking about Pearl Harbor. We knew it would never be the same again."[5]

Ed Fearon, Don James, and Jack Quigg at Topanga Point, December 7, 1941. (Don James/Courtesy Tom Adler.)

Fellow PVSC member E. J. Oshier, 350 miles away in Santa Cruz, was surfing the San Lorenzo River mouth when he got word. He was riding a wave near the cliff when a guy shouted the news at him. Oshier called him "a rotten no-good," his spite born more from the message, perhaps, than the messenger.[6] He had already joined the National Guard and was living in Oakland, traveling down to Santa Cruz to ride waves on weekends. But not anymore, not after that message. He paddled in and reported to Camp Roberts, 120 miles to the south.

The massive changes required to mobilize the nation for war impacted California beach culture in predictable ways. The first was to pull many young people off the beaches and outfit them for military service or defense industry work. Even those with 3-A deferments—men with dependents, which included Grannis and Ball—eventually volunteered for duty. Grannis enlisted in the Army Air Corps, and Ball in the Coast Guard Reserve.[7] Tom Blake, calling it "the thing to do," was forty years old when he joined the Coast Guard Reserve in 1942.[8] War had been at the back of their minds since September 1, 1939, when hostilities began in Europe after Germany attacked Poland. Two days earlier, as Ball was finishing his newsletter, he printed across the top of the front page: "WHILE YE SPINSHEET GOES TO PRESS WE WAIT THE GRIM ANNOUNCEMENT ON THE RADIO***   WAR???????"[9] Two years later, after Japanese planes sank twenty-one ships at Pearl Harbor and destroyed or damaged more than three hundred aircraft, killing more than twenty-four hundred U.S. soldiers and civilians, the war hit home and upended everybody's life.[10]

Lifeguards, the backbone of California beach culture since the time of George Freeth, were among the most enthusiastic volunteers in the war effort. Redondo Beach reported in the summer of 1942, for example, that nine of its seasonal guards were leaving for duty in the Coast Guard; the city had no idea who was going to replace them.[11] Los Angeles County reported in its annual review (1941–1942) that twenty of its seasonal guards had joined various branches of the military. The report also noted two veteran lifeguards who had died in airplane crashes: twenty-five-year-old first lieutenant Rudy J. Binder on a reconnaissance flight, and ensign Edwin Hold, also twenty-five, during a flight-training mission. These were among the 26,019 Californians who ultimately died in the conflict.[12] "Many people owe their lives to the alertness and ability of these two boys as life guards," read the report. "They were fine fellows and will be greatly missed."[13]

The Coast Guard announced in August 1942 that it had begun a program to recruit men aged forty to forty-five for shore-patrol service in Southern California; the older recruits would allow younger men completing those tasks to ship out for duty "on the high seas."[14] The *Wilmington Daily Press Journal* reported that the Coast Guard would take anyone physically able to do the work but preferred war veterans, boatmen, and lifeguards. Tom Blake, who had been working as a lifeguard in Santa Monica, asked captain George Watkins to write him a letter of recommendation so that that he could join the Coast Guard, which he did later that month.[15] After training on Catalina and San Clemente Islands, Blake supervised beach-patrol units at the lifeboat station at Port Arguello in Santa Barbara County. He disenrolled from the Coast Guard Temporary Reserve in November of that year and elected to join the regular Coast Guard Reserve for the remainder of the war. He continued to supervise beach-patrol and canine units in Santa Barbara and at the Naval Air Station on Whidbey Island in Puget Sound. He filled most of his final year in the Coast Guard loading ammunition at the Receiving Station on Bay and Powell streets in San Francisco. Because of his age, he was discharged in July 1945, several months before the end of the war.[16]

"Pete" Peterson left his lifeguarding job in Santa Monica when he was inducted into the navy rather late in the conflict—February 1944.[17] After boot camp at the Naval Training Station in Farragut, Idaho, and extensive training in New Orleans and Little Creek (Virginia) as a diver and shipfitter—plus some anti-aircraft machine gun instruction thrown in for good measure—he steamed to the Pacific theater in April 1945 on the *U.S.S. Pandemus,* a landing craft repair ship.[18] The *Pandemus* joined the battle for

Jom Blake, SP./c. U.S.C.G.
AUG. 1942

Specialist First Class Tom Blake, U.S. Coast Guard, 1942. (The Croul Family Collection.)

Okinawa (April 1 to June 22, 1945), one of the fiercest engagements of the war. An estimated 12,500 U.S. soldiers were killed or missing, and more than two hundred thousand Okinawans (Ryūkyūans) and Japanese died. Hundreds of kamikaze attacks destroyed or damaged navy ships, including one that narrowly missed the *Pandemus* itself.[19] Peterson earned a Bronze Star for his service in the Okinawa Gunto Operation from June 13 to July 15.[20] He continued his ship repair duties at Guam and the Philippines, participating in the final liberation of these latter islands from August 4 to September 6. After Japan surrendered on August 14, 1945, the *Pandemus* spent three months in Shanghai, China before returning to the United States, where Peterson was discharged in March 1946.[21]

"Doc" Ball also served in the Pacific Theater, using his dentistry skills aboard the *U.S.S. General H. L. Scott.* The ship transported soldiers and supplies to and from the southern and western Pacific, plying between San Francisco and New Caledonia, the Marshalls, the New Hebrides, New

"Doc" Ball served in the U.S. Coast Guard Reserve aboard the *U.S.S. General H. L. Scott.* (John Heath "Doc" Ball.)

Guinea, and the Philippines.[22] Always a health nut, Ball "would circle the *Scott*'s boat deck twice daily, scooping a bucket of ocean water from the mess deck bay and taking a sip or two to 'keep him in touch'."[23] Ball recognized the benefits of exercise on reducing stress during the long voyages, the taste of salt water perhaps recalling more carefree days at Bluff Cove.

The most influential surfers of the period—contest organizers, board builders, surfing club enthusiasts—were out of commission for much of the war. "Adie" Bayer, stalwart of the PVSC and perennial president of the West Coast Paddleboard Association, joined the Coast Guard. Meyers Butte, founder of the Pacific System Homes surfboard factory, stopped production and entered the navy. "Whitey" Harrison, with two daughters (Virginia and Rose), worked as a commercial abalone diver in Orange County. Mary

Ann Hawkins, married to Bud Morrissey, had a daughter (Kathleen) and gave swimming lessons in her backyard pool in the San Fernando Valley.[24]

Nationwide gas rationing, imposed in December 1942, also lowered the number of California beachgoers by limiting their access. The measure was intended to reduce wear on automobile tires, whose natural rubber was needed for the war effort after Japan seized control of supply hubs in Malaysia. A similar rationale had prompted a national speed limit of thirty-five miles an hour in May 1942. Because automobile plants converted to building military vehicles full-time, no new civilian cars or trucks were sold beginning in January 1942. California beach culture had flourished in the wake of automobile and highway expansion throughout the 1920s and 1930s. But much of that enthusiasm came to a screeching halt, so to speak. Most regular ("Class A") drivers could only buy three to four gallons of gas per week. Under the best conditions, that supply probably fueled a one-way trip to San Onofre from Santa Monica (about eighty miles). Numbers recorded by Los Angeles County lifeguards on eleven beaches along the Santa Monica Bay tell a dramatic story of the fall and rise of beach attendance during and after the war. The guards reported seventeen million visits in 1942–1943, down from twenty-seven million in 1941–1942, a number that dropped to just under thirteen million in 1944–1945. Then the numbers soared: more than forty million visits in 1945–1946. The annual report attributed the change to "the ending of hostilities and the lifting of gasoline rationing."[25] The busiest beaches were those that offered the most parking. Hermosa Beach, with nearly two miles of ocean frontage, recorded thirteen million visits all by itself in 1945–1946. "Thousands of people could be seen driving up and down the coast," stated the report, "seeking a place where they could park their cars."[26]

A contributing factor to fewer beach visits in Los Angeles County was the quarantine imposed by the California State Board of Public Health from spring 1943 to summer 1947. The Hyperion sewage treatment plant, located midway between Hermosa Beach and Venice, lacked the chlorine to sanitize raw sewage dumped into the Santa Monica Bay. To protect public health, the state board banned ocean bathing along ten miles of coast for more than four years.[27] At times the quarantine stretched into Santa Monica, the very heart of beach-culture activity during the previous two decades.[28] Given the lack of personnel, however, the order was often hard to enforce. Medical reports from area doctors during the war found "large increases in intestinal diseases in proportion to the numbers of ocean swimmers."[29] As soon as the Hyperion plant began regular chemical treatment of sewage rather than simply trying to screen it, ocean bathing, and sports like surfing, started up safely once again.

The imposing military presence on many California beaches probably also deterred visitors. Reports of Japanese aircraft flying over San Francisco on December 8, 1941—supposedly launched from Japanese carriers sitting offshore—had spread fear throughout the state. The *Los Angeles Times* announced the next morning: "ENEMY PLANES SIGHTED OVER CALIFORNIA COAST."[30] A fifteen-mile blackout was ordered around the port of Los Angeles directly after the attack on Pearl Harbor.[31] By the end of the month, a coastal railway gun battery—two eight-inch guns capable of firing a 260-pound shell more than eighteen miles—had been stationed on a spur track between 18th and 19th Streets in Manhattan Beach to protect Los Angeles Harbor.[32]

Fears heightened even more after a Japanese submarine shelled the beach at Ellwood Oil Field, near Santa Barbara, the night of February 23, 1942. Thirty-two hours later, on the morning of February 25, machine-gun fire and anti-aircraft shells pierced the skies of Los Angeles for several hours. Although the incident turned out to be a false alarm—blamed on "war nerves" by Secretary of the Navy Frank Knox—many were convinced that a coastal invasion was imminent.[33] The following month, the Western Defense Command began the forced evacuation of Japanese Americans on the West Coast. More than 112,000 residents were eventually transferred to internment camps.[34] The *Santa Ana Register* reported in May 1942 that about eight hundred people of Japanese ancestry reported to the civil control station near San Onofre, an area known as "Little Tokyo." The group would be evacuated two days later to the internment camp at Poston, Arizona.[35] San Onofre itself had already been taken over by the U.S. Marines as part of the military buildup. The entire Santa Margarita Ranch was acquired through eminent domain to establish Camp Pendleton, which became the largest military camp on the West Coast, stretching seventeen miles between Oceanside and San Clemente.[36] A Coast Guard beach patrol station was set up near the surf break at San Onofre, with two-man foot patrols and their dogs checking the area.

The military commandeered the most strategic positions along the West Coast. At the northern end of Santa Monica Bay, for example, Point Dume housed an early warning air defense radar site and the U.S. Army's 37th Coast Artillery Brigade, which used the area as a training ground and firing range.[37] The army and Coast Guard ran beach patrols along twenty-one miles of Malibu coastline, with the Adamson Pool House at Surfrider Beach serving as the headquarters for eight Coast Guard stations.[38] Moving down the coast toward Palos Verdes and the southern end of Santa Monica Bay, gun batteries were located at Pacific Palisades, Playa del Rey, El Segundo, Manhattan Beach (the railway gun battery), Redondo Beach, and two

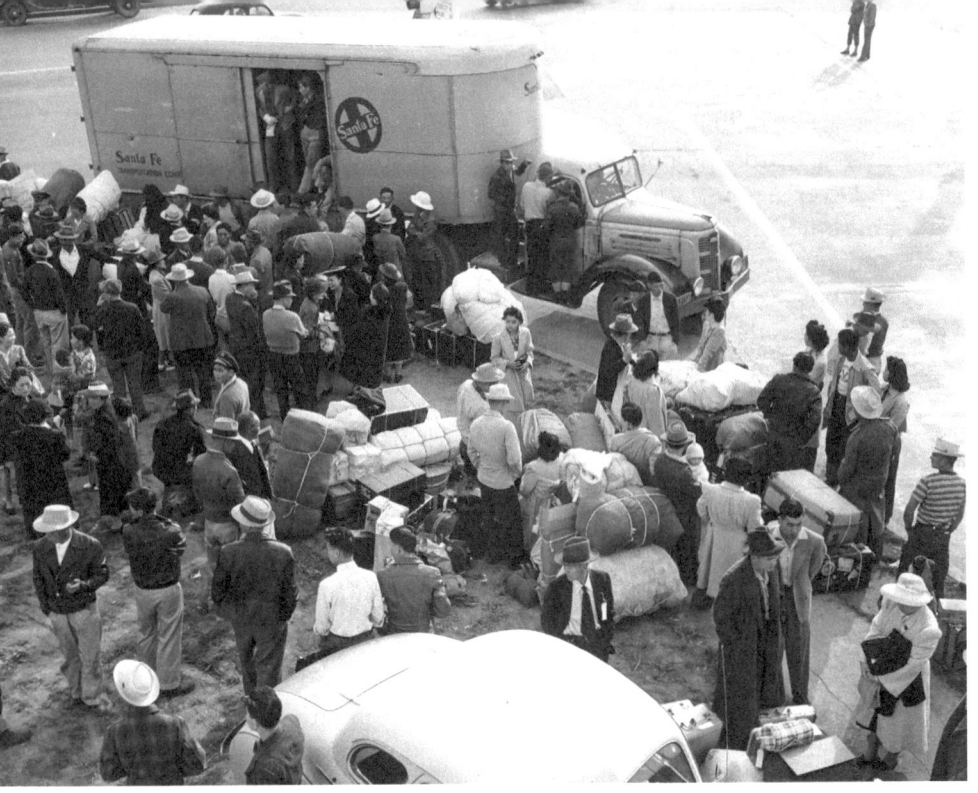

Transportation of Japanese Americans to Manzanar Internment Camp, Venice, California, April 1942. (PhotCL_555_01_1690, The Huntington Library, San Marino, California.)

locations at Palos Verdes: Rocky Point and Point Vicente.[39] In March 1942, several weeks after the shelling near Santa Barbara, the *Long Beach Press-Telegram* announced that antiaircraft batteries would begin target practice for the next month between Malibu and Newport Beach, firing at sleeve targets towed by airplanes.[40] Such piloting missions would be assumed by the Women Airforce Service Pilots (WASP) the following year, a group of more than a thousand women who had volunteered so that male pilots could be released for combat duty.[41] Pilots along the coast also practiced machine-gunning targets, in one case firing on the abandoned barge *Prentice*, lying a mile or so off Malibu. After several weeks of attacks, the barge caught fire and burned; some of its eighty-foot beams washed onto the beach at the Malibu Colony—certainly a deterrent for anybody thinking of paddling out for a surf session at Surfrider Beach.[42]

The thousands of soldiers and defense workers who inundated Los Angeles strained the resources of the county lifeguards. Many of the lifeguards were younger men, sixteen and seventeen, who had been hired in 1942 after 90 percent of the experienced lifeguards had entered the military.[43] The guards were forced to work odd shifts because the defense industry—more than 230,000 men and women in aviation alone by 1944—manufactured planes twenty-four hours a day, so workers came to the beach earlier and later than usual.[44] Moreover, lifeguard captain Theodore V. Warren described the visitors in his annual report as "largely eastern and mid-western people who are entirely unfamiliar with beach and surf conditions, and nearly every one of them constitute a potential rescue. A large portion of our rescues have been from these two groups."[45] Warren also mentioned that the inter-crew competitions that had become a staple of lifeguard programs up and down the coast—"Pete" Peterson had won the last championship in August 1941—were canceled owing to lack of personnel.[46] It was another sign of how the war, thousands of miles away in Europe and across the Pacific, had hit the brakes on California beach culture.

And yet certain activities managed to roll along. The beaches, though dangerous at times and frequently patrolled, remained open. In April and June 1942, the *Los Angeles Times* printed photographs of 1940 PCSRC winner Cliff Tucker and other "surfing cowboys" practicing for summer contests.[47] Early optimism, perhaps, since the events never took place, but surfers continued to enjoy the waves. Bluff Cove barred motorists in July 1942—barricades were installed to prevent cars from descending the cliff road—but surfing was permitted if you didn't mind carrying your board several hundred yards to the break.[48] In September 1942, the *Santa Cruz Sentinel* reported that five members of the local surfing club, including Richard Thompson and Bill Grace, planned a week's safari to San Onofre. Thompson had enlisted in the Coast Guard, and Grace in the Merchant Marines, so it was their bon voyage trip.[49] In June 1944, the *Los Angeles Times* reported the harrowing adventure of two families whose nine-year-old daughters had to drop into fox holes on the beach at San Onofre when U.S. Marines began firing at a target flare near them at dusk. "The tracer bullets were the worst," one of the fathers said. "They looked as big as baseballs and everyone seemed to have our names written on it."[50] The adults, a hundred yards away from the girls, crawled out of the line of fire. They eventually recouped their daughters, unharmed. The group had been informed that one section of the beach was open to the public; they had entered through an unguarded gate and wound up on a practice range. Officially, then, one could still access certain areas of San Onofre, but such newspaper stories would have discouraged the casual visitor, and perhaps even a wave-starved surfer.

Continuity surfaced in other ways, simple yet profound. In August 1944, "Pete" Peterson, on leave from the Amphibious Training Base in Virginia, drove to Palos Verdes with fifteen-year-old Matt Kivlin to enjoy some waves before reporting back. For all of the grand changes caused by the war—historic shifts in so many areas of society that altered the country and its place in the world—there were also meaningful gestures that maintained traditions from one generation to the next. An afternoon of surfing at Bluff Cove was one of those moments. Peterson was the top surfer and lifeguard in California at the time, winner of the most recent PCSRC at San Onofre (1941) and of the Pacific Coast lifeguard championships held at Venice (1941). Kivlin, working as a beachboy at the Jonathan Club in Santa Monica that summer, had some things in common with Peterson: both born in Texas, both interested in shaping boards (Kivlin had recently built a paddleboard in high school). Peterson, with only twelve days of leave to visit his six-year-old son, John, and pick up extra work as a lifeguard, could have hit Palos Verdes by himself. Instead, the most iconic waterman of his era asked a local teen if he wanted to try surfing. "He took me to the Cove," Kivlin recalled fifty-four years later, "and pushed me off on a few waves and I was really hooked."[51] Kivlin went on to become a key contributor to Malibu's postwar fame as a stylish surfer and shaper, ushering in a new era of lightweight balsa boards. Beyond the preference of prewar surfers to enjoy riding waves with others, the moment speaks to Peterson's humility and generosity, and his desire to pass on traditions whose normal channels—contests, surf clubs, and various social gatherings—had all but disappeared.

Despite the military buildup in the Long Beach area after the attack on Pearl Harbor—the arrival of sixty thousand new residents and sudden expansion of ship and aircraft manufacturing around the Port of Los Angeles—Victor Marshall still ran his beach concession on Alamitos Bay during summers, renting paddle boats, umbrellas, and surfboards.[52] Long Beach lifeguard captain Roy Miller managed to hire sixty-eight lifeguards to protect more than a hundred thousand visitors along eight miles of coast during the July 4th holiday in 1943.[53] Los Angeles County and the state of California continued to acquire beaches during the war for future development, including such desirable sites as Zuma in Malibu and Huntington Beach in Orange County.[54] And so, even with all the wartime changes and disruptions, there remained opportunities in Southern California to enjoy surfing, paddleboarding, and other beach-related activities. Beyond any general public spirit that focused individual effort on war-related causes rather than recreational pursuits, the real stalling mechanism to the continued development of beach culture during World War II remained the absence of key people and organized events that had fueled its tremendous growth from the mid-1930s—competitions, club gatherings, camping trips (beach fires were outlawed at night for much of the war), along with the entire social life surrounding such occasions.[55]

~

The *Whittier News,* representing a small community southeast of downtown Los Angeles, ran a column entitled "Our Men In Service" that gave regular updates from locals stationed in distant ports. In August 1944, weather officer Lieutenant Paul Hardin described the "excellent swimming and surf-board riding at Waikiki Beach and at the Hooluana Beach Club on the opposite side of the island."[56] Hardin's missive draws our attention to the state of beach culture at Waikīkī during the war, a place that would continue to influence California coastal communities for decades to come. What happened at Waikīkī invariably established the latest trends on California beaches, from swimwear to surfing styles. Because of its closer proximity to war, Hawai'i adopted measures that were more draconian than California—imposing nearly three years of martial law, for example. And yet, perhaps because of such severe restrictions, there was a greater need for organized public recreation, which included paddleboard, surfing, and outrigger canoe contests.

The Hawaii Surfing Association formed in August 1939 "to help stimulate interest in surf racing in the Islands," according to its president, John M. Lind.[57] Lind was a California transplant and had organized the Long Beach Surfing Club before moving to the islands.[58] The great Hawaiian paddleboard races throughout the 1920s and into the early 1930s, with noted champions Sam Kahanamoku, Thomas Kiakona, and Tom Blake, hadn't been held since 1932. Lind wanted to organize a local team to compete in the popular races at Long Beach in December 1939, a goal admirably fulfilled when Gene "Tarzan" Smith, then working for the Waikiki Beach Patrol, captured third place in the half-mile race, and then first place in both the half-mile and mile events two weeks later in Venice.[59] Lind continued to organize contests throughout the war, working with the Outrigger Canoe Club and the Honolulu Junior Chamber of Commerce. Smith dominated the longer paddleboard events, and beachboy Allen "Turkey" Love reigned as the surfing champion, winning events in 1940, 1941, and 1944.[60] Although the surfing event wasn't held in 1943 because of lack of surf, the organizers included special outrigger canoe races for army and navy crews.[61] Duke Kahanamoku, fifty-three years old, led his six-man team to the winner's circle that year, reinforcing his stature, after four decades, as king of the beach. An estimated ten thousand spectators packed the shore to watch "ancient Hawaiian sports steal the show from the war," a boon for both military and civilian morale.[62]

There was no mistaking that the U.S. military had taken over Waikīkī. All the major hotels—the Royal Hawaiian, the Moana, the Halekulani—boarded

Posing in front of trophies offered during a wartime Waikīkī water carnival (with barbed wire lining the beach) over the July 4th holiday, 1943. Standing: Duke Kahanamoku, enlisted man, Gene "Tarzan" Smith; sitting: Ann Morris, Wanda Grant, Kathleen Patterson. (U.S. Army photo from the collection of John M. Lind.)

officers and men on R&R. The U.S. Army leased the Lalani Hawaiian Village, creating three bathhouses and accommodations for nearly seven hundred men.[63] The *Honolulu Advertiser* reported: "Men of the armed services are promised all the surfing and beach recreation they want with the opening of the new bathing facilities at Waikiki."[64] The U.S. Navy opened its recreation center in Waikīkī—the Breakers—in December 1942, hosting up to forty-four hundred men a day.[65] Barbed wire lined the beaches to protect against a Japanese invasion, but thousands of servicemen packed the sand on annual Kamehameha Day celebrations (June 11), watching the various paddling races and beauty pageants on offer. As David Farber and Beth Bailey observe, soldiers and defense workers essentially became the new tourists in Hawaiʻi. Military and civilian elites had intentionally created this role for them, seeking to defuse potential conflict between newly arrived war personnel and Hawaiʻi's multiracial community, especially Americans of Japanese ancestry who represented more than a third of the population.[66]

Farber and Bailey explain: "Tourists, as sociologist Dean MacCannell has pointed out, see difference as pleasurable, rather than threatening, and the unusual as affirming their own way of life rather than challenging it. The paradigm of the 'fighting-man-as-tourist' enabled wartime visitors to consume the 'otherness' of Hawaii without risking loss of primary identity and without needing to directly confront or reject the 'other.' At least this was what military and civilian authorities hoped would occur."[67] As with the newest beach visitors in California arriving from the East Coast and Midwest—each of whom constituted "a potential rescue" for lifeguards—the hundreds of thousands of soldiers who landed in Hawai'i were entering a realm that the majority of them were entirely unfamiliar with.

Farber and Bailey describe the partial success, challenges, and failures of treating soldiers as tourists, part of which corresponds to the words of Don James that open this chapter: long tantalized by touristic images of paradise, the visitors couldn't help but notice the jarring difference between dreamland Waikīkī and the reality of an island locked down for war. The authors cite the personal account of Edward F. Grier as one example: "Before the war Waikiki was known to ten mainlanders for every one who knew anything about Pearl Harbor. The efficient Hawaii Tourist Bureau and the visible legends of Hollywood had produced the expectation of a vacation paradise. . . . Naturally every service man in Honolulu at once heads for Waikiki." But upon arriving, Grier noted that, in wartime, it was "a pretty shabby neighborhood."[68] The barbed wire, the overcrowding, the wartime rationing and lack of nightlife owing to martial law—it all left more than one soldier feeling lonely and disillusioned.

The situation became grim enough by early 1945 that the military created a booklet to help prepare soldiers and defense workers for island realities—*A Pocket Guide to Hawaii*. The guide provides an overview of Hawai'i's history, its diverse people, and the various resources available to soldiers, including tips on recreation, dating, staying healthy, and rules for writing home (all mail was censored). "There's one primary point to remember," soldiers were told in the guide. "No matter what the color of their skin, no matter how they appear, the civilians you see in the Hawaiian Islands are Americans. They're just as proud of the Stars and Stripes as you are. Never forget that."[69] The no-nonsense language throughout the guide presents what Farber and Bailey call "a democratic, tolerant, and open-minded message."[70] But the authors note that "the illustrations accompanying the text carried a very different message."[71] The figure on the title page, for example—"a cute, naked, dwarfish, dark-skinned man"—reappears several times throughout the booklet, suggesting that Hawaiians, "while interesting, are also primitive, and no threat to white America."[72] The figure likely represented one of the legendary Menehune in Hawaiian tradition, a diminutive race of workers and craftspeople.

Additional images of Native Hawaiians in the booklet—two of them surfers—reinforce stereotypes discussed in previous chapters. The text reminds soldiers not to "let any fantastic fiction you may have read about [Hawaiians] back home throw you off the beam." But the images reproduce those fictions as effectively as any Hollywood movie.[73] The surfers are warrior-like in stature, and yet they clearly represent images of a people who belong to the past (like the Menehune). The white people depicted in the booklet, largely soldiers, are smiling and dressed in contemporary clothing styles, military and civilian. Native Hawaiian men are represented as either infantile or archaic; Native Hawaiian women as exotic or sexualized hula dancers. Despite the military's best intentions to create a democratic message of parity, the visuals sustained social biases and racism of the time that relegated Native Hawaiians either to entertainment or to history. Such images reinforced a century-old push toward political control of Hawai'i and encouraged the disenfranchisement of Native Hawaiians in their own land.

The surfing and paddleboard contests held at Waikīkī during the war performed the same function as those inaugurated by the Hawaii Promotion Committee and the Outrigger Canoe Club thirty-five years earlier: to promote Hawai'i by marketing its most unique qualities—its natural beauty and indigenous traditions. Rather than pitching to mainland tourists, however, the tourism industry now targeted the U.S. military, which had quickly become the biggest spender in the islands. Individual soldiers, for example, dropped more than ten million dollars a year on Hotel Street prostitutes alone. The amount equaled the annual loss of revenue in Hawai'i after tourism was shut down following the attack on Pearl Harbor.[74] The only tourist-related program that continued during the war was the radio show *Hawaii Calls*, performed every Saturday night at the Moana hotel to "keep that nostalgia—the feeling of Hawaiian music, and Webley Edwards [the host], and Al Kealoha Perry and the Singing Surfriders—all that business going so people would think about Hawai'i [and] after the war, want to come back again."[75] The strategy certainly worked. Despite any lingering disappointment in wartime Waikīkī, visitors continued to flock to Hawai'i after the war, though increasingly drawn from the same walks of life as the soldiers themselves—most of them working-class and middle-class travelers rather than society's elite. The settler colonialism imagined by the Hawaii Promotion Committee and figures like Alexander Hume Ford as they promoted Hawai'i in the early twentieth century finally took hold after World War II. In 1900, three years before the advent of the Hawaii Promotion

Committee, the population of whites in Hawai'i was just under thirty thousand, slightly more than Chinese (more than twenty-five thousand) but less than both Native Hawaiians (more than thirty-seven thousand) and Japanese (more than sixty-one thousand). By 1960, one year after statehood, the white population had grown to more than two hundred thousand, outpacing every other ethnicity in the Islands. During the decade after statehood, the white population grew by another one hundred thousand, finally becoming the largest single ethnic group in the Hawaiian Islands.[76]

Waikīkī remained the source of California dreams immediately after the war, with a new crop of surfers—Joe Quigg, Matt Kivlin, Tommy Zahn, among others—booking fares on the *Lurline* and finding inspiration in the progressive wave-riding of beachboy Albert "Rabbit" Kekai. But they would be the last generation to genuflect at the altar of Waikīkī. As the 1940s gave way to the 1950s, the west and north shores of O'ahu—Mākaha, Waimea Bay, Sunset Beach—offered larger and more daring waves, prompting Californians to adjust their dreams and put their shoulder into designing new surfboards to meet the challenge of gigantic surf. California beach culture had managed to endure the disruptions of the war largely because of municipal lifeguard organizations throughout Southern California. Groups like the West Coast Paddleboard Association, however, which had been so important to the growth of surfing and paddleboarding in the 1930s, faltered in their attempts to rekindle the old enthusiasm. In mid-June 1946, for example, Lewis R. Leis of Hermosa Beach penned the following letter to Harry Welch, secretary of the Newport Beach Chamber of Commerce:

> Most all surfing and paddleboard enthusiasts have returned from the service and the West Coast Paddleboard Association is re-organizing.
>
> We are ready to help you with your plans for paddleboard races, which you want to sponsor in your community.
>
> Time is running short, please send us your tentative dates soon, so we can schedule contests for this season.[77]

Ambivalent about planning an event with summer already begun, Welch finally responded on June 24: "Our Committee has decided that we will not hold any Paddleboard Races this year. Perhaps another year we will plan something of this kind."[78] Welch's response seems to have been shared by business owners in other coastal communities. Without the financial support of Southland Chambers of Commerce, competition waned, as did interest in surfing clubs, many of which disbanded or never regrouped after the war.[79]

The few bright spots in competition primarily involved lifeguards. In association with the Catalina-to-Hermosa Beach aquaplane race in August 1946, the Los Angeles County lifeguards won the dory-swim-paddleboard medley.[80] The following year at the same event, Santa Monica lifeguards Tommy Volk and Tommy Zahn captured first and third in the paddleboard race; PVSC member "Tulie" Clark placed second. No further mention of the Palos Verdes Surfing Club occurs in regional newspapers for the rest of the decade, so Clark's affiliation was purely nostalgic.[81] In October 1947, "Pete" Peterson, Volk, and Zahn finished one-two-three in the first annual "Malibu Remuda" paddleboard race, with co-organizer Mary Ann Hawkins placing second behind Georgina Williamson of Santa Monica's Manoa Surfboard Club.[82] In September 1949, the Santa Monica lifeguards triumphed over the Cabrillo Beach lifeguards in a ten-man relay race from Catalina Island to Santa Monica.[83] Lifeguards continued to compete here and there on paddleboards as part of their rescue training, but the annual gatherings at San Onofre and Long Beach that had done so much to unite surfers from San Diego to Los Angeles, giving them a forum for cultural exchange in riding technique, board construction, and general *savoir vivre,* had gone the way of soup lines and gas rationing.

In their place arrived the technological advances of wartime research and manufacturing—plastic foam, fiberglass, polyurethane resins, neoprene (for wetsuits)—that set the stage for a beach-culture revolution that turned Southern California into the world's biggest surf factory during the 1950s. By the time *Gidget* premiered in 1959, all of the building materials were in place to create a new dream for teenagers around the world. Like a starlet ready to take center stage, Malibu didn't so much replace Waikīkī as establish itself as a phenom in its own right, flashing a glamour intrinsic to the shores of Southern California. And because Surfrider Beach, through the gift of geography, reclined in the exact direction of the South Pacific, it was perfectly placed to take those tropical lines and groom them into a dazzling performance.

Notes

Introduction

1. Gabe Sullivan, "Interview with Calvin "Tulie" Clark, 1995. *Encyclopedia of Surfing* (eos.surf).

2. The terms "mainland" and "mainlander" are problematic in terms of furthering a hierarchy that prioritizes the continent and those who live on it. However, I have not yet found terms that better capture the same meaning in a succinct way, so I use them throughout this study.

3. For broad historical overviews of the beach itself, see Lenček and Bosker, *The Beach: The History of Paradise on Earth,* and Ritchie, *The Lure of the Beach: A Global History.*

4. For an overview of settler colonialism in the United States, see Hixson, *American Settler Colonialism.*

5. For more on Freeth's life and accomplishments, see Moser, *Surf and Rescue.*

6. For race issues concerning Freeth and Kahanamoku, and the problematical title of "father of modern surfing," see Gilio-Whitaker, "Appropriating Surfing and the Politics of Indigenous Authenticity," 223–28.

7. Starr, *Material Dreams: Southern California Through the 1920s,* vii–x.

8. For settler colonialism as a structure, see Patrick Wolfe, "Settler colonialism and the elimination of the native," *Journal of Genocide Research,* 387–409.

9. Blake, "Waves and Thrills at Waikiki," 597–604.

10. *Evening Outlook,* September 20, 1935. See the *Honolulu Star-Bulletin* (October 3, 1935) for Granstrom's arrival.

11. *Honolulu Advertiser,* February 2, 1936.

12. *Honolulu Star-Bulletin,* January 4, 1936.

13. *Honolulu Star-Bulletin,* January 4, 1936.

14. The program debuted in Hawai'i on October 7, 1935 (*Honolulu Star-Bulletin,*

October 8, 1935) and in Los Angeles two months later (*Los Angeles Times,* November 8, 1935).

15. Mak, "Creating 'Paradise of the Pacific'," 53–54.

16. For a thorough discussion of this process, see Aileen Moreton-Robinson's *The White Possessive: Property, Power, and Indigenous Sovereignty.*

17. *Honolulu Star-Bulletin,* April 18, 1936. In an interesting connection between the nightclubs and the lifeguards, Stiffler mentions in her column for September 21, 1935, that Ornellas was working as a lifeguard in Santa Monica.

18. *Palos Verdes Peninsula News,* December 31, 1937.

19. *Los Angeles Times,* September 19, 1937.

20. Chapter 9 of this study reviews the tradition in detail.

21. Deloria, *Playing Indian.*

Prologue

1. *Honolulu Star-Bulletin,* June 24, 1925.

2. *Santa Ana Register,* June 15, 1925.

3. *Santa Ana Register,* June 15, 1925.

4. *Santa Ana Register,* June 15, 1925.

5. Davis, *Waterman,* 171.

6. Davis, *Waterman,* 171.

7. In "A Star Was Born," William Oscar Johnson notes that Crabbe was "one thirty-second Polynesian" (*Sports Illustrated,* July 18, 1984, 143).

8. *Santa Ana Register,* June 15, 1925.

9. As quoted in Davis, *Waterman,* 163.

10. *Santa Ana Register,* June 15, 1925.

11. *Santa Ana Register,* June 9, 1924.

12. *Santa Ana Register,* January 1, 1923.

13. *Los Angeles Times,* June 18, 1922 and March 15, 1925.

14. Sabin, *Crude Politics,* 69.

15. Sabin, *Crude Politics,* 163.

16. As quoted in Randall, *The King and Queen of Malibu,* 201.

17. "The Duke—Interview with Duke Kahanamoku," 17.

18. Burnett and Burnett, *Surfing Newport Beach,* 69.

19. *Los Angeles Times,* May 23, 1925.

20. *Santa Ana Register,* June 15, 1925. Sheffield notes in Santa Monica's *Evening Outlook* (August 9, 1934) that he founded the "Corona Del Mar Surf Board Club" in 1926.

21. George Freeth had founded a surf club in Redondo in 1912, but it was short-lived. See the *Los Angeles Evening Express,* November 7, 1912.

22. Lifeguard Charlie Wright had organized surf contests at Mission Beach in the San Diego area in 1925 (*Pomona Progress,* August 28, 1925 and *Evening Tribune,* September 25, 1925), and both Redondo Beach and Hermosa Beach in Los Angeles had held surfing and paddleboard races before Corona del Mar's

contest (*Los Angeles Times*, August 16, 1926 and *Redondo Reflex*, July 6, 1928). The original contest was called the "Pacific Coast Surf Board Championship." I use the term "Pacific Coast Surf Riding Championships" for consistency of reference with later contests.

23. *Los Angeles Times*, May 31, 1925.

24. *Honolulu Star-Bulletin*, July 2 and August 2, 1921. For Sam Kahanamoku's subsequent wins: *Honolulu Star-Bulletin*, June 26, 1922 and February 23, 1923. A big profile on Sam appeared in the same paper on April 21, 1923; Dad Center called him "the greatest surf rider in Hawaii," even better than Duke. For traditional Hawaiian paddleboarding, see Clark, *Hawaiian Surfing*, 37–40. A trio of surfboard races appeared in Los Angeles the year before Sam's win at the Edgewater. These may have been a vestige of George Freeth's influence because some of the people involved—Jerry Witt and Ray Kegeris—had been coached by Freeth. See the *Los Angeles Times*, September 24, 1924 ("Special Surfboard Exhibition to Thrill Fans" at the Club Casa Del Mar in Santa Monica); *Los Angeles Times*, October 20, 1924 ("Something new in racing will be on the program, a fifty-yard dash on surf boards" in Redondo Beach); *Redondo Reflex*, November 21, 1924 ("Men's 50-yard surf board race").

25. Mark, *Our Lifeguard Family*, 2571–73. Tabor had an impressive career after lifeguarding, eventually becoming an aerospace scientist working on the S-5 moon rocket. Tabor said about being the only African American to lifeguard: "If you wanted to compete in the white world, you could not be as good as them, you had to be better. Today [2008] we no longer have that glaring gap in the races. We had an inferiority complex that had been placed on us by our fellow white Americans. I believe that's what took place at the time" (2572).

26. *Los Angeles Times*, April 11, 1993. The article mistakenly lists Walker as the first African American lifeguard in Los Angeles County. Twenty-eight years after being hired, Walker was listed as the only African American out of 107 year-round lifeguards.

27. For the first female lifeguard in Los Angeles County, Wendy Paskin, see the *Redondo Reflex*, May 22, 1974 and the *Los Angeles Times*, August 18, 1974. The *Los Angeles Times* (August 23, 1973) has an article on Kai Nowell, the first female lifeguard hired by the Los Angeles City lifeguard service.

28. For the Black Surfing Association, see https://www.kcet.org/shows/artbound/tony-corley-evolution-of-the-black-surfing-association.

29. *Los Angeles Times*, June 9, 1922. See also Jefferson, *Living the California Dream*, 71–103.

30. *Los Angeles Times*, July 22, 1922.

31. *Los Angeles Times*, October 24, 1922 and July 7, 1923.

32. The Casa Del Mar: *Los Angeles Times*, July 13, 1924; the Edgewater Beach Club: *Los Angeles Times*, September 14, 1924; the Santa Monica Athletic Club was founded earlier but relocated to the beach in 1924: *Los Angeles Times*, April 12, 1924; the Breakers: *Los Angeles Times*, February 1, 1926; the Jonathan Club acquired the Edgewater Beach Club in 1930: *Los Angeles Times*, May 3, 1930; the

Gables: *Los Angeles Times*, February 21, 1926; mention of the "Wave Crest Beach Club" begins in early 1930: *Los Angeles Times*, January 4, 1930; the Deauville Club: *Los Angeles Times*, July 9, 1926.

33. *Los Angeles Times*, January 3, 1925.

34. *Los Angeles Times*, June 18, 1925.

35. Blake, *Hawaiian Surfboard*, 48. The article in *American Anthropologist* was by Stewart Cullin (April 1899, 201–47). Cullin was quoting William Tufts Brigham's *A Preliminary Catalogue of the Bernice Pauahi Bishop Museum of Polynesian Ethnology and Natural History*, Part I (1892), 56 (which Blake also quoted from). See also Burnett and Burnett, *Surfing Newport Beach*, 75.

36. *Los Angeles Times*, July 19, 1926.

37. The following month, Blake won another paddleboard race in Redondo Beach, which included competitors like Gerard Vultee. who would come in second place at Corona del Mar in 1928 and 1929 (*Los Angeles Times*, August 16, 1926). In July 1928, one month before the PCSRC, Blake won a similar paddleboard contest in Hermosa Beach (*Los Angeles Times*, July 15, 1928). See also the *Honolulu Advertiser* (June 12, 1930) for a dual paddleboard/surfing event at Waikīkī that Blake won.

38. *Los Angeles Times*, June 19, 1927.

39. *Los Angeles Times*, September 24, 1928.

40. *Los Angeles Times*, April 4, 1932.

41. Wright tandem surfing with Mary Powers for the Mission Beach Amusement Center (*San Diego Union*, March 25, 1923); an exhibition at Mission Beach with Helen Riser and Hawaiian Tony Comacho (*San Diego Union*, September 24, 1924); holding a "Surf Board Meet" (*Pomona Progress*, August 28, 1925)—the article indicates that Wright started surfing in 1921; surfing in the New Year at the Mission Beach bathhouse (*San Diego Union*, December 31, 1925); another exhibition at the Mission Beach bathhouse (*Evening Tribune*, February 26, 1926); surfing in another New Year with Fay Baird at Mission Beach (*Evening Tribune*, December 29, 1926 and *San Diego Union*, January 2, 1927); Wright tandem surfing with Mary Powers at Mission Beach (*Evening Tribune*, February 27, 1927). For details of early San Diego surfer Ralph Noisat, see Elwell and Schmauss, *Surfing in San Diego*, 11. For the experiences of lifeguard and surfer Emil Sigler during the 1930s, see Aguirre, *Waterman's Eye*.

42. Martino, *Lifeguards of San Diego County*, 9, and *Help!*, 159–81.

43. Martino, *Help!*, 45 (Oceanside) and 109 (Ocean Beach).

44. Duke competed at Coronado in 1922 (*San Diego Union*, July 5, 1922) and again the following summer (*Los Angeles Times*, July 23, 1923). Articles in the *San Diego Union* announce that Duke will surf, but it doesn't appear that he made those trips: May 23, 1924 (at Ocean Beach) and January 17, 1926 (at La Jolla).

45. Lynch and Gault-Williams, *Tom Blake*, 54–55.

46. Starr, *Material Dreams*, 98.

47. https://www.digitalhistory.uh.edu/topic_display.cfm?tcid=124#:~:text =During%20the%201920s%2C%20movie%20attendance,of%20half%20 the%20nation's%20population.

48. *Los Angeles Times*, August 7, 1927.

49. *Pasadena Post*, December 16, 1927. This film does not appear to be extant.

50. *Los Angeles Times*, June 19, 1927.

51. *Los Angeles Times*, May 9, 1926.

52. *Long Beach Telegram*, May 16, 1923.

53. Devienne, "Spectacular Bodies," 6.

54. *Los Angeles Times*, October 27, 1926.

55. For a picture of the Coogan and Colman houses, see https://adamsonhouse
.pastperfectonline.com/photo/192336D9-BD63–4450-B607–149818688695.
Coogan lived at 19 Malibu Colony according to Fleming, *Movieland Directory*.

56. Schmitt, *Hawaii in the Movies*, 310–11.

57. Konzett, *Hollywood's Hawaii*, 35.

58. Hunhdorf, *Going Native*, 3.

59. For a comprehensive historical study of this topic, see Deloria, *Playing Indian*.

60. *Los Angeles Times*, July 12, 1931.

61. In 1927, for example, more than half of the ten thousand tourists who arrived in the islands aboard ships from the Matson Navigation Company and the Los Angeles Steamship Company came from California (5,526). See Mak, "Creating 'Paradise of the Pacific'," 53–54.

62. Mak, "Creating 'Paradise of the Pacific'," 66–67.

63. For details on the *Malolo* and Matson's other vessels, see O'Brien, *White Ships*.

64. The group's name derived from the section of Honolulu (Pā-waʻa junction) that the three men called home (*Honolulu Star-Bulletin*, July 22, 1920).

65. Garrett, *Struggling to Define a Nation*, 178.

66. Garrett, *Struggling to Define a Nation*, 184–85.

67. Garrett, *Struggling to Define a Nation*, 197.

68. Yamashiro, "Ethics in Song," 1.

69. *San Francisco Examiner*, June 13, 1915.

70. Garrett, *Struggling to Define a Nation*, 187.

71. Trask, *Native Daughter*, 144.

72. *Honolulu Star-Bulletin*, August 25 and 31, 1922.

73. *Honolulu Advertiser*, December 3, 1925.

74. *Honolulu Star-Bulletin*, August 25, 1922.

75. For the drownings, see the *Honolulu Advertiser*, October 30, 1916 and the *Honolulu Star-Bulletin*, October 31, 1916; For David Kahanamoku: *Honolulu Star-Bulletin*, October 5, 1917.

76. *Pasadena Post*, June 13, 1929.

77. *Pasadena Post*, June 13, 1929.

78. *Honolulu Star-Bulletin*, November 20, 1930.

79. *Honolulu Star-Bulletin*, August 23, 1965. See also Davis, *Waterman*, 176.

80. *Honolulu Star-Bulletin*, October 26, 1934.

81. Mak, "Creating 'Paradise of the Pacific'," 66–67.

82. *Honolulu Advertiser*, December 11, 1936.

83. Starr, *Material Dreams*, 95.

84. Starr, *Material Dreams*, 96.

85. Timmons, *Waikiki Beachboy*, 30.

86. Skwiot, *The Purposes of Paradise*, 110.

87. Devienne, "Spectacular Bodies," 7–8.

88. *Honolulu Star-Bulletin*, October 19, 1929.

Chapter 1. The Dreamer

1. Gault-Williams, *Legendary Surfers*, 43.

2. *Honolulu Star-Bulletin*, October 19, 1929.

3. *Honolulu Star-Bulletin*, November 8, 1929.

4. Starr, *Material Dreams*, 69.

5. Starr, *Material Dreams*, 69.

6. See the *Detroit Free Press* (October 11, 1920) for a description of Duke racing a local man named Billy Dyer at the Detroit YMCA.

7. Lynch and Gault-Williams, *Tom Blake*, 53.

8. *Los Angeles Times*, December 13, 1923. Blake beat Duke in the 220-yard freestyle.

9. Lynch and Gault-Williams, *Tom Blake*, 53.

10. *Honolulu Star-Bulletin*, January 1, 1930; Blake, "The Royal and Ancient Sport," 5.

11. Lynch and Gault-Williams, *Tom Blake*, 49.

12. Westwick and Neushul, *World in the Curl*, 71.

13. Blake, *Hawaiian Surfboard*, 67.

14. Gault-Williams, "Surf Drunk," 96.

15. *Los Angeles Times*, June 11, 1922.

16. *Los Angeles Times*, June 8, 1924.

17. Harrison, "A Glimpse Inside Lorrin's Barn," 36.

18. Lockwood, "From now on, your name is Burrhead," 52. Blake also credited the influence of the English racing shell on his designs (*Hawaiian Surfboard*, 51).

19. Hine, *The American West*, 331.

20. Starr, *Material Dreams*, 90.

21. *Honolulu Star-Bulletin*, November 4, 1930.

22. Blake, "The Royal and Ancient Sport," 5.

23. Blake, *Hawaiian Surfboard*, 68–69. For an interesting article on the five Hustace brothers using surfboards to save lives at Waikīkī, see the *Honolulu Advertiser*, July 21, 1908.

24. Lynch and Gault-Williams, *Tom Blake*, 104.

25. See Davis, *Waterman* (223) for Duke's similar take on foam boards.

26. Blake, *Hawaiian Surfboard*, 48–49.

27. Lynch and Gault-Williams, *Tom Blake*, 49.

28. Blake, *Tom Blake Scrapbook*, 13.

29. Blake, *Tom Blake Scrapbook*, 13.

30. Blake, *Hawaiian Surfboard*, 41.

31. Blake, *Hawaiian Surfboard*, 40.

32. Blake's verses appear in *Hawaiian Surfboard*, 40.

33. For the development of Blake's hollow boards in Florida and the eastern United States, see Lynch and Gault-Williams, *Tom Blake*, 123–29; in Australia, see Jarratt, *Surfing Australia*, 34–39.

34. Lynch and Gault-Williams, *Tom Blake*, 95–96.

35. *Evening Outlook*, September 20, 1935.

36. See the *Los Angeles Times* (July 27, 1936), for example, where Red Cross examiners voted rescues with the hollow paddleboard "the fastest and most efficient method."

37. Blake, *Hawaiian Surfboard*, 74. See also Blake, "Riding the Breakers!," and Blake, "Improved Hollow Surfboard For All-Around Sport."

38. Blake, "Improved Hollow Surfboard For All-Around Sport," 174.

39. Lockwood, "Granny and Doc," 48.

40. Instructions to build surfboards were also being published by mid-decade. See Hi Sibley's "Better Ways to Build Surf Boards" in *Popular Mechanics* (August 1935: 56–57).

41. *Evening Outlook*, July 30, 1934. See also the *Los Angeles Times* (July 28, 1934) for a photograph of a dozen members practicing for an upcoming contest. Peterson is noted as the president in the caption.

42. The letter from Bayer (April 20, 1940) is part of the Records of the Newport Beach Chamber of Commerce at the Sherman Library and Gardens (Paddleboard Association, File 430, Box 27). The list of member clubs is also in this file, including the Hermosa Girls Club, Palos Verdes Surfing Club, Long Beach Surfing Club, Santa Monica Surfing Club, Venice Surfing Club, Point Conception, Crest Club, Cabrillo Beach Surfing Club, Deauville Paddle Club, San Onofre Surfing Wahines, Manhattan Beach Surfing Club, Hermosa Beach Surfing Club, Surf Riders, and Haole Surfers.

43. For paddleboarding events in 1939: Pacific Beach: *Times Advocate*, July 29; La Jolla: *Times Advocate*, August 8; Long Beach: *Los Angeles Times*, August 28 ("first annual surf and paddleboard tourney"); Newport Beach: *News-Pilot*, October 12; Seal Beach: *Santa Ana Register*, May 22; San Pedro: *News-Pilot*, September 4; Long Beach: *Los Angeles Times*, December 4; Manhattan Beach: *Los Angeles Times*, June 5; Venice: *Los Angeles Times*, December 18; Santa Monica: *Santa Ana Register*, May 2.

44. https://www.federalreservehistory.org/essays/recession_of_1937_38.

45. *Los Angeles Times*, June 29, 1936.

46. *Los Angeles Times*, June 27, 1938. See also the *Times* (June 26, 1938) for information on earlier races: one in 1935 that was called off owing to bad weather; the article states that the PVSC was runner-up in 1937, but I found no confirmation on either the 1935 or 1937 races in the press. The *Times* (June

25, 1937) reports on preparations for the 1937 race for June 27, but no follow-up confirmation. The article lists the sponsor as the Pacific Coast Paddle Board Association, which is likely the West Coast Paddleboard Association.

47. See the *Los Angeles Times* (May 19, 1932) for "the Olympic safety surf sled"—a three-foot board invented by Bill Wheeler that included a fin for stability: "A stabilizer, or rudder, is attached to the underside of the sled at the rear, which prevents 'shimmying' or tipping over when coming in contact with cross currents." The *Times* shows a picture of the finned-board, which weighed eight pounds; see also the *Times* article on June 15, 1932 for a cartoon depiction of Wheeler (who worked in the paper's art department) and the board.

48. For Watson's trip to the Islands, see the *Honolulu Star-Bulletin*, March 10, 1930.

49. *Los Angeles Times*, August 12, 1940.

50. *Los Angeles Times*, November 12, 1938; *News-Pilot*, November 12, 1938.

51. *Los Angeles Times*, December 12, 1938.

52. *Long Beach Independent*, June 19, 1939.

53. Stecyk, "Pacific System," 35.

54. *Honolulu Star-Bulletin*, May 14, 1932.

55. Stecyk, "Pacific System," 36–38.

56. *Honolulu Star-Bulletin*, May 14, 1932.

57. For a broader review of the Massie Affair, and its connection to the Waikīkī beachboys, see Walker, *Waves of Resistance*, 79–81.

58. See, for example, *Honolulu Star-Bulletin*, January 30, 1932 ("Resolutions Demand Quiz Here By Congress Bodies").

59. *Honolulu Star-Bulletin*, January 29, 1932; Timmons, *Waikiki Beachboy*, 33.

60. Thurston had not only wanted to use the beach patrol to banish "beach pests," but he also thought that having one clearing house for beach services would "end the strife" between various factions vying for tourist dollars (*Honolulu Advertiser*, February 2, 1936).

61. https://www.outriggercanoeclubsports.com/occ-archives/oral-histories/william-justin-mullahey/. See also Timmons, *Waikiki Beachboy*, 33.

62. Tom Blake mentions Mullahey in *Hawaiian Surfboard* as having shown New York lifeguards the value of surfboards as lifesaving devices (69).

63. Thurston's group assumed the name "Waikiki Beach Patrol," which had been used since 1917 for the municipal lifeguards who patrolled the beach, first led by David Kahanamoku. Those lifeguards were still working for the city in 1935—three of them along with their captain, John Kauha. This latter group was subsequently referred to as the "Territorial Beach Patrol." The Waikiki Beach Patrol began with six men in 1935, then a dozen the following year. For information on reorganization in the Territorial Beach Patrol, and harbor board chairman Louis S. Cain's firing of Kauha, see the *Honolulu Star-Bulletin*, October 12, 1935.

64. *Honolulu Advertiser*, February 2, 1936.

65. *Honolulu Advertiser*, February 2, 1936.

66. California Surf Museum, A-Z file folders: Pacific System Homes, p. 3.

67. California Surf Museum, A-Z file folders: Pacific System Homes, p. 5.

68. *Hawaiian Star*, October 27, 1906.

69. Mak, "Creating 'Paradise of the Pacific'," 53–54.

70. *Honolulu Advertiser*, May 15, 1935.

71. See Matthew Bird's Youtube video "Streamlined: from hull to home."

72. Stecyk, "Pacific System," 35.

73. See Lynch and Gault-Williams, *Tom Blake* (97–114) for copies of the companies' brochures.

74. Blake, *Hawaiian Surfboard*, 64–65.

75. Stecyk, "Pacific System," 34, and California Surf Museum, A-Z file folders: Pacific System Homes, p. 1.

76. *Honolulu Star-Bulletin*, March 15, 1941.

77. As quoted in Timmons, *Waikiki Beachboy*, 30.

Chapter 2. The Photographer

1. Lockwood, "Granny and Doc," 56.

2. *Los Angeles Times*, January 18, 1931.

3. *Los Angeles Times*, January 18, 1931.

4. Lynch and Gault-Williams, *Tom Blake*, 64–68.

5. Ackerman, *Doc Ball*; see also Lawler, "Southern California's Bohemian Surfers: Roots of American Counterculture," 173.

6. This copy can be found in the California History Room at the California State Library in Sacramento; the inscription is dated February 5, 1947.

7. Ball, "Surf-Boarders Capture California," 355.

8. Blake appears (unidentified) on p. 358 of the September 1944 issue; his name mistakenly appears on p. 362 below a picture of Jim Bailey.

9. Blake, *Hawaiian Surfboard*, 40.

10. Blake, *Hawaiian Surfboard*, 41.

11. James, *Surfing San Onofre to Point Dume*, 11.

12. Ball's family began vacationing in Hermosa Beach in 1917; see Jackson, "Doc Ball," 1.

13. Lockwood, "Granny and Doc," 48.

14. Archibald Ball was born in Michigan; Genevieve Heath Ball in New York (1910 CA census); Martin Peterson (Wisconsin) and Laura Peterson (South Carolina) (1930 CA census and Lockwood, "Waterman," 48); William Hawkins (Illinois) and Beulah Hawkins (Missouri) (1920 CA census); Frederick Harrison (Illinois) and Lillie Harrison (Wisconsin) (1910 census); Thomas Edward Blake Senior (Michigan) and Blanche Blake (Wisconsin) (Lynch and Gault-Williams, *Tom Blake*, 1–2).

15. Lockwood, "Granny and Doc," 47.

16. Ball, "Surf Board Riding in Palos Verdes," 5.

17. California Surf Museum, A–Z folders, "Ball, Doc": loose notes by PVSC member John Gates.

18. See note 66 in this chapter for the newsletter that dates Ball's invention.

19. Gault-Williams, *Legendary Surfers*, 126.

20. For the first known surfers on the mainland, see Finney and Houston, *Surfing: A History of the Ancient Hawaiian Sport*, 82.

21. Starr, *Endangered Dreams*, 224, 239.

22. Mexican deportation: Hine, *The American West*, 333–35; migrant populations and Los Angeles labor camps: Starr, *Endangered Dreams*, 227.

23. Starr, *Endangered Dreams*, 239.

24. Lockwood, "Granny and Doc," 55.

25. Lockwood, "Granny and Doc," 56.

26. Lockwood, "Granny and Doc," 56.

27. Ball, *Early California Surfriders*, 29; this reprint has the same page numbers as the 1946 first edition.

28. The Hawaiian word *malihini* means "stranger," "foreigner," or "newcomer"; *kama'āina* means "native-born." The addition of an "s" on Hawaiian words is an anglicized plural. See note 50 below.

29. Ball, *Early California Surfriders*, 44.

30. Ball, *Early California Surfriders*, 44, 56–57, 84–85, 90–91.

31. Ball, *Early California Surfriders*, 84–85.

32. Ball, *Early California Surfriders*, 63.

33. Lockwood, "Granny and Doc," 47.

34. Ball, *Early California Surfriders*, 70–71. See Kristen Lawler's reading (*American Surfer*, 81–85) of these nicknames in the context of Marxian and Lacanian theories that highlight surfers' refusal of work (identity) and their dedication to pleasure and play.

35. Ball, *Early California Surfriders*, 44–45.

36. Ball, *Early California Surfriders*, 62–63.

37. Ball, *Early California Surfriders*, 88–89.

38. Ball, *Early California Surfriders*, 53–54.

39. Ball, *Ye Weekly Super Illustrated Spintail*, January 18, 1939, 1–2; February 8, 1939, 2. Photocopies of the newsletter appear in a notebook at the Surfing Heritage and Culture Center, San Clemente, California.

40. Ball, *Early California Surfriders*, 88.

41. Ball, *Early California Surfriders*, 5.

42. Ball, *Early California Surfriders*, 56–57; Ball, *Ye Weekly Super Illustrated Spintail*, February 8, 1939, 4.

43. Ball, *Early California Surfriders*, 41.

44. Ball, *Early California Surfriders*, 60–61.

45. Starr, *Material Dreams*, 80.

46. Ball, *Early California Surfriders*, 85. This photograph also appears in *Ye Weekly Super Illustrated Spintail*, October 2, 1940, 2; the date is the weekend of September 26, 1940.

47. Ball, *Early California Surfriders*, 81.

48. Ball, *Ye Weekly Super Illustrated Spintail*, September 22, 1937, 1. Regarding

the origin of the newsletter, Ball wrote in a circa November 24, 1936 issue—referring to himself in the third person: "It was his intent from the beginning to establish a weekly combination of bulletin, announcements, fun, and just plain Kukai Nui as a means of stimulating club interest and activity."

49. *Los Angeles Times*, September 19, 1937.

50. The Hawaiian word *malihini* was often misspelled by Californians as "malahini."

51. Sides, "Surf Slaloms," *Los Angeles Saturday Night*, 7–9, 27, 32–33.

52. *Life*, February 7, 1938, 41–42.

53. *Palos Verdes Peninsula News*, November 26, 1937; February 11, 1938. The publication was called the *Palos Verdes News* at the time. I use the common title for consistency of reference.

54. See, for example, Moser, *Surf and Rescue,* 117–20.

55. *Life*, February 7, 1938, 41.

56. Doss, *Looking at* Life *Magazine,* 2.

57. Baughman, "Who Read *Life?*" 42.

58. *Life*, August 7, 1939, 44–45; the surfing photographs were taken by staff photographer Peter Stackpole.

59. Hamilton, "Surfboards, Ahoy!" 14.

60. "Rolling Waves Provide Thrills for California's Surf Riders," 45.

61. See Clark, *Hawaiian Surfing* (14–16) for several examples, including the following from *Kepelino's Traditions*: "The wife may go hungry, the children, the whole family, but the head of the house does not care. He is all about the sport. That is his food. All day there is nothing but surfing" (16).

62. Ball, *Early California Surfriders,* 27.

63. Ackerman, *Doc Ball.*

64. See this example of the division between work week and weekend play from *Ye Weekly Super Illustrated Spintail,* October 2, 1940, 1: "SWAMPED IS NOT THE WORD FOR WHAT EL JHB HAS BEEN GOING THRU IN THE LAST FEW WEEKS . . . IT'S HELL ME FRANS *** JUST HELL IN THE RAW. HOWEVER WE RECEOVER IN GAWJUS WEEK-ENDS."

65. *Santa Ana Register,* July 10, 1939; *Los Angeles Times,* July 11, 1938.

66. Ball, *Ye Weekly Super Illustrated Spintail,* August 30, 1939, 1.

67. *Los Angeles Times,* August 28, 1939. Ball identifies Art Rogers as the photographer in his newsletter, but Ted Hurley's name appears at the bottom of the photograph.

68. Ball, *Ye Weekly Super Illustrated Spintail,* August 30, 1939, 2. See Ball, *Early California Surfriders,* for a similar shot of Bailey and his dog at the Cove (54).

69. Ball, *Ye Weekly Super Illustrated Spintail,* September 13, 1939, 1.

70. The camera is described in detail in Ball, "The World's Most Rugged Camera Hobby," 38–40, 92–95. The camera I describe is the end product of about six months of refinements, from September 1939 to May 1940. The camera is currently housed in the California Surf Museum in Oceanside, California. See Ball, *Ye Weekly Super Illustrated Spintail,* May 11, 1940, 1.

71. https://surfmuseum.org/current-exhibits/doc-balls-camera/.

72. https://surfmuseum.org/current-exhibits/doc-balls-camera/.

73. Ball, *Ye Weekly Super Illustrated Spintail*, November 8, 1939, 2.

74. Ball, *Ye Weekly Super Illustrated Spintail*, September 27, 1939, 2.

75. Ball, *Ye Weekly Super Illustrated Spintail*, October 18, 1939, 4.

76. Ball, *Early California Surfriders*, 52–53.

77. Ball, "The World's Most Rugged Camera Hobby," 40.

78. Two examples are the picture of Blake surfing Hermosa Beach, which appeared in advertising brochures for the Los Angeles Ladder Company (see Lynch and Gault-Williams, *Tom Blake*, 159) and the picture of Blake, Gard Chapin, and John Gates surfing the Cove (see Ball, *Ye Weekly Super Illustrated Spintail*, December 6, 1939, 3).

79. Ball, *Ye Weekly Super Illustrated Spintail*, November 29, 1939, 1.

80. Lawler, *American Surfer*, 4.

81. Lawler, *American Surfer*, 69. See also 85–96 where she treats Ball's photography and its influence both on the surfer image of the 1930s and on subsequent generations of surfers.

82. Ball, *Ye Weekly Super Illustrated Spintail*, October 2, 1940, 3.

Chapter 3. The Waterman

1. *Evening Outlook*, May 6, 1983. See also Lockwood, "Waterman," 45.

2. *Evening Outlook*, September 7, 1932.

3. *Los Angeles Times*, September 9, 1932.

4. Rogers built custom window screens and doors, and offered various wood-turning and band-sawing services. See the *Santa Monica, Ocean Park, Venice, Sawtelle, and Westgate Directory 1925* (729). He was not affiliated with Rogers Aircraft, Inc., also based in Venice in the early 1920s but that operated planes out of Rogers Airport in Los Angeles.

5. *Los Angeles Times*, July 29, 1932. Blake had already demonstrated the effectiveness of hollow boards the previous summer in Santa Monica: he had picked up work lifeguarding and rescued two men when their skiff swamped nearly a mile offshore. See the *Los Angeles Times*, July 18, 1931.

6. *Los Angeles Times*, April 25, 1932.

7. *Los Angeles Times*, October 3, 1932.

8. *Evening Outlook*, September 7, 1932.

9. http://www.laalmanac.com/population/po02.php.

10. Annual Report for 1927–1928, City of Los Angeles, Department of Playground and Recreation, "Public Beaches—5."

11. Annual Report for 1927–1928, City of Los Angeles, Department of Playground and Recreation, "Public Beaches—1."

12. Annual Report for 1927–1928, City of Los Angeles, Department of Playground and Recreation, "Public Beaches—1."

13. *Los Angeles Times*, July 17, 1932 and Annual Financial Report for 1932, City of Los Angeles, Department of Playground and Recreation, 21.

14. Annual Report for 1931–1932, Department of Parks and Recreation, County of Los Angeles, 29.

15. Annual Report for 1931–1932, Department of Parks and Recreation, County of Los Angeles, 28.

16. Los Angeles County hired lifeguards at Santa Monica Canyon State Beach and Manhattan State Beach, and Long Beach hired lifeguards at Alamitos Bay (Annual Report for 1941, California State Park Commission, 17, 27).

17. Annual Report for 1929–1930, Department of Parks and Recreation, County of Los Angeles, 47 (for list of regulations to enforce), and Annual Report for 1930–1931, 13 (for cooperation with other departments).

18. Annual Report for 1931–1932, Department of Parks and Recreation, County of Los Angeles, 27; Annual Report for 1932–1933, Department of Parks and Recreation, County of Los Angeles, 20.

19. Annual Report for 1931–1932, Department of Parks and Recreation, County of Los Angeles, 3.

20. *Los Angeles Times*, April 4, 1932.

21. *Los Angeles Times*, September 24, 1928.

22. *Los Angeles Times*, September 14, 1928.

23. Blake trained by securing his paddleboard to the Corona del Mar jetty and paddling in place for up to three hours every day. See Lynch and Gault-Williams, *Tom Blake*, 118.

24. *Los Angeles Times*, September 26, 1932.

25. *Los Angeles Times*, October 3, 1932.

26. Lockwood, "Waterman," 54.

27. Lockwood, "Waterman," 46.

28. Lynch and Gault-Williams, *Tom Blake*, 118.

29. Lockwood, "Waterman," 51.

30. *Los Angeles Times*, January 18, 1931.

31. "Honolulu, Hawaii, U.S. Arriving and Departing Passenger and Crew Lists, 1900–1959 for Preston Peterson," Series Description A3422-Arriving at Honolulu, Hawaii, 1900–1953, ancestry.com.

32. Lockwood, "Waterman," 49; Dixon, *Men Who Ride Mountains*, 25. See https://calisphere.org/item/5039c21480e9861240ed478674c4f082/ for a photograph of the Peterson and Smith bathhouse and the Rendezvous ballroom, which the family also owned. Peterson's daughter, Lisa, in an interview with Matt Warshaw, stated that her father was born in 1911; the often-reported date of his birth as 1913 owed to a mistake on Peterson's birth certificate (See Warshaw, "Pete Peterson: So Good He Didn't Need Wax").

33. Dixon quotes Peterson in *Men Who Ride Mountains* that the balsa boards he saw originated with Florida surfers (25–26). The *Honolulu Star-Bulletin* reported on April 28, 1920, that W. P. Roth, vice president and general manager at Matson

Navigation company, had a surfboard made of balsa in New York and planned to bring it to Hawai'i. Tom Blake credits Lorrin Thurston in *Hawaiian Surfboard* with introducing the balsa board to the islands in 1926 (5).

34. Dixon, *Men Who Ride Mountains*, 26: "Later on we added redwood noses and tailblocks for strength and that brought the weight up." See also Kenvin, "General Veneer," 26–27.

35. Harrison, "A Glimpse Inside Lorrin's Barn," 38; Lockwood, "Waterman," 55.

36. Lockwood, "Waterman," 46.

37. Lockwood, "Waterman," 49.

38. Lockwood, "Waterman," 55.

39. See Gault-Williams, "Surf Drunk," for 1937 as the date of the hot curl innovation (95, note 1). Reference to the incorrect date of 1934 can be found in Stecyk, "Hot Curl," 66. For Peterson's arrival on October 21, 1937: "Honolulu, Hawaii, U.S. Arriving and Departing Passenger and Crew Lists, 1900–1959 for Francis Peterson," Series Description A3422-Arriving at Honolulu, Hawaii, 1900–1953, ancestry.com. Peterson departed on October 27, 1937.

40. Gault-Williams, "Surf Drunk," 100.

41. A photograph of Peterson's 1938 account sheet at Pacific Homes records him finishing a board on January 31, 1938. I'm assuming this was not the first board he built at the company's factory and that he had been working there before his October 1937 trip (Stecyk, "Pacific Homes," 38). Harrison indicates that he was working at Pacific Homes in the summer of 1936 (Harrison, "A Glimpse Inside Lorrin's Barn," 42).

42. http://www.legendarysurfers.com/2015/05/fran-heath-1917–2006.html.

43. Walker, *Waves of Resistance*, 1. Walker's chapters 3 and 4 are especially relevant for the time period treated in this study.

44. For an account of a mainlander who endured such beatings, see Paskowitz, "Tarzan at Waikiki."

45. Walker, *Waves of Resistance*, 41.

46. Harrison, "A Glimpse Inside Lorrin's Barn," 42.

47. *Honolulu Star-Bulletin*, March 4, 1936.

48. *Honolulu Star-Bulletin*, March 4, 1936.

49. *Honolulu Star-Bulletin*, March 4, 1936.

50. Harrison stated that he stayed for six months in Hawai'i and then came back with Peterson, which would be the near the end of April 1933 (Gault-Williams, *Legendary Surfers,* 76).

51. *Honolulu Star-Bulletin,* October 12, 1933.

52. Ball, "Surf Board Riding in Palos Verdes," *Palos Verdes Peninsula News*, 5.

53. The same photograph appears in the *Los Angeles Times* on April 18, 1937 with the caption: "Hawaii-Style: Preston Peterson, lieutenant of Santa Monica lifeguards, gives Juanita Blackard, Charlotte Soule and Frank McMahon (bow) ride in outrigger canoe he brought from mid-Pacific islands."

54. *Los Angeles Times*, September 5, 1934.

55. *Evening Outlook*, July 30, 1934. See also the *Los Angeles Times* (July 28, 1934) for a photograph of a dozen members practicing for an upcoming contest. Peterson is noted as the president in the caption.

56. *Evening Outlook*, July 30, 1934.

57. Lockwood, "Waterman," 52–53. One wonders if the surf contest that day, which had to be postponed because of "unsatisfactory surf conditions" (*Evening Outlook,* September 10, 1934) is related to the fourth Pacific Coast Surf Riding Championships, which has remained somewhat of a mystery. No details of the contest have yet emerged save the name of its winner, Gardner Lippencott. But a photograph of Lippencott, Bill Dillehunt, and Peterson appeared in the *Los Angeles Times* on September 5, 1934 (four days before the contest), and the three riders are noted as "preparing for the Pacific Coast paddleboard and surfboard championships." You can clearly see the Malibu pier looming behind the surfers. Another photograph in the Rotogravure section of the *Times* appeared eleven days later, featuring Dillehunt and Peterson at the "west coast trials" of the contest. Similar wave conditions (and background objects) in the two photographs indicate that they were likely taken on the same day. After noting the postponement of the surfing events—the paddleboard races were indeed held, with Chauncey Granstrom taking the three-mile contest and Billy Watkins winning the hundred-yard race—the *Evening Outlook* mentioned that the surf contest would be held at Corona del Mar two weeks later. So the fourth PCSRC, which Lippencott won, may have been that rescheduled surf contest held at Corona del Mar. The previous two PCSRC had been held in September, so the timing was right, and the contests tended to be two years apart (the third one was held in 1932, which Peterson had won), though not exclusively.

58. George Freeth had started a surf club in Redondo Beach in 1912, though it was short-lived after he stopped working at the local bathhouse (*Redondo Reflex*, November 8, 1912). The surf club at Corona del Mar was in Orange County and had disbanded several years earlier.

59. *Evening Outlook*, August 7, 1934; *Los Angeles Times*, August 9, 1934.

60. *Evening Outlook*, April 22, 1935; *Santa Ana Register*, July 25, 1935.

61. James, *Surfing in the 1930s*.

62. *Evening Outlook*, July 30, 1934.

63. *Evening Outlook*, July 30, 1934.

64. *Santa Ana Register*, July 27, 1935; *Los Angeles Times*, December 18, 1935.

65. Cliff Tucker, 1940 winner of the PCSRC at San Onofre, presided as "Paddle Polo Chairman" for 1941. With Blake's paddleboard builder Thomas Rogers as a sponsor, along with the Los Angeles Playground and Recreation Department, Tucker organized an eleven-week schedule that pitted ten separate surfing and paddleboard clubs against one another every Wednesday night from June 25 to September 3. The champion that year would be crowned at the Los Angeles Swimming Stadium on September 14. Hermosa Beach won the title in 1941, succeeding the Palos Verdes Surfing Club (1940 champions) and the Venice Surfing Club (1939 champions). See the *Los Angeles Times*,

September 15, 1941; *San Pedro News Pilot*, September 9, 1940; and *Los Angeles Times*, August 12, 1939.

66. Records of the Newport Beach Chamber of Commerce, Sherman Library and Gardens, Corona del Mar, California: Folder 430, "Paddleboard Assn." The letter dates from April 20, 1940. The two women's clubs were the Hermosa Girls Club and the San Onofre Surfing Wahines.

67. My personal list of named surfers from the 1920s and 1930s, gathered from various sources (books, newspaper articles, archival lists) is currently more than four hundred men and women; according to Gault-Williams, Florida also had up to forty-five surfers in 1938 (*Legendary Surfers*, 160).

68. Ball, *Ye Weekly Super Illustrated Spintail*, July 10, 1940, 1.

69. Ball, *Ye Weekly Super Illustrated Spintail*, July 10, 1940, 1.

70. James, *Surfing San Onofre to Point Dume*, 129.

71. James, *Surfing in the 1930s*. See also James, *Surfing San Onofre to Point Dume*, 122.

72. *Long Beach Telegram and the Long Beach Daily News*, May 23 and June 11, 1912. See also the article describing George Falla and George Holmes making rescues on the last day of the season: *Long Beach Telegram and the Long Beach Daily News*, October 2, 1912.

73. *Long Beach Telegram and the Long Beach Daily News*, October 28, 1922. George Freeth had briefly held such a position in Venice in 1909 and in Redondo Beach in 1913.

74. Centennial History of the Long Beach Lifeguard Service, Part 1, https:// www.youtube.com/watch?v=Zy7cXJ5dOvE, and Part II, https://www.youtube .com/watch?v=RFrvcCihYZg. See Chris Brewster's "Letter to the Editor" in the *International Journal of Aquatic Research and Education* (August 2007; 195–97) for a history of the rescue tube. Brewster notes that the "rescue can" or "rescue cylinder" was first devised by Captain Henry Sheffield in 1897 while visiting Durban, South Africa.

75. *San Francisco Examiner*, May 11, 1934; Mark, *Our Lifeguard Family*, 280, 2059. See the *Santa Cruz Evening News* (May 13, 1935) for mention of the city purchasing "Res-Q tubes" after a fatal drowning. See also Peterson's obituary in Santa Monica's *Evening Outlook* (May 6, 1983) for a description of his innovations. B. Chris Brewster writes that the tube was based on a model designed by Reggie Burton and Captain Watkins (Brewster, "Letter to the Editor," 1).

76. Santa Monica Public Library, Santa Monica Collection Room, City of Santa Monica Budget, 1947–1948 Appropriation, "Recreation—Life Guards." The budget records the price of the rescue tubes at eighteen dollars apiece in 1947–1948, which would be about eleven dollars apiece in 1934 (adjusted for inflation). An example of the rescue tube can be found on display at the Santa Monica Pier, with Peterson's Company's name imprinted on the outside.

77. Tygiel, "Introduction," 3.

78. *Los Angeles Times*, September 7, 1938.

79. *Los Angeles Times*, July 22, 1934.

80. *Los Angeles Times*, August 9, 1934.

81. See the Annual Reports, Department of Parks and Recreation, County of Los Angeles: 1929–1930 (p. 48), 1930–1931 (p. 13), 1939–1940 (pp. 3 & 4 of the unnumbered report).

82. https://www.laalmanac.com/population/po02.php.

Chapter 4. The Waterwoman

1. Lynch, "Interview with Mary Ann Hawkins-Midkiff," 5.

2. Lynch, "Interview with Mary Ann Hawkins-Midkiff," 2.

3. Gault-Williams, "Tarzan Redux," 45.

4. Lynch and Gault-Williams, "The Last Chapter," 46.

5. "Honolulu, Hawaii, U.S. Arriving and Departing Passenger and Crew Lists, 1900–1959 for Gene Smith," Series Description A4156-Arriving at Honolulu, Hawaii, 1900–1953, ancestry.com. The manifest indicates that Smith was a stowaway. He arrived on January 11, 1934.

6. Lynch, "Interview with Mary Ann Hawkins-Midkiff," 3.

7. Lynch, "Interview with Mary Ann Hawkins-Midkiff," 3.

8. *Honolulu Advertiser*, November 7, 1938; *Honolulu-Star Bulletin*, October 17, 1940 and June 8, 1944; *Honolulu Advertiser*, November 2, 1945. See also Lynch and Gault-Williams, "The Last Chapter."

9. *Los Angeles Times*, December 18, 1939.

10. Croul Publications, Mary Ann Hawkins Collection, Book One, "Letter from Lorrin Harrison," December 25, 1934, 2.

11. Croul Publications, Mary Ann Hawkins Collection, Book One, "Letter from Lorrin Harrison," December 25, 1934, 4; I have added some punctuation for clarity.

12. Clark, *Hawaiian Surfing*, 45.

13. Pukui, *Hawaiian Proverbs and Poetical Sayings* (No. 2433).

14. See the *Santa Ana Register* article (July 21, 1930) describing how 1929 Pacific Coast Surf Riding Champion Kellar Watson learned tandem surfing at Waikīkī and brought the practice back to Corona del Mar: "According to the local surf rider about 20 persons from this city [Orange] ride every Sunday at Corona del Mar: Many young couples are now enjoying the sport as the passenger is usually a girl."

15. Lynch, "Interview with Mary Ann Hawkins-Midkiff," 2–3.

16. Lynch, "Interview with Mary Ann Hawkins-Midkiff," 2.

17. *Evening Outlook*, June 22, 1938. For reference to Hawkins dating "Tulie" Clark, see Ball, *Ye Weekly Super Illustrated Spintail*, January 12, 1937, 1; for Hawkins and "E. J." Oshier, see Ball, *Ye Weekly Super Illustrated Spintail*, April 7, 1937, 1; August 25, 1937, 2; and November 17, 1937, 2.

18. *Evening Outlook*, September 14, 1936.

19. *Long Beach Press-Telegram*, December 12, 1938; *Long Beach Sun*, December 12, 1938.

20. "Pete" Peterson's wife, Arlene, won several races herself. The San Onofre Surfing Wahine scrapbook mentions Arlene winning two contests (competing for the SOSW club) in May 1938: at Seal Beach and at the Del Mar club in Santa Monica (*San Onofre Surfing Wahines*, 31). She is also reported winning a race at Seal Beach in May 1939 (*Santa Ana Register*, May 22, 1939).

21. For the marriage license of Hawkins and Morrissey, see the *Ventura County Star*, April 6, 1939; for the Long Beach surfing contest results, see the *Long Beach Sun*, December 4, 1939.

22. Lynch, "Interview with Mary Ann Hawkins-Midkiff," pp. 4–5.

23. Ball, *Ye Weekly Super Illustrated Spintail*, January 15, 1936, 1.

24. Ball, *Ye Weekly Super Illustrated Spintail*, February 23, 1937, 1, and March 17, 1937, 1.

25. *San Onofre Surfing Wahines*, 3. The date appears in a period scrapbook—*San Onofre Surfing Wahines*—housed at Huntington Beach's International Surfing Museum. Much of the scrapbook has been reproduced (with reformatting) in the revised edition of David F. Matuszak's *San Onofre: Memories of a Legendary Surfing Beach*. The International Surfing Museum has no records of who donated the scrapbook, and there is no clear indication within the scrapbook of its authorship. Matuszak suggests Helen Hughes as the most likely author because her name is referenced the least number of times in the book. There are forty-seven pages in the scrapbook with material on them. For reference convenience, I have numbered them from 1 to 47, beginning with the first page that reads "AI NO PAHA IA OE."

26. *San Onofre Surfing Wahines*, 3.

27. *Southwest Wave* (Los Angeles), October 28, 1938.

28. *Southwest Wave* (Los Angeles), December 8, 1939.

29. Ball, *Ye Weekly Super Illustrated Spintail*, June 15, 1938, 2.

30. *San Onofre Surfing Wahines*, 10.

31. *San Onofre Surfing Wahines*, 19.

32. *San Onofre Surfing Wahines*, 30. The information on Waterman can be found on a postcard she sent to Hawkins ("Mrs. Mary Ann Morrissie"), with a date of January 6, 1940, in Croul Publications, Mary Ann Hawkins Collection: Book One.

33. *Evening Outlook*, January 13, 1939.

34. *Evening Outlook*, April 18, 1939.

35. Ball, *Ye Weekly Super Illustrated Spintail*, April 12, 1939, 1.

36. Ball, *Ye Weekly Super Illustrated Spintail*, 3.

37. *San Onofre Surfing Wahines*, 20.

38. *San Onofre Surfing Wahines*, 11.

39. *San Onofre Surfing Wahines*, 22 (volleyball), and 39 (Irene Chovan lobster diving).

40. *San Onofre Surfing Wahines*, 45.

41. *San Onofre Surfing Wahines*, 30.

42. *San Onofre Surfing Wahines*, 47.

43. *San Onofre Surfing Wahines*, 24.

44. Lynch, "Interview with Mary Ann Hawkins-Midkiff," 3–4. A picture of the first group to visit San Onofre indicates that the date was "circa 1934"; Hawkins does not appear in the photograph: Harrison, "A Glimpse Inside Lorrin's Barn," 40.

45. *Life* magazine, February 7, 1938, 42.

46. *Redondo Reflex*, May 27, 1938.

47. *Evening Vanguard*, June 20, 1938; *Evening Outlook*, June 22, 1938.

48. *Los Angeles Times*, August 8, 1938.

49. *Life* magazine, August 22, 1938, 35.

50. For Peterson competing for the Del Mar club, see the *Evening Outlook*, September 13, 1937; for Hawkins, see the *Evening Outlook*, June 22, 1938.

51. Moser, *Surf and Rescue*, 77–83.

52. *Los Angeles Times*, August 21, 1935. See also the club magazine, *Del Mar Club Life* (August 1935), 13, 18, 29.

53. *Palos Verdes Peninsula News*, December 31, 1937.

54. *Palos Verdes Peninsula News*, December 31, 1937.

55. *Palos Verdes Peninsula News,* January 7, 1938.

56. Ball, *Ye Weekly Super Illustrated Spintail*, January 5, 1938, 1.

57. *Palos Verdes Peninsula News*, December 31, 1937.

58. *Palos Verdes Peninsula News*, December 31, 1937.

59. *Palos Verdes Peninsula News*, December 31, 1937.

60. *Honolulu Star-Bulletin*, May 6, May 27, and June 5, 1937.

61. *Honolulu Advertiser*, January 16, 1938. See note 86 below for more details on Costa's column.

62. https://maureenmegowan.com/south-bay-history/history-of-rancho-palos -verdes/.

63. *Palos Verdes Peninsula News*, January 7, 1938.

64. *Palos Verdes Peninsula News*, January 7, 1938.

65. Ball, *Ye Weekly Super Illustrated Spintail*, January 5, 1938, 1.

66. *Los Angeles Times*, November 18, 1935. The radio station had been playing Hawaiian music since the early 1920s, with Sol Hoʻopiʻi often featured: *Los Angeles Times*, May 4, 1923.

67. *Honolulu Star-Bulletin*, April 26, October 4, and October 8, 1935.

68. *Honolulu Star-Bulletin* March 21, 1936.

69. https://www.youtube.com/watch?v=P4bNqECDU84. For more background on the program founding, see https://bb.steelguitarforum.com/viewtopic .php?t=146408. The date of the first show is listed on the site as July 1935, but the first broadcast was on October 7, 1935. See *Honolulu Star-Bulletin*, October 8, 1935.

70. https://en.wikipedia.org/wiki/Hawaii_Calls.

71. *Honolulu Star-Bulletin*, October 7, 1935.

72. Sullivan, "Interview with Calvin 'Tulie' Clark."

73. *Los Angeles Times*, December 15, 1935.

74. Cooley, *Surfing About Music*, 72–76. For a connection between the steel guitar and Leo Fender's surf music Stratocasters, see Troutman, *Kīkā Kila: How the Hawaiian Steel Guitar Changed the Sound of Modern Music*, 194.

75. "Waikiki Willie" in the *Honolulu Star-Bulletin*, October 8, 1935.

76. *Honolulu Star-Bulletin*, October 10, 1936.

77. *Honolulu Star-Bulletin*, December 21, 1935.

78. In September 1936, for example, Stiffler mentions that about seventy-five members of the Hawaiian colony attended a farewell for Edith Kalai (*Honolulu Star-Bulletin*, September 5, 1936); in November of the same year, she mentions "105 Hawaiians" appear as extras at the Republic studio (*Honolulu Star-Bulletin*, November 28, 1936).

79. *Honolulu Star-Bulletin*, September 21, 1935.

80. *Honolulu Star-Bulletin*, January 4, 1936.

81. For background on Don the Beachcomber, see Alexander, *America Goes Hawaiian: The Influence of Pacific Island Culture on the Mainland*, 124–25.

82. *Honolulu Star-Bulletin*, November 28, 1936.

83. *Honolulu Star-Bulletin*, September 25, 1937.

84. *Honolulu Star-Bulletin*, September 25, 1937.

85. Stiffler's column began in the *Honolulu Star-Bulletin* on August 17, 1935 and ended on February 19, 1938.

86. Costa's column began on July 18, 1937 in the *Honolulu Advertiser* under the title, "Hawaiians in Hollywood." The name changed to "Hawaii in Hollywood" on September 19, 1937. The column ran until January 9, 1938.

87. *Honolulu Star-Bulletin*, January 2, 1932.

88. *Honolulu Star-Bulletin*, April 3, 1937.

89. https://www.theelvisforum.org/sweet-leilani-original-version-t3974.html.

90. Giddens, *Bing Crosby*, 479–81.

91. For a copy of the "Hula Luau" announcement, see "Doc" Ball's folder in the California Surf Museum archives. The less common spelling of "McIntyre" appears on the announcement.

92. "Hawaii in Hollywood," *Honolulu Advertiser*, July 25, 1937.

93. Lynch, "Interview with Mary Ann Hawkins-Midkiff," 1–2.

94. *Honolulu Star-Bulletin*, August 16, 1935. Harrison mentions in his December 25, 1934 letter to Hawkins that he and Kukea would be leaving the islands together (3): Croul Publications, Mary Ann Hawkins Collection: Newport Beach, Calif.

95. For similarities between the two indigenous groups, see Hixson, *American Settler Colonialism*, 145–65 and 189–91.

96. Ball, *Ye Weekly Super Illustrated Spintail*, January 5, 1938, 1.

97. Deloria, *Playing Indian*, 25.

98. Sturm, *Becoming Indian*, 177.

99. Sturm, *Becoming Indian*, 177.

100. https://foundationsoflawandsociety.wordpress.com/2016/12/09/anti-miscegenation-in-california/. The law was overturned in 1948. See also Stiffler's

column in the *Honolulu Star-Bulletin* for January 4, 1936: "And since California passed the law against intermarriage of Malay races with the white race (such as Filipino and white, etc.) the Hawaiian has been unable to procure a marriage license at all."

101. Ball, *Ye Weekly Super Illustrated Spintail*, January 5, 1938, 1.

102. *Honolulu Star-Bulletin*, July 3, 1939.

103. The races ran the week of July 13 to 20. Her results can be found in the *Honolulu Advertiser* on July 13, 15, 17, and 20, 1939.

104. Davis, *Waterman*, 201.

105. Lynch, "Interview with Mary Ann Hawkins-Midkiff," 5. The *Pasadena Post* reports Duke giving an exhibition at the Pasadena Athletic Plunge (January 20, 1927). Hawkins would have been almost eight.

106. Lynch, "Interview with Mary Ann Hawkins-Midkiff," 5. The picture of her shaking Duke's hand appears in the *Honolulu Star-Bulletin* on July 4, 1939. See also her interview with the *Honolulu Star-Bulletin* (August 1, 1973). One wonders if Hawkins reconnected with Gene "Tarzan" Smith at Waikīkī; he was working for the Waikiki Beach Patrol and won a paddling race during the Pacific Aquatic Carnival (*Honolulu Advertiser*, July 23, 1939).

107. Lynch, "Interview with Mary Ann Hawkins-Midkiff," 5. As Hawkins states, the surf was small the day the Australians competed in the boat races but there is no mention of contests being canceled: *Honolulu Star-Bulletin*, July 24, 1939.

108. Lynch, "Interview with Mary Ann Hawkins-Midkiff," 5.

109. *Honolulu Star-Bulletin*, August 1, 1973.

110. *Honolulu Star-Bulletin*, April 3, 1937.

111. *Honolulu Star-Bulletin*, June 26. 1937.

112. Lynch, "Interview with Mary Ann Hawkins-Midkiff," 4.

113. Lynch, "Interview with Mary Ann Hawkins-Midkiff," 4.

Chapter 5. The Traveler

1. O'Brien, *The White Ships*, 158–59 et passim.

2. Mak, "Creating 'Paradise of the Pacific'," 66.

3. *Honolulu Star-Bulletin*, September 28, 1932.

4. *Honolulu Star-Bulletin*, September 28, 1932. See also the *San Bernardino County Sun*, October 2, 1932.

5. Harrison, "A Glimpse Inside Lorrin's Barn," 37.

6. Harrison, "A Glimpse Inside Lorrin's Barn," 37.

7. Harrison, "A Glimpse Inside Lorrin's Barn," 37.

8. Harrison, "A Glimpse Inside Lorrin's Barn," 37. For the dates and timing of the ships, see the *Honolulu Star-Bulletin*, September 28, 1932 and the *San Bernardino County Sun*, October 2, 1932. Harrison recalled spending fourteen hours aboard the tugboat (Harrison, "A Glimpse Inside Lorrin's Barn," 37); the *Honolulu Star-Bulletin* article above indicates the period was less than an hour.

9. Harrison, "A Glimpse Inside Lorrin's Barn," 37–38.

10. Harrison, "A Glimpse Inside Lorrin's Barn," 37–38. See also the *San Francisco Examiner*, October 7, 1932.

11. Harrison, "A Glimpse Inside Lorrin's Barn," 38.

12. Harrison, "A Glimpse Inside Lorrin's Barn," 37.

13. Harrison, "A Glimpse Inside Lorrin's Barn," 38.

14. *Honolulu Star-Bulletin*, October 12 and 13, 1932.

15. Harrison, "A Glimpse Inside Lorrin's Barn," 38.

16. Harrison, "A Glimpse Inside Lorrin's Barn," 38.

17. *Honolulu Star-Bulletin*, December 9, 1935.

18. Harrison, "A Glimpse Inside Lorrin's Barn," 37.

19. Harrison, "A Glimpse Inside Lorrin's Barn," 36.

20. Harrison recalled stowing away with Peterson to get home, apparently without getting caught (Harrison, "A Glimpse Inside Lorrin's Barn," 38).

21. *Santa Ana Register*, December 21, 1933.

22. Harrison, "A Glimpse Inside Lorrin's Barn," 38–42.

23. Harrison, "A Glimpse Inside Lorrin's Barn," 42.

24. Laderman, *Empire in Waves*, 7. Chapter 1 details the Americanization of surfing with regard to imperialism and colonialism in Hawai'i.

25. Harrison dates a photograph of his group's first visit to San Onofre as "circa 1934" (Harrison, "A Glimpse Inside Lorrin's Barn," 40). See note 38 for why a dating of 1935 is unlikely.

26. *Los Angeles Times*, July 29, 1935. The event was for the first annual Aquatic Sports Day. See the article Sides wrote for *Saturday Night* ("Surf Slaloms"), illustrated with many of "Doc" Ball's photographs.

27. Blake, *Hawaiian Surfboard*, 62. Blake misspells Granstrom's name as "Cranstrom."

28. Lockwood, "Waterman," 53. The quotation comes from Santa Monica lifeguard Wally Burton.

29. Sides, "Surf Slaloms," 9.

30. Sides arrived in the islands on July 13, 1929 and left on August 24 (*Honolulu Advertiser*, July 15, 1929 and *Honolulu Star-Bulletin*, August 26, 1929); he arrived with his first wife on January 11, 1934 and departed on February 19 (*Honolulu Star-Bulletin*, January 11 and February 21, 1934).

31. Sides, "Surf Slaloms," 9.

32. *Los Angeles Times*, April 1, 1975.

33. Harrison, "A Glimpse Inside Lorrin's Barn," 36–37.

34. Harrison, "A Glimpse Inside Lorrin's Barn," 36–37.

35. Harrison, "A Glimpse Inside Lorrin's Barn," 36.

36. *Santa Ana Register*, August 9, 1935.

37. *Santa Ana Register*, August 9, 1935.

38. The newspaper misspelled his name as "Jo Kokea." Kukea's comment helps to confirm Harrison's first trip to San Onofre prior to 1935; if the trip had been in 1935, Kukea would certainly have gone too (he stayed with the Harrisons from late March to mid-August), but he is not mentioned in any of the accounts.

39. *Santa Ana Register*, August 9, 1935.

40. Pezman, "Turning Points," 73.

41. Harrison, "A Glimpse Inside Lorrin's Barn," 35.

42. Clark, *Let's Go, Let's Go!*, 10.

43. Clark, *Let's Go, Let's Go!*, 10.

44. Clark, *Let's Go, Let's Go!*, 37.

45. The data derives from census figures in Jordan, "Remembering the Forgotten Village of San Onofre," 31.

46. *Weekly Times-Advocate* (Escondido, Calif.), March 23, 1935.

47. Harrison, "A Glimpse Inside Lorrin's Barn," 37.

48. Warshaw, *The History of Surfing*, 78.

49. Ball, *Ye Weekly Super Illustrated Spintail*, April 14, 1937, 1.

50. Harrison, "A Glimpse Inside Lorrin's Barn," 36.

51. Harrison, "A Glimpse Inside Lorrin's Barn," 36.

52. Freeth was last reported in Redondo Beach in late October 1917 "awaiting a call from the New York Engineers Corps to go to the front at any time" (*Redondo Reflex*, October 26, 1917).

53. Clark, *Let's Go, Let's Go!*, 33.

54. Clark, *Let's Go, Let's Go!*, 33.

55. Rosie Harrison Clark relates that the canoe was probably finished when she was ten years old, or about 1950 (*Let's Go, Let's Go!*, 34). Native Americans in Southern California, of course, had their own traditions of crafting dugout canoes as well.

56. One such source, the *Fornander Collection of Hawaiian Antiquities and Folk-Lore*, can be found at https://ulukau.org/index.php ("Building Canoes" in volume 5, part 3: 610–14). See Holmes, *The Hawaiian Canoe* (30–42) for an illuminating description of traditional canoe-building practices.

57. Ford, "Riding the Surf in Hawaii," 17; *Honolulu Advertiser*, November 9, 1941.

58. Harrison, "A Glimpse Inside Lorrin's Barn," 42.

59. Clark, *Let's Go, Let's Go!*, 37.

60. Clark, *Let's Go, Let's Go!*, 30.

Chapter 6. Palos Verdes

1. Ball, *Ye Super Illustrated Weekly Spin Tail*, January 10, 1936, 1.

2. Ball, *Ye Super Illustrated Weekly Spin Tail*, January 10, 1936, 2.

3. The picture and description begin to appear at the top of page one of the *Palos Verdes Peninsula News* in November 1946 and continue until June 1947.

4. *Judging Palos Verdes as a Place to Live*, 16–17.

5. *Judging Palos Verdes as a Place to Live*, 19.

6. *Judging Palos Verdes as a Place to Live*, 3.

7. The firm's founder, Frederick Law Olmsted Senior, had designed, with partner Calvert Vaux, New York's Central Park in 1857; his son, Frederick Law Olmsted Junior, and stepson, John Charles Olmsted, continued his work by

designing Palos Verdes Estates. The Olmsted firm had also consulted on a 1929 report for the state of California ("Report of State Park Survey of California") and on a 1930 report for Los Angeles County ("Parks, Playgrounds and Beaches for the Los Angeles Region").

8. Fogelson, *Bourgeois Nightmares*, 15.

9. Fogelson, *Bourgeois Nightmares*, 15.

10. Fogelson, *Bourgeois Nightmares*, 15.

11. Ball, *Ye Super Illustrated Weekly Spin Tail*, February 28, 1940, 2.

12. I am indebted to Dina Gilio-Whitaker for her knowledge of settler colonialism and her recommendations on the working draft, which extend here to specific wording.

13. *Palos Verdes Peninsula News*, October 28, 1938. See Luck, "Log Jam 1922," 44–45; Ehlers states that he and three others, including Calvin "Tulie" Clark, rode Bluff Cove in 1928 (Ehlers would have been thirteen, and Clark eleven). Ehlers misremembers dates in the article, placing the founding of the Hermosa Beach Surfing Club in 1934, for example, rather than in 1939.

14. Ball, *Ye Weekly Super Illustrated Spintail*, January 18, 1939, 1.

15. Ball, *Ye Weekly Super Illustrated Spintail*, June 19, 1940, 1.

16. Ball, *Ye Weekly Super Illustrated Spintail*, June 19, 1940, 1.

17. Ball, *Ye Weekly Super Illustrated Spintail*, circa December 30, 1936, 1, and January 4, 1939, 2. The former issue indicates that members had also surfed the cove on New Year's Eve, 1935.

18. Ball's ashes were spread at Bluff Cove on September 22, 2004 ("A to Z" file folders, California Surfing Museum, "Doc Ball" folder; notebook for "The Palos Verdes Surfing Club, 1932–2002," last page).

19. In Ball's day, for example, the *Honolulu Star Bulletin* (August 23, 1935) reported that the ashes of Hope Kauha, the father of lifeguard captain John Kauha, would be spread at Waikīkī. Kauha senior (seventy-seven years old) was born on Waikīkī beach and noted as "an expert surf rider." For information on the "paddle-out ceremony," see Moser, "Origins of the Paddle-Out Ceremony."

20. Nicholls, "Lessons in Surfing for Everyman," 22.

21. Ball, *Ye Weekly Super Illustrated Spintail*, November 17, 1937, 1.

22. Ball, *Ye Weekly Super Illustrated Spintail*, September 29, 1937, 3.

23. Ball, *Ye Weekly Super Illustrated Spintail*, October 6, 1937, 2.

24. Ball, *Ye Weekly Super Illustrated Spintail*, September 29, 1937, 3.

25. Ball, *Ye Weekly Super Illustrated Spintail*, November 17, 1937, 1.

26. Ball, *Ye Weekly Super Illustrated Spintail*, November 17, 1937, 2.

27. Starr, *Endangered Dreams*, 318.

28. *Palos Verdes Peninsula News*, November 26, 1937.

29. See the summary by Charles H. Cheney, one of the planners of Palos Verdes Estates, describing the financial problems faced by the community and the pros and cons of incorporation (*Palos Verdes Peninsula News*, May 20, 1938).

30. *Palos Verdes Peninsula News*, November 26, 1937.

31. Los Angeles County, for example, agreed to contribute two thousand

dollars for lifeguard service in Hermosa Beach; the funds were part of an annual contract the city made with the county (Hermosa Beach City Council minutes for February 5, 1935, 113, and March 5, 1935, 120).

32. *Palos Verdes Peninsula News*, November 26, 1937.

33. Ball, *Ye Weekly Super Illustrated Spintail*, August 16, 1939, 1.

34. Lockwood, "From now on, your name is Burrhead," 45.

35. Ball, *Ye Weekly Super Illustrated Spintail*, February 14, 1940, 2.

36. Ball, *Ye Weekly Super Illustrated Spintail*, February 14, 1940, 2.

37. Ball, *Ye Weekly Super Illustrated Spintail*, February 14, 1940, 2.

38. Ball, *Ye Weekly Super Illustrated Spintail*, February 14, 1940, 2.

39. Ball, *Ye Weekly Super Illustrated Spintail*, March 13, 1940, 1.

40. Ball, *Ye Weekly Super Illustrated Spintail*, January 18, 1939, 2.

41. Ball, *Ye Weekly Super Illustrated Spintail*, January 25, 1937, 2.

42. Ball, *Ye Weekly Super Illustrated Spintail*, January 25, 1937, 1.

43. Ball, *Ye Weekly Super Illustrated Spintail*, March 15, 1939, 2–3.

44. Lockwood, *Peanuts*, 42.

45. *Palos Verdes Peninsula News*, October 28, 1938.

46. Ball, *Ye Weekly Super Illustrated Spintail*, March 15, 1939, 2.

47. Ball, *Ye Weekly Super Illustrated Spintail*, circa May 1, 1940, 1. The issue is undated but appears between issues from April 24, 1940 and May 11, 1940.

48. Ball, *Ye Weekly Super Illustrated Spintail*, circa May 1, 1940, 1.

49. Mary Ann Hawkins states in a letter to Gary Lynch that she had written to Oshier from Santa Cruz and told him about the surf (Croul Publications, Mary Ann Hawkins Collection: Gary Lynch, "Interview with Mary Ann Hawkins-Midkiff," 9). This would have been in 1937, when they were dating. Ball's news-letter confirms that Oshier and Dexter Woods (whom Hawkins mentions as visiting Santa Cruz with Oshier after she had written the letter) made a trip to Santa Cruz the weekend of October 16, 1937 (Ball, *Ye Weekly Super Illustrated Spintail*, October 20, 1937, 3).

50. *Santa Cruz Sentinel*, August 7, 1940.

51. *Santa Cruz Sentinel*, July 17, 1938. The paper reported on July 16, 1938, that Duke was scheduled to give a surfing exhibition, but the paper did not report if the event took place.

52. *Santa Cruz Sentinel*, August 7, 1940. The newspaper reported that the club had formed the previous summer (in 1939). See Thompson, *Out of the Blue: The Story of the Santa Cruz Surfing Club*, for interviews with original members who state 1936 as the year of the club's founding.

53. Ball, *Ye Weekly Super Illustrated Spintail*, May 29, 1940, 1.

54. Ball, *Ye Weekly Super Illustrated Spintail*, May 29, 1940, 1.

55. Surf-club member information comes from the *Santa Cruz Sentinel*, August 7, 1940.

56. *The Daily Surf* (Calif.), July 20, 1885. See also Finney and Houston, *Surfing: A History of the Ancient Hawaiian Sport*, 81–82.

57. An earlier mention (*Santa Cruz Surf*, May 25, 1888) reports local interest

in the sport, though it's not clear if or where the surfing took place: "Prof. Joseph P. Fleming, the champion swimmer, who will teach the natorial art here this summer, has already several pupils who desire to perfect themselves in swimming and surf riding before the season fully opens." For later reports, the search term is "surf board riding": *Santa Cruz Surf*, July 23, 1896 (see also Hickenbottom, *Surfing in Santa Cruz*, 11); *Santa Cruz Evening News*, September 8, 1923; *Santa Cruz Evening News*, June 25, 1927; *Santa Cruz Sentinel*, June 23, 1932.

58. *Santa Cruz Evening News*, July 28, 1913.

59. *Santa Cruz Evening News*, July 28, 1913.

60. *Santa Cruz Evening News*, September 8, 1923.

61. *Santa Cruz Sentinel*, June 23, 1932.

62. *Santa Cruz Sentinel*, August 7, 1940.

63. Los Angeles County Regional Planning District, *The Master Plan of Shoreline Development*, 31.

64. Los Angeles County Regional Planning District, *The Master Plan of Shoreline Development*, 8.

65. Los Angeles County Regional Planning District, *The Master Plan of Shoreline Development*, 8.

66. Los Angeles County Regional Planning District, *The Master Plan of Shoreline Development*, 24.

67. Los Angeles County Regional Planning District, *The Master Plan of Shoreline Development*, 31–32.

68. Ball, *Ye Weekly Super Illustrated Spintail*, February 21, 1940, 1.

69. Ball, *Ye Weekly Super Illustrated Spintail*, February 14, 1940, 1.

70. *Palos Verdes Bulletin*, January 1927, 3, no. 1, 1, and February, 1927, 3, no. 2, 1.

71. *Palos Verdes Bulletin*, February, 1927, 2. See also the *Los Angeles Times*, March 22 and April 17, 1927.

72. *Palos Verdes Bulletin*, January 1927, 3, no. 1, 1.

73. *Los Angeles Times*, June 26, 1927.

74. *Los Angeles Times*, June 26, 1927.

75. *Los Angeles Times*, February 9 and April 20, 1938.

76. Mark, *Our Lifeguard Family*, 1278; the story of the Tahitian natives as inspiration for the fins comes from Los Angeles lifeguard Cal Porter. The story of de Corlieu as a source comes from his biography on the International Scuba Diving Hall of Fame website: "In 1938, de Corlieu's friend Henri Lombard took some fins to Tahiti where Owen Churchill, an American Olympic yachtsman, saw them." https://www.visitcaymanislands.com/en-us/isdhf/isdhf-bios/louis-de-corlieu. See also the *Los Angeles Times*, December 9, 1956, which notes Churchill bringing fins back from Tahiti circa 1938. Don James includes a picture of the fins in *Surfing San Onofre to Point Dume, 1936–1942*, and dates the photograph to 1938. He writes: "This was the day Owen Churchill had come down to the beach at Santa Monica and had gifted us with his newly invented swim fins" (128). Arthur C. Verge also dates photographs of Santa Monica lifeguards wearing fins to 1938 in *Santa Monica Lifeguards*, 47.

77. https://patents.google.com/patent/US2321009A/en.

78. https://patents.google.com/patent/US2321009A/en. "I dispense entirely with any and all metal reinforcements. I thereby decrease the weight of the devices and attain such advantages as increased flexibility, which is desirable while walking with the devices on dry land or in riding surf boards and the like, and also while using the devices in the water."

79. Voit worked in the tire business as an agent for the Diamond Rubber Company (*Los Angeles Times*, December 18, 1912) and then as director of sales for the Eno Rubber Company (*Los Angeles Times*, April 30, 1922). He was issued a permit for the W. J. Voit Rubber Company in January 1928 (*Los Angeles Times*, January 18, 1928). The patent for the "inflatable ball" is under the name of Frank Egerer for the Voit Rubber Company (Patent number 1,853,515, filed November 18, 1929 and secured April 12, 1932): https://www.freepatentsonline.com/1853515.html.

80. Mark, *Our Lifeguard Family*, 1280.

81. For the influence of swell forecasting during World War II, see Westwick and Neushul, *World in the Curl*, 82–89.

82. Ball, *Ye Weekly Super Illustrated Spintail*, September 27, 1939, 2.

83. Ball, *Ye Weekly Super Illustrated Spintail*, September 27, 1939, 2.

84. *Los Angeles Times*, September 7, 1934.

85. *Los Angeles Times*, September 7, 1934. Note surfer Robert Sides's article in "Saturday Night," which mentions storms as the cause of waves: "When the long, windless, oily groundswells, born in mid-ocean storms, roll up the Coast, the sport is supreme," 8.

86. For an overview of Munk's experiment, see the documentary *Waves Across the Pacific*, https://waltermunkfoundation.org/uncategorized/waves-across-the-pacific/.

87. Ball, *Ye Weekly Super Illustrated Spintail*, September 29, 1937, 3.

88. Ball, *Ye Weekly Super Illustrated Spintail*, September 29, 1937, 3.

89. Minville also built and advertised custom surfboards: *Honolulu Advertiser*, September 5, 1926.

90. Blake, *Hawaiian Surfboard*, 62–65.

91. Blake, *Hawaiian Surfboard*, 54.

92. Blake, *Hawaiian Surfboard*, 54.

93. Ball, *Ye Weekly Super Illustrated Spintail*, October 4, 1939, 1.

94. Ball, *Ye Weekly Super Illustrated Spintail*, December 13, 1939, 2.

95. Ball, *Ye Weekly Super Illustrated Spintail*, January 31, 1940, 2.

96. Ball, *Ye Weekly Super Illustrated Spintail*, February 14, 1940, 2.

97. Ball, *Ye Weekly Super Illustrated Spintail*, February 14, 1940, 2.

98. See the list of Palos Verdes Surfing Club members that "Tulie" Clark sent to Jane Schmauss in November, 1998 (California Surfing Museum, A–Z Folders, "'Doc' Ball"): the date "5-15-35" is written under "Palos Verdes Surfing Club" at the top of the page. See also the *Southwest Wave*, July 30, 1935, which reported that the club had been formed earlier that year.

99. Copies of the PVSC constitution and bylaws can be found at the back of

the Palos Verdes Surfing Club Notebook at the Surfing Heritage and Culture Center.

100. The charter members are listed in the Palos Verdes Surfing Club Notebook, Surfing Heritage and Culture Center, "Constitution of the Palos Verdes Surfing Club," p. IV. Kay Murray later wrote: "The Palos Verdes Surfing Club was started by the efforts of Adie Bayer, while a member of the swimming team at Los Angeles Jr. College. He actually badgered the swim team members into becoming surfers. . . . As best I can recall, except for Doc Ball, the charter members were all members of that swimming and water polo team" (California Surf Museum, A–Z File Folders, "Doc" Ball, "The Palos Verdes Surfing Club, 1932–2002"). Members, and their approximate year of initiation (if known), were Charles Allen (1937), Art "Gooseneck" Alsten (1938), Jack Ball (charter member 1935), Adolph "Adie" Bayer (charter member 1935), Bob Boice, Calvin "Tulie" Clark (1935–1936), Jean Depue (1937–1938), George Feister (1935), Johnny "The Smokehouse Kid" Gates (1937–1938), Leroy "Granny" Grannis (1936–1937), Al Holland, Gene Hornbeck (charter member 1935), Adolph Huber (1938), Jack Humphreys (1938), Bob Johnson, Hal Landis (1938), Erwin "Dutch" Lenkeit (charter member 1935), Richard "Mo" Meine (1939), Darrell Miller (charter member 1935), Kay Murray (charter member 1935), Truxton Oehrlin (1939), Everett J. Oshier (1935–1936), Hal Pearson (1937), Bill Pierce (1938), Jim Reynolds (charter member 1935), Fenton Scholes (1938), Earl "Hoppy" Swarts (1935–1936), Cliff Tucker (1939), William Turnbull (1936–1937), Bob Westbrook (1935), and Bernie Zeller.

101. Palos Verdes Surfing Club Notebook, Surfing Heritage and Culture Center, "Constitution of the Palos Verdes Surfing Club," IV.

102. Palos Verdes Surfing Club Notebook, Surfing Heritage and Culture Center, "Constitution of the Palos Verdes Surfing Club," IV.

103. See Gault-Williams and Lynch ("Through the Master's Eyes," 55) for a picture of the clubhouse wall decorated with the portraits.

104. Ackerman, *Doc Ball: Surfing's Legendary Lensman*.

105. Dates for the clubs' founding (or the earliest appearance of the club name in newspapers) come from the following sources: the Del Mar Surfing Club (*Daily News* (Los Angeles), July 20, 1936); the Venice Surfing Club (*Los Angeles Times*, April 29, 1938); the San Onofre Surfing Wahines (*San Onofre Surfing Wahines* scrapbook, Huntington Beach International Surfing Museum, 3); the Manhattan Beach Surfing Club (*San Bernardino County Sun*, August 8, 1938); the Long Beach Surfing Club (*Los Angeles Times*, February 10, 1939); the Hermosa Beach Surfing Club (Hermosa Beach City Council Minutes, February 7, 1939, 225); and the Cabrillo Beach Surfing Club (*San Pedro News-Pilot*, September 12, 1939).

106. The Palos Verdes Surfing Club Notebook, Surfing Heritage and Culture Center, "By-Laws of the Palos Verdes Surfing Club," 2.

107. Ball, *Ye Weekly Super Illustrated Spintail*, July 6, 1939, 2.

108. Ball, *Ye Weekly Super Illustrated Spintail*, February 28, 1940, 2.

109. Ball, *Ye Weekly Super Illustrated Spintail*, February 28, 1940, 2.

110. Hermosa Beach City Council Minutes, February 7, 1939, 225.

111. *Redondo Reflex*, March 10, 1939.

112. The PVSC held four of the gatherings: March 19, 1937; March 19, 1938; March 31, 1939, and March 16, 1940.

113. Ball, *Ye Weekly Super Illustrated Spintail*, circa November 24, 1936, 1.

114. Lockwood, "Granny and Doc," 52.

115. The newsletter comprises approximately 156 extant issues: nine issues from 1936 (with a gap between January 26 and November 10); thirty-eight issues from 1937; twenty-nine issues from 1938; forty-six issues from 1939; and thirty-four issues from 1940. Ball was the primary editor, though other members filled in from time to time. The earliest extant issue (January 2, 1936) is called *Weekly Spiny-Tail*, a play on *Weekly Spintail*. Page two of this issue also uses the title *The Illustrated Weekly Spintail* and indicates that the issue is "the second edition," so presumably Ball wrote the first one in late December 1935. Ball edited the newsletter under the pseudonym "JJ Smokehouse" and often referred to himself in the third person as "JBHall." On July 28, 1937, Ball titled the newsletter *Ye Weekly Super Illustrated Spintail*, a name that became permanent along with a more professional-looking printed format.

116. Ball, *Ye Weekly Super Illustrated Spintail*, January 10, 1936, 1.

117. Ball, *Ye Weekly Super Illustrated Spintail*, February 7, 1940, 2.

118. Ball, *Ye Weekly Super Illustrated Spintail*, January 5, 1938, 2.

119. Ball, *Ye Weekly Super Illustrated Spintail*, January 12, 1937, 1.

120. Ball makes an interesting comment about seeing "Manual Lujan former member of ye PVSC" frequenting the cove. I have seen no other references to Lujan in the club (*Ye Weekly Super Illustrated Spintail*, November 8, 1939, 2). Several clubs seemed to have included women in their ranks, including the Hermosa Beach, Manhattan Beach, and Del Mar Surfing Clubs.

121. *Ye Weekly Super Illustrated Spintail*, October 18, 1939, 1. Tucker was perhaps the first surfer to have a "signature" model surfboard, which Thomas Rogers built and sold as a "Slantzwise" (A–Z Folders, Blake, "Pacific Coast Paddle Polo Schedule, Season 1941").

122. *Ye Weekly Super Illustrated Spintail*, January 31, 1940, 1.

123. *Ye Weekly Super Illustrated Spintail*, December 14, 1938, 1. The following appears in the January 2, 1936 newsletter: "Joke—Laho Lio: 'Bet you don't even know what a fairy God father is.' Nellie Bly: 'Fraid I don't, but I got an Uncle I'm not so sure of.'" (1).

Chapter 7. San Onofre

1. Lockwood, "Passing the Torch," 63.

2. Los Angeles County Regional Planning District, *Master Plan*, 31.

3. Haas, *Conquests and Historical Identities in California*, 13–14.

4. https://www.jbmian.com/history.html#/. For additional background,

see Jordan, "Remembering the Forgotten Village of San Onofre," 27–29, and Gamble, *First Coastal Californians*, 31–34; 76–77. An overview of present-day Acjachemen involvement in environmental justice issues can be found in Gilio-Whitaker, *As Long as Grass Grows*, 132–38.

5. Shipek, *Pushed into the Rocks*, 28. For a comprehensive overview of the Spanish, Mexican, and American Periods in Southern California, see Chapter 3, "Postcontact History."

6. Shipek, *Pushed into the Rocks*, 31–32.

7. Shipek, *Pushed into the Rocks*, 35. I've simplified a protracted and complex history, which can be consulted in more detail in Shipek's book. For this period, see also Haas, *Conquests and Historical Identities in California*, 56–68.

8. Jordan, "Remembering the Forgotten Village of San Onofre," 29.

9. Jordan, "Remembering the Forgotten Village of San Onofre," 29.

10. *Los Angeles Evening Post-Record*, July 8, 1926.

11. *Santa Ana Register*, August 11, 1930; *Santa Ana Register*, August 28, 1930: "Mr. and Mrs. Robert Paulus and children, Mr. and Mrs. Jake Timken and children and Mr. and Mrs. Robert Lemke and children motored to San Onofre Saturday evening and camped until Sunday evening."

12. Ball, *Ye Weekly Super Illustrated Spintail*, April 12, 1939, 3.

13. Gault-Williams, *Legendary Surfers*, 235–36.

14. Sullivan, "Interview with Calvin 'Tulie' Clark," 1995, *Encyclopedia of Surfing* (eos.surf).

15. Gault-Williams, *Legendary Surfers*, 236.

16. Gault-Williams, *Legendary Surfers*, 237.

17. Palos Verdes Surfing Club Notebook, "Constitution of the Palos Verdes Surfing Club," 1.

18. Palos Verdes Surfing Club Notebook, "Constitution of the Palos Verdes Surfing Club," 3.

19. "A to Z Folders," California Surf Museum, "'Doc' Ball" folder; note by John Gates.

20. Palos Verdes Surfing Club Notebook, "Amendments to the Constitution," 3.

21. Ball, *Ye Weekly Super Illustrated Spintail*, December 25, 1938, 4.

22. Palos Verdes Surfing Club Notebook, "Constitution of the Palos Verdes Surfing Club," 1.

23. Ball, *Ye Weekly Super Illustrated Spintail*, July 10, 1940, 1.

24. Ball, *Ye Weekly Super Illustrated Spintail*, August 14, 1940, 1.

25. See, for example, *Ye Weekly Super Illustrated Spintail*, November 29, 1939, 1: "Finally after ten years of collectings and neg shooting ye doc finally gets one of his own hide—and on one of the super waves of the day—wound up on the rocks but whatthehell boys whatthehell."

26. Croul Publications, Mary Ann Hawkins Collection: Gary Lynch, "Interview with Mary Ann Hawkins-Midkiff," 5.

27. *San Onofre Surfing Wahines*, 38.

28. Ulrich had applied for a liquor license to sell the beverage the previous year (*Santa Ana Register*, February 3, 1938).

29. *Los Angeles Times*, August 28, 1939.

30. *Santa Ana Register*, May 1, 1930. See also a report from the same paper (April 9, 1930) detailing the club's "initiation tea" at Corona del Mar where members also planned on "surf board riding." Bertolet is mentioned here as well, along with Kenneth Tanaka, Louis Romoff, Jack Dutton, Wayne Garlock, and Nevin Hoy.

31. See Gault-Williams, *Legendary Surfers*, 79, note 293, where he cites Lorrin Harrison's remark that "Laholio" meant "horse balls" in Spanish. In Hawaiian, "laho" translates as "scrotum" and "lio" as "horse."

32. Harrison, "A Glimpse Inside Lorrin's Barn," 42; Ball, *Ye Weekly Super Illustrated Spintail*, November 17, 1936, 1. The "DMC" was Santa Monica's Del Mar Club. The Hawaiian word would have been "kukae" ("excrement").

33. *The Long Beach Sun*, December 16, 1931.

34. Craig Lockwood states in "Waterman" that Peterson and fellow lifeguard Wally Burton were frequenting San Onofre by 1930–31 (53). Describing meeting Peterson at Waikīkī in the winter of 1932–1933, Lorrin Harrison reported in "Lorrin's Barn," "I had heard about Pete Peterson and seen him at San Onofre" (38). If this is true, then both Harrison and Peterson had been frequenting San Onofre well before Harrison's famous trip there circa 1934.

35. One exception could be the 1934 PCSRC, about which little information is known. There were two surfing events in 1935, both at Huntington Beach (*Santa Ana Register*, July 29 and September 2). Bob Sides won the first contest, and Lorrin Harrison the second.

36. Ball wrote: "after allowing as to how other farces had been held at the popular beach spot—old jbh did think mebe he could devise some kind of a meet that couldn't be much worse—and did such . . . then—as usually happens—at the nofre duck pond—no surf appears—but this did not stop that mad Dentist for he had some races all arranged" (*Ye Weekly Super Illustrated Spintail*, August 30, 1939, 1). As noted in Chapter Two, this event was not the annual PCSRC, which had taken place a month earlier and was won by Lorrin Harrison.

37. Warshaw, *The History of Surfing*, 80.

38. *Evening Outlook*, September 3, 1936.

39. *Santa Ana Register*, September 11, 1936. Peterson, Brignell, Wilkes, Harrison and other members of the Del Mar Surfing Club were photographed after their victory in the 1937 Catalina-to-Santa Monica paddleboard race (*Evening Outlook*, June 28, 1937).

40. Peterson as president of the Del Mar Surfing Club: *Evening Outlook*, February 9, 1938; names of the top ten finishers: *Evening Outlook*, July 11, 1938. It's possible that the Del Mar Surfing Club also sponsored the 1936 PCSRC.

41. Verge, *Santa Monica Lifeguards*, 27.

42. For the WCPA sponsoring the contest, see the *Los Angeles Times*, July 4, 1938 and the *Pasadena Post*, August 9, 1940. Ball references Bayer as a swimming

instructor at the club in January 1936 (*Ye Weekly Super Illustrated Spintail*, January 15, 1936, 1); in Bayer's April 20, 1940 letter to Harry Welch, Secretary of the Newport Beach Chamber of Commerce, he lists the Deauville Club as the WCPA's postal address (Records of the Newport Beach Chamber of Commerce, Sherman Library and Gardens, Folder 430, "Paddleboard Assn."). The letter dates from April 29, 1940.

43. *Evening Outlook*, February 9, 1938.

44. Ball, *Ye Weekly Super Illustrated Spintail*, February 9, 1938, 1.

45. *Los Angeles Times*, June 27, 1938. The PVSC had won the inaugural race in 1936 but lost to the Del Mar Surfing Club in 1937. Note the following report the day before the 1938 race from the *Evening Outlook* (June 25): "Palos Verdes was established as the favorite when the Del Mar Surfing Club of Santa Monica, winner a year ago, refused to compete because of the restriction placed on the boards. The ruling, as made by the West Coast Paddleboard Association, is that all boards must be identical. The Del Mar members have their own designs and refused to participate without them."

46. *Evening Outlook*, February 9, 1938.

47. *Evening Outlook*, July 11, 1938 (reported forty-eight contestants); *Los Angeles Times*, July 11, 1938 (reported thirty-six contestants).

48. *Santa Ana Register*, July 10, 1939 (reported eighty contestants); *Los Angeles Times*, August 12, 1940 (reported seventy-five contestants). No newspaper articles have been found that cover the 1941 contest.

49. *Los Angeles Times*, July 11, 1938 and August 12, 1940.

50. *Los Angeles Times*, August 11, 1940.

51. The original date for the contest was July 12, 1940 (*Los Angeles Times*, August 11, 1940).

52. *Evening Outlook*, July 11, 1938.

53. Records of the Newport Beach Chamber of Commerce, Sherman Library and Gardens, Corona del Mar, California: Folder 430, "Paddleboard Assn." The letter dates from April 20, 1940.

54. Events from 1936 where the WCPA is reported as sponsor: Venice (*Los Angeles Times*, June 22); Santa Monica–Catalina (*Los Angeles Times*, June 28); Topanga-Venice (*Daily News* (Los Angeles), July 20); Santa Monica (*Evening Outlook*, September 12); Balboa (*Los Angeles Times*, November 21); probable races sanctioned by the WCPA given the location and/or competitors (though not explicitly stated in newspaper reports): Hermosa Beach—won by Peterson (*Redondo Reflex*, August 7); Balboa—events won by Peterson and Harrison (*Santa Ana Register*, August 31); PCSRC at San Onofre—won by Peterson (*Santa Ana Register*, September 11); 1937 events where the WCPA is reported as sponsor: Topanga-Santa Monica (*Evening Outlook*, May 22); Catalina-Santa Monica (*Evening Outlook*, June 28); probable races sanctioned by the WCPA: Santa Monica (*Evening Vanguard*, June 10); Hermosa Beach—won by "Tulie" Clark (*Evening Outlook*, August 2); Santa Monica team races—PVSC defeats Del Mar and Santa Monica (*Ball, Ye Weekly Super Illustrated Spintail*, September 9, 1937, 1); Santa Monica—won by Peterson (*Evening Outlook*, September 13).

55. Events from 1938 where the WCPA is reported as sponsor: Catalina-Santa Monica (*Los Angeles Times*, June 27); PCSRC (*Los Angeles Times*, July 10); probable races sanctioned by the WCPA: Venice—won by PVSC over Del Mar and Santa Monica (*Evening Outlook*, June 22); Long Beach—surfboard relays won by Manhattan Beach Surfing Club (*San Bernardino County Sun*, August 8); Venice—Venice Paddleboard Club beats the Deauville club (*Evening Vanguard*, September 2); Cabrillo—won by John Kerwin (*News-Pilot*, September 5); Long Beach—won by Peterson and Hawkins (*Los Angeles Times*, November 12). The number of contests held steady at about a dozen a year from 1939 through 1941, so it's likely that the WCPA sanctioned a similar percentage as in 1938.

56. *Evening Outlook*, February 9, 1938; *Ball, Ye Weekly Super Illustrated Spintail*, January 10, 1939, 2.

57. "It was a much wilder group down there . . . These guys were wonderful guys. Barney Wilkes, Doakes [Charles Butler], Laholio, Nellie Blye [*sic*], Joe Bush . . . They would tend to surf all morning and then, in the afternoon, there was a lot of pretty heavy drinking—wine; cheap wine. Party type, you know; hula dancers, singing and all that stuff," Gault-Williams, *Legendary Surfers*, 235.

58. Gault-Williams, *Legendary Surfers*, 235.

59. *Santa Ana Register*, August 6, 1936.

60. *Los Angeles Times*, July 28, 1935.

61. In a sad epilogue, Wilkes died in Mexico in February 1968. His body was discovered in a beach cabin about thirty-five miles south of Tijuana. He had been living alone in his camper, which he had parked on the grounds of a motor court (*Redlands Daily Facts* (Redlands, CA), February 23, 1968).

62. *Los Angeles Times*, August 9, 1992; https://sanonofresurfingclub.org/home ("The Club"/"History of San Onofre").

63. *Los Angeles Times*, June 9, 1922. See also Jefferson, *Living the California Dream*, 71–103.

64. *Del Mar Club Life*, February 1934, 3.

65. *Judging Palos Verdes as a Place to Live*, 3.

66. Wheaton, "Space Invaders in Surfing's White Tribe," 178.

67. Matuszak, *San Onofre* (2018), 771.

68. Matuszak, *San Onofre* (2018), 780, and https://sanonofresurfingclub.org/home ("The Club"/"History of San Onofre").

69. The names of sections along the beach were dubbed the "Ghetto" and "Watts"; the former winning its name due to the lower playing ability of volleyball players, and the latter "because that's where it was known that some of the drug dealers, or some of the drug-deals went down" (Matuszak, *San Onofre* [2018], 316–317).

70. The Santa Cruz Surfing Club did admit female members. See the *Santa Cruz Sentinel*, August 7, 1940. See also the same newspaper (July 18, 1985) where Sue Groff mentions that women weren't allowed in the club house and had to wait outside. ("Of course," she said, "I ran in there when ever possible.")

71. For more on the role of imagination in beach culture, see Wheaton, "Space Invaders in Surfing's White Tribe," 178.

72. Oral History: Ronald Dewolf Higgins and Francis Andrew Imaika-lani Bowers, June 8, 1978, Outrigger Canoe Club, https://www.outrigger canoeclubsports.com/occ-archives/oral-histories/ronald-dewolf-higgins-francis -andrew-imaikalani-bowers/; see also Couvillon, *Sands of Time*, 31.

73. Couvillon, *Sands of Time*, 40. See also Smith and Feinemen, *Kings of the Beach*, 2–3.

74. *Los Angeles Times*, July 19, 1925.

75. Smith and Feinemen, *Kings of the Beach*, 2.

76. See the *Los Angeles Times* (August 7, 1927) for a photograph of the Santa Monica Beach Club competing in a volleyball match against the Santa Monica Athletic Club.

77. *Annual Report, Department of Recreation Camps and Playgrounds*, 1929–1930 (51, 53) and 1930–1931 (13).

78. Smith and Feinemen, *Kings of the Beach*, 4–10.

79. Smith and Feinemen, *Kings of the Beach*, 5.

80. Smith and Feinemen, *Kings of the Beach*, 6.

81. For more on the genesis of building a business life around beach culture, see Holmes, *Hobie: Master of Water, Wind and Waves*, ix.

82. Matuszak, *San Onofre* (2018), 1118.

83. *San Onofre Surfing Wahines*, 22.

84. *Evening Outlook*, June 21, 1937. See also Ball, *Ye Weekly Super Illustrated Spintail*, May 26/June 2, 1937, 2.

85. *Los Angeles Times*, October 27, 1926.

86. *Santa Maria Times*, October 26, 1935.

87. *Santa Ana Register*, September 11, 1936.

88. Ball, *Ye Weekly Super Illustrated Spintail*, April 14, 1937, 1, and May 12, 1937, 1.

89. Besides his acting career, Coogan is best known for suing his mother and stepfather in 1938 for having squandered the millions of dollars he had earned on the big screen. Although Coogan himself recovered just over $126,000 of the total, his lawsuit prompted passage of the Coogan Law, which required fifty percent of a child's net earnings to be placed in a trust. For the Coogan Law, see *Long Beach Sun*, July 19, 1939 and https://www.sagaftra.org/membership-benefits/young-performers/coogan-law.

90. Cain, "The Widow's Mite," 22.

91. James, *Surfing San Onofre to Point Dume*, 124.

Chapter 8. Malibu

1. James, *Surfing San Onofre to Point Dume*, 129. See the *San Bernardino County Sun* (January 21, 1939) for the story of Coogan selling Grable's furniture to purchase a new car.

2. James, *Surfing San Onofre to Point Dume*, 124–25. For more on Coogan's lawsuit against his mother and stepfather, see Cary, *Jackie Coogan*, 167–76.

3. James, *Surfing San Onofre to Point Dume*, 129.

4. See, for example, "Malibu—the stars' playground" (*Vanity Fair,* October 1930, 53) with a picture of Clara Bow, or "On the beach at Malibu" (*Vanity Fair*, January 1932, 52–53), which includes a photograph of Douglas Fairbanks Jr., Joan Crawford, and this detail: "Is it any wonder that the casual visitor on the Malibu sands feels that he is dreaming that he walks along some ancient Grecian shore, peopled by a beautiful dead race of bronzed gods and goddesses?"

5. *Los Angeles Times*, April 6, 1927 and May 29, 1938.

6. Daigle, *American Tan*, 120–21. For a detailed study of tanning in France in the 1920s, including a challenge to Coco Chanel's influence, see Pascal Ory, *L'invention du bronzage. Essai d'une histoire culturelle* (Paris: Complexe, 2008).

7. Daigle, *American Tan*, 153–54.

8. *Detroit Free Press*, June 4, 1939.

9. Samuel K. Rindge was the eldest son of Frederick and May Rindge (Frederick had passed away in 1905). The ranch was owned by May Rindge rather than her son.

10. Reid, "The Days of Great Boards and Real Watermen," 57.

11. Reid, "The Days of Great Boards and Real Watermen," 57.

12. *Los Angeles Times*, June 13 and June 27, 1926; http://www.adamsonhouse .org/tile.php.

13. See the *Los Angeles Times* report that the Roosevelt Highway was paved from Santa Monica to the Las Flores Inn (July 1, 1923: "Route Changes Are Numerous").

14. Lynch and Gault-Williams, *Tom Blake*, 35.

15. *Los Angeles Times*, September 20, 1926.

16. *Los Angeles Times*, September 20, 1926; *Evening Vanguard*, September 20, 1926.

17. The Roosevelt Highway officially opened to the public on June 29, 1929, though it had been in use by the public since the 1923 U.S. Supreme Court decision.

18. http://www.adamsonhouse.org/main.php. May Rindge had also started building a mansion for herself up on the bluff overlooking Surfrider Beach, which was never completed because of the Great Depression. Randall notes that this house also began to take shape in 1929 (*King and Queen of Malibu*, 214).

19. See the *Los Angeles Times* (June 26, 1927) for mention of the "brand new lovely Malibu cottage" of Anna Q. Nilsson, who is generally credited with being the first to lease a house there.

20. Rindge, *Happy Days in Southern California*, 64–65.

21. Randall, *King and Queen of Malibu*, 80–88.

22. Gamble, *The Chumash*, 6–8; 108.

23. Gamble, *The Chumash*, 108–11.

24. Gamble, *The Chumash*, 206.

25. Gamble, *The Chumash*, 204–5.

26. Rindge, *Happy Days in Southern California*, 70.

27. Gamble indicates, for instance, that the Chumash and their neighbors, the Western Tongva, "considered *Humaliwo* an important political center" (108). The name "California" first appears in a Spanish romance, published in Madrid in 1510 (Deverell and Igler, *A Companion to California History*, 5).

28. For details of the Rindge's battle with the homesteaders, see Randall, *The King and Queen of Malibu*, 92–94.

29. Randall, *The King and Queen of Malibu*, 129.

30. Randall, *The King and Queen of Malibu*, 182.

31. The poisoning of the sheep reported by Randall was later determined to be caused by anthrax, noted as a cattle disease rather than intentional poisoning (*Los Angeles Times*, September 12, 1917: "Anthrax Kills Sheep").

32. Nunn penned a trilogy in this genre: *Tapping the Source* (1984), *The Dogs of Winter* (1997), and *Tijuana Straits* (2004). More recent titles include Don Winslow's *The Dawn Patrol* (2008) and two collections edited by David M. Olsen: *The Silver Waves of Summer* (2021) and *The Dark Waves of Winter* (2023).

33. For information on Cain's arrival in California, his Malibu article for *Vanity Fair*, and background on the writing and publication of *The Postman Always Rings Twice*, see Hoopes, *Cain*, 214–47.

34. Cain, "The Widow's Mite, or Queen of the Rancho," 22.

35. Cain, "The Widow's Mite, or Queen of the Rancho," 22.

36. Cain, *The Postman Always Rings Twice*, 36.

37. For an instructive reading of the central themes in Cain's writing, including automobiles and highways, see Fine, "james m. cain and the los angeles novel."

38. Cain, *The Postman Always Rings Twice*, 24.

39. Cain, *The Postman Always Rings Twice*, 24.

40. Cain, *The Postman Always Rings Twice*, 101.

41. Cain, *The Postman Always Rings Twice*, 102.

42. Cain, *The Postman Always Rings Twice*, 102.

43. Cain, *The Postman Always Rings Twice*, 102.

44. Cain, *The Postman Always Rings Twice*, 102.

45. James, *Prewar Surfing Photographs*, 45–46.

46. *Los Angeles Times*, September 7, 1934.

47. Ball, *Ye Weekly Super Illustrated Spintail*, September 13, 1939, 1.

48. Ball, *Ye Weekly Super Illustrated Spintail*, September 27, 1939, 2.

49. Randall, *The King and Queen of Malibu*, 218.

50. Ball, *California Surfriders*, 12.

51. Ball, *Ye Weekly Super Illustrated Spintail*, October 18, 1939, 1; December 13, 1939, 2.

52. This one-page issue of the newsletter has no date but appears between April 24 and May 11, 1940, so perhaps Wednesday, May 1 (the day of the week that Ball usually published the newsletter).

53. Blake, *Hawaiian Surfboard*, 55–58 (for a description of Duke's longest ride in 1917, and Blake and Duke's long rides in 1930); the *Honolulu Advertiser*, June

1, 1936 (for Blake's longest ride of more than a mile). For a detailed description of Duke's longest ride, see Davis, *Waterman*, 108–11.

54. Cain, "The Widow's Mite or Queen of the Rancho," 22.

55. Warshaw, *The History of Surfing*, 109.

Chapter 9. *Hawaiian Surfboard* and the Writing of Surf History

1. Starr, *Material Dreams*, 69.

2. Blake, *Hawaiian Surfboard*, 5–6.

3. The scenario originally appeared in Blake's "Surfriding in Hawaii," where the Hawaiian was named "Miloa," perhaps derived from "mī" ("dream") and "loa" ("long" or "distant"). Blake misspells (and mistranslates) the name of the famous surfing spot "Kalehuawehe" as "Kalahuewehe" throughout his book (his mistranslation is on p. 15). For the correct spelling and translation ("the removed *lehua* lei"), see Pukui, Ebert, and Mookini, *Place Names of Hawaii*, 76.

4. Blake, *Hawaiian Surfboard*, 32.

5. Blake, *Hawaiian Surfboard*, 28.

6. Blake, *Hawaiian Surfboard*, 28. Blake writes on the opening page of the book, "I came from the snow country, of northern Wisconsin, to Waikiki beach, to substitute surfboards for skiis [sic]" 5.

7. Blake, *Hawaiian Surfboard*, 22–23.

8. Blake, *Hawaiian Surfboard*, 23.

9. Blake, *Hawaiian Surfboard*, 24; Kamakau, *Tales and Traditions*, 45.

10. Kamakau, *Tales and Traditions*, 6.

11. Lynch and Gault-Williams, *Tom Blake*, 33. The authors state that Francis Cunningham came from Oklahoma and that her family grew rich from oil, which likely indicates that they were Osage Indians.

12. Lynch and Gault-Williams, *Tom Blake*, 32–33. For the couple's arrival in Honolulu on August 15, 1925: "Honolulu, Hawaii, U.S. Arriving and Departing Passenger and Crew Lists, 1900–1959 for Thomas Blake," Series Description A3422-Arriving at Honolulu, Hawaii, 1900–1953, ancestry.com. Above Blake's name is listed "Frances Blake, 18, from Bartlesville, OKLA." The couple departed on December 5, 1925.

13. Blake, *Hawaiian Surfboard*, 28.

14. Lynch and Gault-Williams, *Tom Blake*, 33.

15. Lynch and Gault-Williams, *Tom Blake*, 33.

16. Lynch and Gault-Williams, *Tom Blake*, 26.

17. Lynch and Gault-Williams, *Tom Blake*, 58.

18. Blake, *Hawaiian Surfboard*, 26.

19. *Tom Blake Scrapbook*, 13.

20. *Tom Blake Scrapbook*, 29.

21. Gault-Williams and Lynch, "Pulling Seaward: Tommy Zahn," 77.

22. Blake, *Hawaiian Surfboard*, 28. For Blake's spelling of "Kalahuawehe," see footnote 3 above.

23. For the origin of the Pan-Pacific Press Bureau, see the *Honolulu Advertiser*, February 21, 1922. The Pan-Pacific Press Bureau originated from the Pan-Pacific Union, organized by Hawai'i booster Alexander Hume Ford.

24. *Honolulu Star-Bulletin*, May 10, 2006. For more on hula dancers and tourism, see Desmond, *Staging Tourism*, 60–78.

25. *Paradise of the Pacific* 1, no. 1 (January 1888): 1.

26. Blake, *Hawaiian Surfboard*, 37.

27. Finney, *Hawaiian Surfing*, 23.

28. Finney and Houston, *Surfing: The Sport of Hawaiian Kings*, 13–14.

29. Blake, *Hawaiian Surfboard*, 5.

30. Blake, *Hawaiian Surfboard*, 39.

31. Blake, *Hawaiian Surfboard*, 41. The phrase "a lost art" also appeared in Alexander Hume Ford's "Aquatic Sports," 19.

32. Finney, *Hawaiian Surfing*, 61, 72–74.

33. Blake, *Hawaiian Surfboard*, 60.

34. Blake, *Hawaiian Surfboard*, 82.

35. Finney and Houston, *Surfing: The Sport of Hawaiian Kings*, 67.

36. Ford had arrived in April 1907, and George Freeth gave surf lessons to both Ford and Jack London. For details on surfing in the nineteenth century, see Clark, *Hawaiian Surfing*, and Moser, "The Endurance of Surfing in 19th-Century Hawai'i."

37. Finney's master's thesis cites only one article by Ford—"Outdoor Allurements"—which appeared in the 1911 edition of Thrum's *Hawaiian Annual*. Ford described the origins of the Outrigger Canoe Club in this article but not his role in "saving" surfing (as he does elsewhere), so it's likely that Finney drew his information from *Hawaiian Surfboard*. Note Ford's comments in 1944 reinforcing his role as surfing's savior: "In 1908 I did get back to Waikiki, learned to ride the surfboard, organized the Outrigger club to revive the then dead sport of surfriding" (*Honolulu Star-Bulletin*, February 15, 1944).

38. Forbes, *Hawaiian National Bibliography*, vol. 2, 94.

39. Bates, *Sandwich Island Notes*, 298.

40. Bates, *Sandwich Island Notes*, 421.

41. Much of this paragraph first appeared in Moser, "The Reports of Surfing's Demise Have Been Greatly Exaggerated," 202.

42. Blake, *Hawaiian Surfboard*, 50; Finney and Houston, *Surfing: The Sport of Hawaiian Kings*, 57. Jarves is noted in this latter work as a missionary, which is incorrect. He was a newspaper editor for *The Polynesian*. The reference comes from his *Scenes and Scenery in the Sandwich Islands* (1844).

43. Emerson, "Causes of Decline of Ancient Hawaiian Sports," 59. Blake mentions Emerson in connection with Native Hawaiian burial traditions but does not cite this specific article. For a reading of Emerson's religious and political agendas, see Laderman, *Empire in Waves*, 8–10, 14–15.

44. London, "My Hawaiian Aloha," 170.

45. Walker, *Waves of Resistance*, 61–62.

46. Laderman, *Empire in Waves*, 19–20.

47. Wood, *Displacing Natives*, 45.

48. *Pacific Commercial Advertiser*, May 29, 1907.

49. For Ford and statehood, see Laderman, *Empire in Waves*, 28. For more information on Ford and the Hawaii Promotion Committee, see Moser, "The Hawaii Promotion Committee and the Appropriation of Surfing," 517–19.

50. Blake, *Hawaiian Surfboard*, 7.

51. Desmond, *Staging Tourism*, 40.

52. One might read a metaphorical example of this dynamic in the story of Moloa: the king was a famous surfer in his youth, but now Moloa has assumed his (surf) crown.

53. Blake, *Hawaiian Surfboard*, 52.

54. Blake, *Hawaiian Surfboard*, iv.

55. Blake, *Hawaiian Surfboard*, 40. Blake is also credited with placing a fin on surfboards in 1935, an innovation that only came into its own with the lighter balsa and fiberglass boards after World War II.

56. Moser, *Surf and Rescue*, 28, 123.

57. Blake mentions Freeth several times in his book, including the following reference (an indication that little was generally known about Freeth's accomplishments in California prior to 1915): "George Freeth rode California surf about the 1915 period" (61).

58. Smith and Feinemen, *Kings of the Beach*, 5.

59. McElvanie, *The Great Depression*, 75.

60. Starr, *The Dream Endures*, 4.

61. *Los Angeles Times*, August 7, 1927. For information on the Hawaiian tradition of bodysurfing, see John R. K. Clark's entries for the sport ("kaha nalu") in *Hawaiian Surfing*, 73–80.

62. Davis, *Waterman*, 67, 133; Jarret, *Surfing Australia*, 23.

63. *Los Angeles Times*, July 10, 1913.

64. The *San Diego Union* (July 30, 1918) reported Freeth and his lifeguards offering free classes every morning at Ocean Beach to beach visitors.

65. Drummond, *The Art of Wave Riding*, 1.

66. Drummond, *The Art of Wave Riding*, 1. The epigraph precedes Drummond's introduction.

67. Ford, "Aquatic Sports," 19.

68. *Los Angeles Times*, September 26, 1932.

69. *San Diego Union*, July 18, 1937. The president of the organization, Lewis C. Tompkins, stated that bodysurfing (also called "Moby coasting") "has been popular among small groups at San Diego County beaches for a long time, but it seems to be little known elsewhere and it has never been given due recognition as an outstanding surf sport." For bodysurfing contests (and their winners) during Huntington Beach's aquatic festivals (July) and Black and Gold Days

(September): *Santa Ana Register*, July 29, 1935—George Farquhar, Mack Beal, John Olson; *Santa Ana Register*, September 2, 1935—Ernie Syracusa; *Santa Ana Register*, July 6, 1936—Bob Read, Bill Farquhar, Earl Conrad; *Santa Ana Register*, September 7, 1937—Art Bermudez, George Bisset, Bud Redline; *Santa Ana Register*, September 6, 1938—Dave McBride, Art Bermudez, Johnny Overmyer.

70. *Life*, "Surf Riding On California Beach Is A Favorite Summertime Sport," 50–51.

71. The article states that the pictures were taken at Palos Verdes, but three of the four on p. 41 were taken from the Hermosa Beach pier. *Life* photographer Bob Wallace snapped the pictures of Mary Ann Hawkins (Ball, *Ye Weekly Super Illustrated Spintail*, December 8, 2).

Epilogue

1. James, *Surfing San Onofre to Point Dume*, 127.

2. https://capitolmuseum.ca.gov/special/ww2/after-the-war; Farber and Bailey, "The Fighting Man as Tourist," 641.

3. James, *Surfing San Onofre to Point Dume*, 138.

4. Lockwood, "Granny and Doc," 52.

5. Lockwood, "Granny and Doc," 52.

6. Lockwood, "Passing the Torch," 59.

7. Lockwood, "Granny and Doc," 54.

8. Lynch and Gault-Williams, *Tom Blake*, 164.

9. Ball, *Ye Weekly Super Illustrated Spintail*, August 30, 1939, 1.

10. https://ww2db.com/battle_spec.php?battle_id=17.

11. *Redondo Reflex*, August 20, 1942.

12. Starr, *Embattled Dreams*, 183. Starr counts battle and non-battle causes beginning from the declaration of a national emergency on May 27, 1941.

13. Annual Report, Department of Parks and Recreation, 1941–1942, 11.

14. *Wilmington Daily Press Journal*, August 14, 1942.

15. Official Military Personnel File of Blake, Thomas Edward.

16. Lynch and Gault-Williams, *Tom Blake*, 164–65.

17. Peterson's military records indicated that he was inducted rather than enlisted ("Notice of Separation From U.S. Naval Service," dated March 13, 1946). Official Military Personnel File of Peterson, Francis P.

18. Lockwood, "Waterman," 58–59.

19. Chalke, *Frank Chalke Oral History Interview*. Chalke served as a Radioman aboard the *U.S.S. Pandemus* during the battle of Okinawa: https://digitalarchive.pacificwarmuseum.org/digital/collection/p16769coll1/id/9729. For a general history of the battle, consult https://www.nationalww2museum.org/war/topics/battle-of-okinawa.

20. Official Military Personnel File of Peterson, Francis P.

21. Lockwood, "Waterman," 58–59; Chalke, *Frank Chalke Oral History Interview*.

22. https://www.history.navy.mil/research/histories/ship-histories/danfs/g/general-h-l-scott-ap-136.html.

23. Lockwood, "Granny and Doc," 54.

24. *San Fernando Valley Times,* July 16, 1945: "In my pool—ages 6 to 16. Mary Ann Hawkins Morrissey, former swim champ 6 lessons $25." The phone number listed on the ad places her in the town of Arleta.

25. Annual Report, Department of Parks and Recreation, 1945–1946, 4; 1941–1942, 13; 1942–1943, 27; 1944–1945, 11.

26. Annual Report, Department of Parks and Recreation, 1945–1946, 4.

27. The quarantine order was issued on April 3, 1943 (Annual Report, Department of Parks and Recreation, 1942–1943, 2). See also the *Los Angeles Times,* April 15, 1943; June 26, 1947, and June 30, 1947. The quarantined area generally stretched from 14th street in Hermosa Beach, just north of the pier, to Brooks Avenue in Venice, just south of the Venice pier.

28. *Los Angeles Times,* October 18, 1945, and February 2, 1946.

29. Verge, "The Impact of the Second World War on Los Angeles," 308.

30. *Los Angeles Times,* December 9, 1941. The reports were soon proved false.

31. Starr, *Embattled Dreams,* 36.

32. http://www.militarymuseum.org/ManhattanBeachMR.html.

33. https://www.nationalguard.mil/News/Article/2858244/washington-guard-helped-defend-us-after-pearl-harbor-attack/#:~:text=Within%20hours%20of%20the%20end,used%20as%20a%20psychological%20warfare.

34. https://www.archives.gov/education/lessons/japanese-relocation#background. Italian-American and German-American residents in California were also forced to leave restricted areas. See D'Amelio, "A Season of Panic," 147–62.

35. *Santa Ana Register,* May 13, 1942.

36. https://www.pendleton.marines.mil/Main-Menu/History-and-Museums/.

37. https://malibutimes.com/wp-content/uploads/2014/07/16/c9821ee5da77fe5cc862f6a40f1d1101.pdf.

38. https://malibutimes.com/wp-content/uploads/2014/07/16/c9821ee5da77fe5cc862f6a40f1d1101.pdf.

39. https://www.northamericanforts.com/West/ca-south2.html.

40. *Long Beach Press-Telegram,* March 17, 1942.

41. https://www.worldwariiaviation.org/women-air-force-service-pilots-wasp/.

42. *Los Angeles Evening Citizen News,* May 9, 1942.

43. Annual Report, Department of Parks and Recreation, 1942–1943, 26.

44. Starr, *Embattled Dreams,* 123.

45. Starr, *Embattled Dreams,* 25.

46. Starr, *Embattled Dreams,* 25. *Los Angeles Times,* August 16, 1941.

47. *Los Angeles Times,* April 10 and June 30, 1942.

48. *Palos Verdes Peninsula News,* July 31 and September 11, 1942.

49. *Santa Cruz Sentinel,* September 2. 1942.

50. *Los Angeles Times,* June 2, 1944.

51. Duclos, "Matt Kivlin," 52.

52. *Long Beach Sun*, June 8, 1942, and July 2, 1943.

53. *Long Beach Sun*, July 12, 1943.

54. Annual Report, Department of Parks and Recreation, 1945–1946, 2; the 1944–1945 report indicates that Zuma was being considered for acquisition (3). Huntington Beach was gifted to the state in 1942: https://www.parks.ca.gov/?page_id=643#:~:text=Huntington%20was%20gifted%20to%20the,California%20state%20beach%20in%201963.

55. The Los Angeles County annual report for 1942–1943 indicates that beach fires were prohibited on public beaches, which actually improved the quality of the sand, clearing it of soot, ashes, and charcoal (26).

56. *Whittier News,* August 11, 1944.

57. *Honolulu Advertiser*, August 24, 1939.

58. *Long Beach Sun*, November 8, 1939. Lind is also mentioned in Ball's newsletter for having driven nine and a half hours from San Francisco for a two-hour surf session at Bluff Cove (*Ye Weekly Super Illustrated Spintail*, March 15, 1939, 2).

59. *Los Angeles Times*, December 4 and 18, 1939.

60. *Honolulu Advertiser*, August 19, 1940 and June 12, 1941; *Honolulu Star-Bulletin*, June 21, 1944.

61. *Honolulu Star-Bulletin*, June 11, 1943.

62. *Honolulu Star-Bulletin*, June 11, 1943.

63. *Honolulu Advertiser*, August 19, 1942. Local businessman George Paele Mossman had opened the Hawaiian Village a decade earlier to preserve traditional Hawaiian culture and crafts, presenting dramatic shows for tourists to enjoy. Pualani Mossman—the "Matson Girl"—was his daughter and an early hula dancer in the program.

64. A sad outcome of soldiers and war workers having access to surfboards was the occasional drowning. Instances included Robert B. Gutherie, a thirty-three-year-old civilian radio operator at Pearl Harbor, who died after renting a surfboard at Waikīkī (*Honolulu Advertiser*, March 24, 1942), and Marine Corps Private Joseph B. Arnoldi, twenty-nine, who was found floating unconscious after trying the sport for the first time (*Honolulu Star-Bulletin*, July 27, 1942).

65. Bailey and Farber, *The First Strange Place*, 50.

66. Farber and Bailey, "The Fighting Man as Tourist," 641.

67. Farber and Bailey, "The Fighting Man as Tourist," 641.

68. Farber and Bailey, "The Fighting Man as Tourist," 651.

69. Army Information Branch, *A Pocket Guide to Hawaii*, 7.

70. Farber and Bailey, "The Fighting Man as Tourist," 649.

71. Farber and Bailey, "The Fighting Man as Tourist," 649.

72. Farber and Bailey, "The Fighting Man as Tourist," 649.

73. Army Information Branch, *A Pocket Guide to Hawaii*, 8.

74. Bailey and Farber, *The First Strange Place*, 100.

75. Kodama-Nishimoto and Nishimoto, "Oral History Interview with Richard 'Kingie' Kimball," 1738.

76. http://www.ohadatabook.com/T01–03–11u.pdf. The 1970 census on this site lists Caucasians as just over 300,000; the second largest ethnic group is Japanese at just over 217,000.

77. Records of the Newport Beach Chamber of Commerce, Sherman Library and Gardens, Corona del Mar, California: Folder 430, "Paddleboard Assn." The letter is dated June 12, 1946.

78. Records of the Newport Beach Chamber of Commerce, Sherman Library and Gardens, Corona del Mar, California: Folder 430, "Paddleboard Assn." Welch's two letters are dated June 21 and June 24, 1946.

79. The *Santa Cruz Sentinel* (December 31, 1946) reported members of the Santa Cruz Surfing Club helping out on a rescue, so the club continued to meet after World War II. See also Hickenbottom, *Surfing in Santa Cruz*, 16–17.

80. *Los Angeles Times*, August 11, 1946.

81. *News-Pilot* (San Pedro), September 6, 1947.

82. *Topanga Journal and Malibu Monitor*, October 3, 1947.

83. *News-Pilot* (San Pedro), September 8, 1949. The article names the Santa Monica Surfing Club as the victor, for which Santa Monica lifeguard Tommy Volk competed. Peterson, Zahn and other lifeguards would have been a part of this team as well.

Bibliography

Archival Sources

A–Z file folders, California Surf Museum, Oceanside, California.

Ball, *Ye Weekly Super Illustrated Spintail*, Surfing Heritage and Culture Center, San Clemente, California

California History Room, California State Library, Sacramento, California

Croul Publications, Mary Ann Hawkins Collection, Newport Beach, California

Del Mar Club Life, Santa Monica History Museum, Santa Monica, California

Hermosa Beach City Council Minutes, 1935–1939, Hermosa Beach City Clerk's Office, Hermosa Beach, California

Newspapers.com

Official Military Personnel File of Peterson, Francis P. SN 8802176. Record Group 24. Records of the Bureau of Naval Personnel. National Archives and Records Administration. National Archives at St. Louis

Official Military Personnel File of Blake, Thomas Edward. SN 633390. Record Group 26. Records of the United States Coast Guard. National Archives and Records Administration. National Archives at St. Louis

Palos Verdes Bulletin, Palos Verdes Public Library, Palos Verdes Estates, California

Records of the Newport Beach Chamber of Commerce, Sherman Library and Gardens, Corona del Mar, California

San Onofre Surfing Wahines, Huntington Beach International Surfing Museum, Huntington Beach, California

Santa Monica Public Library, Santa Monica Collection Room, Santa Monica Budget, 1947–1948 Appropriation

Walter Munk Papers, SMC 17, Special Collections & Archives, UC San Diego, San Diego, California

Other Sources

Ackerman, Carl, dir. *Doc Ball: Surfing's Legendary Lensman*. Carl Ackerman Productions, 1999.

Aguirre, David. *Waterman's Eye: Emil Sigler—Surfing San Diego to San Onofre, 1928–1940*. San Diego: Tabler and Wood, 2007.

Alexander, Geoff. *America Goes Hawaiian: The Influence of Pacific Island Culture on the Mainland*. Jefferson, N.C.: McFarland, 2018.

Annual Financial Report, 1930–41, City of Los Angeles, Department of Playground and Recreation.

Annual Report, California State Park Commission, 1939–45.

Annual Report, City of Los Angeles, Department of Playground and Recreation, 1927–29.

Annual Report, Department of Parks and Recreation, County of Los Angeles, 1928–46.

Army Information Branch, Information and Education Division, Morale Services Section, Central Pacific Base Command. *A Pocket Guide to Hawaii*. Washington D.C.: Army Information Branch, Information and Education Division, 1945.

Bailey, Beth, and David Farber. *The First Strange Place: Race and Sex in World War II Hawaii*. Baltimore: Johns Hopkins University Press, 1992.

Ball, John H. "Surf Board Riding in Palos Verdes." *Palos Verdes Peninsula News*, October 28, 1938, 5.

Ball, John H. "Surf-Boarders Capture California." *National Geographic Magazine*, September, 1944: 355–62.

Ball, John H. *California Surf Riders: 1946*. N.p., 1946. Reprinted as *Early California Surfriders,* with an introduction by Jim Feuling, Ventura, CA: Pacific Publishing, 1995.

Ball, John H. "The World's Most Rugged Camera Hobby." *Modern Photography,* May 1950, 38–40, 92–95.

Bates, G. W. *Sandwich Island Notes. By a Häolé*. New York: Harper & Brothers, 1854.

Baughman, James L. "Who Read *Life*? The Circulation of American's Favorite Magazine." In *Looking at* Life *Magazine*, edited by Erika Doss, 41–51. Washington D.C.: Smithsonian Institution Press, 2001.

Blake, Tom. "Surfriding—The Royal and Ancient Sport." *Mid-Pacific Magazine* 39, no 1. (1930): 3–6.

Blake, Tom. "Surfriding in Hawaii." *Paradise of the Pacific* 44, no. 12 (December 1931): 45–52.

Blake, Tom. "Waves and Thrills at Waikiki." *National Geographic* (May 1935): 597–604.

Blake, Tom. *Hawaiian Surfboard*. Honolulu: Paradise of the Pacific Press, 1935.

Blake, Tom. "Riding the Breakers!" *Popular Mechanics* 68, no. 1 (July 1937): 114–17.

Blake, Tom. "Improved Hollow Surfboard For All-Around Sport." *Popular Science* 134, no. 6 (1939): 174–76.

Blake, Tom. *Tom Blake Scrapbook*. Newport Beach, Calif.: Croul Publications, 2014.

Brewster, B. Chris. "Letter to the Editor" in the *International Journal of Aquatic Research and Education* (August 2007): 195–97.

Burnett, Claudine, and Paul Burnett. *Surfing Newport Beach: The Glory Days of Corona Del Mar*. Charleston, S.C.: The History Press, 2013.

Cain, James M. "The Widow's Mite, or Queen of the Rancho." *Vanity Fair* (August 1933): 22- 23, 54.

Cain, James M. *The Postman Always Rings Twice: Double Indemnity, Mildred Pierce, and Selected Stories*. New York: Alfred A. Knopf, 2003.

California State Park Commission. *Annual Report, 1939, 1941, 1945*.

Cary, Diana Serra. *Jackie Coogan: The World's Boy King: A Biography of Hollywood's Legendary Child Star*. Lanham, Md.: Scarecrow Press, 2007.

Chalke, Frank. *Frank Chalke Oral History Interview*. Fredericksburg, Tex.: National Museum of the Pacific War, April 12, 2018.

Clark, John R. K. *Hawaiian Surfing: Traditions from the Past*. Honolulu: University of Hawai'i Press, 2011.

Clark, Rosie Harrison. *Let's Go, Let's Go! The Biography of Lorrin "Whitey" Harrison: California's Legendary Surf Pioneer*. Choteau, Mt.: Harrison Clark, 1997.

Cooley, Timothy J. *Surfing About Music*. Berkeley: University of California Press, 2014.

Couvillon, Arthur R. *Sands of Time: The History of Beach Volleyball*, vol. 1. Information Guides, 2002.

Daigle, Patricia. "American Tan: Modernism, Eugenics, and the Transformation of Whiteness." Ph.D. thesis, University of California, Santa Barbara, 2015.

Davis, David. *Waterman: The Life and Times of Duke Kahanamoku*. Lincoln: University of Nebraska Press, 2015.

D'Amelio, Dan. A. "A Season of Panic: The Internments of World War II." *Italian Americana* 19, no. 2 (Summer 1999): 147–62.

Deloria, Philip J. *Playing Indian*. New Haven, Conn.: Yale University Press, 1998.

Desmond, Jane C. *Staging Tourism: Bodies on Display from Waikiki to Sea World*. Chicago: University of Chicago Press, 1999.

Deverell, William, and David Igler, eds. *A Companion to California History*. Chichester, U.K.: Wiley Blackwell, 2014.

Devienne, Elsa. "Spectacular Bodies: Los Angeles Beach Cultures and the Making of the 'California Look' (1900s-1960s)." *European Journal of American Studies* 14, no. 4 (2019): 1–25.

Dixon, Peter. *Men Who Ride Mountains: Incredible True Tales of Legendary Surfers, rev. ed*. Guilford, Conn.: Lyons Press, 2001.

Doss, Erika, ed. *Looking at Life Magazine*. Washington D.C.: Smithsonian Institution Press, 2001.

Drummond, Ron. *The Art of Wave Riding*. Hollywood, Calif.: The Cloister Press, 1931.

Duclos, Jeff. "Matt Kivlin: A Precedent of Style." *Longboard Magazine* 6, no. 3 (1998): 50–59.

"The Duke—Interview with Duke Kahanamoku." *Surfer Magazine* 6, no. 1 (1965): 16–20.

Ejiri, Masakazu. "The Development of Waikiki, 1900–1949: The Formative Period of an American Resort Paradise." Ph.D. thesis, University of Hawaiʻi, 1996.

Elwell, John C., and Jane Schmauss. *Surfing in San Diego*. Charleston, S.C.: Arcadia, 2007.

Emerson, N. B. "Causes of Decline of Ancient Hawaiian Sports." *The Friend* 50, no. 8 (August 1892): 57–60.

Farber, David, and Beth Bailey. "The Fighting Man as Tourist: The Politics of Tourist Culture in Hawaii during World War II." *Pacific Historical Review* 65, no. 4 (November 1996): 641–60.

Fine, David M. "james m. cain and the los angeles novel." *American Studies* 20, no. 1 (Spring 1979): 25–34.

Finney, Ben R. "Hawaiian Surfing, A Study of Cultural Change." Master's thesis, University of Hawaiʻi, 1959.

Finney, Ben R., and James D. Houston: *Surfing: The Sport of Hawaiian Kings*. Rutland, Vt.: Charles E. Tuttlepany, 1966. Reprinted as *Surfing: A History of the Ancient Hawaiian Sport*. San Francisco: Pomegranate Artbooks, 1996.

Fleming, E. J. *The Movieland Directory: Nearly 30,000 Addresses of Celebrity Homes, Film Locations and Historical Sites in the Los Angeles Area, 1900–Present*. Jefferson, N.C.: McFarland, 2004.

Fogelson, Robert M. *Bourgeois Nightmares: Suburbia, 1870–1930*. New Haven, Conn.: Yale University Press, 2005.

Forbes, David W. *Hawaiian National Bibliography, 1780–1900*. 4 vols. Honolulu: University of Hawaiʻi Press, 1998–c. 2003.

Ford, Alexander Hume. "Aquatic Sports." *Paradise of the Pacific* 21, no. 12 (December 1908): 19–20.

Ford, Alexander Hume. "Riding the Surf in Hawaii." *Collier's Outdoor America* 43, no. 21 (1909): 17.

Fornander, Alexander. *Fornander Collection of Hawaiian Antiquities and Folk-Lore*. 3 vols. Honolulu: Bishop Museum, 1916–1920.

Gamble, Lynn H. *The Chumash World at European Contact: Power, Trade, and Feasting Among Complex Hunter-Gatherers*. Berkeley: University of California Press, 2008.

Gamble, Lynn H., ed. *First Coastal Californians*. Santa Fe, N.M.: School for Advanced Research Press, 2015.

Garrett, Charles Hiroshi. *Struggling to Define a Nation: American Music and the Twentieth Century*. Berkeley: University of California Press, 2008.

Gault-Williams, Malcolm. "Woody Brown: Pilot, Surfer, Sailor." *The Surfer's Journal* 5, no. 3 (1995): 94–107.

Gault-Williams, Malcolm. "Surf Drunk: The Wallace Froiseth Story." *Surfer's Journal* 6, no. 4 (1996): 94–109.

Gault-Williams, Malcolm. "Tarzan Redux: Chapter Fill-ins from the Life of Gene Smith." *Surfer's Journal* 13, no. 2 (2004): 44–53.

Gault-Williams, Malcolm. *Legendary Surfers, Volume 3: The 1930s.* Lulu.com, 2005.

Gault-Williams, Malcolm, and Gary Lynch. "Through the Master's Eyes." *Longboard Magazine* 6, no. 4 (1998): 51–59.

Gault-Williams, Malcolm, and Gary Lynch. "Pulling Seaward: Tommy Zahn." *Surfer's Journal* 9, no. 2 (1999): 72–87.

Giddens, Gary. *Bing Crosby: A Pocketful of Dreams; The Early Years, 1903–1940.* Boston: Little, Brown, 2001.

Gilio-Whitaker, Dina. *As Long As Grass Grows: The Indigenous Fight for Environmental Justice, from Colonization to Standing Rock.* Boston: Beacon Press, 2019.

Gilio-Whitaker, Dina. "Appropriating Surfing and the Politics of Indigenous Authenticity." In *The Critical Surf Studies Reader*, edited by Dexter Zavalza Hough-Snee and Alexander Sotelo Eastman, 214–32. Durham, N.C.: Duke University Press, 2017.

Haas, Lisbeth. *Conquests and Historical Identities in California.* Berkeley: University of California Press, 1995.

Hamilton, Andy. "Surfboards, Ahoy!" *Los Angeles Times*, September 19, 1937.

Harrison, Lorrin. "A Glimpse Inside Lorrin's Barn." *Surfer's Journal* 2, no. 4 (1992): 34–43.

Hickenbottom, Thomas. *Surfing in Santa Cruz.* Charleston, S.C.: Arcadia, 2009.

Hine, Robert V. et al. *The American West: A New Interpretive History*, 2nd edition. New Haven, Conn.: Yale University Press, 2017.

Historical Committee of the Outrigger Canoe Club. "Oral History: William Justin Mullahey." Interview by Kenneth J. Pratt, Honolulu, Hawai'i, May 6, 1980.

Hixson, Walter L. *American Settler Colonialism.* New York: Palgrave Macmillan, 2013.

Holmes, Paul. *Hobie: Master of Water, Wind and Waves.* Newport Beach, Calif.: Croul Publications, 2013.

Holmes, Tommy. *The Hawaiian Canoe*, rev. ed. Honolulu: Editions Limited, 1993.

Hoopes, Roy. *Cain: The Biography of James M. Cain.* Carbondale: Southern Illinois University Press, 1982.

Howard, Devon. "San Onofre: A Way of Life." *Longboard Magazine* (June 1998): 50–59.

Hunhdorf, Shari M. *Going Native: Indians in the American Cultural Imagination.* Ithaca, N.Y.: Cornell University Press, 2001.

Jackson, John A. "Doc Ball." *Easy Reader*, vol. 34, no. 21 (January 7, 1993): 1, 19–22.

James, Don. *Surfing in the 1930s: A Documentary on the Pioneers of Surfing.* Early Sixties Classic Video Productions, 1994.

James, Don. *Surfing San Onofre to Point Dume: 1936–1942*. San Francisco: Chronicle Books, 1998.

James, Don. *Prewar Surfing Photographs*. Santa Barbara, Calif.: T. Adler Books, 2004.

Jarret, Phil. *Surfing Australia: A Complete History of Surfboard Riding in Australia*. Rev ed. Melbourne: Hardie Grant Books, 2017.

Jefferson, Alison Rose. *Living the California Dream: African American Leisure Sites during the Jim Crow Era*. Lincoln: University of Nebraska Press, 2020.

Johnson, William Oscar. "A Star Was Born." *Sports Illustrated*, July 18, 1984, 137–59.

Jordan, Ryan. "Remembering the Forgotten Village of San Onofre: An Untold Story of Race Relations." *Journal of San Diego History* 60, no. 1 and 2 (2014): 27–44.

Judging Palos Verdes as a Place to Live. Palos Verdes Project: Palos Verdes, California, c. 1936.

Kamakau, Samuel Mānaiakalani. *Tales and Traditions of the People of Old: Nā Moʻolelo a ka Poʻe Kahiko*. Trans. Mary K. Pukui; ed. Dorothy B. Barrère. Honolulu: Bishop Museum Press, 1991: 45–49.

Kenvin, Richard. "General Veneer." *Surfer's Journal* 28, no. 6 (2019): 22–35.

Kodama-Nishimoto, Michi, and Warren Nishimoto. "Oral History Interview with Richard 'Kingie' Kimball (March 27, 1986). In *Waikīkī, 1900–1985: Oral Histories, vol 1*. Honolulu: Oral History Project, June 1985: 1707–86.

Konzett, Delia Malia Caparoso. *Hollywood's Hawaii: Race, Nation, and War*. New Brunswick, N.J.: Rutgers University Press, 2017.

Laderman, Scott. *Empire in Waves: A Political History of Surfing*. Berkeley: University of California Press, 2014.

Lawler, Kristin. *The American Surfer: Radical Culture and Capitalism*. New York: Routledge, 2011.

Lawler, Kristin. "Southern California's Bohemian Surfers: Roots of American Counterculture." In *Bohemia in Southern California*, edited by Jay Ruby. San Diego: San Diego State University Press, 2017.

Lenček, Lena, and Gideon Bosker. *The Beach: The History of Paradise on Earth*. New York: Viking, 1998.

Lockwood, Craig. "From now on, your name is Burrhead." *Surfer's Journal* 11, no. 5 (2002): 40–63.

Lockwood, Craig. "Waterman: Preston 'Pete' Peterson." *Surfer's Journal* 14, no. 4 (2005): 44–69.

Lockwood, Craig. "Granny and Doc." *Surfer's Journal* 15, no. 6 (2006): 46–59.

Lockwood, Craig. "Passing the Torch." *Surfer's Journal* 16, no. 5 (2007): 53–63.

Lockwood, Craig. *Peanuts: An Oral Biography—Exploring Legend, Myth and Archetype in California's Surfing Subculture*. Newport Beach, Calif.: Croul Family Foundation, 2009.

London, Jack. "My Hawaiian Aloha." *Cosmopolitan* (September 1916): 36–37, 170.

Long Beach Lifeguard Association. *Centennial History of the Long Beach Lifeguard Service, Parts 1 and 2.* n.d.

Los Angeles County Regional Planning District. *The Master Plan of Shoreline Development.* Los Angeles: June 1940.

Luck, Chuck A [Charles Ehlers]. "Log Jam 1922." *Surfer's Journal* 1, no. 2 (1991): 42–47.

Lynch, Gary. "Interview with Mary Ann Hawkins-Midkiff," 15 March 1989," tape recorder (transcribed), 5, Croul Publications, Mary Ann Hawkins Collection: Book One, Newport Beach, California.

Lynch, Gary, and Malcolm Gault-Williams. "The Last Chapter: Stories of Gene 'Tarzan' Smith. *Surfer's Journal* 7, no. 4 (1997): 44–51.

Lynch, Gary, and Malcolm Gault-Williams. *Tom Blake: The Uncommon Journey of a Pioneer Waterman.* Corona del Mar, Calif.: Croul Family Foundation, 2001.

Mak, James. "Creating 'Paradise of the Pacific': How Tourism Began in Hawaii." Working Papers 2015–1, University of Hawai'i at Mānoa, Department of Economics. https://uhero.hawaii.edu/RePEc/hae/wpaper/WP_2015-1.pdf.

Mark, Richard. *Our Lifeguard Family: Honoring Your Service, The First 100 Years—An Anthology of the L.A. County Lifeguards.* 2008. Google online.

Martino, Michael T. *Lifeguards of San Diego County.* Charleston, S.C.: Arcadia, 2007.

Martino, Michael T. *Help! San Diego Lifeguards to the Rescue: A History of Their Service, Volume 1: 1868–1941.* San Diego: Sunbelt Publications, 2018.

Matuszak, David F. *San Onofre: Memories of a Legendary Surfing Beach.* Redlands, Calif.: Pacific Sunset Publishing, 2018.

Matuszak, David F. *San Onofre: Memories of a Legendary Surfing Beach,* rev. ed. Redlands, Calif.: Pacific Sunset Publishing, 2020.

McElvanie, Robert S. *The Great Depression: America, 1929–1941.* New York: Times Book, 1993.

Moreton-Robinson, Aileen. *The White Possessive: Property, Power, and Indigenous Sovereignty.* Minneapolis: University of Minnesota Press, 2015.

Moser, Patrick. "The Reports of Surfing's Demise Have Been Greatly Exaggerated." *Bamboo Ridge* 98 (2011): 195–204.

Moser, Patrick. "The Endurance of Surfing in 19th-Century Hawai'i. *Journal of the Polynesian Society* 124, vol. 4 (2016): 411–32.

Moser, Patrick. "The Hawaii Promotion Committee and the Appropriation of Surfing." *Pacific Historical Review* 89, vol. 4 (Fall 2020): 500–27.

Moser, Patrick. "Origins of the paddle-out ceremony." In *Creative writing and surfing*: TEXT Special Issue 65 (October 2021), edited by Nigel Krauth, Sally Breen, Tim Baker and Jake Sandtner, 1–11. https://textjournal.scholasticahq.com/.

Moser, Patrick. *Surf and Rescue: George Freeth and the Birth of California Beach Culture.* Urbana: University of Illinois Press, 2022.

Nicholls, C. P. L. "Lessons in Surfing for Everyman." *Westways* (July 1936): 22–23.

O'Brien, Duncan. *The White Ships: Matson Line to Hawaii–New Zealand–Australia via Samoa–Fiji, 1927–1978*. Victoria, B.C.: Pier 10 Media, 2008.

Ory, Pascal. *L'invention du bronzage: Essai d'une histoire culturelle*. Paris: Complexe, 2008.

Paskowitz, Dorian. "Tarzan at Waikiki." *Surfer's Journal* 2, no. 2 (1992): 18–23.

Pezman, Steve. "Turning Points." *Surfer's Journal* 20, no. 6 (2011): 68–87.

Pukui, Mary Kawena. *'Ōlelo No'eau: Hawaiian Proverbs and Poetical Sayings*. Honolulu: Bishop Museum, Special Publication 71, 1983.

Pukui, Mary Kawena, Samuel H. Ebert, and Esther T. Mookini. *Place Names of Hawaii*. Rev. ed. Honolulu: University of Hawai'i Press, 1974.

Randall, David K. *The King and Queen of Malibu: The True Story of the Battle for Paradise*. New York: W.W. Norton, 2016.

Reid, Sam. "The Days of Great Boards and Real Watermen." *Surfer Magazine* 6, no. 5 (1965): 56–59.

Rindge, Frederick Hastings. *Happy Days in Southern California*. N. p., 1893.

Ritchie, Robert C. *The Lure of the Beach: A Global History*. Berkeley: University of California Press, 2021.

"Rolling Waves Provide Thrills for California's Surf Riders." *Life* (August 7, 1939): 44–45.

Sabin, Paul. *Crude Politics: The California Oil Market, 1900–1949*. Berkeley: University of California Press, 2005.

Santa Monica, Ocean Park, Venice, Sawtelle, and Westgate Directory 1925. Los Angeles: Los Angeles Directory Co., 1925.

Schmitt, Robert. *Hawaii in the Movies, 1898–1959*. Honolulu: Hawaii Historical Society, 1988.

Shipek, Florence Connolly. *Pushed into the Rocks: Southern California Indian Land Tenure, 1769–1986*. Lincoln: University of Nebraska Press, 1987.

Sibley, Hi. "Better Ways To Build Surf Boards." *Popular Mechanics* (August 1935): 56–57.

Sides, Robert. "Surf Slaloms," *Los Angeles Saturday Night* (February 12, 1938): 7–9, 27, 32–33.

Skwiot, Christine. *The Purposes of Paradise: U.S. Tourism and Empire in Cuba and Hawai'i*. Philadelphia: University of Pennsylvania Press, 2011.

Smith, Sinjin, and Neil Feinemen. *Kings of the Beach: The Story of Beach Volleyball*. Los Angeles: Power Books, 1988.

Starr, Kevin. *Material Dreams: Southern California through the 1920s*. New York: Oxford University Press, 1990.

Starr, Kevin. *Endangered Dreams: The Great Depression in California*. New York: Oxford University Press, 1996.

Starr, Kevin. *The Dream Endures: California Enters the 1940s*. New York: Oxford University Press, 1997.

Starr, Kevin. *Embattled Dreams: California in War and Peace, 1940–1950*. New York: Oxford University Press, 2002.

Stecyk, Craig. "Hot Curl." *Surfer's Journal* 3, no. 2 (1993): 64–73.

Stecyk, Craig. "Pacific System: Birth of the Surfboard Factory." *Surfer's Journal* 6, no 4 (1996): 32–39.

Sturm, Circe. *Becoming Indian: The Struggle over Cherokee Identity in the Twenty-first Century.* Santa Fe, N.M.: SAR Press, 2011.

Sullivan, Gabe. "Interview with Calvin 'Tulie' Clark," 1995. *Encyclopedia of Surfing* (eos.surf).

"Surf-Riding is Winter Sport now in California." *Life* (February 7, 1938): 41–42.

"Surf Riding On California Beach Is A Favorite Summertime Sport." *Life* (August 26): 50–51.

Thompson, Chris. *Out of the Blue: The Story of the Santa Cruz Surfing Club.* SoundVision Media Film, 2010.

Timmons, Grady. *Waikiki Beachboy.* Honolulu: Editions Limited, 1989.

Trask, Haunani-Kay. *From a Native Daughter: Colonialism and Sovereignty in Hawai'i*, rev. ed. Honolulu: University of Hawai'i Press, 1999.

Trask, Haunani-Kay. "Lovely Hula Hands: Corporate Tourism and the Prostitution of Hawaiian Culture." *Border/Lines* 23 (Winter 1991/1992): 22–27.

Troutman, John W. *Kīkā Kila: How the Hawaiian Steel Guitar Changed the Sound of Modern Music.* Chapel Hill: University of North Carolina Press, 2016.

Tygiel, Jules. "Introduction." In *Metropolis in the Making: Los Angeles in the 1920s*, edited by Tom Sitton and William Deverill, 1–10. Berkeley: University of California Press, 2001.

Verge, Arthur C. "The Impact of the Second World War on Los Angeles." *Pacific Historical Review* 63, no. 3 (August 1994): 289–314.

Verge, Arthur C. *Santa Monica Lifeguards.* Charleston, S.C.: Arcadia, 2007.

Walker, Isaiah Helekunihi. *Waves of Resistance: Surfing and History in Twentieth-Century Hawai'i.* Honolulu: University of Hawai'i Press, 2011.

Warshaw, Matt. *The History of Surfing.* San Francisco: Chronicle Books, 2010.

Warshaw, Matt. "Pete Peterson: So Good He Didn't Need Wax." *Encyclopedia of Surfing* (blog), July 8, 2014. https://eos.surf/2014/07/08/pete-peterson/.

Westwick, Peter, and Peter Neushul. *The World in the Curl: An Unconventional History of Surfing.* New York: Crown, 2013.

Wheaton, Belinda. "Space Invaders in Surfing's White Tribe: Exploring Surfing, Race, and Identity." In *The Critical Surf Studies Reader*, edited by Dexter Zavalza Hough-Snee and Alexander Sotelo Eastman, 177–95. Durham, N.C.: Duke University Press, 2017.

Wolfe, Patrick "Settler colonialism and the elimination of the native." *Journal of Genocide Research* 8, no. 4 (December 2006): 387–409.

Wood, Houston. *Displacing Natives: The Rhetorical Production of Hawai'i.* Lanham, Md.: Rowman and Littlefield, 1999.

Yamashiro, Aiko. "Ethics in Song: Becoming Kama'āina in Hapa-Haole Music." *Cultural Analysis* 8 (2009): 1–23.

Index

California, 227, 228; enlistments, 222; internments, 228; Okinawa, 224; Pearl Harbor, 221–22, 223; rationing, 226; shore patrol, 223; U. S. troops in Hawai'i, 231–32, 234; WASPs (Women Airforce Service Pilots), 228

Wright, Charlie, 24, 87, 238, 238n22, 240n41

Ye Weekly Super Illustrated Spintail (John "Doc" Ball), 165–67, 246–47n48, 265n115. *See also* Ball, John Heath "Doc"

Zahn, Tommy, 100, 235, 236, 279n83

PATRICK MOSER is professor of writing and French at Drury University. He is the author of *Surf and Rescue: George Freeth and the Birth of California Beach Culture* and the editor of *Pacific Passages: An Anthology of Surf Writing*.

The University of Illinois Press
is a founding member of the
Association of University Presses.

University of Illinois Press
1325 South Oak Street
Champaign, IL 61820-6903
www.press.uillinois.edu